International Debt Statistics 2015

International Debt Statistics 2015

WORLD BANK GROUP

1 2 3 4 18 17 16 15

ISBN (paper): 978-1-4648-0413-7
ISBN (electronic): 978-1-4648-0414-4
DOI: 10.1596/978-1-4648-0413-7
ISSN (paper): 2310-2667
ISSN (electronic): 2310-2675

Cover design: Jomo Tariku, World Bank Group
Cover image by Jomo Tariku, World Bank Group

Library of Congress Cataloging-in-Publication Data has been applied for

Table of Contents

Preface

This year's edition of *International Debt Statistics*, successor to *Global Development Finance* and *World Debt Tables*, and the third in the series, is designed to respond to user demand for timely, comprehensive data on trends in external debt in developing countries. It also provides summary information on the external debt of high-income countries and public (domestic and external) debt for a select group of countries.

The World Bank's Debtor Reporting System (DRS), from which the aggregate and country tables presented in this report are drawn, was established in 1951. *World Debt Tables*, the first publication that included DRS external debt data, appeared in 1973 and gained increased attention during the debt crisis of the 1980s. Since then, the publication and data have undergone numerous revisions and iterations to address the challenges and demands posed by the global economic conditions.

Presentation and access to data have been refined to improve the user experience. The printed edition of *International Debt Statistics 2015* now provides a summary overview and a select set of indicators, while an expanded dataset is available online (datatopics.worldbank.org/debt/ids).

By providing comprehensive and timely data that reflects the latest additions and revisions, and by expanding the scope of the data available online, we aim to serve the needs of our users and to reach a wider audience. Improvements in data dissemination are matched with ongoing efforts to improve the quality and timeliness of data collection. In partnership with the major providers of debt data management systems to developing countries, the Commonwealth Secretariat (COMSEC) and the United Nations Conference on Trade and Development (UNCTAD), we are working toward an established standard code and a set of system links that will enable countries to provide their DRS reports electronically in a seamless and automated data exchange process.

As these changes take place, we welcome your feedback and suggestions for further improvements at data@worldbank.org.

Haishan Fu
Director, Development Data Group

Acknowledgments

This volume was prepared by the Financial Data Team of the Development Data Group (DECDG), led by Ibrahim Levent under the management of Neil Fantom, and comprising Peter Bourke, Wendy Huang, Malvina Pollock, Evis Rucaj, Rubena Sukaj, Sun Hwa Song, Rasiel Vellos, Alagiriswamy Venkatesan, and Molly Watts, who worked closely with other teams in DECDG. The team was assisted by Elysee Kiti. The overview of current developments was prepared by Malvina Pollock, Evis Rucaj, and Rasiel Vellos in consultation with the staff of DECDG; country economists reviewed the data tables. The work was carried out under the direction of Haishan Fu. Valuable advice was provided by the Operations and Strategy unit of the Vice Presidency.

The production of this volume was managed by Azita Amjadi. The online database was prepared by Shelley Fu and William Prince. International Debt Statistics electronic products were prepared by a team led by Malarvizhi Veerappan under the supervision of Soong Sup Lee and comprising Rajesh Danda, Jean-Pierre Djomalieu, Ramgopal Erabelly, Shelley Fu, Gytis Kanchas, Ugendran Machakkalai, Nacer Megherbi, and Manish Rathore. The cover was designed by Jomo Tariku. Susan Graham, Andrés Meneses, and Paola Scalabrin from the Publishing and Knowledge Division of the World Bank coordinated the publication and dissemination of the book.

User Guide to Tables

International Debt Statistics 2015 focuses on financial flows, trends in external debt, and other major financial indicators for developing and advanced economies. The report includes more than 200 time series indicators from 1970 to 2013 for most reporting countries. This edition of *International Debt Statistics* (IDS) has been reconfigured to offer a more condensed presentation of the principal indicators, along with additional tables showcasing Quarterly External Debt Statistics and Public Sector Debt.

Tables

Aggregate Tables

The aggregate tables are labeled by region name. Data are shown for all developing countries and six regional groups (East Asia and Pacific, Europe and Central Asia, Latin America and the Caribbean, Middle East and North Africa, South Asia, and Sub-Saharan Africa).

Country Tables

Country tables are labeled by country name and ordered alphabetically. Data are shown for 124 developing countries that report public and publicly guaranteed external debt to the World Bank's Debtor Reporting System (DRS). The tables also include key debt ratios and the composition of external debt stocks and flows for each country.

Each table shows a time series with the most recent six years, as well as 2000 and 2005 as companion years. Full time series data are available for all countries in the World Bank's Open Data website (http://data.worldbank.org/data-catalog/international-debt-statistics).

Statistics

The general cutoff date for countries to report data for this publication was end-September 2014. The economic aggregates presented in the tables are prepared for the convenience of users. Although debt ratios can give useful information about developments in a debt-servicing capacity, conclusions drawn from them will not be valid unless accompanied by careful economic evaluation.

The macroeconomic data provided are collected from national statistical organizations, which in some cases may be subject to a considerable margin of error. The usual care must be taken in interpreting the ratios, particularly for the most recent years, because figures may be preliminary and subject to revision.

Notes at the bottom of each country table summarize major events that have taken place in the country in recent years; describe the sources of information for short-term and private nonguaranteed external debt if the reports were not provided by the country; and highlight main issues in the data collection process. Unless otherwise specified, data on long-term public and publicly guaranteed external debt for 2013 are based on reports provided by the country.

More detailed information on data sources, methodology, and compilation is provided in the appendix at the back of this book.

Aggregate Measures for Income Groups and Regions

Aggregate measures for income groups and regions include the 124 developing countries that report public and publicly guaranteed external debt to the World Bank's DRS, whenever data are available. The aggregate "All developing countries" is the sum of data for 124 countries.

Classification of Economies

For operational and analytical purposes, the World Bank's main criterion for classifying economies is gross national income (GNI) per capita (calculated by the *World Bank Atlas* method). Every economy is classified as low income, middle income, or high income. Low- and middle-income countries are sometimes referred to as developing countries. The term is used for convenience; it is not intended to imply that all countries in the group are experiencing similar development or that other economies have reached a preferred or final stage of development. Because GNI per capita changes over time, the country composition of income groups may change from one edition of *International Debt Statistics* to the next. Once the classification is fixed for an edition, based on GNI per capita in the most recent year for which data are available, all historical data presented are based on the same country grouping.

Symbols

0 or 0.0 means zero or small enough that the number would round to zero at the displayed number of decimal places.

.. means that data are not available or that aggregates cannot be calculated because of missing data in the years shown.

$ indicates current U.S. dollars unless otherwise specified.

User Guide to IDS Online Tables

The extended version of country tables that were previously available in the *International Debt Statistics* print edition is now available online. Using an automated query process, these reference tables will be updated based on the revisions to the International Debt Statistics database.

Users can access all the online tables, download the PDF version of the publication, view the report as an eBook on ISSUU, as well as access the database and download the archived editions of the publication by going to http://data.worldbank.org/products/ids.

How to Access IDS Online Country Tables

To access the IDS online tables, visit http://datatopics.worldbank.org/debt/ids and select from "Country," "Region," or "Topic" options.

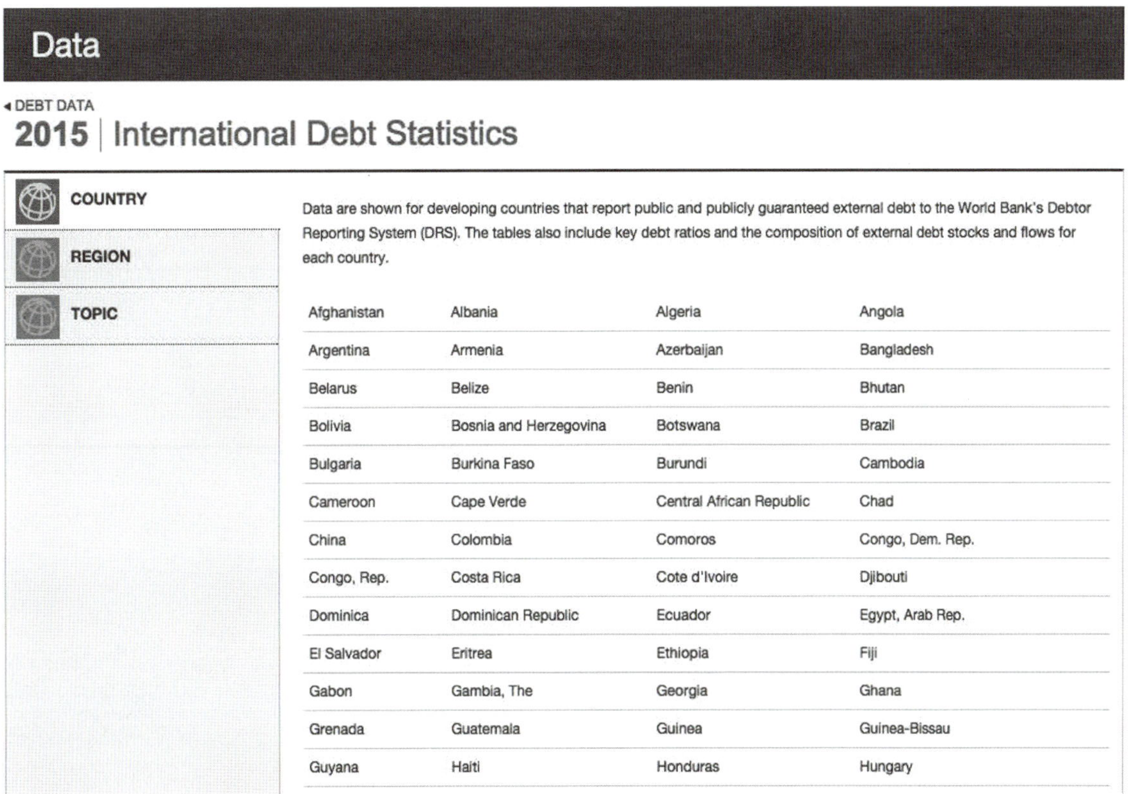
Data

◂ DEBT DATA

2015 | International Debt Statistics

COUNTRY

REGION

TOPIC

Data are shown for developing countries that report public and publicly guaranteed external debt to the World Bank's Debtor Reporting System (DRS). The tables also include key debt ratios and the composition of external debt stocks and flows for each country.

Afghanistan	Albania	Algeria	Angola
Argentina	Armenia	Azerbaijan	Bangladesh
Belarus	Belize	Benin	Bhutan
Bolivia	Bosnia and Herzegovina	Botswana	Brazil
Bulgaria	Burkina Faso	Burundi	Cambodia
Cameroon	Cape Verde	Central African Republic	Chad
China	Colombia	Comoros	Congo, Dem. Rep.
Congo, Rep.	Costa Rica	Cote d'Ivoire	Djibouti
Dominica	Dominican Republic	Ecuador	Egypt, Arab Rep.
El Salvador	Eritrea	Ethiopia	Fiji
Gabon	Gambia, The	Georgia	Ghana
Grenada	Guatemala	Guinea	Guinea-Bissau
Guyana	Haiti	Honduras	Hungary

To access a specific country table directly without going through the above landing page, use the URL http://datatopics.worldbank.org/debt/ids/ and the country name (for example, http://datatopics.worldbank.org/debt/ids/country/argentina to view the table for Argentina). Similarly, to view the regional table, click on the "Region" tab and select one of the listed regions (for example http://datatopics.worldbank.org/debt/ids/region/south-asia to view the table for South Asia).

2015 | International Debt Statistics

Data > Data Topics > Debt Data > Country Tables > Argentina

$ millions, unless otherwise indicated	2009	2010	2011	2012	2013
1. Summary external debt data					
External debt stocks	122,497.0	127,334.7	117,356.9	122,978.2	121,012.7
Long-term external debt	102,023.6	104,324.2	100,355.1	103,083.8	103,929.9
Public and publicly guaranteed	71,123.4	75,952.8	69,252.7	68,338.5	67,597.5
Private nonguaranteed	30,900.2	28,371.3	31,102.4	34,725.3	36,332.4
Use of IMF credit	490.4	3,166.8	3,110.9	3,101.3	3,104.6
Short-term external debt	19,983.0	19,843.7	13,890.9	16,813.1	13,978.2
of which Interest arrears on long-term	10,009.0	10,773.7	5,463.9	6,115.1	6,312.2
Official creditors	896.0	914.7	917.7	916.5	907.4
Private creditors	9,113.0	9,859.0	4,546.2	5,198.6	5,404.7
Memo: principal arrears on LDOD	18,514.8	19,712.4	9,224.9	13,639.4	13,456.5
Official creditors	4,370.1	4,457.9	4,601.0	4,666.3	4,554.6
Private creditors	14,144.7	15,254.5	4,623.9	8,973.0	8,901.9
External debt flows					
Disbursements	7,035.9	7,547.3	6,892.5	10,774.4	7,667.0
Long-term external debt	7,035.9	7,547.3	6,892.5	10,774.4	7,667.0
IMF purchases	0.0	0.0	0.0	0.0	0.0
Principal repayments	4,651.5	11,224.7	10,693.5	11,967.5	9,658.2
Long-term external debt	4,651.5	11,224.7	10,693.5	11,967.5	9,658.2
IMF repurchases	0.0	0.0	0.0	0.0	0.0
Net flows	2,548.4	-4,581.4	-4,443.9	1,078.0	-5,023.2
Long-term external debt	2,384.4	-3,677.4	-3,800.9	-1,193.0	-1,991.2
Short-term external debt	164.0	-904.0	-643.0	2,271.0	-3,032.0
Interest payments	3,192.7	3,477.0	3,644.0	3,552.1	3,310.8
Long-term external debt	2,946.8	3,356.3	3,524.4	3,382.2	3,204.9
IMF charges	4.0	7.3	10.0	3.4	0.9
Short-term external debt	241.9	113.4	109.7	166.5	105.0

Indicators

The indicator codes for each of the indicators online and in the publication are listed below. To view a specific indicator online, go to http://data.worldbank.org/indicator/ and add the indicator code at the end of the url; for example, to view a page for total debt stocks, this line should be in your browser:

http://data.worldbank.org/indicator/DT.DOD.DECT.CD

1. SUMMARY EXTERNAL DEBT DATA			
External debt stocks	DT.DOD.DECT.CD	**External debt flows**	
Long-term external debt	DT.DOD.DLXF.CD	**Disbursements**	DT.DIS.DLTF.CD
Public and publicly guaranteed	DT.DOD.DPPG.CD	Long-term external debt	DT.DIS.DLXF.CD
Private nonguaranteed	DT.DOD.DPNG.CD	IMF purchases	DT.DIS.DIMF.CD
Use of IMF credit	DT.DOD.DIMF.CD	**Principal repayments**	DT.AMT.DLTF.CD
Short-term debt	DT.DOD.DSTC.CD	Long-term external debt	DT.AMT.DLXF.CD
interest arrears on long-term	DT.IXA.DPPG.CD	IMF repurchases	DT.AMT.DIMF.CD
		Net flows	DT.NFL.DECT.CD
		Long-term external debt	DT.NFL.DLXF.CD
Memorandum items		Short-term external debt	DT.NFL.DSTC.CD
Principal arrears on long-term	DT.AXA.DPPG.CD	**Interest payments (INT)**	DT.INT.DECT.CD
Long-term public sector debt	DT.DOD.DPPG.CD	Long-term external debt	DT.INT.DLXF.CD
Long-term private sector debt	DT.DOD.PRVS.CD	IMF charges	DT.INT.DIMF.CD
Public & publicly guaranteed commitments	DT.COM.DPPG.CD	Short-term external debt	DT.INT.DSTC.CD

2. OTHER NON-DEBT RESOURCE FLOWS	
Foreign direct investment (net equity inflows)	BX.KLT.DINV.CD.WD
Portfolio equity flows	BX.PEF.TOTL.CD.WD

3. CURRENCY COMPOSITION OF PUBLIC AND PUBLICLY GUARANTEED DEBT (%)	
Euro	DT.CUR.EURO.ZS
Japanese yen	DT.CUR.JYEN.ZS
Pound sterling	DT.CUR.UKPS.ZS
Swiss franc	DT.CUR.SWFR.ZS
U.S. dollars	DT.CUR.USDL.ZS

4. AVERAGE TERMS OF NEW COMMITMENTS	
Official creditors	
Interest (%)	DT.INR.OFFT
Maturity (years)	DT.MAT.OFFT
Grace period (years)	DT.GPA.OFFT
Private creditors	
Interest (%)	DT.INR.PRVT
Maturity (years)	DT.MAT.PRVT
Grace period (years)	DT.GPA.PRVT

5. MAJOR ECONOMIC AGGREGATES	
Gross national income (GNI)	NY.GNP.MKTP.CD
Exports of goods, services, and primary income	BX.GSR.TOTL.CD
Personal transfers and compensation of employees	BX.TRF.PWKR.CD.DT
Imports of goods, services, and primary income	BM.GSR.TOTL.CD
Primary income on FDI (payments)	BX.KLT.DREM.CD.DT
International reserves	FI.RES.TOTL.CD

6. RATIOS	
External debt stocks to exports (%)	DT.DOD.DECT.EX.ZS
External debt stocks to GNI (%)	DT.DOD.DECT.GN.ZS
Debt service to exports (%)	DT.TDS.DECT.EX.ZS
Short-term to external debt stocks (%)	DT.DOD.DSTC.ZS
Multilateral to external debt stocks (%)	DT.DOD.MLAT.ZS
Reserves to external debt stocks (%)	FI.RES.TOTL.DT.ZS
Current account balance	BN.CAB.XOKA.CD
Reserves to imports (months)	FI.RES.TOTL.MO

7. LONG-TERM EXTERNAL DEBT

Debt outstanding and disbursed	DT.DOD.DLXF.CD	Interest payments	DT.INT.DLXF.CD
Public and publicly guaranteed	DT.DOD.DPPG.CD	**Public and publicly guaranteed**	DT.INT.DPPG.CD
Official creditors	DT.DOD.OFFT.CD	Official creditors	DT.INT.OFFT.CD
Multilateral	DT.DOD.MLAT.CD	Multilateral	DT.INT.MLAT.CD
of which: IBRD	DT.DOD.MIBR.CD	of which: IBRD	DT.INT.MIBR.CD
IDA	DT.DOD.MIDA.CD	IDA	DT.INT.MIDA.CD
Bilateral	DT.DOD.BLAT.CD	Bilateral	DT.INT.BLAT.CD
Private creditors	DT.DOD.PRVT.CD	Private creditors	DT.INT.PRVT.CD
of which: Bonds	DT.DOD.PBND.CD	of which: Bonds	DT.INT.PBND.CD
Commercial banks	DT.DOD.PCBK.CD	Commercial banks	DT.INT.PCBK.CD
Private nonguaranteed	DT.DOD.DPNG.CD	Private nonguaranteed	DT.INT.DPNG.CD
of which: Bonds	DT.DOD.PNGB.CD	of which: Bonds	DT.INT.PNGB.CD
Disbursements	DT.DIS.DLXF.CD	**Principal repayments**	DT.AMT.DLXF.CD
Public and publicly guaranteed	DT.DIS.DPPG.CD	Public and publicly guaranteed	DT.AMT.DPPG.CD
Official creditors	DT.DIS.OFFT.CD	Official creditors	DT.AMT.OFFT.CD
Multilateral	DT.DIS.MLAT.CD	Multilateral	DT.AMT.MLAT.CD
of which: IBRD	DT.DIS.MIBR.CD	of which: IBRD	DT.AMT.MIBR.CD
IDA	DT.DIS.MIDA.CD	IDA	DT.AMT.MIDA.CD
Bilateral	DT.DIS.BLAT.CD	Bilateral	DT.AMT.BLAT.CD
Private creditors	DT.DIS.PRVT.CD	Private creditors	DT.AMT.PRVT.CD
of which: Bonds	DT.DIS.PBND.CD	of which: Bonds	DT.AMT.PBND.CD
Commercial banks	DT.DIS.PCBK.CD	Commercial banks	DT.AMT.PCBK.CD
Private nonguaranteed	DT.DIS.DPNG.CD	**Private nonguaranteed**	DT.AMT.DPNG.CD
of which: Bonds	DT.DIS.PNGB.CD	of which: Bonds	DT.AMT.PNGB.CD

8. DEBT STOCK-FLOW RECONCILATION

Total change in external debt stocks	DT.DOD.DECT.CD.CG
Net flows on external debt	DT.NFL.DECT.CD

9. DEBT STOCK-FLOW RECONCILATION

Total amount rescheduled	DT.DXR.DPPG.CD
Total amount forgiven	DT.DFR.DPPG.CD
Debt buyback	DT.DSB.DPPG.CD

10. CONTRACTUAL OBLIGATIONS ON OUTSTANDING LONG-TERM EXTERNAL DEBT

Official creditors	
Principal	DT.AMT.OFFT.CD
Interest	DT.INT.OFFT.CD
Private creditors	
Principal	DT.AMT.PRVT.CD
Interest	DT.INT.PRVT.CD

How to Use the Databank

DataBank (http://databank.worldbank.org) is an online web resource that provides simple and quick access to collections of time series data. It has advanced functions for selecting and displaying data, performing customized queries, downloading data, and creating charts and maps. Users can create dynamic, custom reports based on their selection of countries, indicators, and years. All these reports can be easily edited, shared, and embedded as widgets on websites or blogs. For more information, see http://databank.worldbank.org/help.

Actions

Click to share the table using either the embed code or the URL

Click to edit and revise the table in DataBank

Click to export all metadata to Excel

Click to export the table to Excel

Click to export the table and corresponding indicator metadata to PDF

Click to print the table and corresponding indicator metadata

Click to access the IDS Online Tables Help file

PART I

Overview

Introduction

International Debt Statistics 2015 presents data and analysis on the external debt of developing countries for 2013, based on actual flows and debt-related transactions reported to the World Bank Debtor Reporting System (DRS) by 124 developing countries. *International Debt Statistics 2015* provides users with comprehensive stock and flow data on the external debt of individual developing countries and for regional and analytical groupings and data on aggregate net capital flows (debt and equity) in 2013. In addition, *International Debt Statistics* (IDS) showcases other debt data collected and compiled by the World Bank. These include the high frequency, quarterly data for high-income and developing countries reported to the joint World Bank—International Monetary Fund (IMF) Quarterly External Debt Statistics (QEDS) and to the Public Sector Debt (PSD) initiatives. The main messages from the 2013 data are:

1. Net debt flows to developing countries increased to $542 billion in 2013, an increase of 28 percent over the comparable figure for 2012. However, the aggregates are heavily impacted by the rise in net debt flows to China, which jumped to $139 billion, four times their 2012 level. Net debt flows to developing countries, excluding China, were $403 billion, only 3 percent higher than in 2012.
2. Long-term debt flows from private creditors rose 24 percent in 2013, to $337 billion, because of an increase in medium-term bank financing and another record year for bond issuance.
3. Net equity inflows, at $643 billion, changed little from 2012. Foreign direct investment proved resilient, rising 6 percent in 2013, but gains were offset by a 29 percent fall in portfolio equity flows. Aggregate net financial flows totaled $1,184 billion, 10 percent higher than 2012, and were considered stable when measured relative to developing countries' gross national income (GNI) at 6 percent.
4. External debt burdens in developing countries remained moderate. The ratio of external debt to GNI averaged 23 percent in 2013, and the ratio of external debt to exports averaged 79 percent. International reserves stood at 111 percent of external debt stocks.
5. Countries reporting to the QEDS confirm that external debt levels in high-income countries are, on average, much higher than in developing countries, but they have moderated somewhat in 2013.

Trends in Debt Stocks and Flows, 2013

Debt stocks accumulated by 10 percent in 2013

Figure O.1 External Debt Stock of Developing Countries, 2008–13

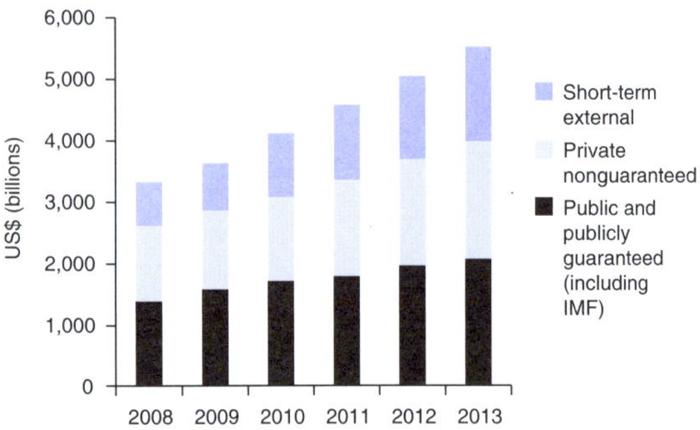

Source: World Bank Debtor Reporting System.

The total debt outstanding to developing countries rose 10 percent in 2013, a similar rate of accumulation to 2012. The combined stock of external debt of developing countries rose from $5 trillion in 2012 to $5.5 trillion at the end of 2013. This reflects net debt inflows of $542 billion, debt forgiveness, and the effect of year-on-year exchange adjustments between local currencies and the U.S. dollar (approximately one-third of developing countries' debt is denominated in U.S. dollars). Short-term debt stocks rose 14 percent, compared with a 9 percent rise in long-term debt, and accounted for 28 percent of the total outstanding external debt at the end of 2013—up from 26 percent the previous year. Private nonguaranteed debt stocks increased by 11 percent, twice the rate of public and publicly guaranteed debt. The stock of long-term debt at end-2013 was almost evenly divided between publicly guaranteed debt and debt owed to private nonguaranteed borrowers.

Net debt flows surged to a record high

Figure O.2 Net Debt Flows to Developing Countries, 2008–13

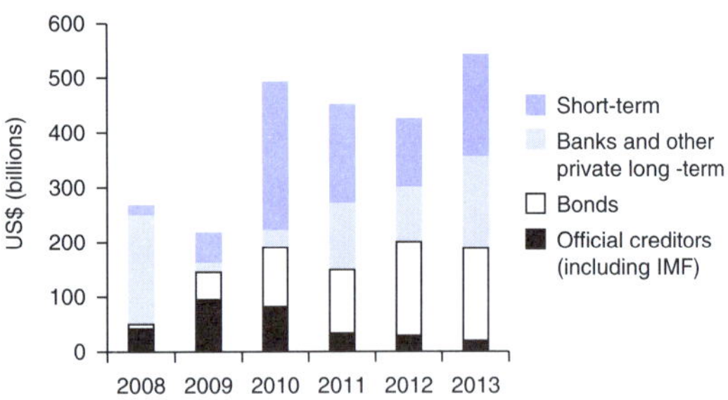

Source: World Bank Debtor Reporting System.

Net debt flows rose to a record high of $542 billion in 2013, 28 percent higher than the comparable figure for 2012. This was driven by a 50 percent increase in net short-term debt flows and a 24 percent rise in long-term debt inflows from private creditors. In contrast, net debt inflows from official creditors fell 32 percent, primarily as a consequence of large repurchases (repayments) by developing countries to the IMF: $24 billion, up 83 percent from their 2012 level. Net debt inflows from other official bilateral and multilateral creditors held steady at $43 billion. Private creditors remained dominant and accounted for 97 percent of net debt flows in 2013. Long-term debt flows from private creditors continued their upward trajectory, rising in 2013 to $337 billion on the back of an increase in medium-term bank financing and another record year for bond issuance by developing country borrowers. The share of short-term debt in total net inflows from private creditors rose to just over one-third in 2013, from approximately 31 percent in 2012.

External debt burdens remain moderate

Figure O.3 Key Debt Indicator Trends in Developing Countries, 2000–13

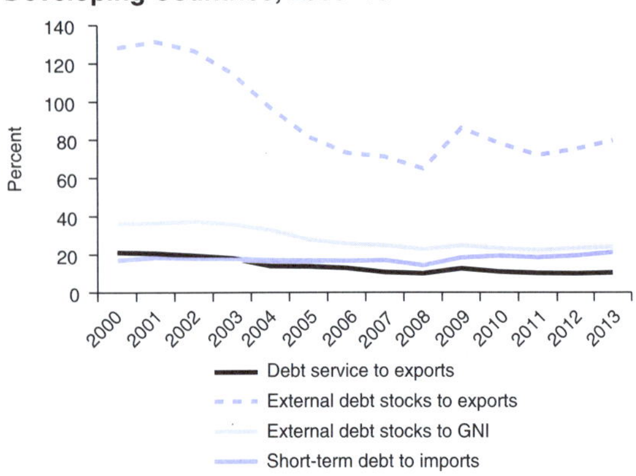

Sources: World Bank Debtor Reporting System and International Monetary Fund.

The majority of developing countries have seen their economies rebound strongly since 2010 with a concomitant improvement in the ratio of outstanding external debt to GNI and to export earnings: an average of 23 percent of GNI and 79 percent of export earnings at end-2013. Risks associated with short-term debt (28 percent of external debt stocks at end-2013) were mitigated by international reserves, which were at 111 percent of external debt stocks for the same period. Short-term debt is primarily trade related; when measured against developing countries' imports, it was at 21 percent, up only slightly from 2012. Developing countries have also seen significant improvement in their external debt payment servicing capacity over the past decade; a consequence of increased export earnings, debt restructuring, and outright debt relief from official and private creditors, and more recently, attractive borrowing terms in international capital markets. The debt service-to-export ratio averaged 10.5 percent in 2013, a marginal increase over the 10 percent recorded in 2012, but, more importantly, it was below half the 21.1 percent at the start of the decade.

Aggregate Financial Flows to Developing Countries, 2013

Net financial flows rise 10 percent in 2013 propelled by net debt inflows

International financial flows, debt and equity combined, totaled $1,184 billion in 2013, 11 percent higher than 2012. The increase was driven by the 28 percent rise in net debt flows. Net equity flows held steady at $643 billion, much the same level as 2012, with the 6 percent increase in foreign direct investment offset by the corresponding 29 percent decline in portfolio equity flows. The global trend was dominated by China, which accounted for more than one-third of net financial flows to developing countries in 2013, and where net financial flows rose by 45 percent compared with their level in the previous year. In contrast, other developing countries saw aggregate net financial flows contract by 2 percent in 2013, with net equity flows down 8 percent from their 2012 level. Although net debt flows to developing countries, excluding China, rose by 3 percent, there was a 22 percent contraction in short-term debt flows.

Figure O.4 Net Financial Flows to Developing Countries, Debt and Equity, 2008–13

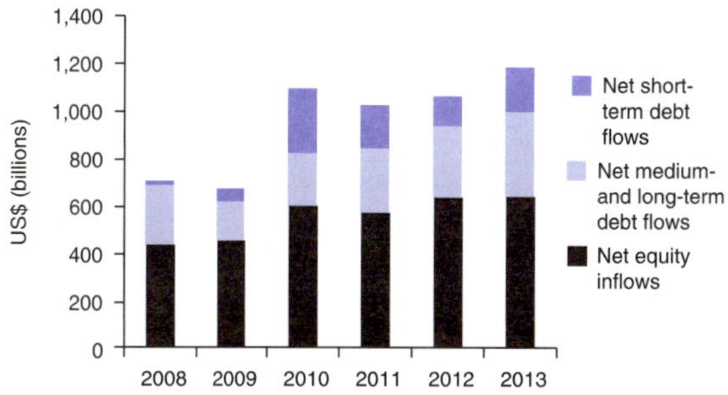

Sources: World Bank Debtor Reporting System, International Monetary Fund, and Bank for International Settlements.

Foreign direct investment accounts for around half of net financial flows - but the picture is mixed

Foreign direct investment proved resilient, accounting for approximately half of net financial inflows in 2013. UNCTAD's *World Investment Report 2014*[1] finds that developing countries were the destination for half of global foreign direct investment in 2013. Investors continue to be attracted by improved business and regulatory environments, growth prospects, and buoyant and expanding domestic markets. Net inflows to all developing countries combined rose 6 percent in 2013, to $574 billion, and close to half of those inflows were directed at China. At the regional and country level, the picture was mixed. Among the top six recipients of net inflows, only Brazil recorded a downturn, and those to Colombia were static. In contrast, Mexico saw net inflows grow 159 percent, to $31 billion, following the $18 billion purchase of Grupo Modele by AB InBev, Belgium. Countries in Europe and Central Asia recorded the sharpest contraction in 2013 (19 percent), while those in South Asia saw the largest (16 percent) increase.

Figure O.5 Net Foreign Direct Investment Inflows to Major Recipients, 2012 and 2013

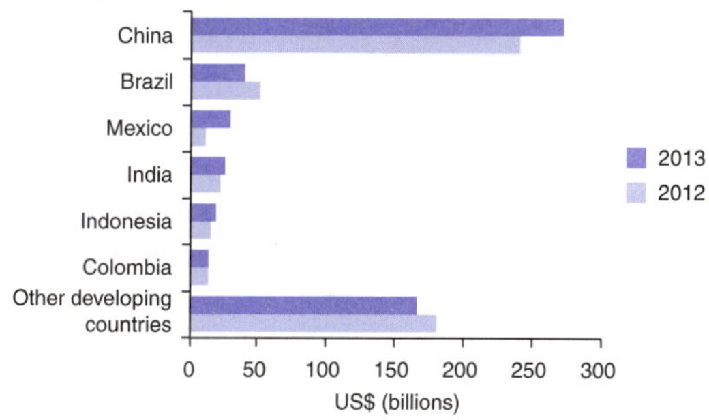

Source: International Monetary Fund.

Portfolio equity flows remain strong but highly concentrated in a small number of countries

The volatility that characterized portfolio equity flows in recent years moderated somewhat in 2013. Although, in aggregate, these flows fell nearly 30 percent from their 2012 level, there had been a sharp drop in 2011 and then a steep rise in 2012 when investors sought emerging markets where growth prospects appeared strong and returns high. This trend broadly continued in 2013, but as always, portfolio equity flows were susceptible to political and economic uncertainty, exemplified by the sharp outflows from Thailand ($6.5 billion) in 2013. Those to Nigeria were also down sharply, although they held up better than expected, given turmoil in the oil sector. Portfolio equity flows benefit only a handful of developing countries and, as with foreign direct investment, China was the destination of choice for half of such inflows in 2013.

Figure O.6 Net Inflow of Portfolio Equity to Major Recipients, 2011–13

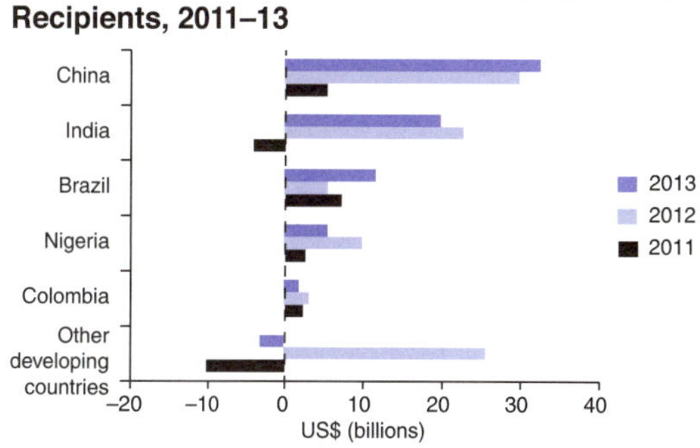

Source: International Monetary Fund.

1. UNCTAD (United Nations Conference on Trade and Development). 2014. *World Investment Report 2014- Investing in the SDGs: An Action Plan*. New York and Geneva.

All Developing Countries

China inflows dominate the global trend in 2013

Figure O.7 **Net Debt Flows for Select Country Groups, 2012 and 2013**

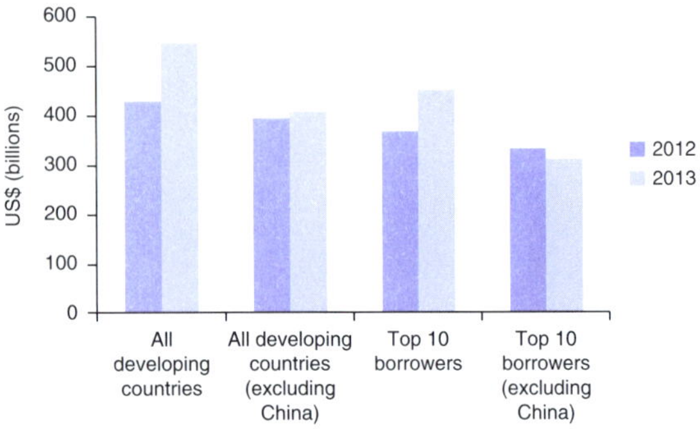

Source: World Bank Debtor Reporting System.

China, the single largest borrower among developing countries, saw net debt flows grow 300 percent in 2013, largely because of a rise in short-term debt inflows, to $115 billion ($33 billion in 2012), with a near ninefold increase in long-term debt inflows from private creditors. These flows dominated the global trend in 2013 and masked disparate changes in the direction of net debt flows for other developing countries. Collectively, there was only a 3 percent rise in net debt flows in 2013 with a 14 percent increase in long-term debt inflows offset by the sharp (22 percent) contraction in short-term debt flows. Major borrowers fared somewhat better with the top ten borrowers, measured on the basis of external debt outstanding at end-2013, recording a 23 percent rise in net debt flows. However, when China is excluded, debt flows to this group reveal a drop of 6 percent.

Net inflows to IDA-only countries increase and diversify

Figure O.8 **IDA-only Countries Net Debt Inflows by Creditor Type, 2013**

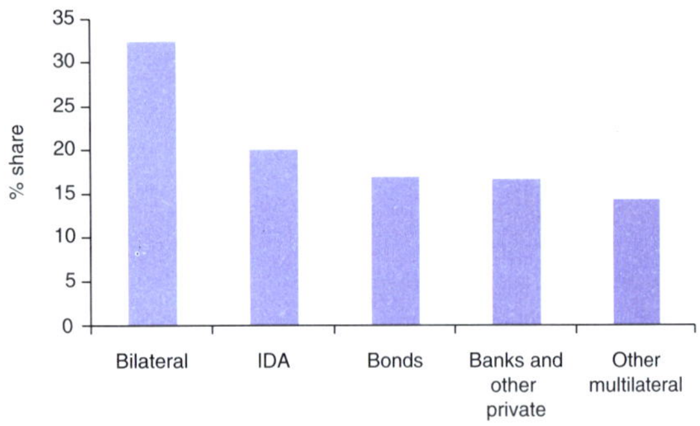

Source: World Bank Debtor Reporting System.

The rise in net financial flows to developing countries is reflected in those directed to 54 countries eligible only for International Development Association (IDA) financing[2]. In 2013, net financial flows to this group rose 21 percent, almost double the 11 percent increase in comparable flows recorded by other developing countries. Net capital inflows in 2013 totaled $56 billion, about one-half of which were accounted for by debt flows. Debt flows have increased by 40 percent over the past three years, and have become increasingly diversified with private creditors now accounting for 33 percent of long-term debt inflows. While most IDA-only countries continue to remain heavily dependent on official, concessional sources of financing, a number have gained market access and issued bonds in international capital markets. Bilateral lenders are the most important category of creditors but IDA remained the single largest creditor to the group, accounting for almost 20 percent of net long-term debt inflows in 2013.

Private sector external borrowing accounts for the greatest share of net debt flows

Figure O.9 **Composition of Net External Debt Flows by Type of Borrower, 2008–13**

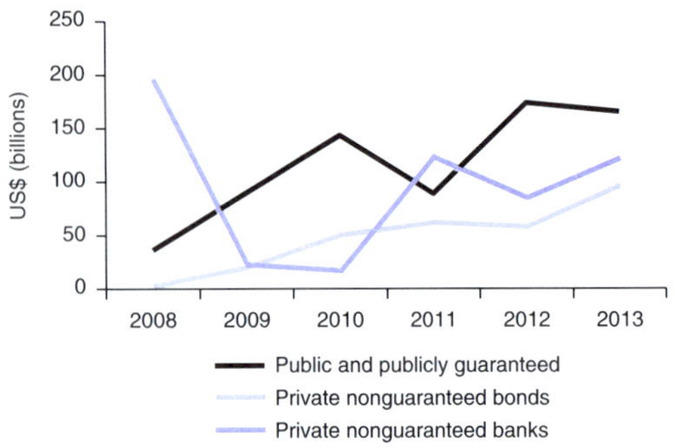

Source: World Bank Debtor Reporting System.

The important economic role played by the private sector in developing countries has led to a significant shift in borrowing patterns in recent years and in the composition of external debt stocks and flows. In 2009, in the wake of the global economic crisis, the nonguaranteed external obligations of private sector borrowers to developing countries accounted for only 31 percent of total long-term external debt stocks. At the end of 2013, their share had increased to more than 55 percent. At the same time, there has been an evolution in the composition of these flows, with bond issuance by private sector entities, an increasingly important component of medium-term debt inflows of private nonguaranteed debt, averaging more than 45 percent in the last four years. Although private-sector borrowing is driven by entities in more advanced emerging market countries, all regions have seen private nonguaranteed debt increase as a share of total external debt.

2. There are 59 countries designated as IDA-only, as of July 1, 2014, of which 54 countries report to the DRS (see page 164).

Bond issuance continues apace

Bond issuance by public and private entities in developing countries reached a record $233 billion in 2013, excluding the $11 billion mega-bond issue by Petrobras, Brazil[3]. In 2012, the larger share of bond issuance was by public borrowers, but in 2013, it was private-sector borrowers that were dominant. Their total issuance rose almost 50 percent, to $123 billion, equivalent to 52 percent of total developing country bond issuance in 2013. Corporate borrowers in Latin America and the Caribbean issued $60 billion in 2013, almost one-half of all issuance by corporate borrowers; two-thirds of the amount was attributable to banks and private companies in Mexico, which issued $43 billion in 2013. Bonds issued by public sector borrowers fell 22 percent in 2013, again driven by the Latin American and Caribbean region, which saw a decline of 35 percent.

Figure O.10 Bond Issuance by Public and Private Sector Borrowers, 2012 and 2013

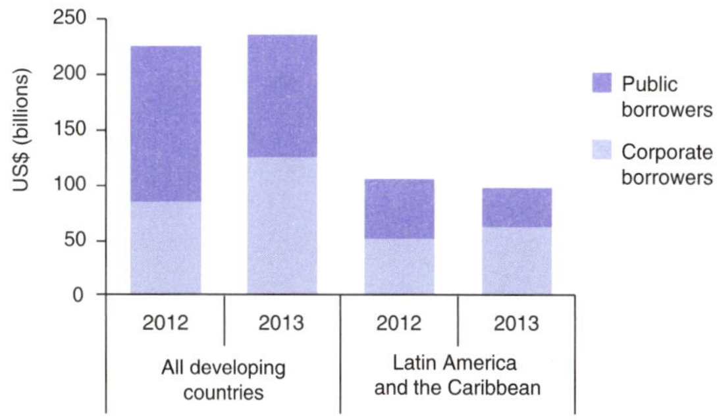

Source: World Bank Debtor Reporting System.

Inflows from bilateral creditors keep official flows steady

Net debt inflows from official creditors were broadly unchanged in 2013, at $43 billion, excluding the IMF, and divided almost evenly between bilateral and multilateral creditors. However, the evolving trend in recent years shows net inflows from bilateral creditors to be on a strong upward trajectory. This continued in 2013 with net inflows rising nearly 80 percent, to $21 billion, triple their 2011 level. In contrast, net inflows from multilateral creditors fell 25 percent in 2013, with a marked downturn in net inflows from a number of regional development banks. The driving force behind the increased bilateral flows is the lending from one developing country to another. Sub-Saharan Africa accounted for almost 40 percent of net inflows from bilateral creditors in 2013, followed by Middle East and North Africa, at 23 percent, primarily from creditors within the region, notably Kuwait, Saudi Arabia, and the United Arab Emirates.

Figure O.11 Bilateral and Multilateral Net Debt Flows, 2007–13

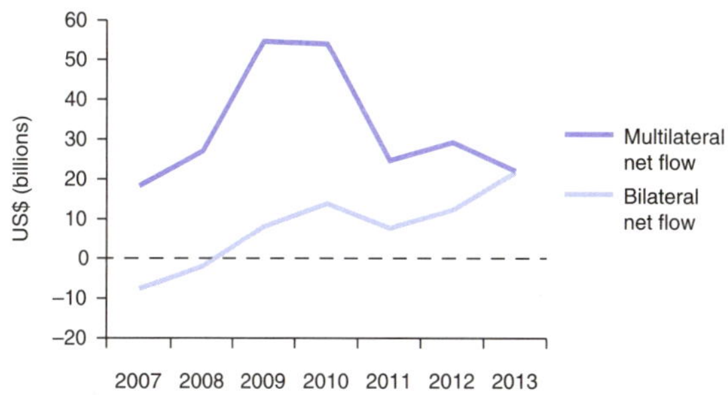

Source: World Bank Debtor Reporting System.

IBRD and IDA dominate inflows from multilateral creditors

Financing from the World Bank (IBRD and IDA) is the most important source of multilateral financing to developing countries. In 2013, net debt flows from the World Bank rose to $15 billion, more than double the comparable figure for 2011 and equivalent to 67 percent of net inflows from all multilateral institutions, excluding the IMF. While disbursements from most multilateral institutions stagnated or declined in 2013, IBRD and IDA rose 12 percent, to $17 billion, and 26 percent, to $10 billion, respectively. IDA resources are reserved for the world's poorest countries, many located in Sub-Saharan Africa, which was the destination for more than half of IDA disbursements in 2013. IDA also provided almost 40 percent of multilateral disbursements to South Asia. Disbursements from IBRD were concentrated in creditworthy countries in Latin America and the Caribbean, East Asia and Pacific, and Europe and Central Asia, and accounted for 34 percent, 41 percent, and 34 percent, respectively, of total multilateral disbursements in each region, in 2013.

Figure O.12 Net Multilateral Disbursements from IBRD and IDA, Regional Distribution, 2013

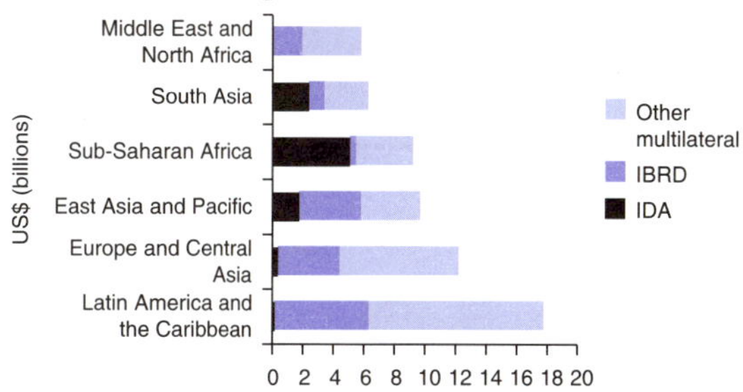

Source: World Bank Debtor Reporting System.

3. The bonds were issued through Petrobras' Dutch finance subsidiary Petrobras Global Finance PV and are considered to be non-resident, albeit 100 percent guaranteed by Petrobras, and not included in Brazil's external debt stocks or flows.

East Asia and Pacific

China drives net financial flows in the region

Figure O.13 Net Capital Flows to East Asia and Pacific Countries, 2007–13

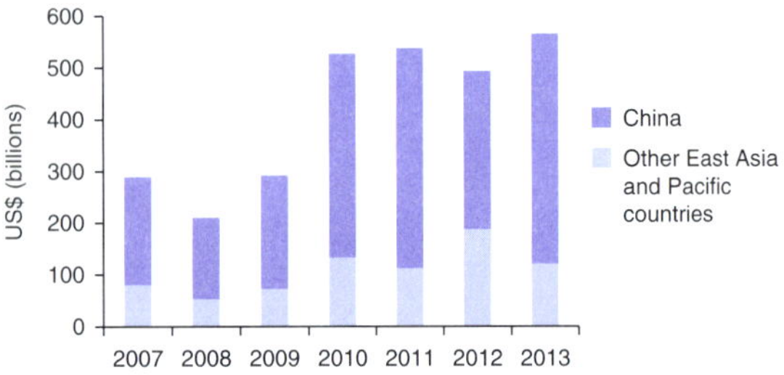

Source: World Bank Debtor Reporting System.

In 2013, net financial flows to the region rose 15 percent, to $563 billion, equivalent to 5 percent of the region's gross national income (GNI), primarily because of the 30 percent increase in net debt flows. Net equity flows rose moderately and were up only 7 percent over their 2012 level. The trend was dominated by China, which accounted for close to 80 percent of all inflows to the region and 52 percent of the combined external debt stock at the end of 2013. China saw net financial flows rise by 45 percent in 2013, to $444 million, of which 69 percent was in the form of equity, and 31 percent constituted net debt flows. In stark contrast, other countries in the region saw net financial flows plummet by 36 percent in 2013, to $119 billion, with net debt flows down by 44 percent, and net equity 18 percent below the 2012 level.

Most countries in the region saw a significant drop in net debt inflows in 2013

Figure O.14 Net Debt Flow To East Asia And Pacific Countries, 2007–13

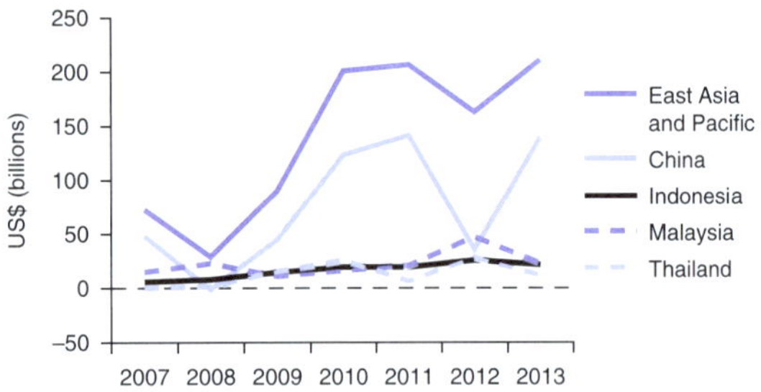

Source: World Bank Debtor Reporting System.

Net debt inflows to the region rose 30 percent in 2013, to $210 billion ($162 billion in 2012), driven by a 300 percent jump in those to China, which accounted for 66 percent of net debt flows to the region in 2013. For other major borrowers, Indonesia, Malaysia, and Thailand, it was a very divergent trend, and all three countries recorded a significant decrease in net debt flows in 2013 compared with the previous year. In Thailand, which had the biggest rise (414 percent) in debt inflows to the region from 2011 to 2012, net debt inflows fell 61 percent in 2013; those to Malaysia were only half their 2012 level; and Indonesia recorded a more modest fall at 16 percent. In all three countries, the decline was attributable to a fall in lending by private creditors and a contraction in short-term debt flows. For smaller borrowers, debt inflows were on an upward trajectory, rising 44 percent in Vietnam, 51 percent in the Solomon Islands, and 223 percent in Lao People's Democratic Republic.

Countries in the region account for twenty four percent of bond issuance by developing countries

Figure O.15 Percent Share Bond Issuance in East Asia And Pacific by Country, 2013

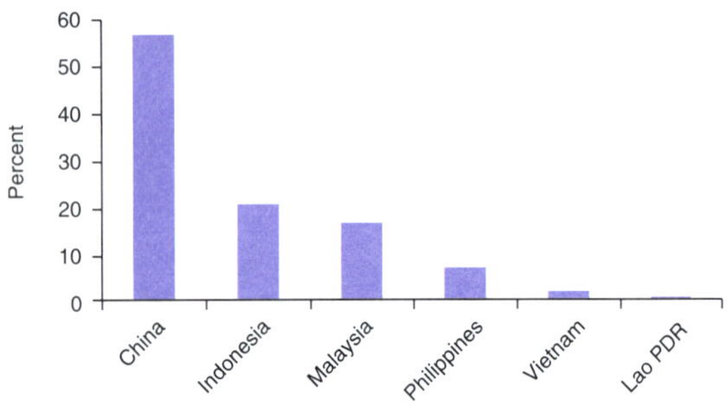

Source: World Bank Debtor Reporting System.

East Asia and Pacific remained the second highest region in terms of bond issuance in 2013, with a 24 percent share among all developing countries. Drops in bond issuance by Thailand and Malaysia were offset by China, which almost tripled its bond issuance from 2012 to 2013, 82 percent of which was issued by corporate borrowers. Lao PDR came to the market for the first time in 2013, with a 3-year unrated $50 million equivalent baht-denominated note; this is the first Thai baht issuance by a foreign government after the Thai authorities removed restrictions on the requirement that foreign issuers have an investment grade rating. Vietnam issued two bonds in 2013, one by Vingroup (ex-Vincom) for a $200 million 4.5-year senior high-yield note and another government guaranteed 12-year note for $626.8 million.

Europe and Central Asia

Sharp increase in 2013 net debt flows

Net financial flows to the region rose 35 percent in 2013, to $139 billion ($103 billion in 2012), as a consequence of a sharp increase in net debt flows. These net debt flows rose 120 percent over their 2012 level, to $95 billion, and served to offset the 26 percent downturn in net equity flows. Foreign direct investment fell by 19 percent, to $42 billion, and portfolio equity flows dropped to one-quarter of its 2012 level, largely because of the collapse in portfolio equity flows to Turkey. The increase in debt flows were underpinned by a near fivefold rise in long-term borrowing by private nonguaranteed entities, to $58 billion, and a comparable increase in short-term debt inflows to $33 billion. Financing from official creditors was negative, with outflows to the IMF climbing to $23 billion ($13 billion in 2012), reflecting repayment of rescue packages extended in the wake of the 2008 global economic crisis; these repayments primarily came from Hungary ($6.7 billion), Romania ($6.2 billion), and Ukraine ($5.6 billion).

Figure O.16 Net Capital Flows to Europe and Central Asia, 2010–13

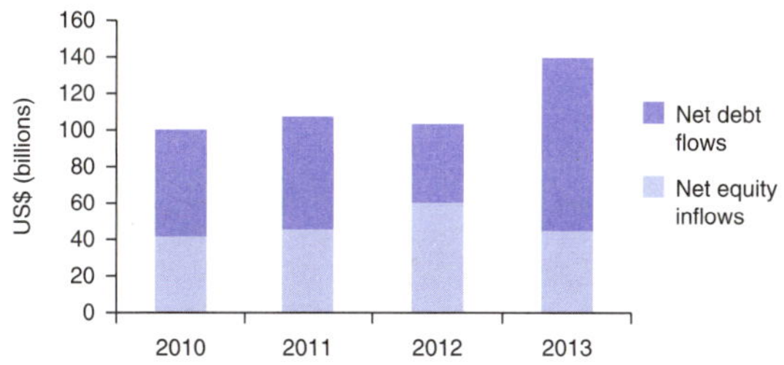

Source: World Bank Debtor Reporting System.

Private sector borrowing has accelerated sharply over the past three years

The financial crisis that began in the last quarter of 2008 made cross-border borrowing from the private sector a lot more costly in 2009, which caused the official creditors, mainly the multilateral organizations, to lend money to the public sector. The net inflows from official creditors doubled in 2009, reaching $49 billion (from $25 billion in 2008), while the private creditors' medium- and long-term net inflows went down to $7.7 billion, from $130 billion in 2008. After 4 years, the situation has reversed. Europe and Central Asia's net medium- and long-term borrowing from foreign private creditors has rapidly increased since 2011, reaching its highest level in 2013 (from –$11.5 billion in 2010 to $80.7 billion in 2013). More than half of those net flows came from borrowing by the commercial banks and other sectors, while the official creditors recorded an outflow of $19 billion. Hungary, Kazakhstan, and Turkey received 81 percent of those net inflows.

Figure O.17 Europe and Central Asia: Net Medium and Long-Term Debt Inflows by Type of Creditor, 2009–13

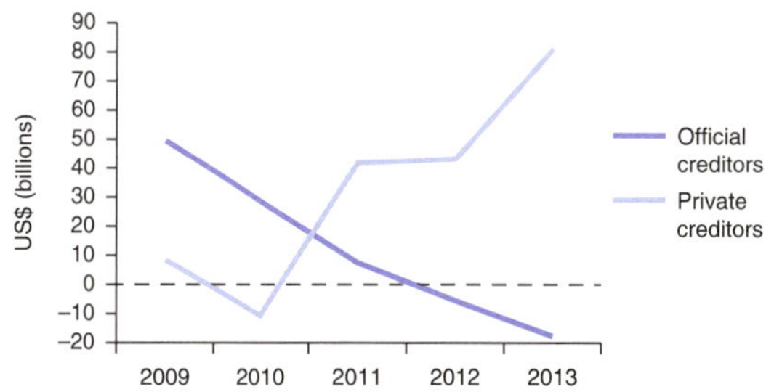

Source: World Bank Debtor Reporting System.

Equity inflows decline but the picture across the region is mixed

The share of equity in net financial flows to the region fell significantly in 2013, to 32 percent, compared with almost 60 percent the previous year. Equity flows to the region are heavily concentrated in five countries: Azerbaijan, Kazakhstan, Turkey, Turkmenistan, and Ukraine, which together account for more than 65 percent of foreign direct investment and 95 percent of portfolio equity flows to the region. When the top five recipients are excluded, inflows of foreign direct investment to the region fell by 21 percent in 2013, although some of the smaller economies, notably Albania, Belarus, Bulgaria, and Romania showed growth. Foreign direct investment inflows to these countries increased between 41 percent (Belarus) to as much as 146 percent (Romania, to $2.5 billion). Net foreign direct investment to Albania, at $1.3 billion, reached its highest level ever and was up 1.9 times over the 2012 level. The majority of these flows constituted reinvestment, targeted mainly at the extractive and processing industries.

Figure O.18 Foreign Direct Investment Equity inflows, 2012 and 2013

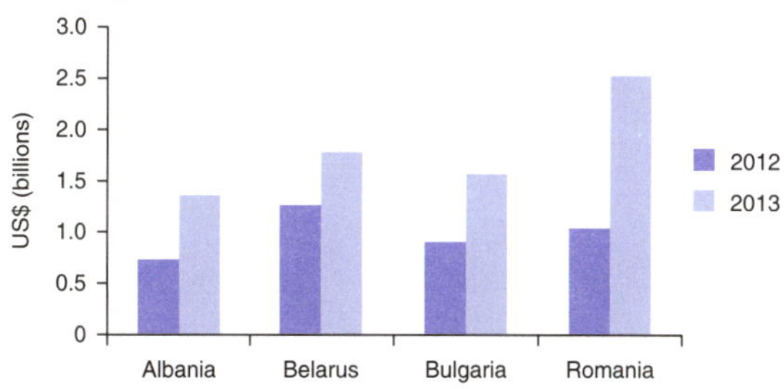

Source: World Bank Debtor Reporting System.

Latin America and the Caribbean

Composition of external debt shift in 2013

Figure O.19 Composition of Net Debt Inflows, 2012 and 2013

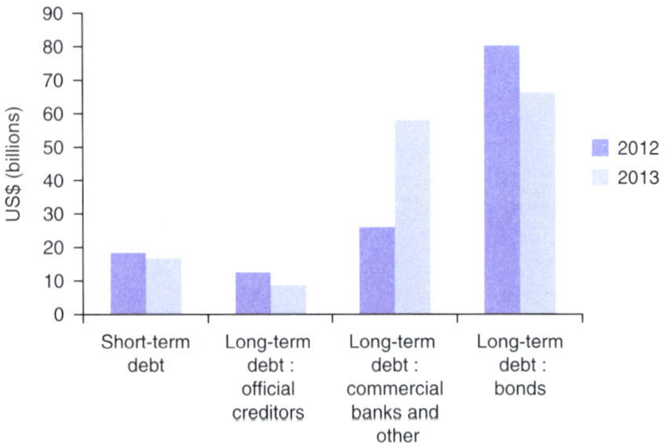

Source: World Bank Debtor Reporting System.

Net debt inflows to the region rose 10 percent in 2013, to $149 billion ($136 billion in 2012), accompanied by some changes in composition. Medium- and long-term net inflows from banks increased, rising by 127 percent over their 2012 level, to $58 billion, offsetting a 17 percent fall in net inflows from bond issuance by public and private entities and a 9 percent contraction in short-term debt inflows. Official creditors account for only a modest share of net debt flows, but these too fell by one-third in 2013, to $8.2 billion. In aggregate, net equity flows held steady with the collapse in portfolio equity flows to Mexico, offset by a doubling of those to Brazil, at $11.6 billion ($5.6 billion in 2012). The 20 percent fall in foreign direct investment to Brazil more than compensated for the tripling of comparable flows into Mexico. Taken together, Brazil and Mexico increased their share of net equity flows to the region to 61 percent (58 percent in 2012).

Equity and private sector borrowing drive financial flows to Mexico

Figure O.20 Mexico: Debt and FDI inflows, 2007–13

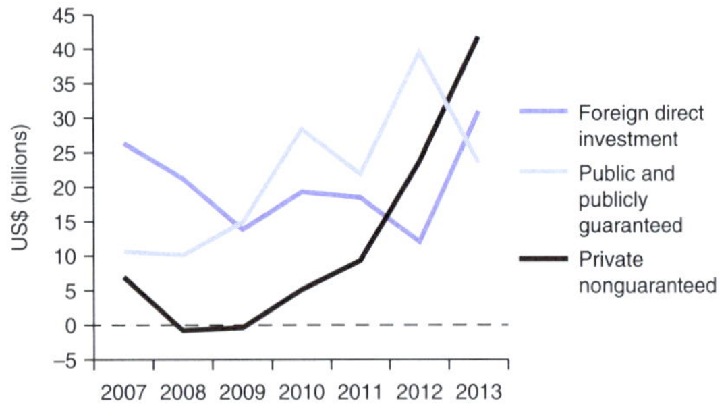

Source: World Bank Debtor Reporting System.

Net financial flows to Mexico totaled $109 billion in 2013, on par with 2012 and equivalent to 38 percent of the comparable flows to countries in Latin America and the Caribbean combined. In contrast to 2012, when net debt flows to public sector borrowers was the most important component of financial flows, 2013 saw high levels of foreign direct investment and debt flows to private sector borrowers. Together they rose 104.2 percent, to $73 billion, more than enough to offset the 42 percent drop in flows to public sector borrowers and a sharp contraction in short-term debt and portfolio equity flows. Foreign direct investment rose by 159 percent, to $31 billion, which made Mexico the third largest developing country recipient in 2013. Net debt inflows to private nonguaranteed borrowers, which have been on a rising trajectory since 2010, jumped by 77 percent in 2013, to $42 billion, equivalent to more than half the total net debt inflows in 2013.

Equity constitutes a significant share of net financial flows

Figure O.21 Net Financial Flows: Share of Debt and Equity, 2013

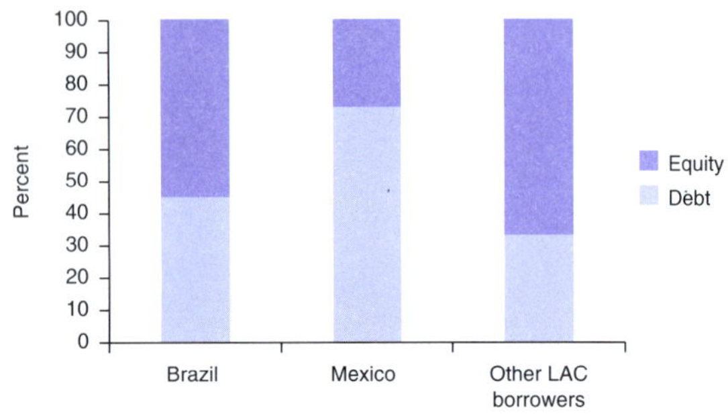

Source: World Bank Debtor Reporting System.

Net financial flows to the region averaged $280 billion per annum in 2012 and 2013, divided roughly equally between debt and equity. Brazil and Mexico combined accounted for 72 percent of these flows in 2013, with inflows to each country at a broadly similar level: $96 billion for Brazil and $109 billion for Mexico. There was, however, a marked difference in the composition flows to each country. In Brazil, the second most important developing country destination after China, equity inflows comprised 55 percent of total inflows in 2013, whereas in Mexico, their share was only 27 percent. For other countries in the region, equity was by far the most important source of financing and made up 67 percent of net financial flows during 2013. This is partially explained by large net debt outflows from República Bolivariana de Venezuela, but it also reflects robust foreign investment across the region, attracted by natural resources, a fast expanding middle class, inter-regional investments, and mega infrastructure projects such as the Panama Canal Expansion Project.

Middle East and North Africa

Net financial flows rise due to increase in debt flows

Net financial flows to the region were up 35 percent, to $31 billion in 2013, entirely because of increased net debt inflows, which rose to $16.7 billion, close to double their 2012 level. Net equity inflows, on which the region has been historically more reliant than debt, were at $14.3 billion—virtually unchanged from their 2012 level, although there were some important shifts in country composition. Foreign direct investment inflows to the Islamic Republic of Iran, the region's primary recipient, fell by one-third in 2013, to $3 billion, while those to Morocco rose by 34 percent, to $3.2 billion. The principal drivers of increased debt flows were lending by official, notably bilateral, creditors; bond issuance by several countries; and, to a lesser degree, a turnaround in short-term debt flows that turned positive in 2013, at $0.4 billion (from an outflow of $1.8 billion in 2012). The combined external debt stock rose by 9 percent, to $191 billion, of which 72 percent constituted public and publicly guaranteed debt.

Figure O.22 Net Financial Flows, 2007–13

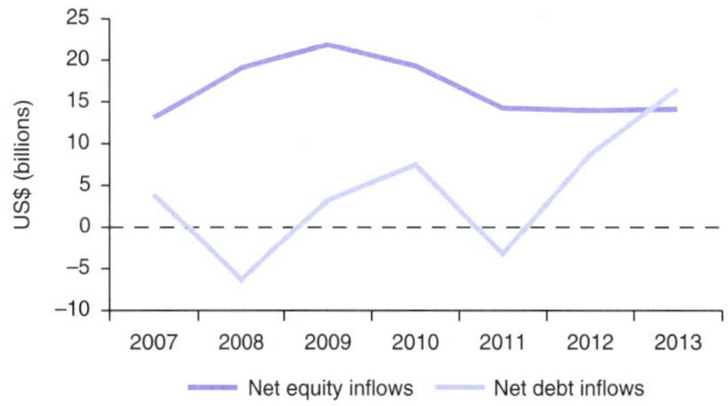

Source: World Bank Debtor Reporting System.

Net debt inflows to the region rise sharply but are heavily concentrated

Long-term debt flows to the region increased over the past two years, to $10.2 billion in 2012 (from an outflow in 2011), and then rose by 51 percent in 2013, to $15.4 billion. In parallel, these flows have become increasingly concentrated in the Arab Republic of Egypt, Jordan, and Morocco. Their combined share jumped from 51 percent of long-term debt inflows in 2012 to 98 percent in 2013. The composition of debt flows to each country vary: for Egypt, two-thirds of the inflows in 2013 came from bilateral creditors, notably Kuwait, Saudi Arabia, and the United Arab Emirates, plus the IMF. In contrast, half the net debt flows to Morocco were from multilateral creditors, while the other half were from private creditors. In Jordan, more than one-third of net long-term debt inflows in 2013 reflected tranche release under the IMF Standby Arrangement, and the remainder came primarily through the issuance of U.S. dollar denominated Treasury Bonds and a $1.25 billion 7-year Eurobond with a 100 percent guarantee by the U.S. government.

Figure O.23 Net Debt Inflows by Country, 2011–13

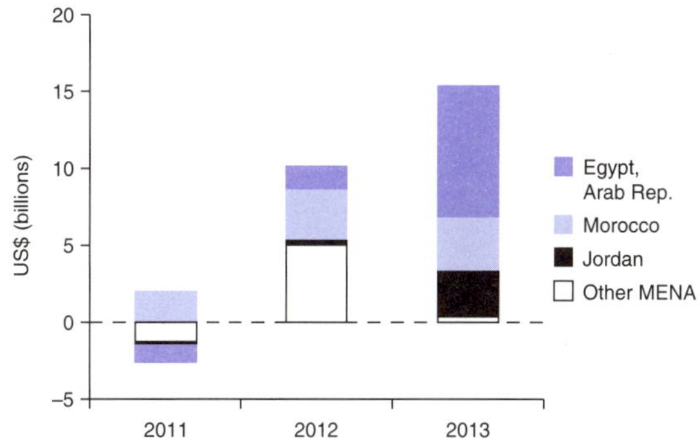

Source: World Bank Debtor Reporting System.

Debt-to-export ratios are, on average, much lower than in other developing countries

The ratios of external debt stock to exports and to GNI for the region averaged 55 percent and 17 percent, respectively, at the end of 2013, up from 41 percent and 14 percent, respectively, in 2012; the increase is attributed to a rise in external debt stock and a contraction in growth and exports. However, debt ratios remain considerably lower than those for other developing countries: 79 percent to exports and 23 percent to GNI at the end of 2013. This level is largely due to the high share of equity in net financial flows in prior years and the robust exports during the past decade. The debt service-to-exports ratio, 5 percent in 2013, was also half that for other developing countries. International reserves were 152 percent of external debt stock at the end of 2013, but the regional aggregate is heavily influenced by Algeria's high level of reserves ($194 billion) and its very low external debt stock ($5 billion). In contrast, Egypt accounted for 23 percent of the region's external debt stock at the end of 2013, but its reserves were only 31 percent of outstanding external debt.

Figure O.24 Debt Ratios for Middle East and North Africa, 2012 and 2013

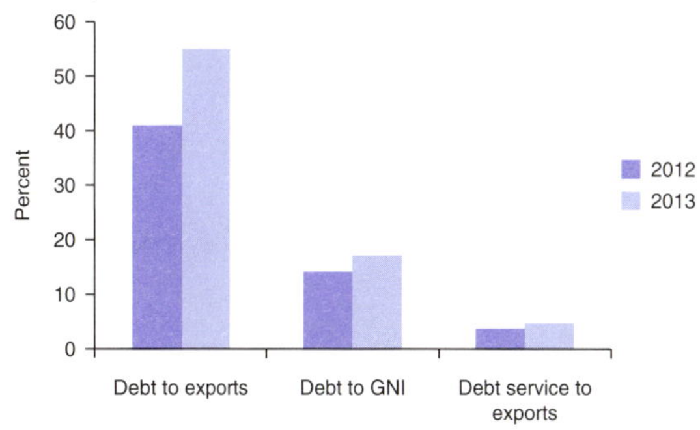

Source: World Bank Debtor Reporting System.

South Asia

Fall in net capital flows due to India

Figure O.25 Net Capital Flows by Type, 2007–13

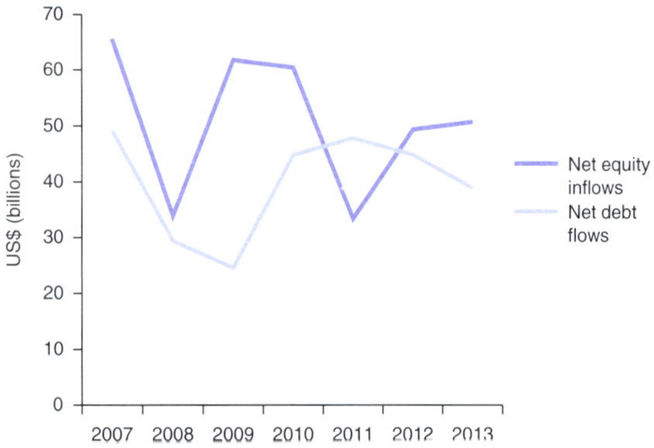

Source: World Bank Debtor Reporting System.

Net capital flows to the region fell 5 percent in 2013 because of a downturn in net debt flows. This downturn was the result of a sharp contraction in short-term debt flows, coupled with a net outflow of $3 billion to holders of Indian bonds (from a $4.5 billion inflow in 2012) and $2.6 billion outflow to the IMF from Pakistan. Outflows were largely offset by a jump in long-term bank lending, directed almost entirely to a wide range of private sector entities in India; long-term bank lending rose to $40 billion, 76 percent over its 2012 level. Net equity inflows at $51 billion were broadly unchanged in aggregate with increased inflows of foreign direct investment offsetting a corresponding downturn in portfolio equity flows. The principle player was India, which accounted for 93 percent of aggregate net capital flows to the region in 2013.

Financial flows to the region rise by 39 percent, excluding India

Figure O.26 Financial Flows to South Asia, Excluding India, 2013

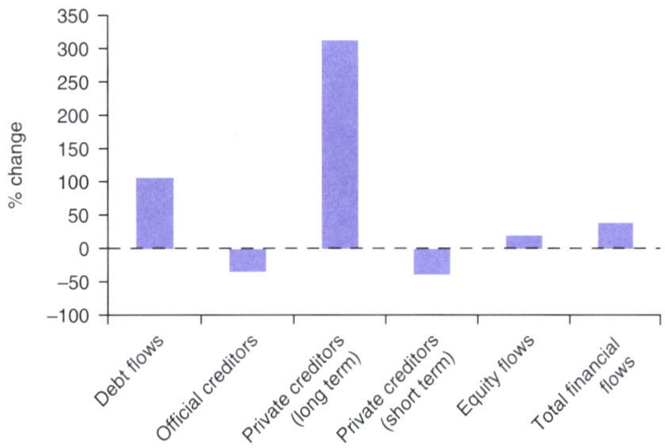

Source: World Bank Debtor Reporting System.

Net financial flows to countries in the South Asia region, excluding India, constitute a very small, 7 percent, share of the region's aggregate flows, but their financing patterns differ from the regional trend. In 2013, net financial flows to this group of countries rose by 39 percent, to $6.3 billion, driven primarily by increased equity inflows. These equity inflows grew by 21 percent, to $4.3 billion, due to increased foreign direct investment flows across the region; in particular, there was a strong showing by Bangladesh, and a sharp rise in Pakistan mainly because of the service (telecom) sector. Despite a $0.7 billion outflow of short-term debt and $2.6 billion net outflow to the IMF from Pakistan, net debt flows doubled to $2.0 billion in 2013, and they accounted for 32 percent of net financial flows. Long-term debt flows were $3.2 billion, little changed from 2012, but with a shift in composition of lending from official sources ($2.5 billion to $1.6 billion) to private sources ($0.4 billion to $1.6 billion).

Debt indicators vary widely across the region

Figure O.27 Debt Ratios for South Asia, 2013

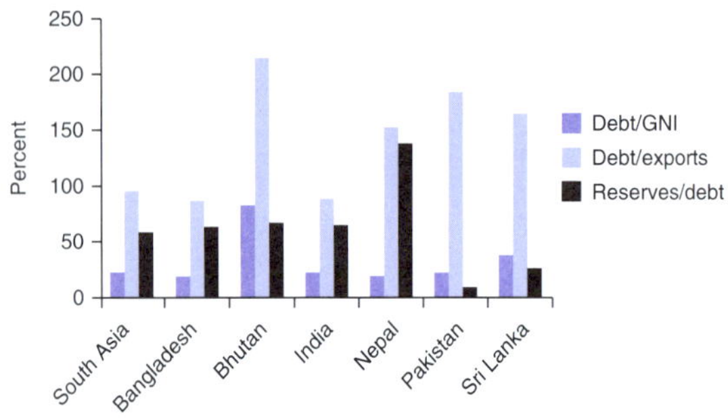

Source: World Bank Debtor Reporting System.

The ratio of external debt stock to GNI for the region, 23 percent, fell in 2013, and the ratio of external debt stock to exports remained virtually unchanged (97 percent) from 2012. These averages were determined by and closely correlated with India's debt ratios (23 percent to GNI and 89 percent to exports), given the weight of the Indian economy compared with that of its neighbors. Across the region, however, there was a wide disparity in ratios. The debt-to-export ratio ranged from highs of 215 percent and 185 percent for Bhutan and Pakistan, respectively, to a low of 88 percent in Bangladesh. Bhutan had the highest ratio of debt to GNI, 84 percent, compared with Bangladesh and Nepal, both at 20 percent. The ratio of international reserves to debt, 58 percent for the region as a whole, was also heavily weighted by India (65 percent), but the ratio varies widely from 138 percent for Nepal to as low as 9 percent for Pakistan.

Sub-Saharan Africa

Net debt inflows offset by net equity flows

Net capital flows to Sub-Saharan Africa stagnated in 2013 with increased net debt inflows offset by a fall in net equity flows, the latter largely because of a steep 44 percent drop in portfolio equity flows to Nigeria. On the debt front, net inflows of long-term debt were up 35 percent over their 2012 level, to $29.5 billon, with official creditors registering close to a 40 percent rise and those from bond issuance tripling to $9 billion. However, these were offset by the fall in medium-term financing from banks and the sharp contraction in short-term debt inflows, which fell to $2.6 billion, around one-third their 2012 level. Overall, net debt flows were up by a moderate 7 percent in 2013. The picture changes radically, however, if South Africa is excluded from the aggregates. With that exclusion, net debt inflows to other countries in the region increased by 63 percent in 2013, to $29 billion ($17.7 billion in 2012). When measured in terms of GNI, net capital flows to the region (excluding South Africa) were 5.9 percent in 2013, down slightly from 2012.

Figure O.28 Net Capital Flows for Sub-Saharan Africa, 2007–13

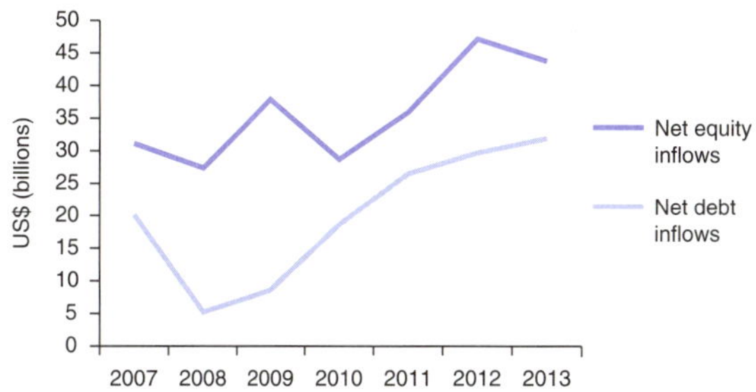

Source: World Bank Debtor Reporting System.

Long- term debt is rising and its composition is changing

The rapid rise in external borrowing by countries in the region is characterized by a marked change in borrowing patterns and creditor composition. Disbursements of long-term debt, excluding South Africa, increased 51 percent in 2013, triple the comparable rise for other developing countries, to $41 billion. Of this, one-half was accounted for by private creditors. Disbursements from private creditors have not only risen, they have also become more diversified. In 2010, all long-term private debt was attributable to banks and other private creditors, but by 2013 one-third was accounted for by bond issuance. Borrowing patterns have also changed, with two-thirds of disbursements from private creditors now directed to publicly guaranteed private-sector borrowers. Disbursements from official creditors have risen moderately, 35 percent since 2010, but they are also characterized by a change in composition. IDA remains the single largest creditor, but overall, multilateral creditors' share of official lending had fallen to 43 percent by 2013, with China the main driver for increased bilateral lending.

Figure O.29 Disbursements to Sub-Saharan Africa, Excluding South Africa, 2007–13

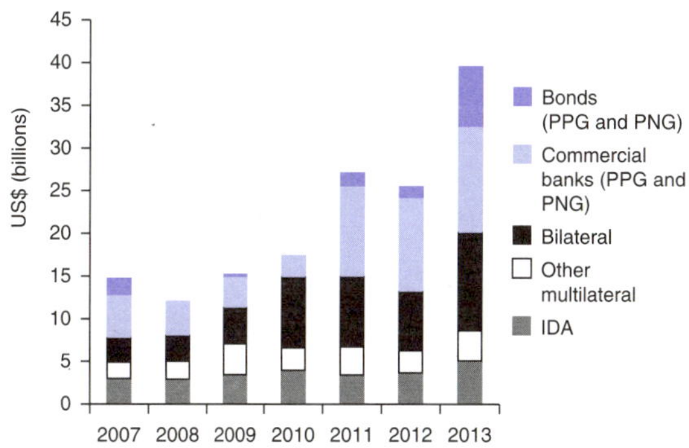

Source: World Bank Debtor Reporting System.

Bond issuance booms

Historically, bond issuance in Sub-Saharan Africa was largely confined to South Africa, but following Ghana's debut sovereign issue in 2007, bond issuance by countries in the region, including those that benefited from HIPC and MDRI debt relief, has become a rapidly rising phenomenon. Access to markets has been facilitated by benign global market conditions and the region's high return potential. Issuance of bonds to the region in 2013, excluding South Africa, totaled $6.9 billion, equivalent to 35 percent of disbursements from official creditors and 19 percent of foreign direct investment inflows to the region. This $6.9 billion included debut issues by Mozambique, Rwanda, and Tanzania. The primary purpose of governments' international sovereign bonds is infrastructure spending, benchmarking for other government and corporate bond markets (as in the case of Nigeria), and public debt management. For example, Rwanda issued a $400 million, 10-year, 6.875 Eurobond in April 2013, which will finance the construction of a convention center and the repayment of some state-owned RwandAir debt.

Figure O.30 Bond Issuance in Sub-Saharan Africa, Excluding South Africa, 2007–13

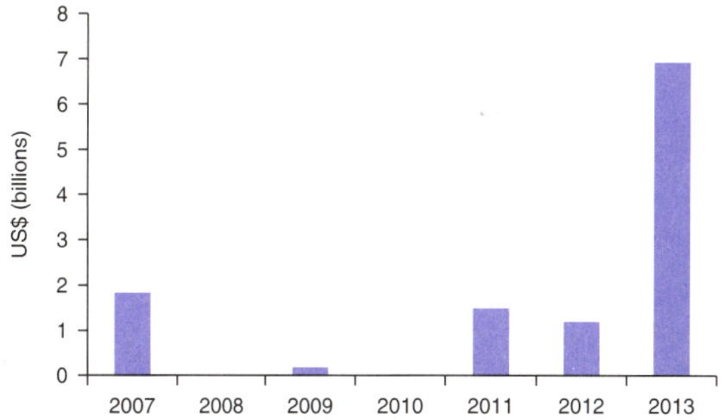

Source: World Bank Debtor Reporting System.

QUARTERLY EXTERNAL DEBT STATISTICS

About the Data

In October 2014, the World Bank, in collaboration with the IMF, launched the new Quarterly External Debt Statistics (QEDS) database in line with the classifications and definitions of the 2013 External Debt Statistics: Guide for Compilers and Users (*2013 EDS Guide* and sixth edition of the *Balance of Payments and International Investment Position Manual* (BPM6). The QEDS database reflects new concepts and definitions, classifications of external debt data, as well as expanded coverage that enhances the analytical use of the data. The database brings together detailed external debt data of countries that subscribe to the IMF's Special Data Dissemination Standard (SDDS) and a select number of countries that participate in the IMF's General Data Dissemination System (GDDS). The benefit of bringing together comparable external debt data is to facilitate macroeconomic analysis and cross-country data comparison.

Trends in the External Debt of High-Income Economies

The external debt stock of high-income economies in 2013 was uneven. Compared with 2012, the debt stock varied from a decline of 23 percent in Finland, to the highest increase, 31 percent, in the Czech Republic. The short-term debt stock remained high, at 41 percent of the total debt. The total external debt stock for high-income economies reporting to the QEDS database rose 2 percent in 2013, to $68 trillion, while the external debt stock of developing countries in the SDDS database during the same time period increased by 1 percent (see Table O.1). The increase in high-income economies' external debt stock was partly driven by the rise in debt of general government, particularly for Cyprus, the Slovak Republic, Slovenia, and Spain. Contributing to the growth was also a moderate increase in external debt by the private sector with debt by "Other sectors" rising by 6 percent, and "Direct investment: intercompany lending" by 8 percent. Issuance of bonds by high-income economies rose by 2 percent, to $29.1 trillion, with Iceland and the Slovak Republic issuing the most.

Table O.1 High-Income Economies, External Debt Stock, 2012 and 2013
Percent share

	2012	2013
Total ($billion)	66,844	68,448
General Government	22%	23%
Central Bank	3%	3%
Deposit-Taking Corporations, except the Central Bank	37%	35%
Other Sectors	26%	27%
Direct Investment: Intercompany Lending	11%	12%

Source: World Bank Quarterly External Debt Statistics.

During 2013, the external debt situation relative to GDP rose marginally for high-income economies to 142 percent. The three most heavily indebted countries were France, Greece, and Portugal, which had debt-to-GDP ratios above 200 percent[4]. On the other hand, the least indebted countries were the Republic of Korea, Israel, and the Russian Federation (each less than 40 percent). During 2013, the largest increase in debt-to-GDP ratio was experienced by the Czech Republic, the Slovak Republic, and Spain, while Finland, Germany, and New Zealand saw their debt-to-GDP ratio decline.

The Group of Seven (G7) countries[5] accounted for 64 percent of the total external debt of high-income economies, totaling $43.7 trillion, during 2013 (see table O.2). The G7 countries' debt stock maintained the 2012 levels, with a slight increase of 0.5 percent. The increase was led by the United States, for which the external debt stock rose by 5 percent in 2013, compared with only 1 percent the previous year. This was followed by Italy and France, which showed external debt stock increases of 4 percent and 3 percent, respectively. Conversely, Japan, Germany, and Canada recorded a reduction in their external debt stock by 7 percent, 5 percent, and 1 percent, respectively.

4. Excludes countries with offshore liabilities.

5. G7 = Group of Seven (Canada, France, Germany, Italy, Japan, the United Kingdom, and the United States).

Table O.2 **G7 Countries, External Debt Stock, 2008–13**
US$ billions

	2008	2009	2010	2011	2012	2013
Canada	848	1,029	1,144	1,248	1,408	1,390
France	4,881	5,180	5,161	5,223	5,377	5,549
Germany	5,220	5,245	5,370	5,494	5,775	5,503
Italy	2,396	2,561	2,445	2,360	2,526	2,629
Japan	2,231	2,086	2,589	3,115	3,017	2,803
United Kingdom	9,003	9,005	9,228	9,667	9,727	9,365
United States	13,757	13,662	14,516	15,508	15,680	16,488
Total G7 Countries	38,335	38,769	40,453	42,615	43,511	43,727

Source: World Bank Quarterly External Debt Statistics.

Figure O.31 **G7 Counties, External Debt-to-GDP Ratio, 2008–13**

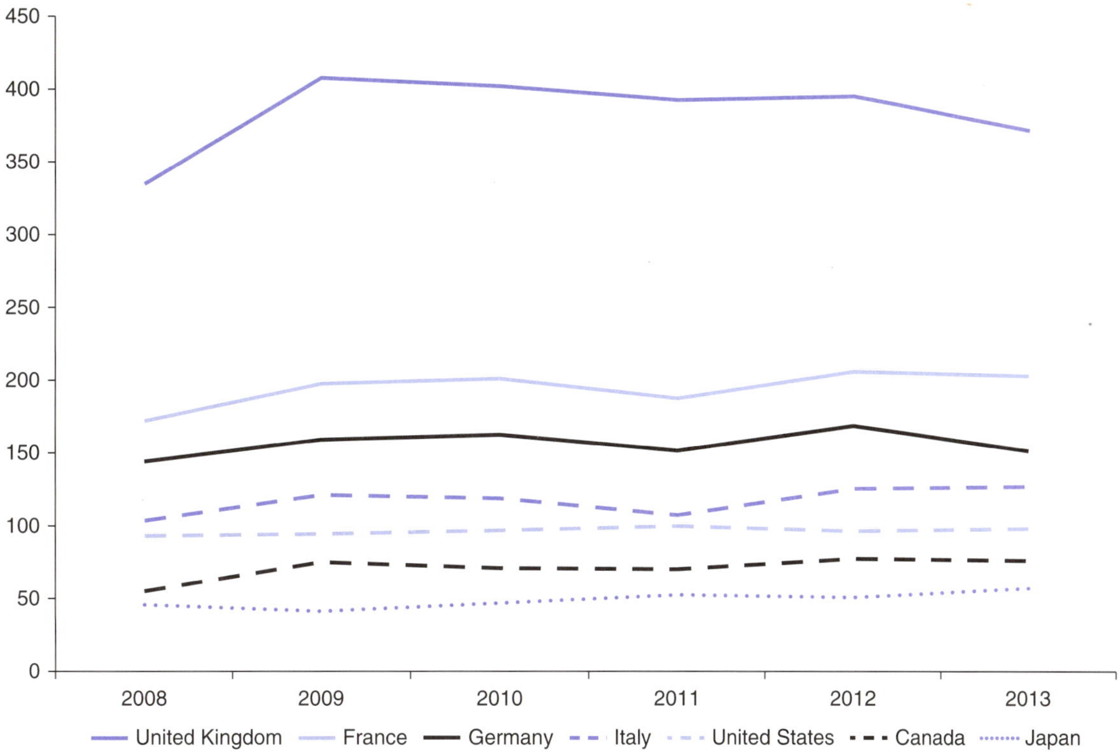

Source: World Bank Quarterly External Debt Statistics.

Despite having recorded a large increase in its debt stock, the external debt-to-GDP ratio in the United States increased slightly to 98 percent. Japan's ratio of external debt-to-GDP ratio rose to 57 percent in 2013 from 51 percent in 2012. In Italy and Canada, the external debt level remained relatively unchanged. Among the G7 countries, Germany had the most significant improvement in their ratio of external debt to GDP, which fell to 151 percent, from 169 percent in 2012. At 371 percent, the United Kingdom had the highest external debt-to-GDP ratio; nonetheless, for 2013 it shows a decline from the previous year. France's debt burden was still above 200 percent, but it recorded a slight improvement in its ratio from 2012 (see figure O.31).

PUBLIC SECTOR DEBT

About the Data

The government and public sector debt data have gained significant attention over the past four years. In 2010, as part of the Open Data Initiative, the World Bank, in partnership with the IMF, mandated by the Inter Agency Group (IAG), launched the online, quarterly, Public Sector Debt database in order to fill the gap between analytical needs and a lack of access to high quality, cross-country data. A continued emphasis on public sector debt was voiced in the 'Communiqué of Meeting of G20 Finance Ministers and Central Bank Governors' on February 16th, 2013, which advocated for "strengthening the public sector balance sheet" and "transparency and comparability of public sector reporting, and monitoring the impact of financial sector vulnerabilities on public debt."

Since the last Task Force on Financial Statistics (TFFS) meeting in March of 2013, the Public Sector Debt Statistics database has experienced a moderate change in membership. Currently 38 developing countries and 35 high-income economies report their data to the Public Sector Debt database.

Trends in 2013

Government debt levels in EU15 economies continued their upward trends in 2013. Despite the programs of fiscal austerity and the new pacts on fiscal discipline, many of the EU15 economies failed to bring their debt down to a more sustainable level. The average government debt-to-GDP ratio rose to 90 percent (87 percent in 2012).

The Government of Greece still owes $443 billion even after three years of strict austerity measures, tax policies, and debt cuts of 53 percent (100 billion euro in March 2012). Greece recorded a government debt of 176.3 percent of GDP, followed by Italy (132.6 percent), Portugal (125.2 percent), and Ireland (125.8 percent). Only 4 countries (Denmark, Finland, Luxembourg, and Sweden) recorded debt ratios below the 60 percent debt default.

High government debt levels were not restricted to EU15 economies only. Cyprus recorded a government debt of $25.3 billion at the end of 2013, up from $19.8 billion in 2012, which accounted for 110 percent of GDP at the end of 2013, compared with 84 percent at the end of 2012. This was the highest increase among all 28 EU members and was primarily the result of borrowing from the European Stability Mechanism in 2013 (see Figure O.32).

When looking at the countries of the Organisation for Economic Co-operation and Development (OECD) outside the Euro Zone, Japan's government debt-to-GDP ratio surpassed 200 percent in 2013, while the ratios of the United States and the United Kingdom stood at 94.5 percent and 85.5 percent, respectively. However, unlike the other two countries, 92 percent of the Japanese government debt has been financed by domestic creditors, recording the highest rate of the leading economies.

The developing economies accumulated less debt during the crisis. The government debt-to-GDP ratios for developing economies in 2013 were more promising than those of high-income economies. Based on the reports to the Public Sector Debt database, the government debt-to-GDP ratio in 2013 ranged from the lowest, 13 percent in Russia, to the highest, 82 percent in Hungary, which was, in most instances, lower than the comparable ratio for 2008. Big economies like Brazil and India saw government debt fall from 55 percent and 68 percent of GDP, respectively, in 2012, to 53 percent and 66.6 percent, respectively, in 2013. Fiscal consolidation in both countries improved the debt burden. Turkey managed to

Figure O.32 Euro Area Government Debt to GDP
Percent

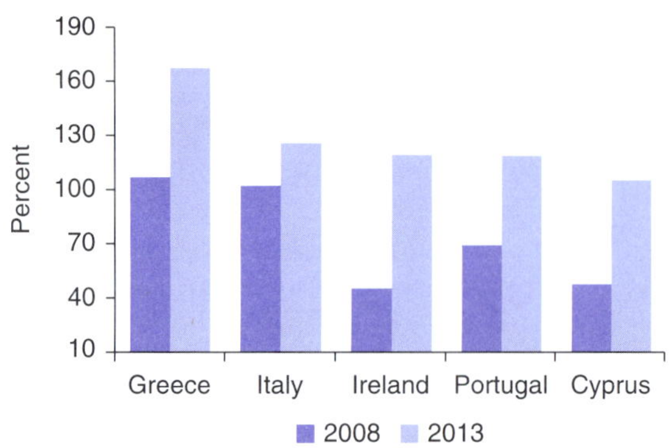

Source: World Bank Public Sector Debt Database.

Figure O.33 Domestic currency debt to total central government debt in select economies
Percent

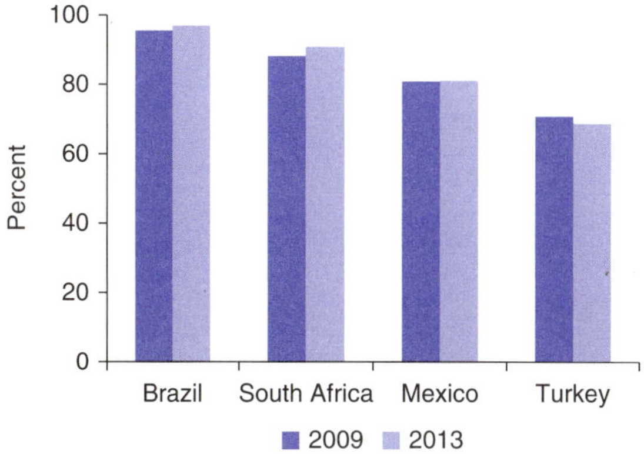

Source: World Bank Public Sector Debt Database.

Figure O.34 Bonds to government debt
Percent

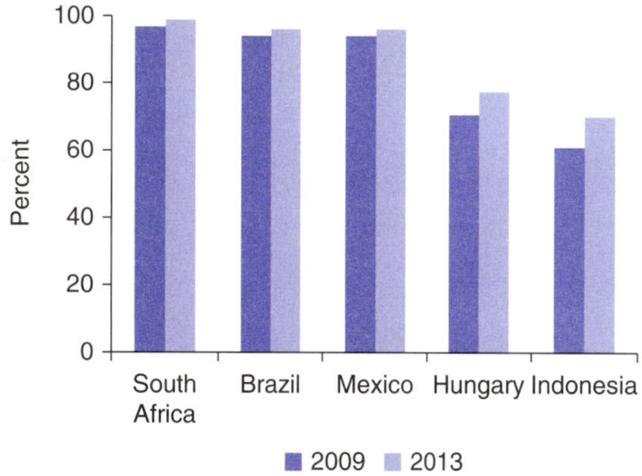

Source: World Bank Public Sector Debt Database.

keep its debt-to-GDP ratio the same as in 2012 (36 percent).

The size of domestic debt markets in developing economies continued to grow in 2013. Learning from the financial crisis, the governments in many developing economies expanded domestic credits, which increased the size of domestic debt dramatically. The majority of this debt is in domestic currency, so countries can avoid the risk of exchange rate fluctuation. As of December 2013, the estimated size of local currency debt among developing economies (excluding China with 99 percent) averaged 78 percent of the total debt. This was a 2 percentage point increase since the financial crisis, although Turkey showed a decrease of 2 percentage points (see Figure O.33).

The government debt is mainly financed by long-term debt securities as a safe opportunity of funding the budget deficits. About 99.8 percent of the central government debt of China is financed by long-term bonds. With the new regulation of Parliament, the local government is authorized to issue bonds. This reflects a reform that will further help the government to finance its projects. Excluding China, the bond issuance from governments in the developing economies that report to the Public Sector Debt database averaged 80 percent of the total debt. From 2009 to 2013, Hungary and Indonesia increased their bond ratios by 9 percentage points, Mexico by 6 percentage points, followed by South Africa and Brazil (an average of 2 percentage points each) (see Figure O.34).

PART II
Aggregate and Country Tables

ALL DEVELOPING COUNTRIES

(US$ billion, unless otherwise indicated)

	2000	2005	2008	2009	2010	2011	2012	2013
Summary external debt data								
External debt stocks	**1,964.0**	**2,352.0**	**3,324.9**	**3,629.7**	**4,109.4**	**4,571.6**	**5,032.1**	**5,506.4**
Long-term external debt	1,633.8	1,807.8	2,557.9	2,705.2	2,909.4	3,194.1	3,540.7	3,854.3
Public and publicly guaranteed	1,183.6	1,240.5	1,346.6	1,440.3	1,561.3	1,638.0	1,823.7	1,956.2
Official creditors	678.4	678.1	705.9	778.9	835.3	868.1	891.3	914.5
Use of IMF credit	60.8	62.8	48.5	149.3	159.0	159.0	145.8	121.2
Private creditors	505.2	562.5	640.7	661.4	725.9	769.9	932.5	1,041.7
of which: Bonds	317.0	404.7	486.1	508.6	568.0	618.8	751.1	818.0
Private nonguaranteed	450.2	567.3	1,211.3	1,264.9	1,348.1	1,556.1	1,717.0	1,898.2
of which: Bonds	81.6	121.9	174.7	193.4	237.0	255.5	293.8	365.5
Short-term external debt	269.4	481.4	718.4	775.1	1,041.0	1,218.5	1,345.6	1,530.8
interest arrears on long-term	27.3	25.5	26.9	26.2	21.5	18.6	21.1	19.8
Long-term external debt								
Disbursements	**225.8**	**340.1**	**622.6**	**551.9**	**645.0**	**756.0**	**784.5**	**930.4**
Public and publicly guaranteed	135.5	141.4	166.9	197.9	248.0	214.6	272.8	292.4
Official creditors	51.1	45.7	74.7	107.3	113.9	92.9	93.0	105.9
Private creditors	84.4	95.7	92.2	90.6	134.1	121.7	179.9	186.5
of which: Bonds	55.4	69.5	66.3	67.1	94.6	92.9	140.1	109.9
Private nonguaranteed	90.4	198.8	455.7	354.0	397.0	541.4	511.6	638.0
of which: Bonds	10.0	32.5	13.8	33.2	66.5	80.3	82.5	122.8
Principal repayments	**200.2**	**264.6**	**390.5**	**422.5**	**437.5**	**485.7**	**471.4**	**550.9**
Public and publicly guaranteed	103.4	124.0	130.4	108.0	104.8	125.7	99.4	127.2
Official creditors	46.2	50.6	50.2	45.2	46.7	61.1	52.1	62.8
Private creditors	57.2	73.3	80.1	62.8	58.0	64.5	47.3	64.4
of which: Bonds	23.6	43.5	55.0	31.5	31.2	33.3	20.6	31.6
Private nonguaranteed	96.8	140.6	260.2	314.5	332.7	360.0	372.0	423.7
of which: Bonds	14.1	14.0	13.7	15.4	18.5	21.5	26.9	28.8
Interest payments	**88.7**	**76.0**	**105.6**	**100.4**	**100.5**	**119.0**	**135.6**	**129.5**
Public and publicly guaranteed	60.6	55.9	54.6	50.3	50.2	54.9	79.9	64.3
Official creditors	24.5	21.4	18.9	16.9	15.8	16.7	18.2	17.9
Private creditors	36.1	34.5	35.8	33.4	34.4	38.2	61.7	46.4
of which: Bonds	24.1	28.3	29.4	27.9	30.0	33.8	56.9	41.1
Private nonguaranteed	28.1	20.2	50.9	50.1	50.3	64.0	55.7	65.2
of which: Bonds	7.2	6.9	10.8	11.0	12.8	18.3	14.4	19.4
Net financial flows								
Net inflows	164.8	442.9	707.7	675.4	1,094.8	1,025.6	1,063.1	1,184.4
Net debt inflows	8.1	124.2	267.1	217.3	491.6	451.2	424.4	541.5
Official creditors	-2.6	-41.5	41.1	93.9	80.6	32.3	27.5	18.6
of which: World Bank	7.4	3.4	7.8	18.3	23.0	7.0	12.4	14.6
of which: IMF	-7.6	-36.6	16.6	31.8	13.4	0.5	-13.3	-24.5
Private creditors	10.7	165.7	226.0	123.4	410.9	418.9	396.9	522.9
Long-term	20.7	80.4	207.7	67.3	140.3	238.6	272.2	336.5
Bonds	27.8	44.5	11.4	53.4	111.4	118.4	175.1	172.3
Banks and other private	-7.1	36.0	196.3	13.9	28.9	119.5	97.1	164.4
Short-term	-10.0	85.3	18.3	56.1	270.6	180.3	124.7	186.4
Net equity inflows	156.7	318.7	440.6	458.1	603.3	574.4	638.7	642.8
Foreign direct investment	142.6	253.6	480.5	345.5	479.7	571.4	541.5	574.2
Portfolio equity	14.1	65.1	-39.9	112.6	123.6	3.0	97.2	68.6
Major economic aggregates								
Gross national income (GNI)	5,512.1	8,695.5	15,069.8	15,080.6	18,270.1	21,105.6	22,316.3	23,698.1
Exports of goods, services & prim. income	1,540.3	2,906.5	5,186.4	4,249.9	5,302.2	6,411.8	6,752.9	6,968.6
Imports of goods, services & prim. income	1,638.6	2,954.3	5,208.6	4,357.2	5,531.0	6,792.4	7,115.7	7,445.2
Primary income on FDI	64.2	177.2	333.4	317.7	434.8	513.7	479.3	419.9
Personal transfers & comp. of employees	76.3	178.6	295.7	280.7	311.9	346.8	352.3	296.8
International reserves	579.5	1,737.3	3,644.6	4,277.4	4,950.8	5,426.5	5,680.0	6,131.3
Ratios								
External debt stocks to exports (%)	127.5	80.9	64.1	85.4	77.5	71.3	74.5	79.0
External debt stocks to GNI (%)	35.6	27.0	22.1	24.1	22.5	21.7	22.5	23.2
Debt service to exports (%)	21.1	13.8	10.0	12.7	11.1	10.3	10.0	10.5
Short-term to external debt stocks (%)	13.7	20.5	21.6	21.4	25.3	26.7	26.7	27.8
Multilateral to external debt stocks (%)	16.2	15.5	11.9	12.4	12.2	11.4	10.8	10.4
Reserves to external debt stocks (%)	29.5	73.9	109.6	117.8	120.5	118.7	112.9	111.3

EAST ASIA AND PACIFIC

(US$ billion, unless otherwise indicated)

	2000	2005	2008	2009	2010	2011	2012	2013
Summary external debt data								
External debt stocks	**497.4**	**641.5**	**815.0**	**937.4**	**1,136.9**	**1,344.3**	**1,508.1**	**1,673.0**
Long-term external debt	418.2	432.7	533.4	564.2	618.4	677.1	760.8	790.1
Public and publicly guaranteed	271.0	277.3	317.4	343.7	371.5	370.5	388.7	401.5
Official creditors	172.0	172.8	193.7	203.0	210.6	216.2	210.7	198.9
Use of IMF credit	17.8	10.0	1.7	20.5	20.4	20.4	20.3	20.3
Private creditors	99.0	104.5	123.6	140.7	160.9	154.3	177.9	202.6
of which: Bonds	35.8	64.9	91.6	104.6	122.1	125.6	154.6	172.1
Private nonguaranteed	147.2	155.4	216.1	220.5	246.9	306.6	372.2	388.6
of which: Bonds	22.1	26.7	25.5	26.9	35.7	53.1	71.9	88.6
Short-term external debt	61.5	198.9	279.8	352.7	498.0	646.8	726.9	862.5
interest arrears on long-term	5.4	1.1	1.2	1.2	1.3	1.4	1.4	1.1
Long-term external debt								
Disbursements	**42.2**	**78.2**	**93.4**	**96.1**	**129.2**	**143.3**	**171.6**	**170.2**
Public and publicly guaranteed	28.8	28.9	28.3	44.1	51.5	38.2	47.5	52.2
Official creditors	15.6	9.0	13.0	16.8	16.9	15.0	15.6	18.3
Private creditors	13.1	19.9	15.3	27.4	34.6	23.2	31.9	33.8
of which: Bonds	4.5	14.5	10.8	19.2	20.7	20.0	29.8	22.1
Private nonguaranteed	13.4	49.3	65.1	51.9	77.7	105.1	124.1	118.0
of which: Bonds	1.1	5.3	0.8	2.9	12.2	15.6	20.3	34.1
Principal repayments	**47.0**	**66.9**	**68.3**	**80.3**	**74.7**	**85.9**	**89.9**	**96.2**
Public and publicly guaranteed	22.8	24.4	22.1	25.5	25.1	29.7	23.0	21.4
Official creditors	10.3	10.8	13.4	12.9	12.9	15.0	13.9	16.5
Private creditors	12.6	13.6	8.7	12.6	12.2	14.7	9.1	4.9
of which: Bonds	1.2	4.3	2.8	5.3	5.1	5.7	1.6	0.4
Private nonguaranteed	24.2	42.5	46.2	54.8	49.7	56.2	66.9	74.7
of which: Bonds	5.2	2.1	1.5	2.9	1.8	3.6	2.2	3.1
Interest payments	**20.5**	**12.6**	**16.4**	**14.1**	**17.1**	**19.7**	**18.3**	**21.7**
Public and publicly guaranteed	12.9	8.5	10.0	9.4	9.6	10.2	11.1	11.3
Official creditors	7.3	4.0	4.7	4.0	3.7	3.8	4.5	4.4
Private creditors	5.7	4.5	5.3	5.4	5.9	6.4	6.6	6.8
of which: Bonds	2.3	3.1	4.0	4.4	4.9	5.4	5.7	6.3
Private nonguaranteed	7.5	4.1	6.4	4.7	7.5	9.5	7.2	10.4
of which: Bonds	1.9	1.3	1.2	1.2	1.3	3.8	3.1	4.6
Net financial flows								
Net inflows	37.3	189.1	208.0	290.3	524.8	535.9	491.0	563.1
Net debt inflows	-14.5	46.7	27.8	88.7	199.7	206.1	161.7	209.9
Official creditors	6.6	-3.3	-0.4	4.0	4.0	0.0	1.6	1.8
of which: World Bank	1.8	-0.6	1.2	2.2	2.7	0.9	1.3	2.5
of which: IMF	1.2	-1.6	0.0	0.1	0.0	0.0	-0.1	-0.1
Private creditors	-21.1	50.0	28.2	84.7	195.7	206.1	160.2	208.2
Long-term	-10.2	13.1	25.5	11.9	50.5	57.4	80.0	72.2
Bonds	-0.7	13.4	7.2	13.8	26.1	26.3	46.3	52.7
Banks and other private	-9.5	-0.3	18.2	-1.9	24.3	30.3	33.7	19.7
Short-term	-10.8	36.9	2.7	72.8	145.2	148.7	80.1	136.0
Net equity inflows	51.8	142.4	180.2	201.6	325.1	329.8	329.3	353.1
Foreign direct investment	45.2	117.6	187.0	170.0	284.4	323.1	291.3	327.5
Portfolio equity	6.6	24.9	-6.8	31.6	40.7	6.7	37.9	25.6
Major economic aggregates								
Gross national income (GNI)	1,688.9	3,037.2	5,904.6	6,338.4	7,585.6	9,170.6	10,227.0	11,296.3
Exports of goods, services & prim. income	636.1	1,297.4	2,364.3	2,015.9	2,603.3	3,106.2	3,368.3	3,578.1
Imports of goods, services & prim. income	606.3	1,195.6	1,988.5	1,768.3	2,393.4	2,987.8	3,196.0	3,440.5
Primary income on FDI	31.7	80.0	117.8	144.5	212.6	260.9	236.4	229.7
Personal transfers & comp. of employees	15.8	34.3	59.2	60.4	75.8	85.9	78.1	80.7
International reserves	275.5	1,003.8	2,265.6	2,779.4	3,315.6	3,708.8	3,871.7	4,344.1
Ratios								
External debt stocks to exports (%)	78.2	49.4	34.5	46.5	43.7	43.3	44.8	46.8
External debt stocks to GNI (%)	29.5	21.1	13.8	14.8	15.0	14.7	14.7	14.8
Debt service to exports (%)	11.4	6.6	3.8	4.9	4.7	4.5	4.3	3.3
Short-term to external debt stocks (%)	12.4	31.0	34.3	37.6	43.8	48.1	48.2	51.6
Multilateral to external debt stocks (%)	13.2	10.0	9.0	8.6	7.6	6.6	6.0	5.6
Reserves to external debt stocks (%)	55.4	156.5	278.0	296.5	291.6	275.9	256.7	259.7

EUROPE AND CENTRAL ASIA

(US$ billion, unless otherwise indicated)

	2000	2005	2008	2009	2010	2011	2012	2013
Summary external debt data								
External debt stocks	**234.1**	**444.1**	**969.5**	**1,023.8**	**1,061.9**	**1,095.1**	**1,143.3**	**1,234.2**
Long-term external debt	173.6	319.2	763.0	797.4	784.4	806.4	859.0	941.3
Public and publicly guaranteed	118.5	152.0	204.9	226.0	246.4	260.6	298.3	326.7
Official creditors	44.8	53.0	76.9	102.1	117.7	123.7	131.1	136.6
Use of IMF credit	16.5	26.0	28.6	58.8	66.8	65.6	52.6	30.0
Private creditors	73.7	99.0	128.0	123.9	128.7	136.9	167.2	190.1
of which: Bonds	40.2	64.1	90.1	88.7	95.3	106.2	137.0	162.1
Private nonguaranteed	55.1	167.2	558.1	571.4	538.0	545.8	560.6	614.6
of which: Bonds	2.1	14.0	47.2	43.2	39.4	31.7	37.2	52.6
Short-term external debt	44.1	98.9	177.9	167.6	210.7	223.1	231.7	262.9
interest arrears on long-term	4.0	0.9	1.1	1.5	2.2	0.6	2.5	0.9
Long-term external debt								
Disbursements	**40.3**	**117.2**	**317.4**	**246.3**	**233.7**	**281.0**	**261.0**	**339.0**
Public and publicly guaranteed	20.7	20.7	29.3	36.6	43.0	41.0	55.1	50.6
Official creditors	6.1	5.3	17.3	28.4	24.2	18.4	15.4	15.2
Private creditors	14.7	15.4	12.0	8.2	18.8	22.6	39.7	35.4
of which: Bonds	8.1	11.7	5.7	5.7	14.6	18.6	36.2	31.2
Private nonguaranteed	19.6	96.5	288.1	209.7	190.7	240.0	205.9	288.5
of which: Bonds	0.5	7.9	4.1	1.0	4.5	4.5	8.5	22.2
Principal repayments	**28.4**	**73.3**	**175.1**	**215.0**	**226.3**	**232.1**	**211.7**	**254.5**
Public and publicly guaranteed	12.8	19.2	22.8	17.9	14.9	21.5	18.0	23.7
Official creditors	4.8	5.1	5.6	4.8	5.2	10.6	8.8	11.3
Private creditors	8.0	14.1	17.2	13.1	9.7	10.9	9.3	12.4
of which: Bonds	3.8	10.1	11.4	8.4	5.6	6.5	5.5	7.0
Private nonguaranteed	15.5	54.1	152.3	197.1	211.4	210.6	193.7	230.8
of which: Bonds	0.1	1.2	1.6	5.1	6.0	8.4	4.5	7.6
Interest payments	**9.3**	**13.5**	**31.7**	**32.8**	**28.5**	**35.5**	**27.9**	**30.6**
Public and publicly guaranteed	6.5	7.6	9.6	8.9	8.4	9.8	10.4	11.2
Official creditors	1.8	1.7	2.6	2.5	2.3	3.0	3.1	2.7
Private creditors	4.6	5.8	7.0	6.4	6.1	6.8	7.4	8.5
of which: Bonds	2.9	4.1	5.0	4.9	4.8	5.6	6.2	7.5
Private nonguaranteed	2.8	5.9	22.1	23.9	20.1	25.7	17.4	19.5
of which: Bonds	0.2	1.0	2.9	2.9	2.6	2.6	1.9	2.2
Net financial flows								
Net inflows	31.3	104.0	265.6	80.5	99.7	106.8	102.8	138.9
Net debt inflows	21.5	58.6	160.9	46.0	58.7	61.9	43.1	94.8
Official creditors	3.7	-6.1	24.6	49.0	27.9	6.8	-6.3	-18.6
of which: World Bank	1.6	-0.1	1.2	3.4	3.9	2.9	2.0	2.1
of which: IMF	2.4	-6.4	12.8	25.5	9.0	-1.0	-13.0	-22.5
Private creditors	17.9	64.7	136.3	-3.0	30.8	55.2	49.4	113.4
Long-term	10.7	43.7	130.6	7.7	-11.5	41.2	42.6	80.7
Bonds	4.7	8.4	-3.2	-6.8	7.5	8.2	34.7	38.8
Banks and other private	6.0	35.3	133.9	14.4	-19.0	32.9	7.9	41.9
Short-term	7.2	21.0	5.7	-10.7	42.3	14.0	6.8	32.7
Net equity inflows	9.8	45.4	104.8	34.5	41.0	44.8	59.7	44.1
Foreign direct investment	9.1	38.8	105.2	30.8	37.2	45.5	51.6	41.9
Portfolio equity	0.7	6.6	-0.4	3.7	3.8	-0.7	8.1	2.2
Major economic aggregates								
Gross national income (GNI)	468.3	984.0	1,699.0	1,417.9	1,602.7	1,781.7	1,814.1	1,931.4
Exports of goods, services & prim. income	163.3	364.4	720.6	545.2	624.6	769.3	788.5	804.6
Imports of goods, services & prim. income	191.5	428.1	853.1	605.9	705.6	875.8	876.4	909.5
Primary income on FDI	2.0	18.2	57.7	44.2	52.6	61.7	59.7	62.2
Personal transfers & comp. of employees	7.9	19.7	41.5	33.2	32.9	37.5	38.5	31.8
International reserves	46.2	137.9	242.7	261.6	283.4	290.7	299.7	314.7
Ratios								
External debt stocks to exports (%)	143.4	121.9	134.5	187.8	170.0	142.3	145.0	153.4
External debt stocks to GNI (%)	50.0	45.1	57.1	72.2	66.3	61.5	63.0	63.9
Debt service to exports (%)	26.1	27.6	30.1	46.7	42.5	36.3	33.3	39.6
Short-term to external debt stocks (%)	18.8	22.3	18.4	16.4	19.8	20.4	20.3	21.3
Multilateral to external debt stocks (%)	9.7	7.6	5.5	7.4	8.4	8.6	9.0	8.8
Reserves to external debt stocks (%)	19.7	31.1	25.0	25.6	26.7	26.5	26.2	25.5

LATIN AMERICA AND THE CARIBBEAN

(US$ billion, unless otherwise indicated)

	2000	2005	2008	2009	2010	2011	2012	2013
Summary external debt data								
External debt stocks	**714.3**	**697.0**	**849.3**	**895.9**	**1,061.8**	**1,206.1**	**1,350.2**	**1,495.4**
Long-term external debt	600.8	572.6	713.4	744.8	850.7	996.4	1,122.3	1,250.8
Public and publicly guaranteed	385.3	405.0	422.2	437.9	478.0	509.4	579.1	632.5
Official creditors	135.9	129.8	126.8	144.5	166.2	169.8	181.4	187.9
Use of IMF credit	11.1	13.4	3.6	23.0	23.6	23.8	23.7	23.5
Private creditors	249.4	275.2	295.5	293.5	311.8	339.6	397.8	444.6
of which: Bonds	213.6	235.9	254.7	256.0	270.9	298.3	341.9	359.2
Private nonguaranteed	215.5	167.6	291.2	306.9	372.7	487.0	543.1	618.3
of which: Bonds	53.7	70.4	77.5	98.0	139.1	146.0	161.0	199.6
Short-term external debt	102.4	111.0	132.3	128.1	187.5	186.0	204.2	221.1
interest arrears on long-term	1.7	8.8	10.9	11.6	6.3	7.0	7.1	7.4
Long-term external debt								
Disbursements	**110.4**	**92.5**	**139.8**	**139.6**	**187.3**	**227.9**	**234.7**	**263.3**
Public and publicly guaranteed	57.1	55.2	61.8	69.5	87.6	75.9	100.3	104.5
Official creditors	15.8	12.3	18.7	29.9	34.9	22.7	24.6	24.4
Private creditors	41.4	42.9	43.1	39.6	52.6	53.2	75.7	80.1
of which: Bonds	34.4	36.8	36.1	34.9	39.7	42.7	54.1	35.4
Private nonguaranteed	53.3	37.2	78.0	70.1	99.7	152.0	134.4	158.8
of which: Bonds	7.6	15.3	8.3	26.4	47.4	55.1	49.4	60.0
Principal repayments	**96.3**	**76.3**	**92.2**	**89.4**	**91.6**	**114.3**	**116.8**	**130.7**
Public and publicly guaranteed	41.5	40.7	46.0	37.0	39.1	44.4	29.2	44.7
Official creditors	16.5	15.9	12.3	13.1	13.6	18.1	12.4	16.0
Private creditors	25.1	24.9	33.7	23.9	25.5	26.3	16.8	28.7
of which: Bonds	17.2	17.6	27.3	13.4	17.6	16.2	8.7	14.5
Private nonguaranteed	54.8	35.6	46.2	52.4	52.5	69.9	87.6	86.0
of which: Bonds	8.8	10.4	8.1	5.6	7.3	6.6	14.9	14.9
Interest payments	**45.5**	**32.2**	**41.0**	**38.8**	**40.1**	**47.0**	**69.3**	**55.5**
Public and publicly guaranteed	29.2	23.9	24.1	22.2	22.4	24.6	46.4	29.2
Official creditors	8.2	5.3	5.3	4.7	4.5	4.6	4.7	4.9
Private creditors	21.0	18.6	18.8	17.5	17.9	20.0	41.7	24.3
of which: Bonds	17.8	17.0	17.4	15.6	16.7	18.6	40.1	22.2
Private nonguaranteed	16.3	8.3	16.9	16.6	17.7	22.4	22.9	26.3
of which: Bonds	4.7	4.2	5.8	6.2	7.9	10.3	8.0	11.4
Net financial flows								
Net inflows	72.2	79.2	124.5	145.6	289.9	227.4	274.6	285.4
Net debt inflows	-1.5	9.6	49.7	45.6	161.7	111.6	135.8	148.9
Official creditors	-11.4	-31.0	6.4	17.2	22.6	4.9	12.1	8.2
of which: World Bank	2.0	-0.6	2.5	6.2	8.3	-2.9	3.6	3.2
of which: IMF	-10.7	-27.4	0.0	0.4	1.3	0.2	-0.1	-0.2
Private creditors	9.9	40.6	43.2	28.4	139.1	106.8	123.7	140.7
Long-term	14.8	19.7	41.2	33.3	74.4	109.0	105.6	124.2
Bonds	16.1	24.1	9.0	42.2	62.3	75.0	80.0	66.0
Banks and other private	-1.3	-4.4	32.2	-8.9	12.1	34.0	25.7	58.3
Short-term	-4.9	20.8	2.1	-4.9	64.7	-2.2	18.1	16.5
Net equity inflows	73.7	69.5	74.8	100.0	128.2	115.8	138.8	136.5
Foreign direct investment	73.8	58.9	86.4	58.8	89.0	112.9	119.3	123.3
Portfolio equity	-0.1	10.6	-11.6	41.2	39.3	2.9	19.5	13.2
Major economic aggregates								
Gross national income (GNI)	2,035.3	2,478.5	4,062.0	3,806.7	4,734.0	5,292.1	5,283.5	5,455.2
Exports of goods, services & prim. income	413.6	599.7	944.7	741.3	921.9	1,137.7	1,166.2	1,175.6
Imports of goods, services & prim. income	481.2	622.5	1,047.1	830.0	1,046.4	1,274.3	1,321.3	1,379.7
Primary income on FDI	20.1	43.2	79.2	65.2	79.8	97.3	95.2	83.0
Personal transfers & comp. of employees	20.1	48.7	62.7	55.1	56.2	59.6	58.6	54.9
International reserves	136.0	228.0	455.8	502.1	583.5	671.4	727.2	729.3
Ratios								
External debt stocks to exports (%)	172.7	116.2	89.9	120.9	115.2	106.0	115.8	127.2
External debt stocks to GNI (%)	35.1	28.1	20.9	23.5	22.4	22.8	25.6	27.4
Debt service to exports (%)	39.5	23.9	14.5	17.6	14.9	14.7	16.5	16.5
Short-term to external debt stocks (%)	14.3	15.9	15.6	14.3	17.7	15.4	15.1	14.8
Multilateral to external debt stocks (%)	12.6	14.3	11.5	12.4	12.0	10.7	10.1	9.4
Reserves to external debt stocks (%)	19.0	32.7	53.7	56.0	55.0	55.7	53.9	48.8

MIDDLE EAST AND NORTH AFRICA

(US$ billion, unless otherwise indicated)

	2000	2005	2008	2009	2010	2011	2012	2013
Summary external debt data								
External debt stocks	**143.8**	**150.6**	**148.7**	**160.6**	**168.1**	**164.0**	**172.9**	**190.6**
Long-term external debt	116.5	122.2	117.7	119.5	121.9	120.6	130.7	147.1
Public and publicly guaranteed	112.5	115.4	110.3	112.6	114.0	112.5	121.3	136.8
Official creditors	88.1	77.7	74.8	78.3	78.1	78.5	82.4	90.5
Use of IMF credit	3.5	1.6	1.3	8.3	8.3	8.2	8.6	9.5
Private creditors	24.4	37.7	35.6	34.3	35.9	34.0	38.8	46.3
of which: Bonds	7.3	21.5	23.6	23.5	26.6	25.9	31.5	39.1
Private nonguaranteed	4.0	6.8	7.4	6.9	7.9	8.0	9.5	10.2
of which: Bonds	0.8	1.0	0.5	0.7	0.5	0.5	0.7	0.7
Short-term external debt	23.9	26.8	29.6	32.8	37.8	35.2	33.5	34.0
interest arrears on long-term	2.6	0.3	0.3	0.3	0.3	0.4	0.5	0.6
Long-term external debt								
Disbursements	**9.2**	**14.9**	**12.0**	**13.6**	**14.8**	**13.5**	**21.8**	**27.3**
Public and publicly guaranteed	7.9	13.0	9.7	12.0	13.5	12.0	18.9	23.8
Official creditors	3.4	5.5	6.3	8.2	7.2	7.6	10.4	13.8
Private creditors	4.5	7.5	3.3	3.9	6.2	4.5	8.5	10.0
of which: Bonds	2.0	4.1	2.3	2.9	5.5	4.0	8.3	9.5
Private nonguaranteed	1.3	1.9	2.3	1.6	1.4	1.5	2.9	3.5
of which: Bonds	0.1	0.5	0.0	0.2	0.0	0.0	0.5	0.0
Principal repayments	**10.6**	**14.2**	**16.2**	**13.2**	**12.2**	**14.0**	**11.6**	**11.9**
Public and publicly guaranteed	10.4	13.3	14.2	11.0	10.3	12.7	9.6	9.0
Official creditors	5.9	7.9	8.0	5.6	6.0	6.5	6.2	6.4
Private creditors	4.5	5.5	6.2	5.4	4.4	6.1	3.4	2.6
of which: Bonds	0.8	1.9	3.0	3.0	2.2	4.6	2.6	1.7
Private nonguaranteed	0.2	0.8	2.0	2.3	1.8	1.3	2.0	2.9
of which: Bonds	0.1	0.3	0.1	0.0	0.2	0.0	0.3	0.0
Interest payments	**4.9**	**4.7**	**4.8**	**4.4**	**4.3**	**4.3**	**4.0**	**4.3**
Public and publicly guaranteed	4.7	4.5	4.5	4.1	4.0	4.0	3.8	4.0
Official creditors	3.1	2.5	2.2	2.0	2.1	1.9	1.9	1.8
Private creditors	1.6	2.0	2.3	2.1	1.9	2.1	1.9	2.2
of which: Bonds	0.5	1.3	1.6	1.7	1.6	1.8	1.7	2.0
Private nonguaranteed	0.2	0.3	0.3	0.3	0.3	0.2	0.2	0.3
of which: Bonds	0.1	0.1	0.0	0.0	0.1	0.0	0.0	0.0
Net financial flows								
Net inflows	4.8	13.5	13.1	25.4	27.1	11.3	23.0	31.0
Net debt inflows	0.8	0.5	-6.2	3.4	7.7	-3.1	8.8	16.7
Official creditors	-2.7	-3.1	-1.7	2.5	1.3	1.0	4.7	8.3
of which: World Bank	-0.3	0.0	-0.3	0.9	0.8	0.9	0.8	1.1
of which: IMF	-0.2	-0.7	-0.1	-0.1	0.0	-0.1	0.5	0.9
Private creditors	3.5	3.7	-4.4	0.9	6.4	-4.1	4.2	8.4
Long-term	1.1	3.1	-2.5	-2.1	1.4	-1.5	6.0	8.0
Bonds	1.3	2.5	-0.8	0.1	3.2	-0.6	5.8	7.8
Banks and other private	-0.2	0.6	-1.7	-2.2	-1.8	-0.8	0.1	0.2
Short-term	2.4	0.6	-1.9	3.1	5.0	-2.6	-1.8	0.4
Net equity inflows	4.0	12.9	19.2	22.0	19.5	14.4	14.1	14.3
Foreign direct investment	3.7	10.5	18.8	20.8	17.5	15.0	15.4	14.0
Portfolio equity	0.3	2.4	0.4	1.2	2.0	-0.6	-1.3	0.3
Major economic aggregates								
Gross national income (GNI)	364.8	543.9	930.7	920.4	1,042.6	1,206.1	1,269.2	1,163.5
Exports of goods, services & prim. income	119.3	206.9	379.2	314.7	328.8	382.7	419.3	345.3
Imports of goods, services & prim. income	110.5	206.7	361.1	341.3	362.2	400.9	419.3	402.4
Primary income on FDI	1.7	10.7	13.4	14.0	17.5	18.1	19.0	5.2
Personal transfers & comp. of employees	10.5	21.7	32.2	30.2	35.9	36.8	42.0	16.2
International reserves	44.1	138.2	260.6	280.5	298.5	274.6	279.2	289.7
Ratios								
External debt stocks to exports (%)	120.6	72.8	39.2	51.0	51.1	42.8	41.2	55.2
External debt stocks to GNI (%)	39.4	27.7	16.0	17.4	16.1	13.6	13.6	16.4
Debt service to exports (%)	14.2	10.2	5.8	5.8	5.2	4.9	3.9	4.9
Short-term to external debt stocks (%)	16.6	17.8	19.9	20.4	22.5	21.5	19.4	17.9
Multilateral to external debt stocks (%)	16.1	17.3	21.0	21.8	21.6	23.3	23.8	23.6
Reserves to external debt stocks (%)	30.7	91.8	175.2	174.7	177.6	167.5	161.5	152.0

SOUTH ASIA

(US$ billion, unless otherwise indicated)

	2000	2005	2008	2009	2010	2011	2012	2013
Summary external debt data								
External debt stocks	**162.4**	**190.1**	**322.7**	**361.5**	**407.3**	**458.7**	**514.5**	**545.7**
Long-term external debt	153.1	174.6	266.3	292.3	324.3	353.5	397.5	433.4
Public and publicly guaranteed	134.5	116.5	156.3	169.6	190.0	203.8	231.6	230.5
Official creditors	101.9	109.8	138.0	145.9	157.4	165.9	167.6	167.2
Use of IMF credit	3.2	3.7	6.9	18.7	20.3	20.3	18.8	16.0
Private creditors	32.7	6.7	18.3	23.7	32.7	37.9	64.0	63.3
of which: Bonds	10.9	2.5	7.7	12.7	18.3	21.1	29.1	26.8
Private nonguaranteed	18.5	58.0	110.1	122.6	134.3	149.7	165.9	202.8
of which: Bonds	1.6	6.5	15.7	16.2	13.5	11.1	8.1	8.3
Short-term external debt	6.1	11.9	49.5	50.5	62.7	84.8	98.3	96.3
interest arrears on long-term	0.1	0.0	0.0	0.0	0.1	0.2	0.2	0.1
Long-term external debt								
Disbursements	**14.0**	**24.4**	**45.7**	**35.2**	**54.7**	**51.9**	**58.4**	**80.5**
Public and publicly guaranteed	13.4	11.0	24.7	17.8	31.9	21.8	25.7	22.4
Official creditors	6.1	7.4	11.3	12.7	14.9	13.7	12.4	13.5
Private creditors	7.3	3.6	13.4	5.1	17.0	8.1	13.3	8.9
of which: Bonds	5.5	2.3	11.5	2.3	12.1	3.0	8.5	3.3
Private nonguaranteed	0.6	13.5	21.0	17.4	22.8	30.1	32.7	58.0
of which: Bonds	0.0	3.5	0.6	2.5	1.3	0.7	0.7	1.3
Principal repayments	**9.3**	**21.8**	**27.1**	**15.2**	**23.7**	**26.0**	**25.2**	**36.8**
Public and publicly guaranteed	8.6	14.5	16.3	8.7	8.9	10.2	10.1	17.1
Official creditors	5.4	4.5	5.6	5.4	6.0	7.1	6.9	7.9
Private creditors	3.3	10.0	10.7	3.3	2.8	3.0	3.2	9.2
of which: Bonds	0.1	8.6	9.5	1.1	0.7	0.2	0.5	5.6
Private nonguaranteed	0.7	7.3	10.8	6.4	14.9	15.8	15.2	19.7
of which: Bonds	0.0	0.1	0.9	1.8	2.5	2.8	3.7	1.1
Interest payments	**5.3**	**5.2**	**7.3**	**6.5**	**6.4**	**7.8**	**9.8**	**10.6**
Public and publicly guaranteed	4.4	3.9	2.9	2.7	2.7	2.7	3.4	3.1
Official creditors	2.3	1.9	2.3	2.2	2.0	2.1	2.5	2.2
Private creditors	2.1	2.0	0.6	0.5	0.7	0.6	0.8	1.0
of which: Bonds	0.2	1.8	0.3	0.3	0.2	0.3	0.4	0.5
Private nonguaranteed	0.9	1.3	4.4	3.8	3.7	5.1	6.4	7.4
of which: Bonds	0.2	0.2	0.3	0.3	0.5	0.9	0.5	0.5
Net financial flows								
Net inflows	10.3	28.1	63.6	86.7	105.6	81.5	94.5	89.9
Net debt inflows	3.5	5.0	29.6	24.7	45.0	48.0	45.0	39.1
Official creditors	0.5	2.9	8.9	10.9	10.8	6.6	4.0	2.9
of which: World Bank	0.7	2.3	1.4	2.4	3.3	2.0	0.9	0.7
of which: IMF	-0.3	0.0	3.2	3.6	2.0	0.0	-1.5	-2.8
Private creditors	3.0	2.0	20.7	13.8	34.2	41.4	41.0	36.2
Long-term	3.9	-0.2	12.9	12.7	22.1	19.3	27.6	38.0
Bonds	5.4	-2.8	1.7	1.9	10.1	0.7	5.0	-2.0
Banks and other private	-1.5	2.6	11.2	10.9	12.0	18.6	22.7	40.0
Short-term	-0.9	2.3	7.9	1.0	12.1	22.0	13.4	-1.8
Net equity inflows	6.9	23.1	34.0	61.9	60.6	33.5	49.5	50.9
Foreign direct investment	4.4	10.7	49.9	37.8	30.8	37.6	26.2	30.3
Portfolio equity	2.5	12.4	-15.9	24.2	29.8	-4.1	23.4	20.5
Major economic aggregates								
Gross national income (GNI)	618.5	1,043.8	1,542.4	1,697.2	2,068.5	2,308.4	2,302.7	2,355.9
Exports of goods, services & prim. income	88.8	202.2	381.2	330.1	429.3	539.7	536.0	565.4
Imports of goods, services & prim. income	117.6	260.5	511.2	440.6	577.9	717.3	753.2	740.6
Primary income on FDI	0.7	8.0	17.0	16.4	25.8	28.0	21.3	18.2
Personal transfers & comp. of employees	17.2	34.2	72.0	75.1	82.4	97.4	108.3	110.4
International reserves	43.3	149.5	268.7	298.8	315.4	310.6	310.8	318.9
Ratios								
External debt stocks to exports (%)	182.9	94.0	84.7	109.5	94.9	85.0	96.0	96.5
External debt stocks to GNI (%)	26.3	18.2	20.9	21.3	19.7	19.9	22.3	23.2
Debt service to exports (%)	17.5	13.7	9.6	6.9	7.3	6.6	7.3	9.4
Short-term to external debt stocks (%)	3.7	6.2	15.3	14.0	15.4	18.5	19.1	17.7
Multilateral to external debt stocks (%)	37.6	36.6	27.6	26.3	25.0	23.3	21.2	20.0
Reserves to external debt stocks (%)	26.7	78.7	83.3	82.7	77.4	67.7	60.4	58.4

SUB-SAHARAN AFRICA

(US$ billion, unless otherwise indicated)

	2000	2005	2008	2009	2010	2011	2012	2013
Summary external debt data								
External debt stocks	**212.0**	**228.7**	**219.7**	**250.5**	**273.4**	**303.4**	**343.1**	**367.5**
Long-term external debt	171.7	186.6	164.0	187.1	209.5	240.1	270.4	291.6
Public and publicly guaranteed	161.8	174.2	135.5	150.4	161.2	181.2	204.7	228.1
Official creditors	135.7	134.9	95.7	105.1	105.3	114.0	118.0	133.3
Use of IMF credit	8.7	8.1	6.3	20.0	19.5	20.8	21.7	22.0
Private creditors	26.1	39.3	39.8	45.3	55.9	67.2	86.7	94.8
of which: Bonds	9.1	15.8	18.5	23.1	34.8	41.8	57.1	58.7
Private nonguaranteed	9.9	12.3	28.5	36.7	48.3	58.9	65.7	63.5
of which: Bonds	1.4	3.2	8.3	8.5	8.8	13.1	15.0	15.7
Short-term external debt	31.5	34.0	49.3	43.4	44.4	42.5	51.0	53.9
interest arrears on long-term	13.6	14.2	13.5	11.5	11.2	9.0	9.4	9.8
Long-term external debt								
Disbursements	**9.6**	**12.9**	**14.4**	**21.1**	**25.2**	**38.3**	**37.1**	**50.1**
Public and publicly guaranteed	7.5	12.6	13.1	17.9	20.6	25.6	25.4	38.8
Official creditors	4.1	6.2	8.1	11.4	15.8	15.4	14.6	20.6
Private creditors	3.4	6.4	5.1	6.5	4.8	10.2	10.7	18.2
of which: Bonds	0.8	0.0	0.0	2.2	2.0	4.5	3.3	8.4
Private nonguaranteed	2.1	0.3	1.2	3.2	4.6	12.7	11.8	11.3
of which: Bonds	0.7	0.0	0.0	0.2	1.1	4.4	3.2	5.1
Principal repayments	**8.5**	**12.2**	**11.6**	**9.3**	**8.9**	**13.4**	**16.1**	**20.9**
Public and publicly guaranteed	7.2	11.8	8.9	7.9	6.5	7.2	9.6	11.3
Official creditors	3.4	6.6	5.4	3.3	3.0	3.8	4.0	4.8
Private creditors	3.7	5.2	3.5	4.6	3.5	3.5	5.6	6.5
of which: Bonds	0.5	1.1	0.9	0.3	0.0	0.1	1.7	2.4
Private nonguaranteed	1.4	0.4	2.7	1.4	2.5	6.1	6.5	9.6
of which: Bonds	0.0	0.0	1.5	0.0	0.8	0.0	1.3	2.1
Interest payments	**3.3**	**7.8**	**4.4**	**3.9**	**4.0**	**4.8**	**6.4**	**6.9**
Public and publicly guaranteed	2.9	7.4	3.5	3.1	3.0	3.6	4.9	5.5
Official creditors	1.8	5.9	1.8	1.5	1.1	1.2	1.6	1.9
Private creditors	1.1	1.5	1.7	1.5	1.9	2.4	3.3	3.7
of which: Bonds	0.6	0.9	1.0	1.1	1.7	2.1	2.7	2.8
Private nonguaranteed	0.4	0.4	0.9	0.8	0.9	1.2	1.5	1.3
of which: Bonds	0.0	0.2	0.5	0.4	0.5	0.7	0.8	0.7
Net financial flows								
Net inflows	8.9	29.1	32.9	46.8	47.7	62.8	77.2	76.0
Net debt inflows	-1.7	3.9	5.4	8.7	18.8	26.7	29.9	32.1
Official creditors	0.8	-0.9	3.4	10.2	14.0	13.0	11.6	16.1
of which: World Bank	1.5	2.4	1.9	3.1	4.0	3.2	3.9	5.0
of which: IMF	0.1	-0.4	0.7	2.2	1.2	1.4	0.9	0.2
Private creditors	-2.5	4.7	2.0	-1.5	4.8	13.6	18.3	16.0
Long-term	0.4	1.1	0.1	3.8	3.5	13.3	10.4	13.4
Bonds	1.0	-1.1	-2.4	2.1	2.3	8.8	3.4	9.0
Banks and other private	-0.6	2.2	2.5	1.7	1.2	4.5	6.9	4.4
Short-term	-2.9	3.6	1.9	-5.3	1.3	0.4	8.0	2.6
Net equity inflows	10.6	25.3	27.5	38.1	28.9	36.1	47.3	43.9
Foreign direct investment	6.5	17.1	33.2	27.3	20.7	37.2	37.7	37.2
Portfolio equity	4.2	8.2	-5.6	10.8	8.2	-1.1	9.6	6.7
Major economic aggregates								
Gross national income (GNI)	335.2	607.9	933.4	903.4	1,223.6	1,369.1	1,440.8	1,510.5
Exports of goods, services & prim. income	114.8	238.1	401.6	303.8	395.5	476.9	472.7	468.2
Imports of goods, services & prim. income	118.7	241.9	455.9	376.4	449.7	538.1	549.4	554.5
Primary income on FDI	8.0	17.2	48.3	33.5	46.6	47.7	47.7	21.5
Personal transfers & comp. of employees	4.8	20.0	28.0	26.8	28.7	29.6	26.9	2.9
International reserves	34.3	79.9	151.3	154.9	154.5	170.4	191.4	134.5
Ratios								
External debt stocks to exports (%)	184.6	96.0	54.7	82.5	69.1	63.6	72.6	78.5
External debt stocks to GNI (%)	63.2	37.6	23.5	27.7	22.3	22.2	23.8	24.3
Debt service to exports (%)	11.8	9.1	4.5	4.8	3.5	4.0	5.0	6.3
Short-term to external debt stocks (%)	14.9	14.9	22.5	17.3	16.2	14.0	14.9	14.7
Multilateral to external debt stocks (%)	25.7	31.7	22.9	21.9	21.4	20.7	19.3	20.1
Reserves to external debt stocks (%)	16.2	34.9	68.9	61.8	56.5	56.2	55.8	36.6

AFGHANISTAN

(US$ million, unless otherwise indicated)

	2000	2005	2008	2009	2010	2011	2012	2013
Summary external debt data								
External debt stocks	..	..	**2,134**	**2,470**	**2,423**	**2,627**	**2,709**	**2,577**
Long-term external debt	..	..	1,985	2,097	1,966	2,023	2,071	2,097
Short-term external debt	..	..	17	20	102	232	250	104
interest arrears on long-term	..	..	17	20	67	210	219	85
Use of IMF credit	..	..	131	353	355	373	388	376
Long-term external debt								
Debt outstanding and disbursed	..	..	**1,985**	**2,097**	**1,966**	**2,023**	**2,071**	**2,097**
Public and publicly guaranteed	..	..	1,985	2,097	1,966	2,023	2,071	2,097
Official creditors	..	..	1,985	2,097	1,966	2,023	2,071	2,097
Private creditors	..	..	0	0	0	0	0	0
of which: Bonds	..	..	0	0	0	0	0	0
Private nonguaranteed	..	..	..	..	..	..	..	..
of which: Bonds	..	..	..	..	..	..	..	..
Disbursements	..	..	**96**	**109**	**76**	**62**	**52**	**36**
Public and publicly guaranteed	..	..	96	109	76	62	52	36
Official creditors	..	..	96	109	76	62	52	36
Private creditors	..	..	0	0	0	0	0	0
of which: Bonds	..	..	0	0	0	0	0	0
Private nonguaranteed	..	..	..	..	..	..	..	..
of which: Bonds	..	..	..	..	..	..	..	..
Principal repayments	..	..	**1**	**3**	**1**	**1**	**1**	**4**
Public and publicly guaranteed	..	..	1	3	1	1	1	4
Official creditors	..	..	1	3	1	1	1	4
Private creditors	..	..	0	0	0	0	0	0
of which: Bonds	..	..	0	0	0	0	0	0
Private nonguaranteed	..	..	..	..	..	..	..	..
of which: Bonds	..	..	..	..	..	..	..	..
Interest payments	..	..	**6**	**7**	**7**	**9**	**8**	**8**
Public and publicly guaranteed	..	..	6	7	7	9	8	8
Official creditors	..	..	6	7	7	9	8	8
Private creditors	..	..	0	0	0	0	0	0
of which: Bonds	..	..	0	0	0	0	0	0
Private nonguaranteed	..	..	..	..	..	..	..	..
of which: Bonds	..	..	..	..	..	..	..	..
Net financial flows								
Net debt inflows	..	..	131	123	84	67	75	7
Official creditors (incl. IMF)	..	..	131	123	84	80	66	19
Private creditors	..	..	..	..	..	-13	9	-12
Long-term	..	..	..	..	..	..	..	..
Public and publicly guaranteed	..	..	..	..	..	..	..	..
Private nonguaranteed	..	..	..	..	..	..	..	..
Short-term	..	..	..	..	..	-13	9	-12
Net equity inflows								
Foreign direct investment	..	..	87	214	76	91	94	69
Portfolio equity	..	..	-1	..	0	0	2	..
Major economic aggregates								
Gross national income (GNI)	..	..	10,234	12,541	15,999	17,953	20,608	20,866
Exports of goods, services & prim. income	..	..	1,935	2,546	3,920	4,300	4,238	..
Imports of goods, services & prim. income	..	..	3,752	4,467	6,840	8,204	11,885	..
Primary income on FDI	..	..	0	0	0	0	2	..
Personal transfers & comp. of employees	..	..	104	152	331	247	385	..
International reserves	..	..	2,431	3,501	4,174	5,268	5,983	6,442
Ratios								
External debt stocks to exports (%)	..	..	110.3	97.0	61.8	61.1	63.9	..
External debt stocks to GNI (%)	..	..	20.9	19.7	15.1	14.6	13.1	12.3
Debt service to exports (%)	..	..	0.4	0.4	0.3	0.3	0.3	..
Reserves to external debt stocks (%)	..	..	113.9	141.8	172.3	200.5	220.9	250.0

Notes:

Short-term debt is based on data from the BIS. Data include the effects of Paris Club debt restructuring agreements signed in 2010 and HIPC and MDRI debt relief.

ALBANIA

(US$ million, unless otherwise indicated)

	2000	2005	2008	2009	2010	2011	2012	2013
Summary external debt data								
External debt stocks	**1,122**	**2,101**	**4,238**	**4,310**	**5,201**	**6,228**	**6,926**	**7,776**
Long-term external debt	937	1,788	2,936	3,485	4,328	5,019	5,349	6,048
Short-term external debt	37	155	1,150	681	743	1,092	1,470	1,632
interest arrears on long-term	3	1	0	0	0	0	0	0
Use of IMF credit	148	158	152	144	129	117	107	97
Long-term external debt								
Debt outstanding and disbursed	**937**	**1,788**	**2,936**	**3,485**	**4,328**	**5,019**	**5,349**	**6,048**
Public and publicly guaranteed	921	1,375	2,298	2,602	3,043	3,287	3,552	3,760
Official creditors	895	1,343	1,868	2,122	2,151	2,289	2,504	2,657
Private creditors	26	32	431	480	893	997	1,049	1,103
of which: Bonds	0	0	79	82	477	556	567	593
Private nonguaranteed	16	413	638	884	1,285	1,732	1,796	2,288
of which: Bonds	..	..	..	..	..	..	..	..
Disbursements	**119**	**489**	**870**	**457**	**820**	**755**	**537**	**623**
Public and publicly guaranteed	119	119	650	291	631	418	336	245
Official creditors	119	119	210	256	184	274	302	235
Private creditors	0	0	440	34	447	144	34	9
of which: Bonds	0	0	84	0	398	101	0	0
Private nonguaranteed	..	370	220	167	189	336	202	378
of which: Bonds	..	..	..	..	..	..	..	..
Principal repayments	**9**	**41**	**74**	**112**	**127**	**143**	**161**	**319**
Public and publicly guaranteed	9	40	58	80	89	102	108	124
Official creditors	8	39	56	78	86	99	105	122
Private creditors	1	1	1	2	3	3	3	2
of which: Bonds	0	0	0	0	0	0	0	0
Private nonguaranteed	..	1	17	32	38	41	53	195
of which: Bonds	..	..	..	..	..	..	..	..
Interest payments	**8**	**25**	**48**	**58**	**47**	**85**	**84**	**80**
Public and publicly guaranteed	7	23	44	50	39	77	74	72
Official creditors	7	23	35	35	31	36	37	36
Private creditors	0	0	9	14	7	41	38	36
of which: Bonds	0	0	0	2	1	32	30	31
Private nonguaranteed	1	1	5	8	8	8	9	8
of which: Bonds	..	..	..	..	..	..	..	..
Net financial flows								
Net debt inflows	130	605	1,428	-134	744	948	745	455
Official creditors (incl. IMF)	122	83	146	168	85	163	187	103
Private creditors	7	522	1,283	-302	658	785	558	352
Long-term	-1	368	642	167	596	437	180	190
Public and publicly guaranteed	-1	-1	439	33	444	141	31	7
Private nonguaranteed	..	369	203	134	151	295	149	183
Short-term	8	154	640	-469	63	349	378	162
Net equity inflows								
Foreign direct investment	143	262	881	1,038	1,052	813	714	1,348
Portfolio equity	..	..	23	-4	7	23	18	2
Major economic aggregates								
Gross national income (GNI)	3,790	8,541	12,946	11,853	11,808	12,855	12,253	12,940
Exports of goods, services & prim. income	819	1,687	3,751	3,439	3,704	4,078	3,800	4,067
Imports of goods, services & prim. income	1,509	3,553	7,149	6,598	6,280	7,010	6,189	6,365
Primary income on FDI	0	2	301	448	381	140	169	174
Personal transfers & comp. of employees	598	1,290	1,495	1,318	1,156	1,126	1,027	804
International reserves	616	1,404	2,320	2,314	2,470	2,394	2,516	2,712
Ratios								
External debt stocks to exports (%)	137.0	124.5	113.0	125.3	140.4	152.7	182.3	191.2
External debt stocks to GNI (%)	29.6	24.6	32.7	36.4	44.0	48.4	56.5	60.1
Debt service to exports (%)	3.7	4.8	4.5	5.7	5.2	5.9	6.7	10.1
Reserves to external debt stocks (%)	54.9	66.8	54.7	53.7	47.5	38.4	36.3	34.9

Notes:

Long-term private nonguaranteed debt data for 2013 are World Bank staff estimates based on reports provided by the country.

ALGERIA

(US$ million, unless otherwise indicated)

	2000	2005	2008	2009	2010	2011	2012	2013
Summary external debt data								
External debt stocks	**25,477**	**17,092**	**6,246**	**7,405**	**7,246**	**6,045**	**5,495**	**5,231**
Long-term external debt	23,369	16,393	4,745	4,035	3,623	3,064	2,449	2,058
Short-term external debt	222	516	1,304	1,492	1,778	1,142	1,205	1,328
interest arrears on long-term	0	0	0	0	0	0	0	0
Use of IMF credit	1,886	184	198	1,878	1,845	1,840	1,842	1,845
Long-term external debt								
Debt outstanding and disbursed	**23,369**	**16,393**	**4,745**	**4,035**	**3,623**	**3,064**	**2,449**	**2,058**
Public and publicly guaranteed	23,369	15,527	3,301	3,053	2,655	2,246	1,627	1,438
Official creditors	17,518	12,500	2,127	2,092	1,889	1,643	1,198	1,117
Private creditors	5,851	3,027	1,174	961	766	603	429	321
of which: Bonds	0	0	0	0	0	0	0	0
Private nonguaranteed	..	866	1,444	982	968	818	822	620
of which: Bonds	..	..	..	..	..	..	..	..
Disbursements	**1,219**	**1,240**	**675**	**211**	**43**	**30**	**29**	**22**
Public and publicly guaranteed	1,219	777	268	88	41	30	28	22
Official creditors	799	446	197	86	40	26	28	22
Private creditors	420	331	71	2	1	4	0	0
of which: Bonds	0	0	0	0	0	0	0	0
Private nonguaranteed	..	463	407	123	2	0	0	..
of which: Bonds	..	..	..	..	..	..		..
Principal repayments	**2,721**	**4,448**	**1,058**	**910**	**557**	**536**	**742**	**459**
Public and publicly guaranteed	2,721	4,219	914	388	324	415	589	257
Official creditors	1,055	3,014	370	155	167	255	488	139
Private creditors	1,666	1,205	544	233	157	160	101	117
of which: Bonds	0	0	0	0	0	0	0	0
Private nonguaranteed	..	229	144	522	234	121	153	203
of which: Bonds	..	..	..	..	..	..	..	..
Interest payments	**1,552**	**889**	**161**	**124**	**95**	**80**	**103**	**51**
Public and publicly guaranteed	1,552	864	113	75	64	58	85	38
Official creditors	1,132	719	50	34	35	32	67	20
Private creditors	421	145	63	41	29	26	18	18
of which: Bonds	0	0	0	0	0	0	0	0
Private nonguaranteed	..	25	48	49	31	22	18	13
of which: Bonds	..	..	..	..	..	..	..	..
Net financial flows								
Net debt inflows	-1,568	-3,734	171	-510	-229	-1,142	-650	-314
Official creditors (incl. IMF)	-349	-3,180	-173	-69	-127	-228	-460	-117
Private creditors	-1,219	-555	345	-441	-101	-914	-190	-197
Long-term	-1,246	-640	-210	-629	-387	-277	-253	-320
Public and publicly guaranteed	-1,246	-874	-473	-231	-155	-157	-101	-117
Private nonguaranteed	..	234	264	-398	-232	-121	-152	-203
Short-term	27	85	554	189	286	-637	63	123
Net equity inflows								
Foreign direct investment	280	1,156	2,520	2,833	2,315	2,628	1,565	1,691
Portfolio equity	..	..	..	..	..	..	..	..
Major economic aggregates								
Gross national income (GNI)	52,080	98,612	169,765	135,812	160,807	197,073	200,431	205,155
Exports of goods, services & prim. income	..	50,268	86,655	52,892	65,259	80,950	79,280	71,940
Imports of goods, services & prim. income	..	31,155	55,409	55,112	55,615	65,958	70,116	73,370
Primary income on FDI	..	5,485	6,152	5,891	4,858	6,313	7,453	..
Personal transfers & comp. of employees	790	170	104	150	197	203	215	..
International reserves	12,024	56,303	143,243	149,041	162,614	182,822	191,297	194,712
Ratios								
External debt stocks to exports (%)	..	34.0	7.2	14.0	11.1	7.5	6.9	7.3
External debt stocks to GNI (%)	48.9	17.3	3.7	5.5	4.5	3.1	2.7	2.5
Debt service to exports (%)	..	11.9	1.4	2.0	1.0	0.8	1.1	0.7
Reserves to external debt stocks (%)	47.2	329.4	2,293.2	2,012.6	2,244.2	3,024.5	3,481.1	3,722.1

ANGOLA

(US$ million, unless otherwise indicated)

	2000	2005	2008	2009	2010	2011	2012	2013
Summary external debt data								
External debt stocks	**9,763**	**12,224**	**15,502**	**17,014**	**16,949**	**19,298**	**20,106**	**24,004**
Long-term external debt	8,085	9,518	12,690	13,635	15,466	17,525	18,203	22,349
Short-term external debt	1,323	2,316	2,391	2,593	181	168	164	176
interest arrears on long-term	874	577	70	85	68	62	58	70
Use of IMF credit	356	390	421	787	1,302	1,606	1,740	1,479
Long-term external debt								
Debt outstanding and disbursed	**8,085**	**9,518**	**12,690**	**13,635**	**15,466**	**17,525**	**18,203**	**22,349**
Public and publicly guaranteed	8,085	9,518	12,690	13,635	15,466	17,525	18,203	22,349
Official creditors	2,703	3,174	4,008	4,822	8,161	9,687	9,615	11,825
Private creditors	5,382	6,344	8,682	8,813	7,305	7,837	8,588	10,525
of which: Bonds	0	0	0	0	0	10	0	0
Private nonguaranteed	..	..	..	..	..	..	..	..
of which: Bonds	..	..	..	..	..	..	..	..
Disbursements	**1,045**	**3,676**	**4,622**	**3,543**	**3,951**	**4,793**	**4,215**	**7,825**
Public and publicly guaranteed	1,045	3,676	4,622	3,543	3,951	4,793	4,215	7,825
Official creditors	34	321	1,101	1,111	3,658	2,353	1,103	3,612
Private creditors	1,011	3,355	3,521	2,432	293	2,440	3,112	4,213
of which: Bonds	0	0	0	0	0	10	51	0
Private nonguaranteed	..	..	..	..	..	..	..	..
of which: Bonds	..	..	..	..	..	..	..	..
Principal repayments	**1,530**	**2,289**	**1,130**	**3,131**	**2,110**	**2,681**	**3,554**	**3,723**
Public and publicly guaranteed	1,530	2,289	1,130	3,131	2,110	2,681	3,554	3,723
Official creditors	268	505	276	310	283	820	1,164	1,380
Private creditors	1,262	1,784	854	2,821	1,827	1,862	2,390	2,344
of which: Bonds	0	0	0	0	0	0	61	0
Private nonguaranteed	..	..	..	..	..	..	..	..
of which: Bonds	..	..	..	..	..	..	..	..
Interest payments	**149**	**257**	**443**	**392**	**176**	**154**	**640**	**873**
Public and publicly guaranteed	149	257	443	392	176	154	640	873
Official creditors	36	61	118	143	114	79	321	414
Private creditors	113	195	325	250	63	75	319	459
of which: Bonds	0	0	0	0	0	0	1	0
Private nonguaranteed	..	..	..	..	..	..	..	..
of which: Bonds	..	..	..	..	..	..	..	..
Net financial flows								
Net debt inflows	-733	2,603	3,632	952	-29	2,421	791	3,840
Official creditors (incl. IMF)	-234	-185	825	1,155	3,900	1,849	70	1,970
Private creditors	-499	2,788	2,807	-203	-3,929	572	722	1,870
Long-term	-251	1,572	2,667	-390	-1,534	579	722	1,870
Public and publicly guaranteed	-251	1,572	2,667	-390	-1,534	579	722	1,870
Private nonguaranteed	..	..	..	..	..	..	..	..
Short-term	-248	1,216	140	187	-2,395	-7	0	0
Net equity inflows								
Foreign direct investment	879	1,140	5,266	2,743	3,326	4,070	4,357	4,184
Portfolio equity	..	..	..	..	..	..	..	..
Major economic aggregates								
Gross national income (GNI)	7,449	24,203	70,461	68,669	74,384	94,419	102,755	109,236
Exports of goods, services & prim. income	8,222	24,312	64,666	41,582	51,586	68,252	72,133	70,381
Imports of goods, services & prim. income	7,454	19,201	57,261	48,784	43,642	53,805	56,518	59,909
Primary income on FDI	929	3,406	13,185	6,130	7,526	9,040	9,722	9,331
Personal transfers & comp. of employees	..	..	82	0	18	0	0	..
International reserves	1,198	3,197	17,869	13,664	19,749	28,786	33,415	32,780
Ratios								
External debt stocks to exports (%)	118.7	50.3	24.0	40.9	32.9	28.3	27.9	34.1
External debt stocks to GNI (%)	131.1	50.5	22.0	24.8	22.8	20.4	19.6	22.0
Debt service to exports (%)	20.9	10.8	2.5	8.5	4.5	4.2	5.8	6.9
Reserves to external debt stocks (%)	12.3	26.2	115.3	80.3	116.5	149.2	166.2	136.6

Notes:

Short-term debt before 2009 is based on data from the BIS.

ARGENTINA

(US$ million, unless otherwise indicated)

	2000	2005	2008	2009	2010	2011	2012	2013
Summary external debt data								
External debt stocks	**147,029**	**128,186**	**122,987**	**127,743**	**120,791**	**132,743**	**133,042**	**136,272**
Long-term external debt	113,234	83,374	102,513	104,732	100,681	103,309	104,085	110,995
Short-term external debt	28,325	34,844	19,983	19,844	16,999	26,333	25,852	22,166
interest arrears on long-term	10	7,738	10,009	10,774	5,464	6,115	6,312	6,607
Use of IMF credit	5,470	9,968	490	3,167	3,111	3,101	3,105	3,111
Long-term external debt								
Debt outstanding and disbursed	**113,234**	**83,374**	**102,513**	**104,732**	**100,681**	**103,309**	**104,085**	**110,995**
Public and publicly guaranteed	87,324	57,013	71,613	76,361	69,579	68,583	67,606	67,462
Official creditors	20,822	20,564	20,785	22,539	23,109	23,804	23,700	24,445
Private creditors	66,503	36,449	50,828	53,822	46,470	44,780	43,905	43,017
of which: Bonds	65,976	35,941	49,864	51,969	45,099	43,729	42,889	42,057
Private nonguaranteed	25,909	26,361	30,900	28,371	31,102	34,725	36,480	43,533
of which: Bonds	11,138	8,772	7,921	6,850	7,855	9,129	8,567	13,917
Disbursements	**18,794**	**4,727**	**7,036**	**7,547**	**6,893**	**10,774**	**7,449**	**10,084**
Public and publicly guaranteed	14,312	3,219	4,046	3,602	2,592	2,612	2,159	3,108
Official creditors	1,971	993	2,020	3,499	2,455	2,588	2,124	2,884
Private creditors	12,341	2,227	2,026	103	137	23	36	225
of which: Bonds	12,339	2,227	2,026	103	90	0	0	213
Private nonguaranteed	4,482	1,507	2,990	3,946	4,300	8,163	5,290	6,976
of which: Bonds	1,408	540	..	476	2,037	1,320	211	375
Principal repayments	**11,689**	**3,491**	**4,733**	**11,306**	**10,775**	**12,049**	**9,677**	**10,131**
Public and publicly guaranteed	6,185	1,724	2,465	5,592	5,120	5,338	3,370	3,213
Official creditors	1,871	1,501	2,380	1,796	1,923	1,907	2,085	1,946
Private creditors	4,314	224	85	3,797	3,196	3,430	1,285	1,267
of which: Bonds	4,097	222	85	1,314	2,909	3,097	1,214	1,214
Private nonguaranteed	5,503	1,766	2,268	5,714	5,655	6,712	6,307	6,918
of which: Bonds	2,309	680	2,009	450	969	26	785	999
Interest payments	**9,837**	**2,170**	**2,958**	**3,366**	**3,532**	**3,388**	**3,199**	**3,158**
Public and publicly guaranteed	7,797	1,454	1,752	2,031	2,443	2,450	2,292	2,336
Official creditors	1,600	756	768	661	614	571	534	603
Private creditors	6,196	698	984	1,370	1,829	1,878	1,758	1,733
of which: Bonds	6,055	697	984	1,247	1,772	1,833	1,731	1,709
Private nonguaranteed	2,041	716	1,206	1,335	1,089	938	907	822
of which: Bonds	1,109	585	710	562	567	717	757	725
Net financial flows								
Net debt inflows	6,820	14,771	2,467	-4,663	-1,417	7,408	-2,906	-4,028
Official creditors (incl. IMF)	915	-4,079	-360	1,703	532	681	39	937
Private creditors	5,905	18,850	2,826	-6,366	-1,949	6,727	-2,944	-4,965
Long-term	7,005	1,744	2,662	-5,462	-4,414	-1,956	-2,267	-984
Public and publicly guaranteed	8,026	2,003	1,941	-3,693	-3,059	-3,407	-1,249	-1,042
Private nonguaranteed	-1,021	-259	722	-1,768	-1,355	1,451	-1,017	58
Short-term	-1,100	17,106	164	-904	2,465	8,683	-678	-3,981
Net equity inflows								
Foreign direct investment	10,418	5,747	4,949	5,027	5,239	8,120	11,821	9,650
Portfolio equity	-3,227	-48	-531	-212	-208	-174	876	462
Major economic aggregates								
Gross national income (GNI)	336,725	216,699	398,837	369,051	452,587	546,906	593,046	599,180
Exports of goods, services & prim. income	38,697	51,204	87,609	69,991	84,380	102,701	97,717	98,449
Imports of goods, services & prim. income	48,076	46,414	81,023	61,706	82,615	104,425	98,172	102,306
Primary income on FDI	3,086	5,456	7,902	8,360	9,964	10,811	10,236	8,844
Personal transfers & comp. of employees	86	432	698	621	639	698	576	526
International reserves	25,147	27,179	44,855	46,093	49,734	43,227	39,920	28,143
Ratios								
External debt stocks to exports (%)	380.0	250.3	140.4	182.5	143.2	129.3	136.2	138.4
External debt stocks to GNI (%)	43.7	59.2	30.8	34.6	26.7	24.3	22.4	22.7
Debt service to exports (%)	64.0	19.7	9.1	21.1	17.1	15.3	13.5	13.7
Reserves to external debt stocks (%)	17.1	21.2	36.5	36.1	41.2	32.6	30.0	20.7

Notes:

Long-term private nonguaranteed debt data before 2008 are World Bank staff estimates. Long-term provincial debt data are World Bank staff estimates. Short-term debt before 2010 is based on data from the BIS.

ARMENIA

(US$ million, unless otherwise indicated)

	2000	2005	2008	2009	2010	2011	2012	2013
Summary external debt data								
External debt stocks	**1,010**	**1,968**	**3,541**	**4,925**	**6,280**	**7,383**	**7,608**	**8,677**
Long-term external debt	675	1,368	2,818	3,679	4,783	5,551	5,889	6,807
Short-term external debt	44	298	453	521	621	869	808	1,150
interest arrears on long-term	6	0	0	0	0	0	0	0
Use of IMF credit	290	302	270	725	876	963	911	720
Long-term external debt								
Debt outstanding and disbursed	**675**	**1,368**	**2,818**	**3,679**	**4,783**	**5,551**	**5,889**	**6,807**
Public and publicly guaranteed	675	923	1,446	2,376	2,557	2,736	2,956	3,312
Official creditors	658	921	1,444	2,375	2,556	2,733	2,942	2,594
Private creditors	17	1	1	1	1	4	14	718
of which: Bonds	0	0	0	0	0	0	0	700
Private nonguaranteed	..	446	1,373	1,302	2,226	2,815	2,933	3,495
of which: Bonds	..	..	..	..	..	..	..	..
Disbursements	**63**	**168**	**776**	**1,247**	**1,734**	**1,476**	**1,610**	**2,785**
Public and publicly guaranteed	63	50	164	941	198	206	280	927
Official creditors	62	50	164	941	198	203	270	234
Private creditors	1	0	0	0	0	2	10	693
of which: Bonds	0	0	0	0	0	0	0	690
Private nonguaranteed	..	117	612	306	1,536	1,271	1,330	1,858
of which: Bonds	..	..	..	..	..	..	..	..
Principal repayments	**15**	**69**	**253**	**300**	**857**	**729**	**834**	**1,582**
Public and publicly guaranteed	15	16	15	21	24	28	30	537
Official creditors	13	16	15	21	24	28	30	537
Private creditors	2	0	0	0	0	0	0	0
of which: Bonds	0	0	0	0	0	0	0	0
Private nonguaranteed	..	53	238	279	833	700	804	1,045
of which: Bonds	..	..	..	..	..	..	..	..
Interest payments	**9**	**23**	**70**	**79**	**60**	**126**	**124**	**123**
Public and publicly guaranteed	9	9	11	23	35	38	43	42
Official creditors	9	9	11	23	35	38	43	42
Private creditors	0	0	0	0	0	0	0	0
of which: Bonds	0	0	0	0	0	0	0	0
Private nonguaranteed	..	14	58	56	25	88	81	81
of which: Bonds	..	..	..	..	..	..	..	..
Net financial flows								
Net debt inflows	21	-38	497	1,458	1,139	1,088	663	1,354
Official creditors (incl. IMF)	34	10	130	1,362	337	266	188	-494
Private creditors	-13	-48	367	96	802	821	475	1,848
Long-term	-2	64	374	28	703	573	536	1,506
Public and publicly guaranteed	-2	..	0	0	0	2	10	693
Private nonguaranteed	..	64	374	28	703	570	526	813
Short-term	-11	-112	-6	68	99	249	-61	342
Net equity inflows								
Foreign direct investment	104	278	1,036	718	361	386	589	399
Portfolio equity	0	0	3	1	7	3	2	-2
Major economic aggregates								
Gross national income (GNI)	1,964	5,033	12,133	8,815	9,599	10,701	10,587	10,926
Exports of goods, services & prim. income	551	1,944	2,894	2,242	3,025	3,533	3,670	4,060
Imports of goods, services & prim. income	1,017	2,520	5,417	4,344	4,950	5,450	5,601	5,984
Primary income on FDI	22	170	270	352	362	379	335	324
Personal transfers & comp. of employees	87	915	1,904	1,440	1,669	1,799	1,915	2,193
International reserves	302	669	1,407	2,004	1,866	1,932	1,799	2,252
Ratios								
External debt stocks to exports (%)	183.4	101.3	122.4	219.7	207.6	209.0	207.3	213.7
External debt stocks to GNI (%)	51.4	39.1	29.2	55.9	65.4	69.0	71.9	79.4
Debt service to exports (%)	9.2	7.3	12.7	18.9	32.0	26.0	31.3	49.9
Reserves to external debt stocks (%)	29.9	34.0	39.7	40.7	29.7	26.2	23.7	25.9

Notes:

Long-term private nonguaranteed debt data from 2011 are World Bank staff estimates based on reports provided by the country.

AZERBAIJAN

(US$ million, unless otherwise indicated)

	2000	2005	2008	2009	2010	2011	2012	2013
Summary external debt data								
External debt stocks	**1,524**	**2,118**	**4,466**	**4,755**	**7,029**	**8,085**	**9,551**	**9,219**
Long-term external debt	832	1,549	2,981	3,642	5,869	6,929	8,448	8,125
Short-term external debt	156	186	1,169	810	878	891	852	852
interest arrears on long-term	0	0	0	0	0	0	0	0
Use of IMF credit	536	383	316	303	282	265	252	242
Long-term external debt								
Debt outstanding and disbursed	**832**	**1,549**	**2,981**	**3,642**	**5,869**	**6,929**	**8,448**	**8,125**
Public and publicly guaranteed	734	1,362	2,654	3,328	3,711	4,312	5,695	6,075
Official creditors	643	1,102	1,838	2,172	2,562	3,144	4,033	4,192
Private creditors	90	260	816	1,157	1,149	1,168	1,662	1,884
of which: Bonds	0	0	0	0	0	0	500	500
Private nonguaranteed	99	187	327	314	2,158	2,616	2,752	2,049
of which: Bonds	..	..	..	..	..	..	..	..
Disbursements	**269**	**431**	**741**	**870**	**2,547**	**1,941**	**2,477**	**1,273**
Public and publicly guaranteed	263	307	526	820	633	878	1,659	1,073
Official creditors	204	71	283	431	453	698	1,069	741
Private creditors	59	236	242	389	180	180	590	333
of which: Bonds	0	0	0	0	0	0	500	0
Private nonguaranteed	6	124	216	50	1,914	1,063	818	200
of which: Bonds	..	..	..	..	..	..	..	..
Principal repayments	**22**	**134**	**149**	**230**	**300**	**856**	**922**	**1,558**
Public and publicly guaranteed	14	37	126	178	228	249	239	646
Official creditors	12	34	46	101	97	116	127	494
Private creditors	2	3	80	76	131	133	111	152
of which: Bonds	0	0	0	0	0	0	0	0
Private nonguaranteed	7	97	23	53	72	608	684	912
of which: Bonds	..	..	..	..	..	..	..	..
Interest payments	**37**	**24**	**88**	**67**	**80**	**948**	**945**	**930**
Public and publicly guaranteed	32	17	77	55	67	77	97	104
Official creditors	31	15	30	35	33	42	43	52
Private creditors	1	2	47	21	35	35	53	52
of which: Bonds	0	0	0	0	0	0	14	27
Private nonguaranteed	5	7	11	12	13	871	848	826
of which: Bonds	..	..	..	..	..	..	..	..
Net financial flows								
Net debt inflows	323	316	697	262	2,300	1,080	1,502	-295
Official creditors (incl. IMF)	141	8	215	312	341	565	928	237
Private creditors	182	308	481	-49	1,959	515	574	-532
Long-term	55	260	355	310	1,891	502	613	-532
Public and publicly guaranteed	57	233	162	312	50	47	479	181
Private nonguaranteed	-2	27	193	-2	1,842	455	134	-712
Short-term	127	48	126	-359	68	13	-39	..
Net equity inflows								
Foreign direct investment	130	4,476	3,521	2,525	3,353	4,485	5,293	2,619
Portfolio equity	..	..	..	..	1	0	0	30
Major economic aggregates								
Gross national income (GNI)	4,987	11,599	43,586	40,772	49,436	61,092	63,181	69,440
Exports of goods, services & prim. income	2,174	8,341	32,484	23,311	28,910	38,058	37,837	36,941
Imports of goods, services & prim. income	2,415	8,658	17,082	13,858	14,379	21,586	22,811	24,650
Primary income on FDI	317	1,582	5,401	3,664	3,815	5,488	4,906	4,507
Personal transfers & comp. of employees	57	623	1,518	1,255	1,410	1,893	1,990	1,733
International reserves	680	1,178	6,467	5,364	6,409	10,274	11,277	14,401
Ratios								
External debt stocks to exports (%)	70.1	25.4	13.7	20.4	24.3	21.2	25.2	25.0
External debt stocks to GNI (%)	30.6	18.3	10.2	11.7	14.2	13.2	15.1	13.3
Debt service to exports (%)	6.4	2.7	0.9	1.4	1.4	4.8	5.0	6.8
Reserves to external debt stocks (%)	44.6	55.6	144.8	112.8	91.2	127.1	118.1	156.2

Notes:

Long-term private nonguaranteed debt data are World Bank staff estimates based on the market data. Short-term debt is based on data from the BIS.

BANGLADESH

(US$ million, unless otherwise indicated)

	2000	2005	2008	2009	2010	2011	2012	2013
Summary external debt data								
External debt stocks	**15,596**	**18,449**	**22,952**	**24,619**	**25,752**	**27,326**	**26,188**	**27,804**
Long-term external debt	14,985	17,385	20,300	21,210	21,400	22,350	23,251	24,850
Short-term external debt	334	688	1,894	1,934	2,949	3,705	1,724	1,458
interest arrears on long-term	0	16	1	1	2	2	2	2
Use of IMF credit	277	376	758	1,475	1,403	1,271	1,213	1,496
Long-term external debt								
Debt outstanding and disbursed	**14,985**	**17,385**	**20,300**	**21,210**	**21,400**	**22,350**	**23,251**	**24,850**
Public and publicly guaranteed	14,985	17,385	20,300	21,210	21,400	22,350	23,251	24,850
Official creditors	14,809	17,209	20,237	21,160	21,367	22,328	23,237	24,838
Private creditors	176	176	63	50	33	22	13	12
of which: Bonds	0	0	0	0	0	0	0	0
Private nonguaranteed	..	..	..	..	..	..	..	..
of which: Bonds	..	..	..	..	..	..	..	..
Disbursements	**861**	**878**	**1,732**	**1,499**	**982**	**1,028**	**2,091**	**3,157**
Public and publicly guaranteed	861	878	1,732	1,499	982	1,028	2,091	3,157
Official creditors	794	878	1,732	1,499	982	1,028	2,091	3,157
Private creditors	67	0	0	0	0	0	0	0
of which: Bonds	0	0	0	0	0	0	0	0
Private nonguaranteed	..	..	..	..	..	..	..	..
of which: Bonds	..	..	..	..	..	..	..	..
Principal repayments	**487**	**566**	**632**	**703**	**743**	**1,050**	**988**	**1,232**
Public and publicly guaranteed	487	566	632	703	743	1,050	988	1,232
Official creditors	465	551	612	691	732	1,039	980	1,230
Private creditors	22	16	20	13	11	11	9	2
of which: Bonds	0	0	0	0	0	0	0	0
Private nonguaranteed	..	..	..	..	..	..	..	..
of which: Bonds	..	..	..	..	..	..	..	..
Interest payments	**165**	**197**	**203**	**197**	**201**	**258**	**296**	**253**
Public and publicly guaranteed	165	197	203	197	201	258	296	253
Official creditors	156	195	200	196	199	257	295	252
Private creditors	9	2	2	1	2	1	1	1
of which: Bonds	0	0	0	0	0	0	0	0
Private nonguaranteed	..	..	..	..	..	..	..	..
of which: Bonds	..	..	..	..	..	..	..	..
Net financial flows								
Net debt inflows	368	370	1,826	812	1,207	603	-938	1,938
Official creditors (incl. IMF)	244	425	1,319	785	204	-142	1,052	2,205
Private creditors	125	-56	507	27	1,003	745	-1,990	-268
Long-term	45	-16	-20	-13	-11	-11	-9	-2
Public and publicly guaranteed	45	-16	-20	-13	-11	-11	-9	-2
Private nonguaranteed	..	..	..	..	..	..	..	..
Short-term	80	-40	527	40	1,014	756	-1,981	-266
Net equity inflows								
Foreign direct investment	280	626	980	754	805	961	1,202	1,258
Portfolio equity	1	20	-130	-104	-104	132	97	270
Major economic aggregates								
Gross national income (GNI)	48,857	63,355	86,607	97,482	109,698	122,091	127,320	142,929
Exports of goods, services & prim. income	7,293	11,322	17,692	17,622	23,756	28,458	28,249	31,716
Imports of goods, services & prim. income	10,018	15,970	26,250	24,984	34,315	41,294	39,716	43,788
Primary income on FDI	149	669	1,028	1,083	1,258	1,365	1,789	1,951
Personal transfers & comp. of employees	1,968	4,642	9,223	10,739	11,282	12,960	14,236	13,857
International reserves	1,486	2,767	5,689	10,219	10,564	8,510	12,031	17,564
Ratios								
External debt stocks to exports (%)	213.9	162.9	129.7	139.7	108.4	96.0	92.7	87.7
External debt stocks to GNI (%)	31.9	29.1	26.5	25.3	23.5	22.4	20.6	19.5
Debt service to exports (%)	10.5	7.1	5.0	5.4	4.3	5.2	5.3	5.2
Reserves to external debt stocks (%)	9.5	15.0	24.8	41.5	41.0	31.1	45.9	63.2

Notes:

Long-term public and publicly guaranteed debt for 2013 are World Bank staff estimates based on the original terms of the loans. Short-term debt before 2012 is based on data from the BIS.

BELARUS

(US$ million, unless otherwise indicated)

	2000	2005	2008	2009	2010	2011	2012	2013
Summary external debt data								
External debt stocks	**2,604**	**5,284**	**15,122**	**22,054**	**28,397**	**33,926**	**33,756**	**39,108**
Long-term external debt	771	1,254	6,996	9,528	12,470	16,430	18,532	23,586
Short-term external debt	1,239	3,503	7,558	9,076	11,864	13,446	11,635	13,590
interest arrears on long-term	14	1	2	3	4	4	4	4
Use of IMF credit	594	527	568	3,449	4,063	4,050	3,588	1,932
Long-term external debt								
Debt outstanding and disbursed	**771**	**1,254**	**6,996**	**9,528**	**12,470**	**16,430**	**18,532**	**23,586**
Public and publicly guaranteed	673	769	5,407	6,217	7,999	10,609	12,559	14,622
Official creditors	384	552	3,539	4,689	5,725	8,380	7,303	8,540
Private creditors	289	217	1,868	1,529	2,274	2,228	5,256	6,082
of which: Bonds	0	0	19	19	1,019	1,800	1,800	1,800
Private nonguaranteed	98	485	1,589	3,311	4,471	5,821	5,973	8,964
of which: Bonds	..	..	..	..	..	..	..	..
Disbursements	**237**	**647**	**3,306**	**1,984**	**3,810**	**5,406**	**3,542**	**4,675**
Public and publicly guaranteed	131	252	2,165	1,264	2,679	3,926	2,223	3,108
Official creditors	13	188	1,563	1,254	1,580	2,826	1,050	1,603
Private creditors	118	64	602	10	1,099	1,100	1,173	1,505
of which: Bonds	0	0	0	0	1,000	800	0	0
Private nonguaranteed	106	395	1,141	720	1,132	1,479	1,320	1,567
of which: Bonds	..	..	..	..	..	..	..	..
Principal repayments	**193**	**508**	**850**	**1,275**	**1,257**	**2,339**	**3,412**	**1,938**
Public and publicly guaranteed	121	175	175	450	455	1,310	2,649	1,064
Official creditors	39	92	95	97	108	167	2,551	379
Private creditors	82	83	80	352	347	1,143	97	685
of which: Bonds	0	0	0	0	0	19	0	0
Private nonguaranteed	71	333	675	825	802	1,029	763	874
of which: Bonds	..	..	..	..	..	..	..	..
Interest payments	**37**	**53**	**236**	**185**	**208**	**572**	**851**	**783**
Public and publicly guaranteed	36	37	180	114	127	460	729	603
Official creditors	17	16	158	96	114	312	431	267
Private creditors	19	21	21	17	14	148	298	336
of which: Bonds	0	0	1	2	4	129	159	159
Private nonguaranteed	1	15	56	71	80	112	121	181
of which: Bonds	..	..	..	..	..	..	..	..
Net financial flows								
Net debt inflows	-87	696	2,654	5,051	6,008	4,648	-2,143	3,043
Official creditors (incl. IMF)	-81	87	1,468	3,982	2,141	2,659	-1,965	-423
Private creditors	-6	608	1,185	1,069	3,867	1,990	-178	3,467
Long-term	70	42	988	-448	1,081	408	1,632	1,512
Public and publicly guaranteed	36	-19	521	-343	752	-42	1,075	820
Private nonguaranteed	35	61	466	-105	329	450	556	693
Short-term	-76	566	198	1,517	2,786	1,582	-1,810	1,954
Net equity inflows								
Foreign direct investment	119	314	2,016	1,823	1,348	3,773	1,251	1,766
Portfolio equity	1	1	1	1	1	0	-4	2
Major economic aggregates								
Gross national income (GNI)	12,690	30,220	59,975	48,095	54,058	59,052	62,145	68,970
Exports of goods, services & prim. income	7,667	17,705	36,878	24,818	29,805	47,242	52,827	44,673
Imports of goods, services & prim. income	8,160	17,411	42,007	31,224	38,402	49,812	51,443	49,373
Primary income on FDI	5	135	682	872	1,039	1,186	1,258	2,374
Personal transfers & comp. of employees	139	199	583	504	575	891	1,053	1,150
International reserves	350	1,137	2,687	4,831	3,431	6,011	5,809	4,938
Ratios								
External debt stocks to exports (%)	34.0	29.8	41.0	88.9	95.3	71.8	63.9	87.5
External debt stocks to GNI (%)	20.5	17.5	25.2	45.9	52.5	57.5	54.3	56.7
Debt service to exports (%)	4.9	3.9	3.3	6.5	5.8	6.8	9.4	10.4
Reserves to external debt stocks (%)	13.5	21.5	17.8	21.9	12.1	17.7	17.2	12.6

BELIZE

(US$ million, unless otherwise indicated)

	2000	2005	2008	2009	2010	2011	2012	2013
Summary external debt data								
External debt stocks	**528**	**989**	**1,252**	**1,271**	**1,287**	**1,261**	**1,196**	**1,249**
Long-term external debt	455	956	1,217	1,226	1,245	1,219	1,158	1,214
Short-term external debt	50	7	7	10	7	8	6	7
interest arrears on long-term	0	7	7	10	7	8	6	7
Use of IMF credit	23	26	28	35	35	35	32	28
Long-term external debt								
Debt outstanding and disbursed	**455**	**956**	**1,217**	**1,226**	**1,245**	**1,219**	**1,158**	**1,214**
Public and publicly guaranteed	455	956	998	1,017	1,002	1,001	984	1,052
Official creditors	228	348	386	412	402	406	412	504
Private creditors	226	608	612	605	600	595	573	548
of which: Bonds	75	482	22	21	21	21	3	527
Private nonguaranteed	..	..	219	209	243	218	173	162
of which: Bonds	..	..	..	..	..	..	..	..
Disbursements	**195**	**213**	**109**	**79**	**39**	**53**	**41**	**165**
Public and publicly guaranteed	195	213	41	66	32	36	37	164
Official creditors	27	48	40	65	32	36	37	123
Private creditors	169	165	2	1	0	0	0	41
of which: Bonds	86	143	0	0	0	0	0	41
Private nonguaranteed	..	..	68	13	7	18	4	1
of which: Bonds	..	..	..	..	..	..	..	..
Principal repayments	**41**	**152**	**84**	**66**	**66**	**69**	**103**	**102**
Public and publicly guaranteed	41	152	49	47	46	37	54	89
Official creditors	20	21	38	39	41	32	31	31
Private creditors	21	131	11	9	5	5	22	58
of which: Bonds	11	36	2	1	0	0	18	54
Private nonguaranteed	..	..	35	18	20	32	49	13
of which: Bonds	..	..	..	..	..	..	..	..
Interest payments	**22**	**70**	**57**	**54**	**56**	**57**	**49**	**30**
Public and publicly guaranteed	22	70	45	43	45	46	40	22
Official creditors	12	15	17	15	13	10	9	10
Private creditors	11	54	28	28	32	36	31	12
of which: Bonds	1	41	2	2	2	2	1	11
Private nonguaranteed	..	..	12	11	11	11	9	8
of which: Bonds	..	..	..	..	..	..	..	..
Net financial flows								
Net debt inflows	153	61	25	21	-26	-16	-64	59
Official creditors (incl. IMF)	7	27	2	33	-9	3	3	89
Private creditors	146	34	23	-13	-17	-19	-67	-29
Long-term	147	34	23	-13	-17	-19	-67	-29
Public and publicly guaranteed	147	34	-10	-7	-5	-5	-22	-17
Private nonguaranteed	..	..	33	-6	-12	-14	-45	-12
Short-term	-1	..	..	..	..	..	..	..
Net equity inflows								
Foreign direct investment	23	106	162	102	94	94	194	89
Portfolio equity	..	..	2	..	..	..	..	..
Major economic aggregates								
Gross national income (GNI)	898	1,242	1,205	1,253	1,329	1,444	1,520	1,551
Exports of goods, services & prim. income	441	622	872	733	834	949	1,040	1,063
Imports of goods, services & prim. income	661	824	1,129	895	972	1,052	1,148	1,208
Primary income on FDI	31	35	107	56	102	40	68	85
Personal transfers & comp. of employees	26	45	76	79	78	75	76	74
International reserves	123	71	166	214	218	237	289	403
Ratios								
External debt stocks to exports (%)	119.6	159.0	143.5	173.4	154.3	133.0	115.0	117.5
External debt stocks to GNI (%)	58.8	79.6	104.0	101.5	96.9	87.3	78.7	80.5
Debt service to exports (%)	15.3	35.7	16.2	16.3	14.6	13.3	14.9	12.7
Reserves to external debt stocks (%)	23.3	7.2	13.3	16.8	16.9	18.8	24.2	32.2

Notes:

Long-term private nonguaranteed debt data from 2008 are based on Central Bank data.

BENIN

(US$ million, unless otherwise indicated)

	2000	2005	2008	2009	2010	2011	2012	2013
Summary external debt data								
External debt stocks	**1,400**	**1,552**	**976**	**1,319**	**1,599**	**1,869**	**2,054**	**2,367**
Long-term external debt	1,237	1,445	850	974	1,113	1,194	1,302	1,593
Short-term external debt	66	41	89	213	341	497	542	549
interest arrears on long-term	1	2	4	32	25	28	47	54
Use of IMF credit	96	66	37	132	146	177	210	225
Long-term external debt								
Debt outstanding and disbursed	**1,237**	**1,445**	**850**	**974**	**1,113**	**1,194**	**1,302**	**1,593**
Public and publicly guaranteed	1,237	1,445	850	974	1,113	1,194	1,302	1,593
Official creditors	1,234	1,445	850	974	1,113	1,194	1,302	1,593
Private creditors	3	0	0	0	0	0	0	0
of which: Bonds	0	0	0	0	0	0	0	0
Private nonguaranteed	..	..	..	..	..	..	..	..
of which: Bonds	..	..	..	..	..	..	..	..
Disbursements	**39**	**97**	**143**	**142**	**184**	**116**	**116**	**337**
Public and publicly guaranteed	39	97	143	142	184	116	116	337
Official creditors	39	97	143	142	184	116	116	337
Private creditors	0	0	0	0	0	0	0	0
of which: Bonds	0	0	0	0	0	0	0	0
Private nonguaranteed	..	..	..	..	..	..	..	..
of which: Bonds	..	..	..	..	..	..	..	..
Principal repayments	**43**	**24**	**16**	**25**	**25**	**29**	**39**	**68**
Public and publicly guaranteed	43	24	16	25	25	29	39	68
Official creditors	43	20	16	25	25	29	39	68
Private creditors	0	4	0	0	0	0	0	0
of which: Bonds	0	0	0	0	0	0	0	0
Private nonguaranteed	..	..	..	..	..	..	..	..
of which: Bonds	..	..	..	..	..	..	..	..
Interest payments	**16**	**14**	**41**	**12**	**13**	**13**	**16**	**18**
Public and publicly guaranteed	16	14	41	12	13	13	16	18
Official creditors	16	14	41	12	13	13	16	18
Private creditors	0	0	0	0	0	0	0	0
of which: Bonds	0	0	0	0	0	0	0	0
Private nonguaranteed	..	..	..	..	..	..	..	..
of which: Bonds	..	..	..	..	..	..	..	..
Net financial flows								
Net debt inflows	-54	82	231	229	309	274	135	284
Official creditors (incl. IMF)	-6	71	146	133	175	120	109	284
Private creditors	-48	11	85	96	134	154	26	0
Long-term	..	-4	..	..	..	..	..	..
Public and publicly guaranteed	..	-4	..	..	..	..	..	..
Private nonguaranteed	..	..	..	..	..	..	..	..
Short-term	-48	15	85	96	134	154	26	0
Net equity inflows								
Foreign direct investment	60	-31	-49	-32	-26	149	282	320
Portfolio equity	0	2	-2	9	5	1	..	..
Major economic aggregates								
Gross national income (GNI)	2,347	4,340	6,622	6,552	6,505	7,260	7,512	8,238
Exports of goods, services & prim. income	552	797	1,675	1,489	1,707	1,765	..	..
Imports of goods, services & prim. income	744	1,188	2,456	2,310	2,393	2,423	..	..
Primary income on FDI	-1	9	30	32	55	66	..	..
Personal transfers & comp. of employees	87	147	207	126	139	172	..	..
International reserves	459	655	1,263	1,230	1,200	887	713	695
Ratios								
External debt stocks to exports (%)	253.6	194.6	58.3	88.6	93.7	105.8	..	..
External debt stocks to GNI (%)	59.6	35.8	14.7	20.1	24.6	25.7	27.3	28.7
Debt service to exports (%)	13.6	6.0	3.7	3.6	3.3	4.0	..	..
Reserves to external debt stocks (%)	32.8	42.2	129.4	93.2	75.0	47.5	34.7	29.4

Notes:

Data include the effects of Paris Club debt restructuring agreement and HIPC and MDRI debt relief.

BHUTAN

(US$ million, unless otherwise indicated)

	2000	2005	2008	2009	2010	2011	2012	2013
Summary external debt data								
External debt stocks	**212**	**657**	**694**	**723**	**868**	**1,015**	**1,420**	**1,480**
Long-term external debt	202	636	676	708	852	998	1,311	1,470
Short-term external debt	2	12	8	5	6	8	100	0
interest arrears on long-term	0	4	0	0	0	0	0	0
Use of IMF credit	8	9	9	9	9	9	9	9
Long-term external debt								
Debt outstanding and disbursed	**202**	**636**	**676**	**708**	**852**	**998**	**1,311**	**1,470**
Public and publicly guaranteed	202	636	676	708	852	988	1,303	1,465
Official creditors	202	636	676	703	832	959	1,265	1,416
Private creditors	0	0	0	5	21	29	38	49
of which: Bonds	0	0	0	0	0	0	0	0
Private nonguaranteed	..	..	..	..	..	10	8	5
of which: Bonds	..	..	..	..	..	..	..	..
Disbursements	**35**	**82**	**32**	**56**	**178**	**270**	**409**	**293**
Public and publicly guaranteed	35	82	32	56	178	260	409	293
Official creditors	35	82	32	51	162	251	400	283
Private creditors	0	0	0	5	16	9	9	9
of which: Bonds	0	0	0	0	0	0	0	0
Private nonguaranteed	..	..	..	..	..	10	..	..
of which: Bonds	..	..	..	..	..	..	..	..
Principal repayments	**5**	**5**	**43**	**41**	**47**	**45**	**69**	**39**
Public and publicly guaranteed	5	5	43	41	47	45	67	37
Official creditors	5	5	43	41	47	45	67	37
Private creditors	0	0	0	0	0	0	0	0
of which: Bonds	0	0	0	0	0	0	0	0
Private nonguaranteed	..	..	..	..	..	..	2	2
of which: Bonds	..	..	..	..	..	..	..	..
Interest payments	**2**	**2**	**38**	**34**	**37**	**37**	**58**	**36**
Public and publicly guaranteed	2	2	38	34	37	37	57	36
Official creditors	2	2	38	34	37	35	55	33
Private creditors	0	0	0	0	1	2	2	2
of which: Bonds	0	0	0	0	0	0	0	0
Private nonguaranteed	..	..	..	..	..	..	0	0
of which: Bonds	..	..	..	..	..	..	..	..
Net financial flows								
Net debt inflows	30	85	-22	12	132	227	432	153
Official creditors (incl. IMF)	30	77	-12	10	115	206	334	246
Private creditors	0	8	-10	2	17	21	98	-93
Long-term	..	..	..	5	16	19	6	7
Public and publicly guaranteed	..	..	..	5	16	9	9	9
Private nonguaranteed	..	..	..	..	..	10	-2	-2
Short-term	0	8	-10	-3	1	2	92	-100
Net equity inflows								
Foreign direct investment	..	6	2	6	20	20	11	20
Portfolio equity	..	..	..	..	..	..	..	..
Major economic aggregates								
Gross national income (GNI)	439	807	1,226	1,220	1,514	1,760	1,770	1,771
Exports of goods, services & prim. income	..	..	688	595	607	762	746	687
Imports of goods, services & prim. income	..	..	835	735	1,024	1,425	1,343	945
Primary income on FDI	..	..	3	-1	4	5	2	20
Personal transfers & comp. of employees	..	..	4	5	8	10	18	12
International reserves	318	467	765	891	1,002	790	955	991
Ratios								
External debt stocks to exports (%)	..	..	100.8	121.4	143.0	133.2	190.2	215.5
External debt stocks to GNI (%)	48.2	81.3	56.6	59.2	57.3	57.7	80.2	83.6
Debt service to exports (%)	..	..	11.9	12.7	13.9	10.8	17.0	10.9
Reserves to external debt stocks (%)	150.1	71.2	110.3	123.3	115.5	77.8	67.2	67.0

Notes:

Short-term debt is based on data from the BIS.

BOLIVIA, PLURINATIONAL STATE OF

(US$ million, unless otherwise indicated)

	2000	2005	2008	2009	2010	2011	2012	2013
Summary external debt data								
External debt stocks	**5,875**	**6,908**	**5,904**	**5,995**	**6,017**	**6,448**	**6,905**	**7,895**
Long-term external debt	5,218	6,445	5,345	5,170	5,137	5,561	5,933	6,929
Short-term external debt	402	182	518	568	628	635	720	713
interest arrears on long-term	2	0	0	0	0	0	0	0
Use of IMF credit	255	282	41	257	253	252	252	253
Long-term external debt								
Debt outstanding and disbursed	**5,218**	**6,445**	**5,345**	**5,170**	**5,137**	**5,561**	**5,933**	**6,929**
Public and publicly guaranteed	4,192	4,531	2,376	2,523	2,779	3,388	4,138	5,149
Official creditors	4,159	4,504	2,279	2,431	2,755	3,299	3,618	4,130
Private creditors	33	27	97	92	24	89	520	1,019
of which: Bonds	0	0	10	0	0	0	500	1,000
Private nonguaranteed	1,026	1,914	2,969	2,647	2,358	2,173	1,795	1,781
of which: Bonds	..	..	..	..	..	..	..	..
Disbursements	**745**	**880**	**1,263**	**512**	**538**	**776**	**1,250**	**1,405**
Public and publicly guaranteed	277	434	590	415	509	776	1,250	1,180
Official creditors	264	429	524	408	506	709	683	680
Private creditors	13	4	67	7	3	67	567	500
of which: Bonds	0	0	0	0	0	0	500	500
Private nonguaranteed	468	447	673	97	30	..	..	225
of which: Bonds	..	..	..	..	..	..	..	..
Principal repayments	**438**	**309**	**761**	**448**	**562**	**351**	**514**	**419**
Public and publicly guaranteed	156	178	369	190	240	166	368	179
Official creditors	153	176	364	178	170	164	366	177
Private creditors	4	2	5	13	70	2	2	2
of which: Bonds	0	0	0	10	0	0	0	0
Private nonguaranteed	281	131	392	257	322	185	146	240
of which: Bonds	..	..	..	..	..	..	..	..
Interest payments	**160**	**155**	**173**	**117**	**75**	**77**	**79**	**115**
Public and publicly guaranteed	113	96	96	69	52	57	65	95
Official creditors	111	96	95	65	49	53	64	71
Private creditors	1	0	1	4	4	4	0	25
of which: Bonds	0	0	0	0	0	0	0	24
Private nonguaranteed	47	59	77	48	22	20	14	20
of which: Bonds	..	..	..	..	..	..	..	..
Net financial flows								
Net debt inflows	292	454	465	114	37	432	820	979
Official creditors (incl. IMF)	106	227	159	231	336	545	317	502
Private creditors	186	227	306	-116	-299	-113	504	476
Long-term	196	318	343	-166	-359	-120	419	483
Public and publicly guaranteed	9	2	62	-6	-67	65	564	498
Private nonguaranteed	187	316	281	-161	-292	-185	-146	-15
Short-term	-10	-91	-37	50	60	7	85	-7
Net equity inflows								
Foreign direct investment	736	-91	280	505	774	902	1,224	1,750
Portfolio equity	..	..	..	..	..	..	..	..
Major economic aggregates								
Gross national income (GNI)	8,172	9,173	16,138	16,666	18,786	22,788	25,406	28,693
Exports of goods, services & prim. income	1,610	3,401	7,369	5,663	6,919	9,260	12,332	..
Imports of goods, services & prim. income	2,443	3,362	6,661	6,062	7,126	9,900	11,460	..
Primary income on FDI	148	271	681	769	863	977	1,649	..
Personal transfers & comp. of employees	127	337	1,135	1,058	960	1,043	1,111	..
International reserves	926	1,328	6,927	7,584	8,134	9,911	11,659	12,783
Ratios								
External debt stocks to exports (%)	365.0	203.2	80.1	105.9	87.0	69.6	56.0	..
External debt stocks to GNI (%)	71.9	75.3	36.6	36.0	32.0	28.3	27.2	27.5
Debt service to exports (%)	39.8	15.4	12.8	10.3	9.5	4.8	5.0	..
Reserves to external debt stocks (%)	15.8	19.2	117.3	126.5	135.2	153.7	168.8	161.9

Notes:

Long-term private nonguaranteed debt data are World Bank staff estimates based on reports provided by the country. Data include the effects of HIPC and MDRI debt relief.

BOSNIA AND HERZEGOVINA

(US$ million, unless otherwise indicated)

	2000	2005	2008	2009	2010	2011	2012	2013
Summary external debt data								
External debt stocks	**2,800**	**6,378**	**9,815**	**11,328**	**9,935**	**10,165**	**10,577**	**11,078**
Long-term external debt	2,619	5,326	8,876	9,111	8,128	8,091	8,427	8,920
Short-term external debt	49	960	907	1,678	1,038	1,308	1,262	1,309
interest arrears on long-term	1	0	0	0	0	0	0	0
Use of IMF credit	131	91	32	539	769	766	888	848
Long-term external debt								
Debt outstanding and disbursed	**2,619**	**5,326**	**8,876**	**9,111**	**8,128**	**8,091**	**8,427**	**8,920**
Public and publicly guaranteed	1,957	2,559	3,008	3,570	3,733	3,874	4,202	4,732
Official creditors	1,832	2,404	2,808	3,042	3,267	3,451	3,798	4,338
Private creditors	125	155	200	527	466	423	404	394
of which: Bonds	0	0	0	322	273	241	221	205
Private nonguaranteed	663	2,767	5,868	5,541	4,395	4,216	4,225	4,188
of which: Bonds	..	..	..	..	..	..	..	..
Disbursements	**103**	**540**	**471**	**394**	**510**	**491**	**526**	**728**
Public and publicly guaranteed	98	153	189	321	441	382	450	643
Official creditors	98	153	163	309	427	370	433	625
Private creditors	0	0	26	12	14	12	17	18
of which: Bonds	0	0	0	0	0	0	0	0
Private nonguaranteed	5	386	282	73	69	108	77	85
of which: Bonds	..	..	..	..	..	..	..	..
Principal repayments	**170**	**95**	**137**	**171**	**537**	**594**	**758**	**669**
Public and publicly guaranteed	170	54	91	110	145	171	167	200
Official creditors	170	51	82	97	108	129	124	155
Private creditors	0	3	9	13	37	43	43	46
of which: Bonds	0	0	0	0	25	26	24	25
Private nonguaranteed	1	41	46	61	392	423	591	468
of which: Bonds	..	..	..	..	..	..	..	..
Interest payments	**119**	**136**	**257**	**217**	**177**	**186**	**183**	**178**
Public and publicly guaranteed	89	53	80	63	55	66	65	58
Official creditors	86	48	70	56	47	55	56	53
Private creditors	2	6	10	8	9	11	9	5
of which: Bonds	0	0	0	0	5	6	5	2
Private nonguaranteed	30	83	176	153	121	120	118	120
of which: Bonds	..	..	..	..	..	..	..	..
Net financial flows								
Net debt inflows	-41	1,052	-448	1,276	-429	166	-158	64
Official creditors (incl. IMF)	-56	63	79	494	556	241	428	429
Private creditors	15	989	-526	782	-985	-75	-586	-365
Long-term	4	342	254	11	-345	-345	-540	-412
Public and publicly guaranteed	..	-3	17	-1	-23	-30	-26	-28
Private nonguaranteed	4	346	236	12	-322	-315	-514	-384
Short-term	11	647	-780	771	-640	270	-46	47
Net equity inflows								
Foreign direct investment	146	314	588	-202	149	338	185	230
Portfolio equity	..	..	..	..	..	..	..	..
Major economic aggregates								
Gross national income (GNI)	6,096	11,416	19,250	17,761	17,056	18,406	17,006	18,176
Exports of goods, services & prim. income	2,247	4,227	6,189	5,187	5,492	6,374	5,780	6,270
Imports of goods, services & prim. income	4,234	8,103	11,705	8,701	8,910	10,654	9,736	9,692
Primary income on FDI	..	97	187	-104	79	272	205	53
Personal transfers & comp. of employees	1,607	2,038	2,718	2,127	1,822	1,958	1,844	1,893
International reserves	497	2,548	4,480	4,529	4,366	4,150	4,283	4,868
Ratios								
External debt stocks to exports (%)	124.6	150.9	158.6	218.4	180.9	159.5	183.0	176.7
External debt stocks to GNI (%)	45.9	55.9	51.0	63.8	58.3	55.2	62.2	60.9
Debt service to exports (%)	14.2	7.3	7.7	9.1	14.6	13.6	18.4	17.9
Reserves to external debt stocks (%)	17.7	39.9	45.6	40.0	43.9	40.8	40.5	43.9

Notes:

Long-term private nonguaranteed debt data from 2005 are World Bank staff estimates. Short-term debt is based on data from the BIS.

BOTSWANA

(US$ million, unless otherwise indicated)

	2000	2005	2008	2009	2010	2011	2012	2013
Summary external debt data								
External debt stocks	**458**	**454**	**440**	**1,707**	**1,797**	**2,396**	**2,488**	**2,430**
Long-term external debt	438	412	391	1,388	1,352	1,897	2,015	1,896
Short-term external debt	15	35	43	229	357	411	385	446
interest arrears on long-term	0	0	0	0	0	0	0	0
Use of IMF credit	6	6	7	90	88	88	88	88
Long-term external debt								
Debt outstanding and disbursed	**438**	**412**	**391**	**1,388**	**1,352**	**1,897**	**2,015**	**1,896**
Public and publicly guaranteed	438	412	391	1,388	1,352	1,897	1,935	1,816
Official creditors	410	401	389	1,387	1,351	1,896	1,935	1,816
Private creditors	28	12	2	2	1	1	0	0
of which: Bonds	0	0	0	0	0	0	0	0
Private nonguaranteed	..	..	..	..	..	..	80	80
of which: Bonds	..	..	..	..	..	..	80	80
Disbursements	**28**	**11**	**54**	**1,006**	**17**	**595**	**149**	**29**
Public and publicly guaranteed	28	11	54	1,006	17	595	69	29
Official creditors	24	11	54	1,006	17	595	69	29
Private creditors	4	0	0	0	0	0	0	0
of which: Bonds	0	0	0	0	0	0	0	0
Private nonguaranteed	..	..	..	..	..	..	80	..
of which: Bonds	..	..	..	..	..	..	80	..
Principal repayments	**52**	**40**	**61**	**36**	**56**	**51**	**28**	**148**
Public and publicly guaranteed	52	40	61	36	56	51	28	148
Official creditors	45	38	56	35	55	51	27	148
Private creditors	7	2	5	1	1	0	1	0
of which: Bonds	0	0	0	0	0	0	0	0
Private nonguaranteed	..	..	..	..	..	..	..	..
of which: Bonds	..	..	..	..	..	..	..	..
Interest payments	**15**	**12**	**7**	**9**	**16**	**16**	**20**	**32**
Public and publicly guaranteed	15	12	7	9	16	16	20	28
Official creditors	14	11	7	9	16	16	20	28
Private creditors	1	0	0	0	0	0	0	0
of which: Bonds	0	0	0	0	0	0	0	0
Private nonguaranteed	..	..	..	..	..	..	..	5
of which: Bonds	..	..	..	..	..	..	..	5
Net financial flows								
Net debt inflows	-29	-17	15	1,156	89	598	94	-59
Official creditors (incl. IMF)	-21	-27	-1	971	-38	544	42	-120
Private creditors	-8	11	16	186	128	54	53	61
Long-term	-3	-2	-5	-1	-1	0	79	..
Public and publicly guaranteed	-3	-2	-5	-1	-1	0	-1	..
Private nonguaranteed	..	..	..	..	..	..	80	..
Short-term	-5	13	21	186	128	54	-26	61
Net equity inflows								
Foreign direct investment	57	211	397	133	141	1,134	134	188
Portfolio equity	-6	27	-37	18	11	-17	-9	..
Major economic aggregates								
Gross national income (GNI)	5,436	9,096	10,481	9,845	13,193	15,233	14,458	14,621
Exports of goods, services & prim. income	3,378	5,739	5,474	3,870	5,168	7,213	6,492	..
Imports of goods, services & prim. income	3,050	4,737	6,691	5,856	7,158	8,406	8,799	..
Primary income on FDI	658	1,066	1,045	471	731	285	116	..
Personal transfers & comp. of employees	26	118	47	15	22	20	18	..
International reserves	6,318	6,309	9,119	8,704	7,885	8,082	7,628	7,726
Ratios								
External debt stocks to exports (%)	13.6	7.9	8.0	44.1	34.8	33.2	38.3	..
External debt stocks to GNI (%)	8.4	5.0	4.2	17.3	13.6	15.7	17.2	16.6
Debt service to exports (%)	2.0	0.9	1.3	1.2	1.5	1.0	0.8	..
Reserves to external debt stocks (%)	1,378.2	1,391.1	2,070.1	509.8	438.8	337.3	306.6	317.9

Notes:

Short-term debt is based on data from the BIS.

BRAZIL

(US$ million, unless otherwise indicated)

	2000	2005	2008	2009	2010	2011	2012	2013
Summary external debt data								
External debt stocks	**242,512**	**188,365**	**262,951**	**281,648**	**352,364**	**404,046**	**440,507**	**482,470**
Long-term external debt	209,303	163,859	225,755	237,336	282,425	357,473	403,486	444,517
Short-term external debt	30,973	23,993	36,644	39,786	65,492	42,140	32,583	33,507
interest arrears on long-term	176	0	0	0	0	0	0	27
Use of IMF credit	2,235	513	552	4,526	4,446	4,432	4,437	4,446
Long-term external debt								
Debt outstanding and disbursed	**209,303**	**163,859**	**225,755**	**237,336**	**282,425**	**357,473**	**403,486**	**444,517**
Public and publicly guaranteed	96,622	94,354	79,912	87,510	97,485	94,712	116,657	135,262
Official creditors	29,845	26,160	29,269	32,595	41,460	36,516	38,959	39,333
Private creditors	66,776	68,194	50,643	54,916	56,025	58,196	77,697	95,928
of which: Bonds	54,096	59,077	43,237	47,350	46,806	45,408	48,465	50,784
Private nonguaranteed	112,682	69,505	145,842	149,826	184,940	262,761	286,830	309,255
of which: Bonds	16,846	35,969	37,855	53,342	83,032	79,363	69,053	61,384
Disbursements	**44,079**	**27,414**	**69,559**	**57,675**	**85,379**	**111,458**	**79,638**	**107,238**
Public and publicly guaranteed	19,664	13,207	16,696	13,732	19,957	13,655	27,987	36,344
Official creditors	5,272	3,327	4,353	6,845	11,317	3,250	4,985	5,253
Private creditors	14,391	9,880	12,342	6,887	8,640	10,405	23,002	31,091
of which: Bonds	10,836	8,252	10,254	5,100	5,433	3,631	6,587	8,680
Private nonguaranteed	24,415	14,207	52,863	43,943	65,422	97,803	51,652	70,894
of which: Bonds	2,886	6,579	6,754	17,015	32,384	30,765	8,822	4,780
Principal repayments	**34,746**	**25,788**	**40,353**	**30,470**	**32,024**	**41,777**	**30,598**	**65,008**
Public and publicly guaranteed	10,932	9,481	16,351	7,784	9,626	15,851	6,697	16,154
Official creditors	7,093	3,334	2,402	3,447	2,662	8,349	2,316	4,470
Private creditors	3,839	6,147	13,949	4,338	6,965	7,502	4,380	11,684
of which: Bonds	2,056	4,187	12,001	2,760	5,770	4,281	3,275	5,561
Private nonguaranteed	23,813	16,306	24,002	22,685	22,398	25,925	23,901	48,853
of which: Bonds	2,775	7,063	2,420	1,585	2,656	3,666	7,154	11,459
Interest payments	**15,297**	**10,314**	**15,046**	**13,554**	**13,157**	**16,615**	**14,259**	**17,833**
Public and publicly guaranteed	6,943	6,700	6,057	5,656	5,172	5,446	5,019	6,010
Official creditors	1,932	1,058	1,291	1,083	967	1,012	962	920
Private creditors	5,010	5,642	4,766	4,573	4,205	4,434	4,057	5,090
of which: Bonds	4,212	5,033	4,406	4,148	3,864	3,902	3,392	3,805
Private nonguaranteed	8,355	3,614	8,989	7,898	7,985	11,169	9,240	11,823
of which: Bonds	1,562	2,161	2,842	2,936	4,207	5,859	3,107	3,722
Net financial flows								
Net debt inflows	4,471	-23,457	26,604	30,347	79,061	46,329	39,483	43,127
Official creditors (incl. IMF)	-8,514	-23,817	1,951	3,399	8,655	-5,099	2,668	783
Private creditors	12,985	360	24,653	26,948	70,406	51,428	36,815	42,344
Long-term	11,154	1,634	27,255	23,806	44,699	74,780	46,372	41,448
Public and publicly guaranteed	10,552	3,733	-1,606	2,549	1,675	2,903	18,622	19,407
Private nonguaranteed	602	-2,099	28,861	21,257	43,024	71,878	27,750	22,041
Short-term	1,831	-1,274	-2,602	3,142	25,706	-23,352	-9,557	897
Net equity inflows								
Foreign direct investment	32,779	15,045	30,064	19,906	40,117	54,782	52,838	41,644
Portfolio equity	3,076	6,451	-7,565	37,071	37,671	7,174	5,600	11,636
Major economic aggregates								
Gross national income (GNI)	626,889	856,883	1,614,369	1,588,139	2,104,398	2,429,989	2,213,546	2,203,225
Exports of goods, services & prim. income	68,205	136,200	240,904	189,564	240,920	305,002	293,331	291,385
Imports of goods, services & prim. income	93,950	125,773	273,320	217,207	291,094	360,466	350,424	375,814
Primary income on FDI	4,238	11,035	28,773	21,029	26,584	31,716	24,564	27,536
Personal transfers & comp. of employees	1,649	2,805	3,643	2,889	2,754	2,798	2,583	2,537
International reserves	32,434	53,245	192,844	237,364	287,056	350,356	369,566	356,214
Ratios								
External debt stocks to exports (%)	355.6	138.3	109.2	148.6	146.3	132.5	150.2	165.6
External debt stocks to GNI (%)	38.7	22.0	16.3	17.7	16.7	16.6	19.9	21.9
Debt service to exports (%)	85.9	46.2	23.5	23.5	19.0	19.4	15.5	28.6
Reserves to external debt stocks (%)	13.4	28.3	73.3	84.3	81.5	86.7	83.9	73.8

BULGARIA

(US$ million, unless otherwise indicated)

	2000	2005	2008	2009	2010	2011	2012	2013
Summary external debt data								
External debt stocks	**12,009**	**18,507**	**52,632**	**55,375**	**50,318**	**47,175**	**50,656**	**52,995**
Long-term external debt	8,440	12,532	33,357	36,620	34,234	33,389	35,937	38,614
Short-term external debt	1,451	4,442	18,334	17,797	15,143	12,848	13,780	13,440
interest arrears on long-term	1	0	0	0	0	0	0	0
Use of IMF credit	2,118	1,533	941	958	941	938	939	941
Long-term external debt								
Debt outstanding and disbursed	**8,440**	**12,532**	**33,357**	**36,620**	**34,234**	**33,389**	**35,937**	**38,614**
Public and publicly guaranteed	7,671	5,075	4,397	4,772	4,466	4,137	5,209	5,359
Official creditors	2,603	3,045	3,019	3,322	3,151	3,140	3,094	3,232
Private creditors	5,068	2,030	1,378	1,450	1,314	997	2,114	2,127
of which: Bonds	4,982	1,920	1,342	1,430	1,301	991	2,109	2,121
Private nonguaranteed	769	7,457	28,960	31,848	29,768	29,253	30,728	33,255
of which: Bonds	..	526	522	146	134	0	150	689
Disbursements	**719**	**4,895**	**17,394**	**8,625**	**1,569**	**10,803**	**5,992**	**6,007**
Public and publicly guaranteed	405	402	370	520	199	292	1,439	770
Official creditors	381	383	362	520	199	292	228	380
Private creditors	24	19	8	0	0	0	1,211	389
of which: Bonds	0	0	0	0	0	0	1,211	389
Private nonguaranteed	313	4,493	17,024	8,105	1,370	10,511	4,553	5,237
of which: Bonds	..	249	0	0	0	0	150	539
Principal repayments	**573**	**3,349**	**3,960**	**3,989**	**3,550**	**3,597**	**3,720**	**4,115**
Public and publicly guaranteed	345	1,761	733	404	268	258	263	563
Official creditors	297	255	715	266	261	251	263	269
Private creditors	48	1,507	19	138	7	7	0	294
of which: Bonds	46	1,496	0	123	0	0	0	294
Private nonguaranteed	229	1,588	3,227	3,585	3,282	3,338	3,457	3,551
of which: Bonds	..	10	287	372	0	139	0	0
Interest payments	**456**	**479**	**929**	**800**	**607**	**785**	**749**	**838**
Public and publicly guaranteed	424	327	292	208	177	188	161	210
Official creditors	139	93	148	106	71	83	82	69
Private creditors	285	234	144	102	106	105	79	141
of which: Bonds	284	229	139	101	106	105	79	141
Private nonguaranteed	32	152	637	592	430	598	588	628
of which: Bonds	..	30	36	29	11	6	0	12
Net financial flows								
Net debt inflows	465	2,308	17,731	4,099	-4,635	4,911	3,204	1,552
Official creditors (incl. IMF)	221	-315	-352	254	-62	41	-35	111
Private creditors	244	2,623	18,084	3,845	-4,573	4,871	3,239	1,441
Long-term	61	1,418	13,786	4,382	-1,919	7,166	2,307	1,781
Public and publicly guaranteed	-24	-1,488	-11	-138	-7	-7	1,211	95
Private nonguaranteed	85	2,905	13,797	4,520	-1,912	7,173	1,096	1,686
Short-term	183	1,206	4,298	-537	-2,654	-2,296	932	-340
Net equity inflows								
Foreign direct investment	1,002	2,017	5,821	2,249	1,528	1,268	889	1,554
Portfolio equity	5	449	-106	8	9	-42	5	-19
Major economic aggregates								
Gross national income (GNI)	12,580	28,979	49,257	46,903	46,225	51,025	49,432	50,531
Exports of goods, services & prim. income	7,321	17,674	31,897	24,384	27,944	36,606	34,960	38,305
Imports of goods, services & prim. income	8,314	22,034	45,096	29,966	30,711	38,836	38,137	40,482
Primary income on FDI	107	912	2,725	1,823	1,573	2,521	1,876	2,273
Personal transfers & comp. of employees	58	1,613	1,919	1,592	1,333	1,483	1,449	1,667
International reserves	3,155	8,041	16,816	17,127	15,421	15,252	18,371	18,335
Ratios								
External debt stocks to exports (%)	164.0	104.7	165.0	227.1	180.1	128.9	144.9	138.3
External debt stocks to GNI (%)	95.5	63.9	106.9	118.1	108.9	92.5	102.5	104.9
Debt service to exports (%)	18.2	25.3	17.7	20.0	15.1	12.2	12.9	13.0
Reserves to external debt stocks (%)	26.3	43.4	31.9	30.9	30.6	32.3	36.3	34.6

Notes:

Long-term private nonguaranteed debt data from 2008 are World Bank staff estimates based on reports provided by the country. Short-term debt before 2009 is World Bank staff estimates based on Central Bank data. The data may include long-term public and publicly guaranteed debt owed by the state-owned railway.

BURKINA FASO

(US$ million, unless otherwise indicated)

	2000	2005	2008	2009	2010	2011	2012	2013
Summary external debt data								
External debt stocks	**1,435**	**2,000**	**1,583**	**1,917**	**2,148**	**2,290**	**2,519**	**2,564**
Long-term external debt	1,226	1,861	1,506	1,716	1,931	2,057	2,218	2,260
Short-term external debt	84	22	9	0	0	0	0	0
interest arrears on long-term	5	0	0	0	0	0	0	0
Use of IMF credit	124	117	69	201	217	233	301	304
Long-term external debt								
Debt outstanding and disbursed	**1,226**	**1,861**	**1,506**	**1,716**	**1,931**	**2,057**	**2,218**	**2,260**
Public and publicly guaranteed	1,226	1,861	1,506	1,716	1,931	2,057	2,218	2,260
Official creditors	1,223	1,861	1,484	1,694	1,913	2,043	2,205	2,249
Private creditors	3	0	22	22	18	15	13	11
of which: Bonds	0	0	0	0	0	0	0	0
Private nonguaranteed	..	..	..	..	..	..	..	..
of which: Bonds	..	..	..	..	..	..	..	..
Disbursements	**91**	**208**	**293**	**217**	**276**	**171**	**159**	**60**
Public and publicly guaranteed	91	208	293	217	276	171	159	60
Official creditors	91	208	293	217	276	171	159	60
Private creditors	0	0	0	0	0	0	0	0
of which: Bonds	0	0	0	0	0	0	0	0
Private nonguaranteed	..	..	..	..	..	..	..	..
of which: Bonds	..	..	..	..	..	..	..	..
Principal repayments	**26**	**24**	**27**	**28**	**30**	**43**	**43**	**48**
Public and publicly guaranteed	26	24	27	28	30	43	43	48
Official creditors	26	24	24	28	27	40	41	46
Private creditors	0	0	3	0	2	3	2	2
of which: Bonds	0	0	0	0	0	0	0	0
Private nonguaranteed	..	..	..	..	..	..	..	..
of which: Bonds	..	..	..	..	..	..	..	..
Interest payments	**12**	**16**	**14**	**15**	**18**	**21**	**21**	**22**
Public and publicly guaranteed	12	16	14	15	18	21	21	22
Official creditors	12	16	14	15	18	21	21	22
Private creditors	0	0	0	0	0	0	0	0
of which: Bonds	0	0	0	0	0	0	0	0
Private nonguaranteed	..	..	..	..	..	..	..	..
of which: Bonds	..	..	..	..	..	..	..	..
Net financial flows								
Net debt inflows	47	194	138	235	266	145	184	14
Official creditors (incl. IMF)	66	196	287	244	269	147	186	17
Private creditors	-19	-2	-149	-9	-2	-3	-2	-2
Long-term	0	0	-3	0	-2	-3	-2	-2
Public and publicly guaranteed	0	0	-3	0	-2	-3	-2	-2
Private nonguaranteed	..	..	..	..	..	..	..	..
Short-term	-19	-2	-147	-8	..	..	..	..
Net equity inflows								
Foreign direct investment	23	21	28	9	-32	144	329	374
Portfolio equity	-3	-4	-2	0	3	-132	209	..
Major economic aggregates								
Gross national income (GNI)	2,606	5,442	8,348	8,343	9,203	10,392	10,721	11,030
Exports of goods, services & prim. income	251	583	1,069	1,140	1,981	2,913	3,484	..
Imports of goods, services & prim. income	691	1,452	2,442	2,035	2,655	3,618	4,165	..
Primary income on FDI	3	7	38	35	26	..	..	..
Personal transfers & comp. of employees	67	57	99	96	120	..	..	..
International reserves	243	438	928	1,296	1,068	957	1,025	628
Ratios								
External debt stocks to exports (%)	572.8	343.0	148.1	168.1	108.5	78.6	72.3	..
External debt stocks to GNI (%)	55.1	36.8	19.0	23.0	23.3	22.0	23.5	23.2
Debt service to exports (%)	18.8	7.8	3.9	3.8	2.5	2.3	2.0	..
Reserves to external debt stocks (%)	16.9	21.9	58.6	67.6	49.7	41.8	40.7	24.5

Notes:

Short-term debt before 2009 is based on data from the BIS. Data include HIPC and MDRI debt relief.

BURUNDI

(US$ million, unless otherwise indicated)

	2000	2005	2008	2009	2010	2011	2012	2013
Summary external debt data								
External debt stocks	**1,125.9**	**1,287.9**	**1,390.3**	**607.2**	**620.9**	**604.4**	**667.3**	**682.7**
Long-term external debt	1,036.0	1,176.1	1,234.3	393.5	381.8	363.2	411.4	397.2
Short-term external debt	65.0	34.1	18.0	7.0	15.7	0.4	7.3	31.3
interest arrears on long-term	19.7	33.1	4.0	0.0	0.7	0.4	0.3	0.3
Use of IMF credit	24.9	77.7	138.0	206.7	223.4	240.7	248.7	254.2
Long-term external debt								
Debt outstanding and disbursed	**1,036.0**	**1,176.1**	**1,234.3**	**393.5**	**381.8**	**363.2**	**411.4**	**397.2**
Public and publicly guaranteed	1,036.0	1,176.1	1,234.3	393.5	381.8	363.2	411.4	397.2
Official creditors	1,032.0	1,174.0	1,234.3	388.5	376.8	358.2	407.0	392.8
Private creditors	4.0	2.1	0.0	5.0	5.0	5.0	4.4	4.4
of which: Bonds	0.0	0.0	0.0	0.0	0.0	0.0	0.0	0.0
Private nonguaranteed	..	..	..	..	..	..	..	..
of which: Bonds	..	..	..	..	..	..	..	..
Disbursements	**41.3**	**42.1**	**24.8**	**29.3**	**31.6**	**28.0**	**60.2**	**6.9**
Public and publicly guaranteed	41.3	42.1	24.8	29.3	31.6	28.0	60.2	6.9
Official creditors	38.2	42.1	24.8	24.3	31.6	28.0	60.2	6.9
Private creditors	3.0	0.0	0.0	5.0	0.0	0.0	0.0	0.0
of which: Bonds	0.0	0.0	0.0	0.0	0.0	0.0	0.0	0.0
Private nonguaranteed	..	..	..	..	..	..	..	..
of which: Bonds	..	..	..	..	..	..	..	..
Principal repayments	**9.4**	**27.2**	**11.3**	**8.5**	**2.4**	**5.8**	**10.2**	**19.2**
Public and publicly guaranteed	9.4	27.2	11.3	8.5	2.4	5.8	10.2	19.2
Official creditors	9.4	22.6	11.3	8.5	2.4	5.8	9.6	19.2
Private creditors	0.0	4.6	0.0	0.0	0.0	0.0	0.6	0.0
of which: Bonds	0.0	0.0	0.0	0.0	0.0	0.0	0.0	0.0
Private nonguaranteed	..	..	..	..	..	..	..	..
of which: Bonds	..	..	..	..	..	..	..	..
Interest payments	**4.5**	**11.9**	**7.4**	**3.6**	**1.4**	**2.0**	**3.0**	**3.2**
Public and publicly guaranteed	4.5	11.9	7.4	3.6	1.4	2.0	3.0	3.2
Official creditors	4.5	11.9	7.4	3.6	1.4	2.0	3.0	3.2
Private creditors	0.0	0.0	0.0	0.0	0.0	0.0	0.0	0.0
of which: Bonds	0.0	0.0	0.0	0.0	0.0	0.0	0.0	0.0
Private nonguaranteed	..	..	..	..	..	..	..	..
of which: Bonds	..	..	..	..	..	..	..	..
Net financial flows								
Net debt inflows	18.4	34.1	48.3	27.2	57.3	25.8	64.6	16.7
Official creditors (incl. IMF)	24.3	40.7	35.3	29.2	49.3	40.8	58.2	-7.3
Private creditors	-5.9	-6.6	13.0	-2.0	8.0	-15.0	6.4	24.0
Long-term	3.0	-4.6	..	5.0	..	..	-0.6	..
Public and publicly guaranteed	3.0	-4.6	..	5.0	..	..	-0.6	..
Private nonguaranteed	..	..	..	..	..	..	..	..
Short-term	-8.9	-2.0	13.0	-7.0	8.0	-15.0	7.0	24.0
Net equity inflows								
Foreign direct investment	11.7	0.6	3.8	0.3	0.8	3.4	0.6	6.8
Portfolio equity	..	..	..	..	..	..	..	..
Major economic aggregates								
Gross national income (GNI)	884.8	1,099.6	1,607.3	1,722.8	2,014.8	2,338.2	2,463.3	2,904.7
Exports of goods, services & prim. income	55.4	98.7	163.9	119.7	181.9	243.1	239.0	..
Imports of goods, services & prim. income	164.9	343.9	609.4	538.0	618.7	790.3	940.6	..
Primary income on FDI	0.4	2.1	..	..	..	..	..	..
Personal transfers & comp. of employees	..	0.1	3.6	28.2	34.5	45.5	46.4	..
International reserves	32.9	100.1	265.7	322.0	330.7	294.0	307.2	328.2
Ratios								
External debt stocks to exports (%)	2031.9	1304.3	848.5	507.2	341.4	248.6	279.3	..
External debt stocks to GNI (%)	127.2	117.1	86.5	35.2	30.8	25.8	27.1	23.5
Debt service to exports (%)	40.9	40.5	12.0	16.6	2.4	4.2	8.8	..
Reserves to external debt stocks (%)	2.9	7.8	19.1	53.0	53.3	48.6	46.0	48.1

Notes:

Short-term debt is based on data from the BIS. Data include the effects of Paris Club debt restructuring agreement and HIPC and MDRI debt relief.

CABO VERDE

(US$ million, unless otherwise indicated)

	2000	2005	2008	2009	2010	2011	2012	2013
Summary external debt data								
External debt stocks	**320**	**477**	**626**	**727**	**892**	**1,039**	**1,248**	**1,484**
Long-term external debt	315	463	611	700	868	1,017	1,229	1,467
Short-term external debt	4	1	1	2	2	2	2	2
interest arrears on long-term	4	1	1	2	2	2	2	2
Use of IMF credit	1	13	13	25	23	20	18	16
Long-term external debt								
Debt outstanding and disbursed	**315**	**463**	**611**	**700**	**868**	**1,017**	**1,229**	**1,467**
Public and publicly guaranteed	315	463	611	700	868	1,017	1,229	1,467
Official creditors	308	442	601	693	816	944	1,110	1,277
Private creditors	7	22	10	6	53	73	118	190
of which: Bonds	0	0	0	0	0	0	0	0
Private nonguaranteed	..	..	..	..	..	..	..	..
of which: Bonds	..	..	..	..	..	..	..	..
Disbursements	**29**	**74**	**75**	**102**	**208**	**191**	**224**	**237**
Public and publicly guaranteed	29	74	75	102	208	191	224	237
Official creditors	29	65	75	102	158	165	181	173
Private creditors	0	9	0	0	50	25	43	64
of which: Bonds	0	0	0	0	0	0	0	0
Private nonguaranteed	..	..	..	..	..	..	..	..
of which: Bonds	..	..	..	..	..	..	..	..
Principal repayments	**11**	**29**	**24**	**25**	**26**	**26**	**20**	**22**
Public and publicly guaranteed	11	29	24	25	26	26	20	22
Official creditors	10	23	20	21	22	24	20	22
Private creditors	2	5	4	4	3	2	0	0
of which: Bonds	0	0	0	0	0	0	0	0
Private nonguaranteed	..	..	..	..	..	..	..	..
of which: Bonds	..	..	..	..	..	..	..	..
Interest payments	**5**	**7**	**7**	**7**	**8**	**10**	**13**	**16**
Public and publicly guaranteed	5	7	7	7	8	10	13	16
Official creditors	4	6	6	7	8	9	12	13
Private creditors	1	1	0	0	0	1	2	2
of which: Bonds	0	0	0	0	0	0	0	0
Private nonguaranteed	..	..	..	..	..	..	..	..
of which: Bonds	..	..	..	..	..	..	..	..
Net financial flows								
Net debt inflows	2	49	50	76	180	162	201	213
Official creditors (incl. IMF)	19	45	54	79	134	138	159	149
Private creditors	-18	4	-4	-4	46	23	43	64
Long-term	-2	4	-4	-4	46	23	43	64
Public and publicly guaranteed	-2	4	-4	-4	46	23	43	64
Private nonguaranteed	..	..	..	..	..	..	..	..
Short-term	-16	..	..	..	..	..	..	..
Net equity inflows								
Foreign direct investment	33	63	210	124	95	91	98	66
Portfolio equity	..	..	..	2	..	..	..	..
Major economic aggregates								
Gross national income (GNI)	525	938	1,742	1,668	1,591	1,792	1,725	1,833
Exports of goods, services & prim. income	151	373	738	590	644	796	790	856
Imports of goods, services & prim. income	344	695	1,259	1,149	1,207	1,459	1,265	1,176
Primary income on FDI	5	11	38	26	56	42	23	13
Personal transfers & comp. of employees	87	137	155	137	131	177	167	176
International reserves	28	174	361	398	382	339	376	475
Ratios								
External debt stocks to exports (%)	211.8	128.0	84.8	123.1	138.6	130.5	158.0	173.3
External debt stocks to GNI (%)	60.9	50.9	35.9	43.6	56.1	58.0	72.3	80.9
Debt service to exports (%)	10.7	9.6	4.2	5.7	5.6	4.9	4.6	4.6
Reserves to external debt stocks (%)	8.8	36.4	57.7	54.8	42.8	32.6	30.1	32.0

CAMBODIA

(US$ million, unless otherwise indicated)

	2000	2005	2008	2009	2010	2011	2012	2013
Summary external debt data								
External debt stocks	**2,648**	**3,525**	**3,181**	**3,439**	**3,755**	**4,356**	**5,652**	**6,427**
Long-term external debt	2,328	3,141	2,832	3,036	3,345	3,741	4,484	5,064
Short-term external debt	227	280	325	272	281	486	1,038	1,234
interest arrears on long-term	131	243	197	208	215	221	209	152
Use of IMF credit	93	103	24	132	129	129	129	129
Long-term external debt								
Debt outstanding and disbursed	**2,328**	**3,141**	**2,832**	**3,036**	**3,345**	**3,741**	**4,484**	**5,064**
Public and publicly guaranteed	2,328	3,141	2,832	3,036	3,345	3,741	4,484	5,064
Official creditors	2,328	3,141	2,832	3,036	3,345	3,741	4,484	5,064
Private creditors	0	0	0	0	0	0	0	0
of which: Bonds	0	0	0	0	0	0	0	0
Private nonguaranteed	..	..	..	..	..	..	..	..
of which: Bonds	..	..	..	..	..	..	..	..
Disbursements	**79**	**155**	**348**	**207**	**344**	**431**	**789**	**596**
Public and publicly guaranteed	79	155	348	207	344	431	789	596
Official creditors	79	155	348	207	344	431	789	596
Private creditors	0	0	0	0	0	0	0	0
of which: Bonds	0	0	0	0	0	0	0	0
Private nonguaranteed	..	..	..	..	..	..	..	..
of which: Bonds	..	..	..	..	..	..	..	..
Principal repayments	**7**	**8**	**19**	**26**	**33**	**41**	**47**	**60**
Public and publicly guaranteed	7	8	19	26	33	41	47	60
Official creditors	7	8	19	26	33	41	47	60
Private creditors	0	0	0	0	0	0	0	0
of which: Bonds	0	0	0	0	0	0	0	0
Private nonguaranteed	..	..	..	..	..	..	..	..
of which: Bonds	..	..	..	..	..	..	..	..
Interest payments	**12**	**12**	**19**	**21**	**26**	**31**	**42**	**51**
Public and publicly guaranteed	12	12	19	21	26	31	42	51
Official creditors	12	12	19	21	26	31	42	51
Private creditors	0	0	0	0	0	0	0	0
of which: Bonds	0	0	0	0	0	0	0	0
Private nonguaranteed	..	..	..	..	..	..	..	..
of which: Bonds	..	..	..	..	..	..	..	..
Net financial flows								
Net debt inflows	128	141	395	117	313	589	1,306	789
Official creditors (incl. IMF)	76	138	329	181	311	390	742	536
Private creditors	52	3	66	-64	2	199	564	253
Long-term	..	..	..	..	..	..	..	..
Public and publicly guaranteed	..	..	..	..	..	..	..	..
Private nonguaranteed	..	..	..	..	..	..	..	..
Short-term	52	3	66	-64	2	199	564	253
Net equity inflows								
Foreign direct investment	149	379	815	511	735	795	1,441	1,345
Portfolio equity	..	..	..	..	..	..	..	..
Major economic aggregates								
Gross national income (GNI)	3,534	6,006	9,916	9,931	10,698	12,261	13,403	14,491
Exports of goods, services & prim. income	1,893	4,094	5,129	5,015	6,026	7,826	8,893	10,087
Imports of goods, services & prim. income	2,453	4,921	6,560	5,981	7,075	8,882	10,343	12,075
Primary income on FDI	123	227	403	351	414	460	617	700
Personal transfers & comp. of employees	121	164	188	142	153	160	172	176
International reserves	502	953	2,292	2,851	3,255	3,450	4,267	4,516
Ratios								
External debt stocks to exports (%)	139.9	86.1	62.0	68.6	62.3	55.7	63.6	63.7
External debt stocks to GNI (%)	74.9	58.7	32.1	34.6	35.1	35.5	42.2	44.4
Debt service to exports (%)	1.7	0.8	0.9	1.0	1.0	1.1	1.4	1.5
Reserves to external debt stocks (%)	18.9	27.0	72.0	82.9	86.7	79.2	75.5	70.3

Notes:

Short-term debt is based on data from the BIS. Data include MDRI debt relief.

CAMEROON

(US$ million, unless otherwise indicated)

	2000	2005	2008	2009	2010	2011	2012	2013
Summary external debt data								
External debt stocks	**10,561**	**7,700**	**2,826**	**3,238**	**3,194**	**3,110**	**3,751**	**4,922**
Long-term external debt	9,070	7,059	2,723	2,783	2,740	2,598	3,154	4,041
Short-term external debt	1,224	334	41	3	9	70	157	444
interest arrears on long-term	205	280	41	3	9	2	24	62
Use of IMF credit	267	307	62	453	445	442	440	437
Long-term external debt								
Debt outstanding and disbursed	**9,070**	**7,059**	**2,723**	**2,783**	**2,740**	**2,598**	**3,154**	**4,041**
Public and publicly guaranteed	8,753	6,467	2,087	2,167	2,163	2,137	2,786	3,816
Official creditors	8,436	6,384	2,082	2,153	2,143	2,114	2,741	3,578
Private creditors	317	83	6	14	20	23	45	239
of which: Bonds	0	0	0	0	0	0	0	0
Private nonguaranteed	317	592	636	615	577	461	368	225
of which: Bonds	..	..	..	..	..	..	..	..
Disbursements	**286**	**227**	**276**	**356**	**278**	**178**	**609**	**1,005**
Public and publicly guaranteed	247	130	189	147	278	178	609	1,005
Official creditors	247	130	189	139	272	173	587	814
Private creditors	0	0	0	8	6	5	22	191
of which: Bonds	0	0	0	0	0	0	0	0
Private nonguaranteed	39	98	87	209	..	..	..	..
of which: Bonds	..	..	..	..	..	..	..	..
Principal repayments	**253**	**537**	**353**	**334**	**154**	**233**	**176**	**154**
Public and publicly guaranteed	166	396	160	105	116	122	83	61
Official creditors	162	396	160	105	116	121	82	57
Private creditors	4	0	0	0	0	1	1	4
of which: Bonds	0	0	0	0	0	0	0	0
Private nonguaranteed	86	141	192	229	38	111	93	93
of which: Bonds	..	..	..	..	..	..	..	..
Interest payments	**215**	**228**	**91**	**57**	**42**	**86**	**60**	**55**
Public and publicly guaranteed	198	178	47	26	27	57	35	29
Official creditors	198	177	47	26	27	56	34	28
Private creditors	1	1	0	0	0	1	1	2
of which: Bonds	0	0	0	0	0	0	0	0
Private nonguaranteed	17	51	44	31	15	28	25	25
of which: Bonds	..	..	..	..	..	..	..	..
Net financial flows								
Net debt inflows	-21	-683	-268	170	124	12	495	1,096
Official creditors (incl. IMF)	136	-301	37	182	156	51	503	754
Private creditors	-157	-382	-304	-12	-32	-39	-8	343
Long-term	-52	-44	-105	-12	-32	-107	-73	94
Public and publicly guaranteed	-4	..	0	8	6	4	20	187
Private nonguaranteed	-48	-44	-105	-20	-38	-111	-93	-93
Short-term	-105	-339	-199	..	..	68	65	249
Net equity inflows								
Foreign direct investment	159	120	56	811	527	138	276	572
Portfolio equity	0	-4	-1	0	0	0	0	..
Major economic aggregates								
Gross national income (GNI)	8,694	16,099	23,323	22,051	22,229	25,184	26,028	28,715
Exports of goods, services & prim. income	2,694	4,248	7,372	5,438	5,692	7,648	7,582	..
Imports of goods, services & prim. income	3,021	4,977	8,419	6,835	6,694	8,654	8,801	..
Primary income on FDI	41	289	165	436	166	282	503	..
Personal transfers & comp. of employees	30	77	162	184	115	219	210	..
International reserves	212	949	3,087	3,676	3,643	3,199	3,381	..
Ratios								
External debt stocks to exports (%)	392.0	181.3	38.3	59.5	56.1	40.7	49.5	..
External debt stocks to GNI (%)	121.5	47.8	12.1	14.7	14.4	12.4	14.4	17.1
Debt service to exports (%)	20.8	19.3	6.1	7.2	3.5	4.2	3.2	..
Reserves to external debt stocks (%)	2.0	12.3	109.2	113.5	114.1	102.8	90.1	..

Notes:

Short-term debt is based on data from the BIS. Data include the effects of HIPC and MDRI debt relief.

CENTRAL AFRICAN REPUBLIC

(US$ million, unless otherwise indicated)

	2000	2005	2008	2009	2010	2011	2012	2013
Summary external debt data								
External debt stocks	**872.1**	**1,033.0**	**990.0**	**537.6**	**614.2**	**547.3**	**551.5**	**574.4**
Long-term external debt	797.3	877.2	827.0	293.8	361.9	271.2	288.3	307.0
Short-term external debt	41.2	106.6	85.6	81.7	79.7	104.1	80.3	86.4
interest arrears on long-term	26.1	97.6	73.6	77.7	77.7	71.1	73.3	80.4
Use of IMF credit	33.6	49.2	77.4	162.1	172.6	172.0	182.9	181.0
Long-term external debt								
Debt outstanding and disbursed	**797.3**	**877.2**	**827.0**	**293.8**	**361.9**	**271.2**	**288.3**	**307.0**
Public and publicly guaranteed	797.3	877.2	827.0	293.8	361.9	271.2	288.3	307.0
Official creditors	764.8	843.1	792.5	259.4	325.3	244.1	261.2	280.8
Private creditors	32.6	34.1	34.5	34.4	36.6	27.1	27.1	26.2
of which: Bonds	0.0	0.0	0.0	0.0	0.0	0.0	0.0	0.0
Private nonguaranteed	..	..	..	..	..	..	..	..
of which: Bonds	..	..	..	..	..	..	..	..
Disbursements	**16.1**	**0.0**	**1.9**	**18.7**	**19.2**	**17.1**	**18.4**	**20.2**
Public and publicly guaranteed	16.1	0.0	1.9	18.7	19.2	17.1	18.4	20.2
Official creditors	16.1	0.0	1.9	18.7	19.2	17.1	18.4	20.2
Private creditors	0.0	0.0	0.0	0.0	0.0	0.0	0.0	0.0
of which: Bonds	0.0	0.0	0.0	0.0	0.0	0.0	0.0	0.0
Private nonguaranteed	..	..	..	..	..	..	..	..
of which: Bonds	..	..	..	..	..	..	..	..
Principal repayments	**7.5**	**0.7**	**11.3**	**8.4**	**1.0**	**0.8**	**2.1**	**3.7**
Public and publicly guaranteed	7.5	0.7	11.3	8.4	1.0	0.8	2.1	3.7
Official creditors	7.4	0.7	11.3	8.4	1.0	0.7	2.1	2.4
Private creditors	0.0	0.0	0.0	0.0	0.0	0.1	0.1	1.2
of which: Bonds	0.0	0.0	0.0	0.0	0.0	0.0	0.0	0.0
Private nonguaranteed	..	..	..	..	..	..	..	..
of which: Bonds	..	..	..	..	..	..	..	..
Interest payments	**4.3**	**0.2**	**6.1**	**3.0**	**1.2**	**0.2**	**1.9**	**0.5**
Public and publicly guaranteed	4.3	0.2	6.1	3.0	1.2	0.2	1.9	0.5
Official creditors	4.3	0.2	6.1	3.0	1.2	0.2	1.9	0.5
Private creditors	0.0	0.0	0.0	0.0	0.0	0.0	0.0	0.0
of which: Bonds	0.0	0.0	0.0	0.0	0.0	0.0	0.0	0.0
Private nonguaranteed	..	..	..	..	..	..	..	..
of which: Bonds	..	..	..	..	..	..	..	..
Net financial flows								
Net debt inflows	-13.8	-5.6	17.9	22.6	29.4	47.3	0.9	13.3
Official creditors (incl. IMF)	7.8	-5.6	5.9	30.6	31.4	16.4	26.9	15.5
Private creditors	-21.6	..	12.0	-8.0	-2.0	30.9	-26.1	-2.2
Long-term	0.0	..	..	..	..	-0.1	-0.1	-1.2
Public and publicly guaranteed	0.0	..	..	..	..	-0.1	-0.1	-1.2
Private nonguaranteed	..	..	..	..	..	..	..	..
Short-term	-21.6	..	12.0	-8.0	-2.0	31.0	-26.0	-1.0
Net equity inflows								
Foreign direct investment	0.9	10.1	117.1	42.3	61.5	36.9	71.2	0.8
Portfolio equity	..	..	..	..	..	..	..	..
Major economic aggregates								
Gross national income (GNI)	901.4	1,340.1	1,962.5	1,960.6	1,981.5	2,190.4	2,168.6	1,537.1
Exports of goods, services & prim. income	..	..	..	..	..	..	..	..
Imports of goods, services & prim. income	..	..	..	..	..	..	..	..
Primary income on FDI	..	..	..	..	..	..	..	..
Personal transfers & comp. of employees	..	..	..	..	..	..	..	..
International reserves	133.3	139.2	121.8	210.6	181.2	154.5	157.9	..
Ratios								
External debt stocks to exports (%)	..	..	..	..	..	..	..	..
External debt stocks to GNI (%)	96.7	77.1	50.4	27.4	31.0	25.0	25.4	37.4
Debt service to exports (%)	..	..	..	..	..	..	..	..
Reserves to external debt stocks (%)	15.3	13.5	12.3	39.2	29.5	28.2	28.6	..

Notes:

Short-term debt is based on data from the BIS. Data include the effects of HIPC and MDRI debt relief.

CHAD

(US$ million, unless otherwise indicated)

	2000	2005	2008	2009	2010	2011	2012	2013
Summary external debt data								
External debt stocks	**1,101**	**1,630**	**1,802**	**1,866**	**2,157**	**2,165**	**2,166**	**2,216**
Long-term external debt	986	1,526	1,743	1,750	2,049	2,054	2,052	2,123
Short-term external debt	25	11	4	4	8	20	27	8
interest arrears on long-term	10	6	4	4	7	8	8	8
Use of IMF credit	90	93	55	113	99	91	87	85
Long-term external debt								
Debt outstanding and disbursed	**986**	**1,526**	**1,743**	**1,750**	**2,049**	**2,054**	**2,052**	**2,123**
Public and publicly guaranteed	986	1,526	1,743	1,750	2,049	2,054	2,052	2,123
Official creditors	971	1,494	1,710	1,718	2,019	2,029	2,027	2,099
Private creditors	15	32	33	32	30	25	25	23
of which: Bonds	0	0	0	0	0	0	0	0
Private nonguaranteed	..	..	..	..	..	..	..	..
of which: Bonds	..	..	..	..	..	..	..	..
Disbursements	**46**	**143**	**97**	**34**	**366**	**65**	**55**	**159**
Public and publicly guaranteed	46	143	97	34	366	65	55	159
Official creditors	46	143	97	34	366	65	55	159
Private creditors	0	0	0	0	0	0	0	0
of which: Bonds	0	0	0	0	0	0	0	0
Private nonguaranteed	..	..	..	..	..	..	..	..
of which: Bonds	..	..	..	..	..	..	..	..
Principal repayments	**13**	**24**	**105**	**42**	**46**	**56**	**49**	**84**
Public and publicly guaranteed	13	24	105	42	46	56	49	84
Official creditors	13	23	105	41	44	51	49	83
Private creditors	1	1	0	1	2	5	0	2
of which: Bonds	0	0	0	0	0	0	0	0
Private nonguaranteed	..	..	..	..	..	..	..	..
of which: Bonds	..	..	..	..	..	..	..	..
Interest payments	**9**	**16**	**18**	**23**	**17**	**18**	**16**	**20**
Public and publicly guaranteed	9	16	18	23	17	18	16	20
Official creditors	9	16	18	23	17	18	16	20
Private creditors	0	0	0	0	0	0	0	0
of which: Bonds	0	0	0	0	0	0	0	0
Private nonguaranteed	..	..	..	..	..	..	..	..
of which: Bonds	..	..	..	..	..	..	..	..
Net financial flows								
Net debt inflows	44	109	-44	-20	311	12	9	53
Official creditors (incl. IMF)	46	114	-21	-19	312	6	2	73
Private creditors	-2	-4	-23	-1	-1	6	7	-21
Long-term	-1	-1	..	-1	-2	-5	..	-2
Public and publicly guaranteed	-1	-1	..	-1	-2	-5	..	-2
Private nonguaranteed	..	..	..	..	..	..	..	..
Short-term	-2	-3	-23	..	1	11	7	-19
Net equity inflows								
Foreign direct investment	115	-99	466	376	313	282	343	538
Portfolio equity	..	..	..	..	..	..	..	..
Major economic aggregates								
Gross national income (GNI)	1,283	5,708	10,085	8,867	10,302	11,842	12,228	12,888
Exports of goods, services & prim. income	..	..	..	..	..	..	..	..
Imports of goods, services & prim. income	..	..	..	..	..	..	..	..
Primary income on FDI	..	..	..	..	..	..	..	..
Personal transfers & comp. of employees	..	..	..	..	..	..	..	..
International reserves	111	226	1,345	617	632	951	1,156	..
Ratios								
External debt stocks to exports (%)	..	..	..	..	..	..	..	..
External debt stocks to GNI (%)	85.8	28.6	17.9	21.0	20.9	18.3	17.7	17.2
Debt service to exports (%)	..	..	..	..	..	..	..	..
Reserves to external debt stocks (%)	10.1	13.8	74.6	33.0	29.3	43.9	53.3	..

Notes:

Long-term public and publicly guaranteed debt data for 2013 are World Bank staff estimates. Short-term debt is based on data from the BIS. Data include the effects of HIPC debt relief.

CHINA

(US$ million, unless otherwise indicated)

	2000	2005	2008	2009	2010	2011	2012	2013
Summary external debt data								
External debt stocks	**145,648**	**281,114**	**378,469**	**445,942**	**559,772**	**710,234**	**750,746**	**874,463**
Long-term external debt	132,259	132,508	190,916	194,475	201,484	222,592	230,411	238,981
Short-term external debt	13,080	148,267	187,188	240,509	347,524	476,911	509,592	624,718
interest arrears on long-term	0	0	0	0	0	0	0	0
Use of IMF credit	309	338	365	10,958	10,764	10,731	10,743	10,764
Long-term external debt								
Debt outstanding and disbursed	**132,259**	**132,508**	**190,916**	**194,475**	**201,484**	**222,592**	**230,411**	**238,981**
Public and publicly guaranteed	94,470	82,016	89,142	92,318	90,637	75,176	70,741	78,211
Official creditors	50,374	52,421	63,349	68,358	67,204	67,684	66,201	60,532
Private creditors	44,096	29,595	25,793	23,960	23,433	7,492	4,540	17,679
of which: Bonds	11,371	13,859	14,032	9,905	10,730	2,486	2,630	8,130
Private nonguaranteed	37,789	50,492	101,774	102,157	110,847	147,416	159,671	160,771
of which: Bonds	1,068	3,574	5,970	7,020	17,153	28,203	38,819	49,133
Disbursements	**19,006**	**28,228**	**38,188**	**23,648**	**42,423**	**46,950**	**37,375**	**56,801**
Public and publicly guaranteed	11,924	8,776	5,449	6,481	10,125	7,785	3,629	16,871
Official creditors	5,790	2,170	3,893	3,310	4,348	3,848	3,408	2,716
Private creditors	6,133	6,606	1,556	3,171	5,777	3,937	222	14,155
of which: Bonds	848	3,208	0	0	0	3,098	0	5,500
Private nonguaranteed	7,082	19,452	32,739	17,167	32,298	39,165	33,746	39,930
of which: Bonds	390	1,622	..	925	11,592	12,133	10,903	25,897
Principal repayments	**19,362**	**20,936**	**23,959**	**33,448**	**27,237**	**36,277**	**35,519**	**33,395**
Public and publicly guaranteed	10,235	6,659	6,750	6,473	8,400	12,199	8,132	6,680
Official creditors	4,270	1,413	2,809	2,594	3,643	5,301	4,491	5,650
Private creditors	5,965	5,246	3,940	3,878	4,757	6,898	3,641	1,029
of which: Bonds	443	550	742	500	0	2,092	318	0
Private nonguaranteed	9,127	14,277	17,209	26,976	18,837	24,078	27,387	26,715
of which: Bonds	534	370	350	464	..	1,083	..	1,821
Interest payments	**6,064**	**3,157**	**4,733**	**3,045**	**5,316**	**6,920**	**4,380**	**5,270**
Public and publicly guaranteed	4,140	2,140	2,513	2,030	1,651	1,792	2,139	2,155
Official creditors	2,386	1,375	1,407	1,090	944	1,070	1,832	1,932
Private creditors	1,754	765	1,106	940	707	722	307	223
of which: Bonds	521	369	418	480	317	310	59	151
Private nonguaranteed	1,924	1,017	2,220	1,015	3,665	5,127	2,241	3,114
of which: Bonds	93	248	431	445	672	1,972	1,184	2,360
Net financial flows								
Net debt inflows	-2,457	39,789	-2,280	43,521	122,201	140,060	34,538	138,533
Official creditors (incl. IMF)	1,520	757	1,084	716	705	-1,453	-1,083	-2,934
Private creditors	-3,977	39,032	-3,364	42,805	121,496	141,513	35,621	141,467
Long-term	-1,877	6,535	13,146	-10,516	14,481	12,126	2,940	26,341
Public and publicly guaranteed	168	1,360	-2,384	-707	1,020	-2,961	-3,419	13,126
Private nonguaranteed	-2,045	5,175	15,530	-9,809	13,461	15,087	6,359	13,215
Short-term	-2,100	32,497	-16,510	53,321	107,015	129,387	32,681	115,126
Net equity inflows								
Foreign direct investment	38,399	94,959	150,490	147,356	240,537	279,762	241,544	273,189
Portfolio equity	6,912	20,569	8,464	29,117	31,357	5,308	29,903	32,595
Major economic aggregates								
Gross national income (GNI)	1,183,809	2,240,794	4,550,407	4,981,701	5,904,606	7,251,604	8,187,349	9,196,168
Exports of goods, services & prim. income	292,111	809,731	1,605,353	1,368,583	1,790,140	2,134,931	2,355,310	2,548,141
Imports of goods, services & prim. income	277,904	701,218	1,227,941	1,156,985	1,593,015	2,023,344	2,143,352	2,356,600
Primary income on FDI	20,198	47,566	72,637	105,948	159,637	204,476	171,845	206,381
Personal transfers & comp. of employees	5,237	8,832	22,694	22,903	33,440	40,483	39,221	38,819
International reserves	168,278	821,514	1,949,260	2,416,044	2,866,079	3,202,789	3,331,120	3,839,548
Ratios								
External debt stocks to exports (%)	49.9	34.7	23.6	32.6	31.3	33.3	31.9	34.3
External debt stocks to GNI (%)	12.3	12.5	8.3	9.0	9.5	9.8	9.2	9.5
Debt service to exports (%)	9.1	3.4	2.1	2.9	3.4	3.5	3.2	1.5
Reserves to external debt stocks (%)	115.5	292.2	515.0	541.8	512.0	450.9	443.7	439.1

Notes:

Long-term private nonguaranteed and short-term debt data are World Bank staff estimates based on reports provided by the country and market data.

COLOMBIA

(US$ million, unless otherwise indicated)

	2000	2005	2008	2009	2010	2011	2012	2013
Summary external debt data								
External debt stocks	**33,159**	**37,162**	**46,245**	**53,045**	**63,815**	**76,902**	**79,871**	**91,978**
Long-term external debt	30,139	30,823	40,436	47,875	54,765	65,172	68,403	78,878
Short-term external debt	2,871	6,176	5,633	4,013	7,912	10,596	10,334	11,963
interest arrears on long-term	0	0	0	0	0	0	0	0
Use of IMF credit	149	163	176	1,157	1,137	1,134	1,135	1,137
Long-term external debt								
Debt outstanding and disbursed	**30,139**	**30,823**	**40,436**	**47,875**	**54,765**	**65,172**	**68,403**	**78,878**
Public and publicly guaranteed	19,880	21,834	28,624	35,126	36,688	39,244	43,706	50,428
Official creditors	6,805	9,834	13,386	14,984	16,151	16,683	19,695	20,688
Private creditors	13,075	12,000	15,238	20,142	20,537	22,561	24,011	29,740
of which: Bonds	8,201	10,927	12,280	17,159	17,686	20,099	21,729	25,555
Private nonguaranteed	10,259	8,989	11,812	12,749	18,078	25,928	24,697	28,451
of which: Bonds	762	370	809	2,709	3,329	6,049	8,649	10,125
Disbursements	**3,753**	**6,518**	**7,083**	**13,148**	**12,831**	**16,529**	**17,598**	**21,797**
Public and publicly guaranteed	2,889	4,397	3,851	8,107	3,491	4,690	7,150	9,014
Official creditors	610	1,469	2,555	2,415	2,125	1,559	4,040	2,180
Private creditors	2,279	2,928	1,296	5,691	1,365	3,131	3,110	6,833
of which: Bonds	1,804	2,304	1,000	5,491	1,335	2,829	2,489	4,778
Private nonguaranteed	865	2,121	3,232	5,041	9,340	11,839	10,448	12,783
of which: Bonds	..	..	..	1,900	620	2,720	2,600	4,200
Principal repayments	**2,882**	**7,272**	**4,733**	**5,769**	**6,430**	**6,403**	**11,361**	**6,129**
Public and publicly guaranteed	2,049	4,580	2,028	1,644	2,183	2,210	2,788	2,011
Official creditors	543	2,095	742	793	981	1,022	1,067	1,114
Private creditors	1,507	2,486	1,286	850	1,202	1,188	1,721	897
of which: Bonds	469	1,723	953	623	983	481	847	809
Private nonguaranteed	832	2,692	2,705	4,126	4,248	4,193	8,573	4,118
of which: Bonds	110	..	..	..	..	..	..	..
Interest payments	**1,948**	**2,513**	**2,722**	**2,694**	**2,824**	**3,187**	**3,640**	**3,329**
Public and publicly guaranteed	1,330	1,875	2,066	1,976	2,117	2,087	2,145	2,155
Official creditors	458	502	615	573	540	516	531	558
Private creditors	872	1,374	1,451	1,403	1,577	1,571	1,614	1,597
of which: Bonds	515	1,284	1,112	1,073	1,282	1,315	1,395	1,392
Private nonguaranteed	618	637	656	718	707	1,100	1,495	1,174
of which: Bonds	84	36	68	129	221	308	461	385
Net financial flows								
Net debt inflows	-222	302	2,822	5,758	10,300	12,810	5,975	17,297
Official creditors (incl. IMF)	67	-626	1,813	1,622	1,144	537	2,973	1,066
Private creditors	-290	928	1,009	4,137	9,156	12,273	3,002	16,231
Long-term	804	-128	537	5,757	5,257	9,589	3,264	14,602
Public and publicly guaranteed	772	443	9	4,841	164	1,943	1,389	5,937
Private nonguaranteed	32	-571	527	916	5,093	7,646	1,875	8,665
Short-term	-1,094	1,056	472	-1,620	3,900	2,684	-262	1,629
Net equity inflows								
Foreign direct investment	2,436	10,267	10,135	7,095	6,771	13,138	14,290	14,403
Portfolio equity	17	86	-86	67	1,318	2,288	3,180	1,926
Major economic aggregates								
Gross national income (GNI)	97,597	141,059	233,900	224,541	274,994	319,384	354,666	363,489
Exports of goods, services & prim. income	16,850	25,289	44,285	39,338	46,336	65,547	70,268	69,066
Imports of goods, services & prim. income	17,728	31,257	56,604	48,994	59,713	80,236	86,681	86,359
Primary income on FDI	655	3,565	8,706	7,628	9,959	14,758	14,959	13,475
Personal transfers & comp. of employees	1,610	3,346	4,827	4,125	4,031	4,101	4,019	4,119
International reserves	8,916	14,787	23,479	24,748	27,766	31,386	36,444	42,758
Ratios								
External debt stocks to exports (%)	196.8	147.0	104.4	134.8	137.7	117.3	113.7	133.2
External debt stocks to GNI (%)	34.0	26.3	19.8	23.6	23.2	24.1	22.5	25.3
Debt service to exports (%)	29.7	39.7	17.4	22.0	20.8	15.4	22.0	14.5
Reserves to external debt stocks (%)	26.9	39.8	50.8	46.7	43.5	40.8	45.6	46.5

COMOROS

(US$ million, unless otherwise indicated)

	2000	2005	2008	2009	2010	2011	2012	2013
Summary external debt data								
External debt stocks	**226.7**	**280.8**	**278.8**	**288.4**	**280.6**	**277.9**	**251.2**	**146.3**
Long-term external debt	204.0	255.3	267.4	260.2	250.7	245.5	219.0	111.9
Short-term external debt	20.3	24.5	5.2	4.7	4.4	4.7	4.1	1.6
interest arrears on long-term	11.3	21.5	5.2	4.7	4.4	4.7	4.1	1.6
Use of IMF credit	2.4	1.0	6.2	23.4	25.4	27.7	28.0	32.9
Long-term external debt								
Debt outstanding and disbursed	**204.0**	**255.3**	**267.4**	**260.2**	**250.7**	**245.5**	**219.0**	**111.9**
Public and publicly guaranteed	204.0	255.3	267.4	260.2	250.7	245.5	219.0	111.9
Official creditors	204.0	255.3	267.4	260.2	250.7	245.5	219.0	111.9
Private creditors	0.0	0.0	0.0	0.0	0.0	0.0	0.0	0.0
of which: Bonds	0.0	0.0	0.0	0.0	0.0	0.0	0.0	0.0
Private nonguaranteed	..	..	..	..	..	..	..	..
of which: Bonds	..	..	..	..	..	..	..	..
Disbursements	**2.1**	**3.3**	**1.4**	**0.3**	**0.0**	**0.0**	**0.0**	**0.0**
Public and publicly guaranteed	2.1	3.3	1.4	0.3	0.0	0.0	0.0	0.0
Official creditors	2.1	3.3	1.4	0.3	0.0	0.0	0.0	0.0
Private creditors	0.0	0.0	0.0	0.0	0.0	0.0	0.0	0.0
of which: Bonds	0.0	0.0	0.0	0.0	0.0	0.0	0.0	0.0
Private nonguaranteed	..	..	..	..	..	..	..	..
of which: Bonds	..	..	..	..		..	..	..
Principal repayments	**1.2**	**2.6**	**8.1**	**7.2**	**3.1**	**2.2**	**5.1**	**0.3**
Public and publicly guaranteed	1.2	2.6	8.1	7.2	3.1	2.2	5.1	0.3
Official creditors	1.2	2.6	8.1	7.2	3.1	2.2	5.1	0.3
Private creditors	0.0	0.0	0.0	0.0	0.0	0.0	0.0	0.0
of which: Bonds	0.0	0.0	0.0	0.0	0.0	0.0	0.0	0.0
Private nonguaranteed	..	..	..	..	..	..	..	..
of which: Bonds	..	..	..	..	..	..	..	..
Interest payments	**0.8**	**1.3**	**4.2**	**2.9**	**1.1**	**1.7**	**2.3**	**0.1**
Public and publicly guaranteed	0.8	1.3	4.2	2.9	1.1	1.7	2.3	0.1
Official creditors	0.8	1.3	4.2	2.9	1.1	1.7	2.3	0.1
Private creditors	0.0	0.0	0.0	0.0	0.0	0.0	0.0	0.0
of which: Bonds	0.0	0.0	0.0	0.0	0.0	0.0	0.0	0.0
Private nonguaranteed	..	..	..	..	..	..	..	..
of which: Bonds	..	..	..	..	..	..	..	..
Net financial flows								
Net debt inflows	2.3	0.7	-5.5	-2.1	-0.7	0.2	-4.9	4.4
Official creditors (incl. IMF)	0.3	0.7	-1.5	-2.1	-0.7	0.2	-4.9	4.4
Private creditors	2.0	..	-4.0	..	..	..	..	..
Long-term	..	..	..	..	..	..	..	..
Public and publicly guaranteed	..	..	..	..	..	..	..	..
Private nonguaranteed	..	..	..	..	..	..	..	..
Short-term	2.0	..	-4.0	..	..	..	..	..
Net equity inflows								
Foreign direct investment	0.1	0.6	4.6	13.8	8.3	23.1	10.4	13.9
Portfolio equity	..	..	..	..	..	..	..	..
Major economic aggregates								
Gross national income (GNI)	202.2	385.9	528.4	534.7	541.1	608.6	594.9	656.7
Exports of goods, services & prim. income	..	44.7	59.8	60.7	68.0	79.1	70.0	..
Imports of goods, services & prim. income	..	108.2	197.0	193.5	206.6	233.7	245.3	..
Primary income on FDI	..	..	..	..	..	..	..	..
Personal transfers & comp. of employees	..	..	..	..	..	..	..	..
International reserves	43.2	85.8	112.2	150.3	145.3	155.2	194.1	173.4
Ratios								
External debt stocks to exports (%)	..	628.8	466.6	475.3	412.6	351.2	358.9	..
External debt stocks to GNI (%)	112.1	72.8	52.8	53.9	51.9	45.7	42.2	22.3
Debt service to exports (%)	..	9.0	20.7	19.6	6.3	5.0	17.0	..
Reserves to external debt stocks (%)	19.1	30.6	40.2	52.1	51.8	55.8	77.3	118.5

Notes:

Data include the effects of Paris Club debt restructuring agreements signed in 2010 and 2013, and the HIPC debt relief.

CONGO, DEMOCRATIC REPUBLIC OF

(US$ million, unless otherwise indicated)

	2000	2005	2008	2009	2010	2011	2012	2013
Summary external debt data								
External debt stocks	**11,805**	**10,715**	**12,322**	**13,083**	**6,188**	**5,531**	**5,591**	**6,082**
Long-term external debt	7,880	9,403	10,862	10,880	4,597	4,022	4,103	4,373
Short-term external debt	3,421	397	673	603	481	250	229	446
interest arrears on long-term	3,042	359	467	489	267	73	71	71
Use of IMF credit	503	914	787	1,601	1,110	1,258	1,260	1,262
Long-term external debt								
Debt outstanding and disbursed	**7,880**	**9,403**	**10,862**	**10,880**	**4,597**	**4,022**	**4,103**	**4,373**
Public and publicly guaranteed	7,880	9,403	10,862	10,880	4,597	4,022	4,103	4,373
Official creditors	7,384	9,033	10,511	10,548	4,472	4,008	4,075	4,356
Private creditors	496	370	351	332	126	14	27	18
of which: Bonds	3	1	0	0	0	0	0	0
Private nonguaranteed	..	..	..	..	..	..	..	..
of which: Bonds	..	..	..	..	..	..	..	..
Disbursements	**0**	**249**	**110**	**131**	**78**	**152**	**242**	**495**
Public and publicly guaranteed	0	249	110	131	78	152	242	495
Official creditors	0	249	110	131	58	152	226	494
Private creditors	0	0	0	0	20	0	17	1
of which: Bonds	0	0	0	0	0	0	0	0
Private nonguaranteed	..	..	..	..	..	..	..	..
of which: Bonds	..	..	..	..	..	..	..	..
Principal repayments	**0**	**112**	**170**	**226**	**89**	**133**	**108**	**181**
Public and publicly guaranteed	0	112	170	226	89	133	108	181
Official creditors	0	110	163	205	85	128	105	171
Private creditors	0	2	7	21	4	5	4	10
of which: Bonds	0	1	0	0	0	0	0	0
Private nonguaranteed	..	..	..	..	..	..	..	..
of which: Bonds	..	..	..	..	..	..	..	..
Interest payments	**0**	**97**	**275**	**242**	**125**	**120**	**168**	**153**
Public and publicly guaranteed	0	97	275	242	125	120	168	153
Official creditors	0	95	272	240	124	120	168	153
Private creditors	0	1	3	2	0	0	0	0
of which: Bonds	0	0	0	0	0	0	0	0
Private nonguaranteed	..	..	..	..	..	..	..	..
of which: Bonds	..	..	..	..	..	..	..	..
Net financial flows								
Net debt inflows	20	95	-171	-55	107	138	115	530
Official creditors (incl. IMF)	0	178	-191	58	-8	180	121	323
Private creditors	20	-83	19	-113	116	-42	-6	207
Long-term	..	-2	-7	-21	16	-5	13	-10
Public and publicly guaranteed	..	-2	-7	-21	16	-5	13	-10
Private nonguaranteed	..	..	..	..	..	..	..	..
Short-term	20	-81	26	-92	100	-37	-19	217
Net equity inflows								
Foreign direct investment	72	180	1,727	-243	2,736	1,687	3,312	2,098
Portfolio equity	..	..	..	..	..	..	..	..
Major economic aggregates								
Gross national income (GNI)	18,700	11,458	17,876	17,477	19,613	22,535	25,857	27,819
Exports of goods, services & prim. income	..	2,756	7,716	5,047	8,915	10,379	8,840	..
Imports of goods, services & prim. income	..	3,892	8,863	7,571	11,931	13,071	11,703	..
Primary income on FDI	..	..	..	..	131	..	..	..
Personal transfers & comp. of employees	..	9	15	20	16	115	12	..
International reserves	83	131	78	1,035	1,300	1,268	1,633	1,678
Ratios								
External debt stocks to exports (%)	..	388.8	159.7	259.2	69.4	53.3	63.2	..
External debt stocks to GNI (%)	63.1	93.5	68.9	74.9	31.6	24.5	21.6	21.9
Debt service to exports (%)	..	7.9	7.7	12.4	3.1	2.5	3.2	..
Reserves to external debt stocks (%)	0.7	1.2	0.6	7.9	21.0	22.9	29.2	27.6

Notes:

Short-term debt is based on data from the BIS. Data include the effects of Paris Club debt restructuring agreement and HIPC and MDRI debt relief.

CONGO, REPUBLIC OF

(US$ million, unless otherwise indicated)

	2000	2005	2008	2009	2010	2011	2012	2013
Summary external debt data								
External debt stocks	**4,865**	**6,258**	**5,488**	**4,939**	**2,406**	**2,638**	**2,829**	**3,452**
Long-term external debt	3,735	5,471	5,071	4,610	2,063	2,329	2,492	3,075
Short-term external debt	1,076	747	364	162	193	155	185	228
interest arrears on long-term	655	736	227	95	76	61	60	69
Use of IMF credit	54	40	53	168	150	155	152	148
Long-term external debt								
Debt outstanding and disbursed	**3,735**	**5,471**	**5,071**	**4,610**	**2,063**	**2,329**	**2,492**	**3,075**
Public and publicly guaranteed	3,735	5,471	5,071	4,610	2,063	2,329	2,492	3,075
Official creditors	2,920	3,293	3,964	3,656	1,224	1,402	1,479	1,980
Private creditors	815	2,179	1,107	954	840	927	1,013	1,095
of which: Bonds	0	0	454	454	454	454	449	436
Private nonguaranteed	..	..	..	..	..	..	..	..
of which: Bonds	..	..	..	..	..	..	..	..
Disbursements	**1**	**183**	**19**	**7**	**504**	**356**	**472**	**836**
Public and publicly guaranteed	1	183	19	7	504	356	472	836
Official creditors	1	183	14	7	502	244	251	632
Private creditors	0	0	5	0	2	112	221	204
of which: Bonds	0	0	0	0	0	0	0	0
Private nonguaranteed	..	..	..	..	..	..	..	..
of which: Bonds	..	..	..	..	..	..	..	..
Principal repayments	**6**	**65**	**107**	**114**	**116**	**114**	**141**	**265**
Public and publicly guaranteed	6	65	107	114	116	114	141	265
Official creditors	6	65	79	80	104	92	106	138
Private creditors	0	0	27	34	12	22	35	126
of which: Bonds	0	0	24	0	0	0	5	14
Private nonguaranteed	..	..	..	..	..	..	..	..
of which: Bonds	..	..	..	..	..	..	..	..
Interest payments	**7**	**34**	**57**	**63**	**23**	**20**	**23**	**31**
Public and publicly guaranteed	7	34	57	63	23	20	23	31
Official creditors	7	34	57	48	9	6	7	13
Private creditors	0	0	0	14	14	14	16	18
of which: Bonds	0	0	0	14	14	14	14	16
Private nonguaranteed	..	..	..	..	..	..	..	..
of which: Bonds	..	..	..	..	..	..	..	..
Net financial flows								
Net debt inflows	-52	128	-54	-174	439	224	359	601
Official creditors (incl. IMF)	9	117	-64	-70	400	158	142	489
Private creditors	-61	11	10	-104	39	66	217	112
Long-term	..	..	-22	-34	-11	89	186	78
Public and publicly guaranteed	..	..	-22	-34	-11	89	186	78
Private nonguaranteed	..	..	..	..	..	..	..	..
Short-term	-61	11	32	-70	50	-23	31	34
Net equity inflows								
Foreign direct investment	166	801	2,526	1,862	2,211	3,056	2,758	2,038
Portfolio equity	0	..	..	..	..	..	..	..
Major economic aggregates								
Gross national income (GNI)	2,275	4,032	8,768	6,979	9,024	10,713	10,832	11,354
Exports of goods, services & prim. income	2,642	4,983	..	..	..	..	..	..
Imports of goods, services & prim. income	2,013	4,318	..	..	..	..	..	..
Primary income on FDI	466	1,296	..	..	..	..	..	..
Personal transfers & comp. of employees	10	11	..	..	..	..	..	..
International reserves	222	732	3,872	3,806	4,447	5,641	5,550	..
Ratios								
External debt stocks to exports (%)	184.1	125.6	..	..	..	..	..	..
External debt stocks to GNI (%)	213.8	155.2	62.6	70.8	26.7	24.6	26.1	30.4
Debt service to exports (%)	1.7	2.3	..	..	..	..	..	..
Reserves to external debt stocks (%)	4.6	11.7	70.5	77.1	184.8	213.8	196.1	..

Notes:

Short-term debt is based on data from the BIS. Data include the effects of Paris Club debt restructuring agreement and HIPC and MDRI debt relief.

COSTA RICA

(US$ million, unless otherwise indicated)

	2000	2005	2008	2009	2010	2011	2012	2013
Summary external debt data								
External debt stocks	**4,738**	**6,519**	**9,242**	**8,156**	**8,547**	**10,723**	**14,510**	**17,443**
Long-term external debt	3,745	4,388	5,217	5,668	5,875	7,673	11,365	14,715
Short-term external debt	962	2,097	3,989	2,243	2,431	2,810	2,904	2,486
interest arrears on long-term	27	2	0	0	0	0	0	0
Use of IMF credit	31	34	37	245	241	240	241	241
Long-term external debt								
Debt outstanding and disbursed	**3,745**	**4,388**	**5,217**	**5,668**	**5,875**	**7,673**	**11,365**	**14,715**
Public and publicly guaranteed	3,509	3,157	3,223	3,208	3,822	3,968	4,977	7,470
Official creditors	1,918	1,366	1,411	1,578	2,196	2,196	2,192	1,933
Private creditors	1,591	1,791	1,812	1,630	1,626	1,773	2,786	5,537
of which: Bonds	1,542	1,669	1,660	1,435	1,435	1,435	2,435	5,185
Private nonguaranteed	236	1,231	1,994	2,459	2,053	3,704	6,388	7,246
of which: Bonds	..	..	..	..	..	..	..	..
Disbursements	**758**	**986**	**1,178**	**1,329**	**1,458**	**1,878**	**3,838**	**5,936**
Public and publicly guaranteed	749	75	394	559	928	773	1,784	3,648
Official creditors	249	75	383	419	845	269	351	418
Private creditors	500	0	11	141	82	504	1,433	3,230
of which: Bonds	500	0	0	75	0	250	1,250	3,000
Private nonguaranteed	9	910	785	770	531	1,105	2,053	2,288
of which: Bonds	..	..	..	..	..	..	..	..
Principal repayments	**391**	**569**	**1,122**	**856**	**623**	**1,176**	**1,697**	**2,262**
Public and publicly guaranteed	374	365	846	573	342	641	742	1,125
Official creditors	338	306	473	250	256	283	323	646
Private creditors	37	59	373	323	86	357	420	479
of which: Bonds	30	41	240	300	0	250	250	250
Private nonguaranteed	17	204	276	284	282	536	955	1,137
of which: Bonds	..	..	..	..	..	..	..	..
Interest payments	**206**	**179**	**352**	**366**	**329**	**415**	**580**	**683**
Public and publicly guaranteed	191	105	248	218	213	200	202	253
Official creditors	105	62	80	77	86	85	77	70
Private creditors	86	43	168	142	127	115	125	183
of which: Bonds	80	39	152	131	116	105	111	169
Private nonguaranteed	16	74	104	147	116	215	378	430
of which: Bonds	..	..	..	..	..	..	..	..
Net financial flows								
Net debt inflows	546	842	811	-1,272	1,023	1,081	2,234	3,257
Official creditors (incl. IMF)	-88	-231	-91	169	590	-14	29	-228
Private creditors	634	1,072	902	-1,441	433	1,095	2,205	3,484
Long-term	455	647	147	304	246	716	2,112	3,902
Public and publicly guaranteed	463	-59	-362	-182	-4	147	1,013	2,751
Private nonguaranteed	-8	706	509	486	249	569	1,098	1,150
Short-term	179	425	755	-1,745	188	379	93	-417
Net equity inflows								
Foreign direct investment	409	575	2,040	1,521	1,316	1,465	1,574	2,527
Portfolio equity	..	..	..	..	..	..	..	..
Major economic aggregates								
Gross national income (GNI)	14,694	19,756	29,414	28,299	35,553	40,648	44,545	48,526
Exports of goods, services & prim. income	7,992	7,535	10,863	9,890	10,797	11,849	13,012	13,545
Imports of goods, services & prim. income	8,793	8,787	14,092	10,825	12,445	14,400	15,735	16,361
Primary income on FDI	1,141	743	749	986	606	505	609	829
Personal transfers & comp. of employees	136	420	605	513	531	520	562	596
International reserves	1,318	2,313	3,799	4,066	4,627	4,756	6,857	7,331
Ratios								
External debt stocks to exports (%)	59.3	86.5	85.1	82.5	79.2	90.5	111.5	128.8
External debt stocks to GNI (%)	32.2	33.0	31.4	28.8	24.0	26.4	32.6	35.9
Debt service to exports (%)	8.2	11.2	14.6	13.0	9.4	14.1	18.1	22.3
Reserves to external debt stocks (%)	27.8	35.5	41.1	49.9	54.1	44.4	47.3	42.0

Notes:

Long-term private nonguaranteed debt data are World Bank staff estimates based on reports provided by the country. Short-term debt before 2005 is based on data from the BIS, and 2013 is based on Central Bank data.

COTE D'IVOIRE

(US$ million, unless otherwise indicated)

	2000	2005	2008	2009	2010	2011	2012	2013
Summary external debt data								
External debt stocks	**12,187**	**11,178**	**12,016**	**13,431**	**10,665**	**12,334**	**9,168**	**11,288**
Long-term external debt	10,546	10,129	10,541	12,530	9,489	10,424	7,729	9,666
Short-term external debt	1,043	797	1,228	62	314	821	174	204
interest arrears on long-term	79	797	1,228	62	7	5	1	0
Use of IMF credit	599	252	247	839	861	1,090	1,265	1,418
Long-term external debt								
Debt outstanding and disbursed	**10,546**	**10,129**	**10,541**	**12,530**	**9,489**	**10,424**	**7,729**	**9,666**
Public and publicly guaranteed	9,063	9,228	9,803	11,682	8,472	9,092	5,239	7,599
Official creditors	6,669	6,977	7,352	9,690	8,426	9,023	4,017	4,969
Private creditors	2,394	2,252	2,452	1,992	46	68	1,222	2,630
of which: Bonds	2,343	2,159	2,346	1,931	0	0	0	0
Private nonguaranteed	1,482	900	738	848	1,018	1,332	2,490	2,067
of which: Bonds	..	..	..	..	..	..	..	..
Disbursements	**148**	**55**	**310**	**423**	**715**	**1,243**	**2,104**	**3,273**
Public and publicly guaranteed	148	21	35	103	360	840	1,284	3,273
Official creditors	148	21	35	103	334	806	106	1,830
Private creditors	0	0	0	0	26	34	1,178	1,443
of which: Bonds	0	0	0	0	0	0	0	0
Private nonguaranteed	..	34	275	320	355	402	820	..
of which: Bonds	..	..	..	..	..		..	..
Principal repayments	**442**	**164**	**782**	**696**	**615**	**561**	**565**	**966**
Public and publicly guaranteed	329	21	586	531	430	341	299	542
Official creditors	283	21	586	531	430	332	290	507
Private creditors	46	0	0	0	0	9	10	35
of which: Bonds	46	0	0	0	0	0	0	0
Private nonguaranteed	113	143	196	165	185	220	266	423
of which: Bonds	..	..	..	..	..	..	..	..
Interest payments	**462**	**46**	**216**	**287**	**113**	**130**	**169**	**291**
Public and publicly guaranteed	342	3	183	240	57	60	50	200
Official creditors	189	3	183	240	57	59	50	55
Private creditors	153	0	0	0	0	0	0	145
of which: Bonds	153	0	0	0	0	0	0	0
Private nonguaranteed	120	43	33	48	56	70	119	91
of which: Bonds	..	..	..	..	..	..	..	..
Net financial flows								
Net debt inflows	-617	-307	-452	-116	452	1,429	1,068	2,487
Official creditors (incl. IMF)	-174	-90	-531	-271	-51	713	-12	1,471
Private creditors	-442	-217	79	155	503	716	1,079	1,015
Long-term	-159	-109	79	155	196	207	1,722	984
Public and publicly guaranteed	-46	0	..	..	26	25	1,168	1,408
Private nonguaranteed	-113	-109	79	155	170	182	554	-423
Short-term	-283	-108	0	..	307	509	-643	31
Net equity inflows								
Foreign direct investment	235	302	431	400	371	302	322	371
Portfolio equity	1	14	2	2	2	..	..	..
Major economic aggregates								
Gross national income (GNI)	9,715	15,643	22,434	22,055	21,923	23,035	23,683	29,796
Exports of goods, services & prim. income	4,512	8,717	11,643	12,562	12,811	13,868	..	..
Imports of goods, services & prim. income	4,423	8,215	10,859	10,845	11,907	10,672	..	..
Primary income on FDI	284	370	581	572	562	..	..	..
Personal transfers & comp. of employees	119	163	199	315	373	..	..	..
International reserves	674	1,367	2,253	3,267	3,624	4,316	3,928	4,243
Ratios								
External debt stocks to exports (%)	270.1	128.2	103.2	106.9	83.2	88.9	..	..
External debt stocks to GNI (%)	125.4	71.5	53.6	60.9	48.6	53.5	38.7	37.9
Debt service to exports (%)	22.7	3.5	9.0	9.0	5.8	5.2	..	..
Reserves to external debt stocks (%)	5.5	12.2	18.7	24.3	34.0	35.0	42.8	37.6

Notes:

Long-term public and publicly guaranteed debt data for 2012 are World Bank staff estimates based on the original terms of the loans. Long-term private nonguaranteed debt data are World Bank staff estimates. Short-term debt is based on data from the BIS. Data include the effects of Paris Club agreement signed in 2011, 2012 and HIPC and MDRI debt relief.

DJIBOUTI

(US$ million, unless otherwise indicated)

	2000	2005	2008	2009	2010	2011	2012	2013
Summary external debt data								
External debt stocks	**298.6**	**485.1**	**843.3**	**894.1**	**769.7**	**775.9**	**807.7**	**832.8**
Long-term external debt	238.3	376.9	678.3	735.3	619.7	650.6	641.9	672.8
Short-term external debt	45.4	87.9	145.7	119.3	114.5	85.6	108.3	102.4
interest arrears on long-term	6.4	8.9	0.7	2.3	0.5	0.6	1.3	1.4
Use of IMF credit	14.9	20.4	19.2	39.5	35.5	39.7	57.5	57.6
Long-term external debt								
Debt outstanding and disbursed	**238.3**	**376.9**	**678.3**	**735.3**	**619.7**	**650.6**	**641.9**	**672.8**
Public and publicly guaranteed	238.3	376.9	678.3	735.3	619.7	650.6	641.9	672.8
Official creditors	238.3	371.3	651.0	711.1	599.3	633.4	628.1	662.4
Private creditors	0.0	5.6	27.4	24.2	20.4	17.2	13.8	10.4
of which: Bonds	0.0	0.0	0.0	0.0	0.0	0.0	0.0	0.0
Private nonguaranteed	..	..	..	..	..	..	..	..
of which: Bonds	..	..	..	..	..	..	..	..
Disbursements	**7.7**	**26.5**	**45.9**	**67.4**	**35.2**	**55.7**	**25.2**	**64.0**
Public and publicly guaranteed	7.7	26.5	45.9	67.4	35.2	55.7	25.2	64.0
Official creditors	7.7	26.5	45.9	67.4	35.2	55.7	25.2	64.0
Private creditors	0.0	0.0	0.0	0.0	0.0	0.0	0.0	0.0
of which: Bonds	0.0	0.0	0.0	0.0	0.0	0.0	0.0	0.0
Private nonguaranteed	..	..	..	..	..	..	..	..
of which: Bonds	..	..	..	..	..	..	..	..
Principal repayments	**8.4**	**11.0**	**17.5**	**22.3**	**22.2**	**24.8**	**30.8**	**31.7**
Public and publicly guaranteed	8.4	11.0	17.5	22.3	22.2	24.8	30.8	31.7
Official creditors	8.4	11.0	13.6	17.3	19.8	21.9	27.3	28.1
Private creditors	0.0	0.0	3.9	5.1	2.4	2.9	3.5	3.7
of which: Bonds	0.0	0.0	0.0	0.0	0.0	0.0	0.0	0.0
Private nonguaranteed	..	..	..	..	..	..	..	..
of which: Bonds	..	..	..	..	..	..	..	..
Interest payments	**2.2**	**3.7**	**7.7**	**8.1**	**8.2**	**9.2**	**9.3**	**9.5**
Public and publicly guaranteed	2.2	3.7	7.7	8.1	8.2	9.2	9.3	9.5
Official creditors	2.2	3.7	7.2	7.6	7.5	8.5	8.8	9.1
Private creditors	0.0	0.0	0.5	0.6	0.6	0.7	0.5	0.4
of which: Bonds	0.0	0.0	0.0	0.0	0.0	0.0	0.0	0.0
Private nonguaranteed	..	..	..	..	..	..	..	..
of which: Bonds	..	..	..	..	..	..	..	..
Net financial flows								
Net debt inflows	39.7	56.7	29.2	15.1	6.6	6.2	34.1	26.3
Official creditors (incl. IMF)	0.7	14.7	34.1	48.2	12.0	38.2	15.7	35.9
Private creditors	39.0	42.0	-4.9	-33.1	-5.4	-31.9	18.5	-9.7
Long-term	..	..	-3.9	-5.1	-2.4	-2.9	-3.5	-3.7
Public and publicly guaranteed	..	..	-3.9	-5.1	-2.4	-2.9	-3.5	-3.7
Private nonguaranteed	..	..	..	..	..	..	..	..
Short-term	39.0	42.0	-1.0	-28.0	-3.0	-29.0	22.0	-6.0
Net equity inflows								
Foreign direct investment	3.3	22.2	227.7	96.9	36.5	79.0	110.0	286.0
Portfolio equity	..	..	..	..	..	..	..	..
Major economic aggregates								
Gross national income (GNI)	567.0	775.8	..	..	..	..	..	..
Exports of goods, services & prim. income	218.4	319.8	398.3	422.7	439.0	440.3	487.7	..
Imports of goods, services & prim. income	287.1	372.3	703.5	580.0	493.8	686.3	700.7	..
Primary income on FDI	4.2	5.9	5.0	6.5	6.8	18.0	7.2	..
Personal transfers & comp. of employees	12.3	25.8	30.3	32.5	32.6	32.4	33.3	..
International reserves	67.8	89.3	175.5	241.8	249.0	244.1	248.6	425.0
Ratios								
External debt stocks to exports (%)	136.7	151.7	211.7	211.5	175.3	176.2	165.6	..
External debt stocks to GNI (%)	52.7	62.5	..	..	..	..	..	..
Debt service to exports (%)	6.9	5.6	8.4	8.5	8.1	8.6	8.8	..
Reserves to external debt stocks (%)	22.7	18.4	20.8	27.0	32.4	31.5	30.8	51.0

Notes:

Short-term debt is based on data from the BIS. Data include the effects of Paris Club debt restructuring agreement signed in 2008.

DOMINICA

(US$ million, unless otherwise indicated)

	2000	2005	2008	2009	2010	2011	2012	2013
Summary external debt data								
External debt stocks	**183.3**	**277.4**	**304.4**	**270.9**	**250.5**	**263.6**	**287.9**	**292.9**
Long-term external debt	163.6	224.4	205.4	201.1	218.8	230.7	255.8	263.6
Short-term external debt	19.0	40.6	83.0	37.9	1.5	5.6	5.6	5.5
interest arrears on long-term	0.0	8.6	17.0	17.9	1.5	1.5	1.5	1.5
Use of IMF credit	0.8	12.4	15.9	31.9	30.2	27.3	26.6	23.8
Long-term external debt								
Debt outstanding and disbursed	**163.6**	**224.4**	**205.4**	**201.1**	**218.8**	**230.7**	**255.8**	**263.6**
Public and publicly guaranteed	163.6	224.4	205.4	201.1	218.8	230.7	255.8	263.6
Official creditors	114.3	173.0	156.8	155.3	173.0	182.3	216.6	227.1
Private creditors	49.2	51.4	48.6	45.8	45.8	48.4	39.2	36.5
of which: Bonds	49.2	48.9	44.0	40.3	40.3	42.1	11.5	11.5
Private nonguaranteed	..	..	..	..	..	..	..	..
of which: Bonds	..	..	..	..	..	..	..	..
Disbursements	**56.2**	**4.5**	**8.0**	**8.9**	**29.7**	**21.1**	**36.3**	**21.5**
Public and publicly guaranteed	56.2	4.5	8.0	8.9	29.7	21.1	36.3	21.5
Official creditors	25.7	4.5	6.2	8.6	29.7	18.3	36.3	21.5
Private creditors	30.5	0.0	1.9	0.3	0.0	2.8	0.0	0.0
of which: Bonds	30.5	0.0	0.1	0.0	0.0	1.8	0.0	0.0
Private nonguaranteed	..	..	..	..	..	..	..	..
of which: Bonds	..		..	..	..	..	..	..
Principal repayments	**6.8**	**9.6**	**12.9**	**14.8**	**9.8**	**9.4**	**7.8**	**9.9**
Public and publicly guaranteed	6.8	9.6	12.9	14.8	9.8	9.4	7.8	9.9
Official creditors	6.8	9.6	12.9	12.9	9.8	9.2	7.6	8.0
Private creditors	0.0	0.0	0.0	1.9	0.1	0.2	0.2	1.9
of which: Bonds	0.0	0.0	0.0	1.9	0.0	0.0	0.0	0.0
Private nonguaranteed	..	..	..	..	..	..	..	..
of which: Bonds	..	..	..	..	..	..	..	..
Interest payments	**3.1**	**4.7**	**4.3**	**4.5**	**4.3**	**4.2**	**7.8**	**5.9**
Public and publicly guaranteed	3.1	4.7	4.3	4.5	4.3	4.2	7.8	5.9
Official creditors	2.9	4.3	4.1	3.9	3.8	3.9	4.2	4.7
Private creditors	0.2	0.4	0.3	0.6	0.5	0.3	3.7	1.1
of which: Bonds	0.2	0.4	0.3	0.3	0.4	0.3	2.7	0.3
Private nonguaranteed	..	..	..	..	..	..	..	..
of which: Bonds	..	..	..	..	..	..	..	..
Net financial flows								
Net debt inflows	49.5	-37.0	15.3	-47.6	-1.2	12.8	27.7	8.7
Official creditors (incl. IMF)	18.8	-2.0	-3.5	0.0	18.8	6.1	27.9	10.8
Private creditors	30.7	-35.0	18.9	-47.6	-20.0	6.7	-0.2	-2.0
Long-term	30.5	0.0	1.9	-1.6	0.0	2.6	-0.2	-1.9
Public and publicly guaranteed	30.5	0.0	1.9	-1.6	0.0	2.6	-0.2	-1.9
Private nonguaranteed	..	..	..	..	..	..	..	..
Short-term	0.2	-35.0	17.0	-46.0	-20.0	4.1	..	-0.1
Net equity inflows								
Foreign direct investment	17.6	21.7	45.1	26.3	10.0	6.8	15.7	10.0
Portfolio equity	..	..	..	..	..	..	..	..
Major economic aggregates								
Gross national income (GNI)	285.1	332.6	433.7	468.9	465.6	480.7	477.4	493.3
Exports of goods, services & prim. income	149.2	135.3	165.1	154.5	180.2	195.9	165.0	174.3
Imports of goods, services & prim. income	227.1	231.0	314.1	284.7	280.1	280.3	274.0	267.7
Primary income on FDI	33.0	22.7	12.5	13.4	7.8	5.0	5.1	5.4
Personal transfers & comp. of employees	16.3	21.8	22.7	22.1	22.9	22.9	23.2	23.6
International reserves	29.4	49.2	55.2	75.5	76.1	81.1	94.6	87.1
Ratios								
External debt stocks to exports (%)	122.9	205.0	184.3	175.3	139.0	134.6	174.5	168.1
External debt stocks to GNI (%)	64.3	83.4	70.2	57.8	53.8	54.8	60.3	59.4
Debt service to exports (%)	7.4	12.1	11.6	13.5	8.6	8.5	11.9	10.7
Reserves to external debt stocks (%)	16.0	17.7	18.1	27.9	30.4	30.8	32.8	29.7

DOMINICAN REPUBLIC

(US$ million, unless otherwise indicated)

	2000	2005	2008	2009	2010	2011	2012	2013
Summary external debt data								
External debt stocks	**4,652**	**7,752**	**10,609**	**11,851**	**13,497**	**15,096**	**22,100**	**23,831**
Long-term external debt	3,381	6,419	8,129	9,003	10,281	11,673	18,834	20,761
Short-term external debt	1,178	887	1,940	1,755	1,754	1,800	1,753	1,753
interest arrears on long-term	28	20	3	0	0	0	0	0
Use of IMF credit	93	446	541	1,094	1,461	1,623	1,513	1,317
Long-term external debt								
Debt outstanding and disbursed	**3,381**	**6,419**	**8,129**	**9,003**	**10,281**	**11,673**	**18,834**	**20,761**
Public and publicly guaranteed	3,381	6,418	7,285	8,160	9,439	10,760	11,982	14,177
Official creditors	2,625	3,257	4,458	5,505	6,376	7,119	8,159	9,088
Private creditors	756	3,160	2,828	2,655	3,063	3,641	3,823	5,088
of which: Bonds	506	1,147	1,201	1,076	1,721	2,412	2,412	3,834
Private nonguaranteed	..	2	843	843	843	913	6,852	6,584
of which: Bonds	..	..	843	843	843	843	1,137	887
Disbursements	**314**	**665**	**1,310**	**1,481**	**2,111**	**2,165**	**2,840**	**3,558**
Public and publicly guaranteed	314	664	1,310	1,481	2,111	2,120	1,843	3,112
Official creditors	150	372	1,023	1,392	1,176	1,117	1,458	1,554
Private creditors	164	292	287	89	935	1,003	385	1,558
of which: Bonds	0	0	0	0	750	750	0	1,500
Private nonguaranteed	..	2	..	..	..	45	998	446
of which: Bonds	..	..	..	..	..	..	550	..
Principal repayments	**264**	**462**	**823**	**896**	**798**	**796**	**1,521**	**1,642**
Public and publicly guaranteed	264	462	823	896	798	788	624	928
Official creditors	223	184	311	354	311	376	407	608
Private creditors	40	278	512	541	487	412	217	319
of which: Bonds	4	20	125	125	105	58	0	78
Private nonguaranteed	..	..	1	0	0	8	897	714
of which: Bonds	..	..	..	..	..	..	431	250
Interest payments	**211**	**212**	**448**	**433**	**444**	**584**	**919**	**958**
Public and publicly guaranteed	211	212	339	325	336	473	448	484
Official creditors	159	109	136	150	156	176	198	204
Private creditors	53	103	204	174	181	297	250	280
of which: Bonds	38	16	125	113	134	249	198	230
Private nonguaranteed	..	0	108	108	108	111	471	475
of which: Bonds	..	..	108	108	108	108	90	95
Net financial flows								
Net debt inflows	316	400	-90	664	1,695	1,586	1,163	1,718
Official creditors (incl. IMF)	-73	407	670	1,299	1,247	912	941	748
Private creditors	389	-7	-759	-635	448	674	222	971
Long-term	124	16	-225	-453	448	628	269	971
Public and publicly guaranteed	124	14	-225	-452	449	591	168	1,239
Private nonguaranteed	..	2	-1	0	0	37	101	-268
Short-term	265	-23	-534	-182	-1	46	-47	0
Net equity inflows								
Foreign direct investment	953	1,172	2,593	1,070	1,820	2,198	3,416	1,600
Portfolio equity	..	..	..	..	..	..	..	..
Major economic aggregates								
Gross national income (GNI)	22,955	32,069	43,982	44,728	49,319	53,354	56,713	57,806
Exports of goods, services & prim. income	9,264	8,013	9,999	8,444	13,525	14,889	15,754	16,851
Imports of goods, services & prim. income	12,193	11,183	18,031	13,986	20,983	23,081	23,634	23,463
Primary income on FDI	1,068	1,765	1,669	1,518	1,698	1,949	1,972	2,670
Personal transfers & comp. of employees	1,839	2,719	3,606	3,415	3,887	4,241	4,262	4,486
International reserves	627	1,920	2,679	3,560	3,849	4,086	3,528	4,679
Ratios								
External debt stocks to exports (%)	50.2	96.7	106.1	140.4	99.8	101.4	140.3	141.4
External debt stocks to GNI (%)	20.3	24.2	24.1	26.5	27.4	28.3	39.0	41.2
Debt service to exports (%)	5.7	9.1	15.1	16.7	10.5	10.8	16.5	16.8
Reserves to external debt stocks (%)	13.5	24.8	25.2	30.0	28.5	27.1	16.0	19.6

Notes:

Long-term private nonguaranteed debt data before 2013 only cover Inter-American Development Bank and Bonds. Short-term debt before 2009 is based on data from the BIS. Data include the effects of Paris Club debt restructuring agreement signed in 2005.

ECUADOR

(US$ million, unless otherwise indicated)

	2000	2005	2008	2009	2010	2011	2012	2013
Summary external debt data								
External debt stocks	**13,338**	**17,408**	**15,818**	**13,263**	**14,963**	**16,497**	**16,931**	**20,280**
Long-term external debt	12,350	15,564	14,084	11,426	13,715	15,309	15,815	19,182
Short-term external debt	797	1,719	1,683	1,386	804	745	673	653
interest arrears on long-term	3	1	31	37	37	46	44	43
Use of IMF credit	191	125	51	452	444	443	443	444
Long-term external debt								
Debt outstanding and disbursed	**12,350**	**15,564**	**14,084**	**11,426**	**13,715**	**15,309**	**15,815**	**19,182**
Public and publicly guaranteed	10,915	10,896	10,095	6,960	8,633	9,929	10,065	12,028
Official creditors	5,922	5,993	6,006	5,895	7,610	8,939	9,106	10,997
Private creditors	4,993	4,902	4,088	1,065	1,023	990	959	1,031
of which: Bonds	3,950	4,600	3,860	873	868	868	868	868
Private nonguaranteed	1,435	4,668	3,990	4,466	5,082	5,380	5,750	7,154
of which: Bonds	..	..	..	..	..	..	..	..
Disbursements	**983**	**3,154**	**1,369**	**1,180**	**2,977**	**3,370**	**2,322**	**5,608**
Public and publicly guaranteed	602	991	353	384	2,307	2,342	1,336	3,145
Official creditors	531	318	343	382	2,305	2,342	1,336	3,044
Private creditors	71	674	10	2	2	1	0	101
of which: Bonds	0	650	0	0	0	0	0	0
Private nonguaranteed	381	2,162	1,016	796	670	1,028	986	2,463
of which: Bonds	..	..	..			..	..	..
Principal repayments	**1,067**	**3,048**	**1,485**	**4,187**	**1,260**	**1,837**	**1,894**	**2,263**
Public and publicly guaranteed	550	923	964	3,529	637	1,048	1,174	1,172
Official creditors	399	803	915	503	593	1,015	1,143	1,142
Private creditors	151	120	49	3,025	44	33	31	30
of which: Bonds	0	0	0	2,987	6	0	0	0
Private nonguaranteed	517	2,125	521	659	623	789	720	1,091
of which: Bonds	..	..	..	..	..	..	..	..
Interest payments	**708**	**843**	**847**	**521**	**464**	**534**	**674**	**839**
Public and publicly guaranteed	536	658	656	330	326	361	481	647
Official creditors	296	275	311	227	255	292	414	575
Private creditors	240	383	345	103	71	69	67	72
of which: Bonds	140	367	331	91	61	61	61	61
Private nonguaranteed	172	185	191	191	139	174	193	192
of which: Bonds	..	..	..	..	..	..	..	..
Net financial flows								
Net debt inflows	-189	-235	-334	-3,310	1,135	1,466	358	3,327
Official creditors (incl. IMF)	282	-680	-572	-121	1,712	1,326	194	1,901
Private creditors	-471	445	238	-3,189	-577	139	164	1,426
Long-term	-216	590	456	-2,886	5	207	235	1,444
Public and publicly guaranteed	-80	553	-39	-3,023	-42	-33	-31	72
Private nonguaranteed	-136	37	495	138	47	239	266	1,372
Short-term	-254	-145	-218	-303	-582	-68	-71	-18
Net equity inflows								
Foreign direct investment	-23	519	527	534	478	580	528	703
Portfolio equity	0	2	1	2	0	2	5	..
Major economic aggregates								
Gross national income (GNI)	16,916	39,692	60,330	61,239	66,474	75,547	82,734	88,650
Exports of goods, services & prim. income	6,163	11,693	21,218	15,854	19,686	24,754	26,569	..
Imports of goods, services & prim. income	6,403	13,880	22,692	18,366	23,757	27,700	29,231	..
Primary income on FDI	329	1,004	785	821	546	701	676	..
Personal transfers & comp. of employees	1,322	2,460	3,089	2,742	2,599	2,681	2,456	..
International reserves	947	1,714	3,738	2,873	1,435	1,664	1,080	3,328
Ratios								
External debt stocks to exports (%)	216.4	148.9	74.6	83.7	76.0	66.6	63.7	..
External debt stocks to GNI (%)	78.8	43.9	26.2	21.7	22.5	21.8	20.5	22.9
Debt service to exports (%)	30.6	35.9	11.1	30.2	9.1	9.7	9.8	..
Reserves to external debt stocks (%)	7.1	9.8	23.6	21.7	9.6	10.1	6.4	16.4

Notes:

Short-term debt is World Bank staff estimates based on Central Bank data.

EGYPT, ARAB REPUBLIC OF

(US$ million, unless otherwise indicated)

	2000	2005	2008	2009	2010	2011	2012	2013
Summary external debt data								
External debt stocks	**29,178**	**29,948**	**33,574**	**35,068**	**36,542**	**35,147**	**39,998**	**44,430**
Long-term external debt	24,897	28,098	30,522	31,098	32,009	30,742	31,960	40,230
Short-term external debt	4,104	1,656	2,842	2,561	3,149	3,026	6,657	2,816
interest arrears on long-term	0	2	0	0	0	0	0	0
Use of IMF credit	177	194	209	1,408	1,384	1,379	1,381	1,384
Long-term external debt								
Debt outstanding and disbursed	**24,897**	**28,098**	**30,522**	**31,098**	**32,009**	**30,742**	**31,960**	**40,230**
Public and publicly guaranteed	24,325	28,005	30,442	31,024	31,955	30,726	31,940	40,218
Official creditors	23,785	25,777	28,100	28,675	28,236	27,454	28,686	34,007
Private creditors	540	2,228	2,341	2,350	3,719	3,272	3,254	6,211
of which: Bonds	0	1,250	1,893	1,883	3,133	2,750	2,750	5,850
Private nonguaranteed	573	93	80	74	54	16	20	12
of which: Bonds	100	..	..	..	..	..	..	..
Disbursements	**569**	**3,090**	**1,133**	**2,131**	**3,617**	**1,510**	**3,681**	**11,100**
Public and publicly guaranteed	362	3,090	1,063	2,122	3,612	1,480	3,656	11,083
Official creditors	218	1,114	962	2,016	1,903	1,459	3,601	7,958
Private creditors	144	1,976	101	107	1,709	21	55	3,125
of which: Bonds	0	1,250	0	0	1,500	0	0	3,100
Private nonguaranteed	207	..	70	9	5	30	25	17
of which: Bonds	..	..	..	..	..	..	..	..
Principal repayments	**1,098**	**1,573**	**2,342**	**2,050**	**2,162**	**2,650**	**2,247**	**2,616**
Public and publicly guaranteed	982	1,573	2,331	2,030	2,137	2,582	2,225	2,591
Official creditors	861	1,344	1,855	1,911	2,063	2,122	2,151	2,413
Private creditors	121	229	476	119	74	460	74	178
of which: Bonds	0	0	0	0	0	383	0	0
Private nonguaranteed	116	..	11	20	25	68	22	25
of which: Bonds	..	..	..	..	..	..	..	..
Interest payments	**619**	**569**	**802**	**779**	**735**	**757**	**719**	**704**
Public and publicly guaranteed	603	565	799	776	734	757	719	704
Official creditors	572	547	714	654	581	563	557	531
Private creditors	31	18	85	123	152	194	161	173
of which: Bonds	0	0	56	112	140	181	147	160
Private nonguaranteed	16	4	3	2	1	0	0	0
of which: Bonds	12	..	..	..	..	..	..	..
Net financial flows								
Net debt inflows	-718	1,453	-602	-200	2,043	-1,263	5,066	4,643
Official creditors (incl. IMF)	-643	-230	-893	105	-160	-663	1,450	5,544
Private creditors	-75	1,683	292	-305	2,203	-600	3,616	-901
Long-term	115	1,747	-315	-24	1,615	-477	-15	2,940
Public and publicly guaranteed	23	1,747	-375	-13	1,635	-439	-19	2,947
Private nonguaranteed	91	..	59	-11	-20	-38	4	-8
Short-term	-189	-64	607	-281	588	-123	3,632	-3,841
Net equity inflows								
Foreign direct investment	1,235	..	390	1,008	1,360	540	209	202
Portfolio equity	269	729	-674	393	1,724	-711	-983	..
Major economic aggregates								
Gross national income (GNI)	100,770	89,432	165,655	191,178	217,727	229,429	256,347	266,219
Exports of goods, services & prim. income	18,735	32,141	57,826	45,601	49,365	47,371	48,834	..
Imports of goods, services & prim. income	23,878	35,787	68,999	56,910	66,308	68,076	75,597	..
Primary income on FDI	92	647	680	2,101	5,268	5,079	5,704	..
Personal transfers & comp. of employees	2,852	5,017	8,694	7,150	12,453	14,324	19,236	..
International reserves	13,118	20,609	32,216	32,253	33,612	14,916	11,628	13,608
Ratios								
External debt stocks to exports (%)	155.7	93.2	58.1	76.9	74.0	74.2	81.9	..
External debt stocks to GNI (%)	29.0	33.5	20.3	18.3	16.8	15.3	15.6	16.7
Debt service to exports (%)	9.8	6.9	5.6	6.4	6.1	7.5	6.6	..
Reserves to external debt stocks (%)	45.0	68.8	96.0	92.0	92.0	42.4	29.1	30.6

EL SALVADOR

(US$ million, unless otherwise indicated)

	2000	2005	2008	2009	2010	2011	2012	2013
Summary external debt data								
External debt stocks	**4,535**	**9,317**	**10,651**	**10,368**	**11,059**	**11,995**	**13,189**	**13,372**
Long-term external debt	2,858	7,425	9,070	9,248	9,971	10,521	11,411	11,266
Short-term external debt	1,645	1,856	1,542	863	836	1,223	1,526	1,853
interest arrears on long-term	0	0	0	0	0	0	0	0
Use of IMF credit	33	36	38	257	252	251	252	252
Long-term external debt								
Debt outstanding and disbursed	**2,858**	**7,425**	**9,070**	**9,248**	**9,971**	**10,521**	**11,411**	**11,266**
Public and publicly guaranteed	2,746	4,802	5,754	6,109	6,402	6,537	7,371	7,275
Official creditors	2,541	3,083	3,487	3,845	4,182	4,301	4,338	4,242
Private creditors	205	1,719	2,267	2,264	2,220	2,237	3,033	3,033
of which: Bonds	82	1,636	2,174	2,174	2,199	2,217	2,362	2,336
Private nonguaranteed	111	2,622	3,316	3,139	3,569	3,983	4,040	3,992
of which: Bonds	..	..	..	..	..	..	38	38
Disbursements	**372**	**1,222**	**1,042**	**1,216**	**1,055**	**874**	**1,603**	**839**
Public and publicly guaranteed	321	682	666	910	707	476	1,173	364
Official creditors	201	337	601	910	707	476	522	337
Private creditors	120	345	65	0	0	0	652	27
of which: Bonds	32	343	0	0	0	0	0	0
Private nonguaranteed	51	540	376	306	348	398	429	475
of which: Bonds	..	..	..	..	..	..	38	..
Principal repayments	**163**	**406**	**490**	**687**	**604**	**757**	**628**	**559**
Public and publicly guaranteed	130	245	351	559	455	587	453	391
Official creditors	126	230	347	555	388	367	452	390
Private creditors	4	16	4	4	68	220	1	1
of which: Bonds	0	0	0	0	0	219	0	0
Private nonguaranteed	33	160	139	127	149	170	175	167
of which: Bonds	..	..	..	..	..	..	..	..
Interest payments	**140**	**344**	**484**	**475**	**465**	**515**	**503**	**532**
Public and publicly guaranteed	133	257	369	374	350	386	373	403
Official creditors	124	119	136	139	117	119	121	121
Private creditors	9	139	232	235	233	267	252	282
of which: Bonds	8	133	232	232	232	266	251	251
Private nonguaranteed	7	87	116	102	115	129	130	129
of which: Bonds	..	..	..	..	..	..	..	2
Net financial flows								
Net debt inflows	802	892	803	-150	423	504	1,278	607
Official creditors (incl. IMF)	75	107	254	354	320	109	70	-53
Private creditors	726	785	548	-504	104	395	1,208	660
Long-term	134	709	298	175	131	8	904	333
Public and publicly guaranteed	116	329	61	-4	-68	-220	650	26
Private nonguaranteed	18	380	237	178	199	229	254	308
Short-term	592	77	250	-679	-27	387	304	327
Net equity inflows								
Foreign direct investment	173	512	538	241	282	169	533	108
Portfolio equity	..	..	..	..	..	..	..	..
Major economic aggregates								
Gross national income (GNI)	12,881	16,604	21,042	20,105	20,868	22,507	22,932	23,418
Exports of goods, services & prim. income	3,803	3,517	4,989	4,293	5,028	5,940	6,164	6,472
Imports of goods, services & prim. income	6,031	7,173	10,268	8,047	9,190	10,882	11,472	12,148
Primary income on FDI	60	181	39	175	190	203	577	614
Personal transfers & comp. of employees	1,765	3,029	3,755	3,402	3,472	3,644	3,910	3,971
International reserves	1,773	1,721	2,442	2,867	2,568	2,151	2,805	2,476
Ratios								
External debt stocks to exports (%)	119.3	264.9	213.5	241.5	220.0	201.9	214.0	206.6
External debt stocks to GNI (%)	35.2	56.1	50.6	51.6	53.0	53.3	57.5	57.1
Debt service to exports (%)	9.9	24.2	20.2	27.4	21.5	21.6	18.6	17.1
Reserves to external debt stocks (%)	39.1	18.5	22.9	27.7	23.2	17.9	21.3	18.5

Notes:

Long-term private nonguaranteed debt data from 2005 are World Bank staff estimates based on reports provided by the country.

ERITREA

(US$ million, unless otherwise indicated)

	2000	2005	2008	2009	2010	2011	2012	2013
Summary external debt data								
External debt stocks	**329.7**	**757.2**	**997.8**	**1,050.7**	**1,041.5**	**1,055.2**	**994.1**	**945.5**
Long-term external debt	298.0	723.0	957.0	1,013.0	1,002.0	1,013.6	952.1	895.9
Short-term external debt	12.0	12.6	17.5	13.9	16.2	18.4	18.6	26.3
interest arrears on long-term	2.0	1.6	4.5	5.9	6.2	7.4	12.6	16.3
Use of IMF credit	19.8	21.7	23.3	23.8	23.3	23.3	23.3	23.3
Long-term external debt								
Debt outstanding and disbursed	**298.0**	**723.0**	**957.0**	**1,013.0**	**1,002.0**	**1,013.6**	**952.1**	**895.9**
Public and publicly guaranteed	298.0	723.0	957.0	1,013.0	1,002.0	1,013.6	952.1	895.9
Official creditors	298.0	690.1	917.4	972.1	964.1	976.9	914.7	856.7
Private creditors	0.0	32.9	39.5	40.9	38.0	36.8	37.5	39.2
of which: Bonds	0.0	0.0	0.0	0.0	0.0	0.0	0.0	0.0
Private nonguaranteed	..	..	..	..	..	..	..	..
of which: Bonds	..	..	..	..	..	..	..	..
Disbursements	**50.7**	**70.6**	**104.9**	**57.6**	**8.6**	**24.2**	**26.8**	**26.7**
Public and publicly guaranteed	50.7	70.6	104.9	57.6	8.6	24.2	26.8	26.7
Official creditors	50.7	70.6	104.1	57.6	8.6	24.2	26.8	26.7
Private creditors	0.0	0.0	0.8	0.0	0.0	0.0	0.0	0.0
of which: Bonds	0.0	0.0	0.0	0.0	0.0	0.0	0.0	0.0
Private nonguaranteed	..	..	..	..	..	..	..	..
of which: Bonds	..	..	..	..	..	..	..	..
Principal repayments	**0.5**	**11.8**	**6.5**	**11.3**	**13.3**	**14.0**	**86.0**	**81.1**
Public and publicly guaranteed	0.5	11.8	6.5	11.3	13.3	14.0	86.0	81.1
Official creditors	0.5	11.8	6.5	11.3	13.3	14.0	86.0	81.1
Private creditors	0.0	0.0	0.0	0.0	0.0	0.0	0.0	0.0
of which: Bonds	0.0	0.0	0.0	0.0	0.0	0.0	0.0	0.0
Private nonguaranteed	..	..	..	..	..	..	..	..
of which: Bonds	..	..	..	..	..	..	..	..
Interest payments	**2.5**	**8.4**	**9.1**	**10.3**	**9.3**	**7.9**	**8.5**	**6.4**
Public and publicly guaranteed	2.5	8.4	9.1	10.3	9.3	7.9	8.5	6.4
Official creditors	2.5	8.4	9.1	10.3	9.3	7.9	8.3	6.2
Private creditors	0.0	0.0	0.0	0.0	0.0	0.0	0.2	0.2
of which: Bonds	0.0	0.0	0.0	0.0	0.0	0.0	0.0	0.0
Private nonguaranteed	..	..	..	..	..	..	..	..
of which: Bonds	..	..	..	..	..	..	..	..
Net financial flows								
Net debt inflows	60.2	38.9	98.3	41.3	-2.7	11.2	-64.3	-50.4
Official creditors (incl. IMF)	50.2	58.9	97.5	46.3	-4.7	10.2	-59.3	-54.4
Private creditors	10.0	-20.0	0.8	-5.0	2.0	1.0	-5.0	4.0
Long-term	..	..	0.8	..	..	..	..	..
Public and publicly guaranteed	..	..	0.8	..	..	..	..	..
Private nonguaranteed	..	..	..	..	..	..	..	..
Short-term	10.0	-20.0	..	-5.0	2.0	1.0	-5.0	4.0
Net equity inflows								
Foreign direct investment	27.9	1.4	39.0	91.0	91.0	39.0	41.4	43.9
Portfolio equity	..	..	..	..	..	..	..	..
Major economic aggregates								
Gross national income (GNI)	706.8	1,089.0	1,368.4	1,840.5	2,097.4	2,584.2	3,063.9	3,412.9
Exports of goods, services & prim. income	106.9	..	..	..	..	..	..	..
Imports of goods, services & prim. income	510.3	..	..	..	..	..	..	..
Primary income on FDI	4.4	..	..	..	..	..	..	..
Personal transfers & comp. of employees	3.3	..	..	..	..	..	..	..
International reserves	25.5	27.9	57.9	90.0	114.1	114.8	..	..
Ratios								
External debt stocks to exports (%)	308.5	..	..	..	..	..	..	..
External debt stocks to GNI (%)	46.6	69.5	72.9	57.1	49.7	40.8	32.4	27.7
Debt service to exports (%)	4.3	..	..	..	..	..	..	..
Reserves to external debt stocks (%)	7.7	3.7	5.8	8.6	11.0	10.9	..	..

Notes:

Long-term public and publicly guaranteed debt from 2010 are World Bank staff estimates. Short-term debt is based on data from the BIS.

ETHIOPIA

(US$ million, unless otherwise indicated)

	2000	2005	2008	2009	2010	2011	2012	2013
Summary external debt data								
External debt stocks	**5,509**	**6,224**	**2,896**	**5,232**	**7,347**	**8,604**	**10,462**	**12,557**
Long-term external debt	5,339	5,928	2,829	4,819	6,547	7,945	9,941	11,886
Short-term external debt	79	120	50	45	314	175	37	186
interest arrears on long-term	65	36	32	32	30	30	26	28
Use of IMF credit	92	176	17	368	485	484	484	485
Long-term external debt								
Debt outstanding and disbursed	**5,339**	**5,928**	**2,829**	**4,819**	**6,547**	**7,945**	**9,941**	**11,886**
Public and publicly guaranteed	5,339	5,928	2,829	4,819	6,547	7,945	9,941	11,886
Official creditors	5,226	5,564	2,590	3,556	4,638	5,685	7,218	8,980
Private creditors	113	364	239	1,263	1,909	2,259	2,723	2,905
of which: Bonds	0	0	0	0	0	0	0	0
Private nonguaranteed	..	..	..	..	..	..	..	..
of which: Bonds	..	..	..	..	..	..	..	..
Disbursements	**185**	**527**	**379**	**2,148**	**1,760**	**1,693**	**2,309**	**2,399**
Public and publicly guaranteed	185	527	379	2,148	1,760	1,693	2,309	2,399
Official creditors	184	400	379	1,098	1,021	1,157	1,645	1,889
Private creditors	2	127	0	1,050	739	537	664	510
of which: Bonds	0	0	0	0	0	0	0	0
Private nonguaranteed	..	..	..	..	..	..	..	..
of which: Bonds	..	..	..	..	..	..	..	..
Principal repayments	**72**	**36**	**72**	**62**	**130**	**259**	**328**	**503**
Public and publicly guaranteed	72	36	72	62	130	259	328	503
Official creditors	62	25	39	34	39	80	122	162
Private creditors	10	11	33	27	91	179	206	341
of which: Bonds	0	0	0	0	0	0	0	0
Private nonguaranteed	..	..	..	..	..	..	..	..
of which: Bonds	..	..	..	..	..	..	..	..
Interest payments	**52**	**49**	**39**	**40**	**50**	**91**	**103**	**159**
Public and publicly guaranteed	52	49	39	40	50	91	103	159
Official creditors	48	40	27	33	35	52	58	96
Private creditors	4	10	11	8	15	38	46	63
of which: Bonds	0	0	0	0	0	0	0	0
Private nonguaranteed	..	..	..	..	..	..	..	..
of which: Bonds	..	..	..	..	..	..	..	..
Net financial flows								
Net debt inflows	90	478	309	2,246	2,023	1,295	1,847	2,043
Official creditors (incl. IMF)	109	371	340	1,228	1,105	1,077	1,524	1,727
Private creditors	-19	107	-32	1,018	918	219	324	316
Long-term	-8	116	-33	1,023	647	358	458	169
Public and publicly guaranteed	-8	116	-33	1,023	647	358	458	169
Private nonguaranteed	..	..	..	..	..	..	..	..
Short-term	-11	-9	1	-5	271	-139	-134	147
Net equity inflows								
Foreign direct investment	135	265	109	221	288	627	279	953
Portfolio equity	..	..	..	..	..	..	..	..
Major economic aggregates								
Gross national income (GNI)	8,031	12,138	26,591	31,801	29,277	31,298	42,709	46,772
Exports of goods, services & prim. income	1,008	1,973	3,533	3,436	4,652	5,824	6,003	..
Imports of goods, services & prim. income	1,673	4,943	9,634	9,086	9,982	11,736	14,235	..
Primary income on FDI	9	21	17	18	35	23	6	..
Personal transfers & comp. of employees	53	174	387	262	345	513	624	..
International reserves	306	1,043	871	1,781	..	..	..	..
Ratios								
External debt stocks to exports (%)	546.3	315.5	82.0	152.3	157.9	147.7	174.3	..
External debt stocks to GNI (%)	68.6	51.3	10.9	16.5	25.1	27.5	24.5	26.8
Debt service to exports (%)	13.7	4.8	3.1	3.0	3.9	6.1	7.2	..
Reserves to external debt stocks (%)	5.6	16.8	30.1	34.0	..	..	..	..

Notes:

Short-term debt is based on data from the BIS. Data include the effects of HIPC and MDRI debt relief.

FIJI

(US$ million, unless otherwise indicated)

	2000	2005	2008	2009	2010	2011	2012	2013
Summary external debt data								
External debt stocks	**181.7**	**195.7**	**390.6**	**535.9**	**553.2**	**859.4**	**730.6**	**797.5**
Long-term external debt	172.4	185.4	360.5	360.7	388.8	544.3	609.4	654.6
Short-term external debt	0.2	0.4	19.4	70.1	61.1	212.1	18.1	39.6
interest arrears on long-term	0.2	0.4	0.4	0.1	0.1	0.1	0.1	0.6
Use of IMF credit	9.1	9.9	10.7	105.2	103.3	103.0	103.1	103.3
Long-term external debt								
Debt outstanding and disbursed	**172.4**	**185.4**	**360.5**	**360.7**	**388.8**	**544.3**	**609.4**	**654.6**
Public and publicly guaranteed	172.4	185.4	360.1	360.1	388.3	543.8	608.9	654.1
Official creditors	172.4	185.4	210.1	210.1	238.3	293.8	358.9	404.1
Private creditors	0.0	0.0	150.0	150.0	150.0	250.0	250.0	250.0
of which: Bonds	0.0	0.0	150.0	150.0	150.0	250.0	250.0	250.0
Private nonguaranteed	..	..	0.4	0.5	0.5	0.5	0.5	0.5
of which: Bonds	..	..	..	..	..	..	..	..
Disbursements	**7.1**	**14.1**	**13.4**	**15.2**	**32.6**	**315.4**	**78.3**	**60.5**
Public and publicly guaranteed	7.1	14.1	13.2	15.0	32.6	315.4	78.2	60.4
Official creditors	7.1	14.1	13.2	15.0	32.6	65.4	78.2	60.4
Private creditors	0.0	0.0	0.0	0.0	0.0	250.0	0.0	0.0
of which: Bonds	0.0	0.0	0.0	0.0	0.0	250.0	0.0	0.0
Private nonguaranteed	..	..	0.2	0.3	0.0	0.0	0.1	0.0
of which: Bonds	..	..	..	..	..	..	..	..
Principal repayments	**16.9**	**8.5**	**7.8**	**10.4**	**9.1**	**163.6**	**11.2**	**15.1**
Public and publicly guaranteed	16.9	8.5	7.7	10.3	9.1	163.6	11.2	15.0
Official creditors	16.9	8.5	7.7	10.3	9.1	13.6	11.2	15.0
Private creditors	0.0	0.0	0.0	0.0	0.0	150.0	0.0	0.0
of which: Bonds	0.0	0.0	0.0	0.0	0.0	150.0	0.0	0.0
Private nonguaranteed	..	..	0.0	0.0	0.0	0.1	0.1	0.1
of which: Bonds	..	..	..	..	..	..	..	..
Interest payments	**7.7**	**5.5**	**15.8**	**14.4**	**13.3**	**24.9**	**26.7**	**27.9**
Public and publicly guaranteed	7.7	5.5	15.8	14.4	13.3	24.9	26.7	27.9
Official creditors	7.7	5.5	5.5	4.1	3.0	3.3	4.2	5.4
Private creditors	0.0	0.0	10.3	10.3	10.3	21.6	22.5	22.5
of which: Bonds	0.0	0.0	10.3	10.3	10.3	21.6	22.5	22.5
Private nonguaranteed	..	..	0.0	0.0	0.0	0.0	0.0	0.0
of which: Bonds	..	..	..	..	..	..	..	..
Net financial flows								
Net debt inflows	-9.8	-47.5	2.6	55.9	14.5	302.8	-126.9	66.4
Official creditors (incl. IMF)	-9.8	5.5	5.5	4.6	23.5	51.8	67.1	45.4
Private creditors	0.0	-53.0	-2.9	51.2	-9.0	251.0	-194.0	21.0
Long-term	0.0	..	0.1	0.2	0.0	100.0	0.0	0.0
Public and publicly guaranteed	0.0	..	..	..	..	100.0	..	..
Private nonguaranteed	..	..	0.1	0.2	0.0	0.0	0.0	0.0
Short-term	..	-53.0	-3.0	51.0	-9.0	151.0	-194.0	21.0
Net equity inflows								
Foreign direct investment	0.6	155.5	350.5	136.9	350.3	404.6	261.0	272.1
Portfolio equity	..	1.7	1.4	-1.1	0.1	-0.1	..	..
Major economic aggregates								
Gross national income (GNI)	1,717.4	3,050.1	3,542.8	2,914.0	3,125.2	3,636.4	3,755.5	3,855.8
Exports of goods, services & prim. income	1,023.2	1,693.0	2,089.8	1,482.8	1,898.2	2,330.2	2,510.4	2,354.5
Imports of goods, services & prim. income	1,136.4	2,046.1	2,768.0	1,785.3	2,189.2	2,668.4	2,777.9	3,159.2
Primary income on FDI	7.5	132.8	122.3	48.0	143.4	171.2	172.7	..
Personal transfers & comp. of employees	44.0	203.7	146.7	171.2	173.8	160.4	190.6	..
International reserves	411.8	320.9	321.5	569.1	719.4	832.2	920.0	940.9
Ratios								
External debt stocks to exports (%)	17.8	11.6	18.7	36.1	29.1	36.9	29.1	33.9
External debt stocks to GNI (%)	10.6	6.4	11.0	18.4	17.7	23.6	19.5	20.7
Debt service to exports (%)	2.4	0.8	1.2	1.7	1.2	8.2	1.5	1.9
Reserves to external debt stocks (%)	226.7	164.0	82.3	106.2	130.0	96.8	125.9	118.0

Notes:

Long-term private nonguaranteed debt data for 2012 are World Bank staff estimates. Short-term debt is based on data from the BIS.

GABON

(US$ million, unless otherwise indicated)

	2000	2005	2008	2009	2010	2011	2012	2013
Summary external debt data								
External debt stocks	**3,920**	**3,898**	**2,153**	**2,324**	**2,524**	**2,798**	**2,870**	**4,316**
Long-term external debt	3,457	3,564	2,016	1,991	2,128	2,388	2,533	3,817
Short-term external debt	355	246	115	104	170	185	111	273
interest arrears on long-term	63	186	5	1	0	0	0	0
Use of IMF credit	107	88	22	230	226	225	225	226
Long-term external debt								
Debt outstanding and disbursed	**3,457**	**3,564**	**2,016**	**1,991**	**2,128**	**2,388**	**2,533**	**3,817**
Public and publicly guaranteed	3,457	3,564	2,016	1,991	2,128	2,388	2,533	3,817
Official creditors	3,338	3,444	954	893	884	929	981	1,250
Private creditors	119	119	1,062	1,098	1,244	1,459	1,552	2,567
of which: Bonds	0	0	946	901	879	879	875	1,718
Private nonguaranteed	..	..	..	..	..	..	..	..
of which: Bonds	..	..	..	..	..	..	..	..
Disbursements	**34**	**18**	**107**	**261**	**466**	**549**	**385**	**2,103**
Public and publicly guaranteed	34	18	107	261	466	549	385	2,103
Official creditors	13	18	62	147	189	216	165	308
Private creditors	21	0	45	114	276	333	221	1,795
of which: Bonds	0	0	0	0	0	0	0	1,500
Private nonguaranteed	..	..	..	..	..	..	..	..
of which: Bonds	..	..	..	..	..	..	..	..
Principal repayments	**188**	**112**	**2,246**	**261**	**291**	**256**	**259**	**877**
Public and publicly guaranteed	188	112	2,246	261	291	256	259	877
Official creditors	160	63	2,185	222	171	165	118	64
Private creditors	27	48	61	39	120	91	142	813
of which: Bonds	0	0	0	0	23	0	4	657
Private nonguaranteed	..	..	..	..	..	..	..	..
of which: Bonds	..	..	..	..	..	..	..	..
Interest payments	**124**	**52**	**359**	**141**	**131**	**127**	**130**	**246**
Public and publicly guaranteed	124	52	359	141	131	127	130	246
Official creditors	118	46	274	49	32	30	28	31
Private creditors	7	7	85	91	99	97	102	215
of which: Bonds	0	0	80	75	74	72	73	191
Private nonguaranteed	..	..	..	..	..	..	..	..
of which: Bonds	..	..	..	..	..	..	..	..
Net financial flows								
Net debt inflows	-363	-58	-2,268	-7	242	307	52	1,388
Official creditors (incl. IMF)	-140	-70	-2,147	-75	19	51	47	244
Private creditors	-223	12	-121	69	223	257	5	1,144
Long-term	-7	-48	-16	76	156	242	79	982
Public and publicly guaranteed	-7	-48	-16	76	156	242	79	982
Private nonguaranteed	..	..	..	..	..	..	..	..
Short-term	-216	60	-105	-7	67	15	-74	162
Net equity inflows								
Foreign direct investment	-43	321	773	573	499	696	696	856
Portfolio equity	..	..	..	..	..	..	..	..
Major economic aggregates								
Gross national income (GNI)	4,289	7,708	13,836	11,021	12,870	16,566	16,042	17,298
Exports of goods, services & prim. income	3,547	5,639	..	..	..	..	..	..
Imports of goods, services & prim. income	2,483	3,387	..	..	..	..	..	..
Primary income on FDI	473	765	..	..	..	..	..	..
Personal transfers & comp. of employees	6	11	..	..	..	..	..	..
International reserves	190	669	1,923	1,993	1,736	2,157	2,352	..
Ratios								
External debt stocks to exports (%)	110.5	69.1	..	..	..	..	..	..
External debt stocks to GNI (%)	91.4	50.6	15.6	21.1	19.6	16.9	17.9	25.0
Debt service to exports (%)	9.9	3.4	..	..	..	..	..	..
Reserves to external debt stocks (%)	4.8	17.2	89.3	85.8	68.8	77.1	81.9	..

Notes:

Long-term public and publicly guaranteed debt data before 2008 are World Bank staff estimates based on reports provided by the country. Short-term debt is based on data from the BIS. Data include the effects of Paris Club debt buyback agreement signed in 2007.

GAMBIA, THE

(US$ million, unless otherwise indicated)

	2000	2005	2008	2009	2010	2011	2012	2013
Summary external debt data								
External debt stocks	**490.1**	**667.1**	**373.0**	**506.2**	**512.3**	**475.8**	**512.8**	**522.7**
Long-term external debt	438.0	616.5	336.8	387.6	391.0	394.4	395.8	415.4
Short-term external debt	27.3	22.4	15.9	43.4	44.3	1.1	22.6	11.8
interest arrears on long-term	0.0	1.4	1.9	2.4	2.3	1.1	1.6	1.8
Use of IMF credit	24.8	28.1	20.2	75.2	77.0	80.3	94.4	95.5
Long-term external debt								
Debt outstanding and disbursed	**438.0**	**616.5**	**336.8**	**387.6**	**391.0**	**394.4**	**395.8**	**415.4**
Public and publicly guaranteed	438.0	616.5	336.8	387.6	391.0	394.4	395.8	415.4
Official creditors	437.0	616.5	334.3	384.2	384.6	390.3	386.2	404.4
Private creditors	1.0	0.0	2.5	3.4	6.4	4.1	9.6	11.0
of which: Bonds	0.0	0.0	0.0	0.0	0.0	0.0	0.0	0.0
Private nonguaranteed	..	..	..	..	..	..	..	..
of which: Bonds	..	..	..	..	..	..	..	..
Disbursements	**20.7**	**54.3**	**37.3**	**33.5**	**43.2**	**24.3**	**25.2**	**40.0**
Public and publicly guaranteed	20.7	54.3	37.3	33.5	43.2	24.3	25.2	40.0
Official creditors	20.7	54.3	35.8	32.7	36.8	24.3	17.9	36.9
Private creditors	0.0	0.0	1.5	0.8	6.4	0.0	7.3	3.1
of which: Bonds	0.0	0.0	0.0	0.0	0.0	0.0	0.0	0.0
Private nonguaranteed	..	..	..	..	..	..	..	..
of which: Bonds	..	..	..	..	..	..	..	..
Principal repayments	**12.7**	**16.1**	**10.3**	**11.3**	**15.8**	**18.5**	**17.8**	**20.1**
Public and publicly guaranteed	12.7	16.1	10.3	11.3	15.8	18.5	17.8	20.1
Official creditors	12.3	15.8	10.3	11.3	12.6	16.2	15.8	17.9
Private creditors	0.4	0.3	0.0	0.0	3.2	2.2	2.1	2.2
of which: Bonds	0.0	0.0	0.0	0.0	0.0	0.0	0.0	0.0
Private nonguaranteed	..	..	..	..	..	..	..	..
of which: Bonds	..	..	..	..	..	..	..	..
Interest payments	**6.0**	**9.4**	**5.8**	**7.0**	**6.6**	**6.3**	**6.1**	**5.1**
Public and publicly guaranteed	6.0	9.4	5.8	7.0	6.6	6.3	6.1	5.1
Official creditors	5.9	9.4	5.8	7.0	6.6	6.2	5.9	4.9
Private creditors	0.1	0.0	0.0	0.0	0.0	0.1	0.2	0.1
of which: Bonds	0.0	0.0	0.0	0.0	0.0	0.0	0.0	0.0
Private nonguaranteed	..	..	..	..	..	..	..	..
of which: Bonds	..	..	..	..	..	..	..	..
Net financial flows								
Net debt inflows	20.6	33.2	26.3	64.9	31.5	-32.5	42.4	9.7
Official creditors (incl. IMF)	15.8	36.5	31.8	37.1	27.3	11.7	16.1	19.8
Private creditors	4.8	-3.3	-5.5	27.8	4.2	-44.2	26.3	-10.1
Long-term	-0.4	-0.3	1.5	0.8	3.2	-2.2	5.3	0.9
Public and publicly guaranteed	-0.4	-0.3	1.5	0.8	3.2	-2.2	5.3	0.9
Private nonguaranteed	..	..	..	..	..	..	..	..
Short-term	5.2	-3.0	-7.0	27.0	1.0	-42.0	21.0	-11.0
Net equity inflows								
Foreign direct investment	..	53.7	78.6	39.4	37.4	36.2	33.5	25.3
Portfolio equity	..	..	..	..	..	..	..	..
Major economic aggregates								
Gross national income (GNI)	752.7	601.7	940.2	872.6	921.9	865.2	886.4	886.6
Exports of goods, services & prim. income	..	189.8	335.8	290.1	284.9	318.9	343.8	..
Imports of goods, services & prim. income	..	305.0	407.4	362.3	341.3	392.8	467.6	..
Primary income on FDI	..	26.9	42.8	11.7	11.5	11.3	10.2	..
Personal transfers & comp. of employees	..	59.3	64.8	79.8	115.7	107.9	141.0	..
International reserves	109.4	98.3	116.5	224.2	201.6	223.2	236.2	210.6
Ratios								
External debt stocks to exports (%)	..	351.5	111.1	174.5	179.8	149.2	149.2	..
External debt stocks to GNI (%)	65.1	110.9	39.7	58.0	55.6	55.0	57.9	59.0
Debt service to exports (%)	..	15.1	5.1	6.5	8.1	7.9	7.1	..
Reserves to external debt stocks (%)	22.3	14.7	31.2	44.3	39.4	46.9	46.1	40.3

Notes:

Short-term debt is based on data from the BIS. Data include the effects of HIPC and MDRI debt relief.

GEORGIA

(US$ million, unless otherwise indicated)

	2000	2005	2008	2009	2010	2011	2012	2013
Summary external debt data								
External debt stocks	**1,826**	**2,151**	**7,633**	**8,556**	**9,519**	**11,359**	**13,149**	**13,694**
Long-term external debt	1,316	1,663	6,003	6,736	7,284	8,605	10,024	10,744
Short-term external debt	44	50	948	808	963	1,545	2,159	2,369
interest arrears on long-term	1	11	7	7	7	84	389	361
Use of IMF credit	466	438	682	1,012	1,272	1,210	965	580
Long-term external debt								
Debt outstanding and disbursed	**1,316**	**1,663**	**6,003**	**6,736**	**7,284**	**8,605**	**10,024**	**10,744**
Public and publicly guaranteed	1,274	1,531	2,974	3,529	4,141	4,343	4,876	4,986
Official creditors	1,272	1,529	1,780	2,155	2,450	2,706	3,097	3,384
Private creditors	2	2	1,194	1,375	1,691	1,637	1,778	1,603
of which: Bonds	0	0	500	500	750	815	1,065	1,000
Private nonguaranteed	42	132	3,029	3,207	3,143	4,262	5,149	5,758
of which: Bonds	..	..	..	..	..	..	750	900
Disbursements	**65**	**146**	**893**	**1,147**	**1,190**	**1,785**	**2,375**	**1,380**
Public and publicly guaranteed	37	76	725	678	815	843	690	332
Official creditors	37	76	225	427	401	343	431	326
Private creditors	0	0	500	250	414	500	258	6
of which: Bonds	0	0	500	0	250	500	250	0
Private nonguaranteed	28	69	168	469	375	942	1,685	1,048
of which: Bonds		..	..	..	..	..	750	150
Principal repayments	**42**	**103**	**423**	**474**	**510**	**1,199**	**956**	**940**
Public and publicly guaranteed	41	80	110	140	169	620	165	238
Official creditors	41	80	40	70	71	67	48	56
Private creditors	0	0	70	70	97	553	118	182
of which: Bonds	0	0	0	0	0	435	0	65
Private nonguaranteed	2	23	314	334	342	579	790	702
of which: Bonds	..	..	..	..	..	..	..	..
Interest payments	**43**	**28**	**225**	**251**	**247**	**307**	**404**	**365**
Public and publicly guaranteed	42	24	54	77	87	139	112	130
Official creditors	42	24	28	31	39	35	38	43
Private creditors	0	0	27	45	47	104	73	87
of which: Bonds	0	0	19	38	38	94	64	79
Private nonguaranteed	1	4	171	174	160	167	292	235
of which: Bonds	..	..	..	..	..	..	29	70
Net financial flows								
Net debt inflows	33	-30	1,065	846	1,111	1,031	1,484	295
Official creditors (incl. IMF)	-29	-17	406	670	605	216	139	-113
Private creditors	62	-14	659	176	505	815	1,345	408
Long-term	26	46	285	316	350	310	1,036	170
Public and publicly guaranteed	..	0	430	181	316	-53	141	-176
Private nonguaranteed	26	47	-145	136	34	363	895	347
Short-term	36	-60	374	-140	156	505	309	238
Net equity inflows								
Foreign direct investment	131	383	1,175	565	698	840	908	978
Portfolio equity	..	3	115	12	-22	-7	74	1
Major economic aggregates								
Gross national income (GNI)	3,175	6,473	12,680	10,679	11,416	14,012	15,700	15,840
Exports of goods, services & prim. income	1,007	2,415	4,244	3,672	4,591	6,000	7,099	8,098
Imports of goods, services & prim. income	1,433	3,469	8,115	5,779	6,885	9,169	10,357	10,516
Primary income on FDI	36	116	358	262	470	800	747	805
Personal transfers & comp. of employees	274	446	1,065	1,112	1,184	1,547	1,770	1,945
International reserves	116	479	1,480	2,110	2,264	2,818	2,873	2,823
Ratios								
External debt stocks to exports (%)	181.3	89.1	179.8	233.0	207.4	189.3	185.2	169.1
External debt stocks to GNI (%)	57.5	33.2	60.2	80.1	83.4	81.1	83.7	86.4
Debt service to exports (%)	12.5	8.1	16.7	21.0	17.5	26.8	23.2	22.0
Reserves to external debt stocks (%)	6.4	22.2	19.4	24.7	23.8	24.8	21.8	20.6

GHANA

(US$ million, unless otherwise indicated)

	2000	2005	2008	2009	2010	2011	2012	2013
Summary external debt data								
External debt stocks	**6,254**	**7,168**	**5,679**	**7,182**	**9,300**	**11,282**	**12,568**	**15,832**
Long-term external debt	5,307	6,045	4,074	5,024	6,100	7,386	8,701	11,039
Short-term external debt	572	616	1,346	1,332	2,263	2,795	2,614	3,570
interest arrears on long-term	10	38	8	50	27	105	143	231
Use of IMF credit	375	507	259	826	937	1,101	1,253	1,223
Long-term external debt								
Debt outstanding and disbursed	**5,307**	**6,045**	**4,074**	**5,024**	**6,100**	**7,386**	**8,701**	**11,039**
Public and publicly guaranteed	5,050	6,045	4,074	5,024	6,100	7,386	8,701	11,039
Official creditors	4,705	5,495	2,596	3,325	4,217	5,133	6,116	6,902
Private creditors	345	551	1,478	1,699	1,882	2,253	2,585	4,137
of which: Bonds	0	0	750	750	750	750	750	1,531
Private nonguaranteed	257	..	..	..	..	..	..	..
of which: Bonds	250	..	..	..	..	..	..	..
Disbursements	**417**	**558**	**756**	**1,006**	**1,297**	**1,534**	**1,546**	**2,807**
Public and publicly guaranteed	417	558	756	1,006	1,297	1,534	1,546	2,807
Official creditors	342	484	600	726	999	1,025	1,073	900
Private creditors	75	74	156	279	299	509	473	1,907
of which: Bonds	0	0	0	0	0	0	0	1,000
Private nonguaranteed	..	..	..	..	..	..	..	..
of which: Bonds	..	..	..	..	..	..	..	..
Principal repayments	**217**	**188**	**135**	**136**	**146**	**198**	**270**	**563**
Public and publicly guaranteed	214	188	135	136	146	198	270	563
Official creditors	141	127	64	56	75	88	117	163
Private creditors	73	61	71	80	71	109	153	401
of which: Bonds	0	0	0	0	0	0	0	219
Private nonguaranteed	3	..	..	..	..	..	..	..
of which: Bonds	..	..	..	..	..	..	..	..
Interest payments	**95**	**87**	**129**	**107**	**159**	**97**	**170**	**265**
Public and publicly guaranteed	80	87	129	107	159	97	170	265
Official creditors	64	57	34	46	72	61	79	113
Private creditors	16	29	95	60	87	36	91	151
of which: Bonds	0	0	64	32	64	0	32	54
Private nonguaranteed	14	..	..	..	..	..	..	..
of which: Bonds	14	..	..	..	..	..	..	..
Net financial flows								
Net debt inflows	62	269	704	918	2,230	1,962	1,206	3,079
Official creditors (incl. IMF)	199	365	536	775	1,048	1,108	1,106	705
Private creditors	-137	-96	168	143	1,182	854	101	2,374
Long-term	-1	13	85	199	228	400	320	1,506
Public and publicly guaranteed	2	13	85	199	228	400	320	1,506
Private nonguaranteed	-3	..	..	..	..	..	..	..
Short-term	-136	-109	83	-56	954	454	-219	868
Net equity inflows								
Foreign direct investment	166	145	1,429	1,940	2,527	3,222	3,295	3,226
Portfolio equity	..	..	..	535	18	1	..	..
Major economic aggregates								
Gross national income (GNI)	4,836	10,601	28,412	25,885	31,640	38,309	39,594	46,796
Exports of goods, services & prim. income	2,456	3,952	7,156	7,735	9,490	14,712	16,858	16,490
Imports of goods, services & prim. income	3,473	6,851	12,695	11,710	14,560	20,813	24,186	24,134
Primary income on FDI	17	94	-80	495	396	1,062	1,915	..
Personal transfers & comp. of employees	32	99	126	114	136	152	138	..
International reserves	232	1,753	1,770	3,386	4,763	5,483	5,368	5,249
Ratios								
External debt stocks to exports (%)	254.6	181.4	79.4	92.9	98.0	76.7	74.6	96.0
External debt stocks to GNI (%)	129.3	67.6	20.0	27.7	29.4	29.5	31.7	33.8
Debt service to exports (%)	16.0	8.4	4.2	3.6	3.8	2.3	3.1	5.6
Reserves to external debt stocks (%)	3.7	24.5	31.2	47.2	51.2	48.6	42.7	33.2

Notes:

Long-term private nonguaranteed debt data only cover bonds. Short-term debt is based on data from the BIS. Data include the effects of MDRI debt relief.

GRENADA

(US$ million, unless otherwise indicated)

	2000	2005	2008	2009	2010	2011	2012	2013
Summary external debt data								
External debt stocks	**203.5**	**407.2**	**551.8**	**571.4**	**578.1**	**566.9**	**590.6**	**585.6**
Long-term external debt	180.7	391.3	477.2	494.6	493.3	487.2	489.9	489.5
Short-term external debt	21.6	6.3	60.2	36.3	38.6	33.8	55.2	51.0
interest arrears on long-term	4.5	4.3	11.2	13.3	14.6	15.8	39.2	47.0
Use of IMF credit	1.2	9.7	14.4	40.5	46.3	45.9	45.5	45.1
Long-term external debt								
Debt outstanding and disbursed	**180.7**	**391.3**	**477.2**	**494.6**	**493.3**	**487.2**	**489.9**	**489.5**
Public and publicly guaranteed	180.7	391.3	477.2	494.6	493.3	487.2	489.9	489.5
Official creditors	116.8	172.4	257.2	274.6	277.7	273.2	275.8	275.5
Private creditors	63.9	218.9	219.9	219.9	215.6	214.0	214.0	214.0
of which: Bonds	27.4	214.3	210.3	210.3	210.3	210.3	210.3	210.3
Private nonguaranteed	..	..	..	..	..	..	..	..
of which: Bonds	..	..	..	..	..	..	..	..
Disbursements	**77.6**	**38.5**	**30.5**	**25.7**	**21.1**	**6.3**	**8.7**	**28.3**
Public and publicly guaranteed	77.6	38.5	30.5	25.7	21.1	6.3	8.7	28.3
Official creditors	19.8	38.5	30.5	25.7	21.1	6.3	8.7	28.3
Private creditors	57.8	0.0	0.0	0.0	0.0	0.0	0.0	0.0
of which: Bonds	26.6	0.0	0.0	0.0	0.0	0.0	0.0	0.0
Private nonguaranteed	..	..	..	..	..	..	..	..
of which: Bonds	..	..	..	..	..	..	..	..
Principal repayments	**10.1**	**5.6**	**8.9**	**9.4**	**15.4**	**13.5**	**6.3**	**28.9**
Public and publicly guaranteed	10.1	5.6	8.9	9.4	15.4	13.5	6.3	28.9
Official creditors	6.3	5.3	8.9	9.4	11.0	10.6	6.3	28.9
Private creditors	3.7	0.4	0.0	0.0	4.4	2.9	0.0	0.0
of which: Bonds	0.0	0.0	0.0	0.0	0.0	0.0	0.0	0.0
Private nonguaranteed	..	..	..	..	..	..	..	..
of which: Bonds	..	..	..	..	..	..	..	..
Interest payments	**3.4**	**3.3**	**8.3**	**11.1**	**10.9**	**11.5**	**8.2**	**5.9**
Public and publicly guaranteed	3.4	3.3	8.3	11.1	10.9	11.5	8.2	5.9
Official creditors	2.3	3.3	5.6	5.8	5.7	6.4	3.6	5.8
Private creditors	1.1	0.0	2.6	5.4	5.2	5.1	4.6	0.0
of which: Bonds	0.0	0.0	2.1	5.1	5.1	5.1	4.6	0.0
Private nonguaranteed	..	..	..	..	..	..	..	..
of which: Bonds	..	..	..	..	..	..	..	..
Net financial flows								
Net debt inflows	63.4	-28.1	39.3	0.0	13.1	-13.4	-0.1	-13.1
Official creditors (incl. IMF)	13.4	33.2	27.3	26.0	16.5	-4.5	1.9	-1.1
Private creditors	50.0	-61.4	12.0	-26.0	-3.4	-8.9	-2.0	-12.0
Long-term	54.1	-0.4	..	..	-4.4	-2.9	..	..
Public and publicly guaranteed	54.1	-0.4	..	..	-4.4	-2.9	..	..
Private nonguaranteed	..	..	..	..	..	..	..	..
Short-term	-4.1	-61.0	12.0	-26.0	1.0	-6.0	-2.0	-12.0
Net equity inflows								
Foreign direct investment	37.4	49.6	115.7	82.8	42.3	29.4	16.5	58.0
Portfolio equity	..	..	..	..	..	..	..	..
Major economic aggregates								
Gross national income (GNI)	489.5	672.1	783.3	708.1	731.1	747.0	767.4	806.3
Exports of goods, services & prim. income	240.8	160.3	215.9	195.4	190.9	202.0	213.5	216.7
Imports of goods, services & prim. income	349.0	435.9	502.5	432.1	426.6	433.0	437.0	455.9
Primary income on FDI	27.8	22.7	31.7	55.4	30.8	20.6	18.8	19.6
Personal transfers & comp. of employees	46.4	26.8	28.9	27.7	28.5	28.9	29.3	29.6
International reserves	57.7	94.3	105.3	129.1	119.2	120.7	119.5	150.6
Ratios								
External debt stocks to exports (%)	84.5	254.0	255.6	292.5	302.8	280.7	276.6	270.2
External debt stocks to GNI (%)	41.6	60.6	70.4	80.7	79.1	75.9	77.0	72.6
Debt service to exports (%)	6.0	6.6	10.0	12.0	14.0	12.6	7.2	16.5
Reserves to external debt stocks (%)	28.3	23.1	19.1	22.6	20.6	21.3	20.2	25.7

Notes:

Short-term debt is based on data from the BIS.

GUATEMALA

(US$ million, unless otherwise indicated)

	2000	2005	2008	2009	2010	2011	2012	2013
Summary external debt data								
External debt stocks	**3,948**	**9,506**	**13,821**	**14,822**	**15,039**	**16,277**	**14,053**	**16,823**
Long-term external debt	2,740	8,014	11,627	13,281	13,144	13,703	13,049	15,800
Short-term external debt	1,172	1,453	2,151	1,226	1,585	2,265	695	714
interest arrears on long-term	317	414	0	0	0	0	0	0
Use of IMF credit	36	40	43	315	309	308	309	309
Long-term external debt								
Debt outstanding and disbursed	**2,740**	**8,014**	**11,627**	**13,281**	**13,144**	**13,703**	**13,049**	**15,800**
Public and publicly guaranteed	2,598	3,720	4,383	4,923	5,555	5,349	6,298	7,058
Official creditors	2,156	2,484	3,427	3,968	4,600	4,719	4,968	5,311
Private creditors	442	1,237	955	955	955	630	1,330	1,748
of which: Bonds	245	1,105	955	955	955	630	1,330	1,730
Private nonguaranteed	142	4,294	7,245	8,358	7,589	8,354	6,751	8,741
of which: Bonds	..	50	55	5	5	155	355	355
Disbursements	**220**	**1,639**	**958**	**941**	**1,471**	**1,025**	**1,748**	**3,375**
Public and publicly guaranteed	220	144	396	807	879	393	1,247	1,392
Official creditors	220	144	396	807	879	393	547	674
Private creditors	0	0	0	0	0	0	700	718
of which: Bonds	0	0	0	0	0	0	700	700
Private nonguaranteed	..	1,495	562	135	592	633	502	1,983
of which: Bonds	..	..	5	..	..	150	200	..
Principal repayments	**192**	**570**	**917**	**1,086**	**949**	**1,347**	**853**	**624**
Public and publicly guaranteed	172	200	260	269	264	604	273	596
Official creditors	139	199	260	269	264	279	273	296
Private creditors	32	1	0	0	0	325	0	300
of which: Bonds	31	0	0	0	0	325	0	300
Private nonguaranteed	20	371	656	817	685	743	580	28
of which: Bonds	..	..	..	50	..	..	..	..
Interest payments	**153**	**420**	**621**	**657**	**636**	**684**	**598**	**601**
Public and publicly guaranteed	134	203	257	258	284	284	274	291
Official creditors	112	102	169	170	196	196	199	207
Private creditors	23	101	88	88	88	88	75	84
of which: Bonds	22	101	88	88	88	88	75	84
Private nonguaranteed	19	217	365	399	352	401	324	310
of which: Bonds	..	5	5	0	0	7	20	26
Net financial flows								
Net debt inflows	62	906	188	-1,070	881	359	-675	2,770
Official creditors (incl. IMF)	80	-56	136	537	615	114	273	378
Private creditors	-18	961	52	-1,607	266	245	-948	2,392
Long-term	-52	1,124	-95	-682	-93	-435	622	2,373
Public and publicly guaranteed	-32	-1	0	0	0	-325	700	418
Private nonguaranteed	-20	1,125	-95	-682	-93	-110	-78	1,955
Short-term	34	-163	147	-925	359	680	-1,570	19
Net equity inflows								
Foreign direct investment	230	392	679	581	907	968	1,026	913
Portfolio equity	..	..	..	..	..	..	..	..
Major economic aggregates								
Gross national income (GNI)	19,065	26,726	38,199	36,632	40,127	46,004	49,091	52,557
Exports of goods, services & prim. income	4,077	7,069	10,548	9,792	11,165	13,171	12,985	13,168
Imports of goods, services & prim. income	5,991	11,886	16,888	14,145	16,674	19,904	19,939	20,631
Primary income on FDI	248	370	886	951	1,001	1,453	1,112	1,020
Personal transfers & comp. of employees	596	3,067	4,460	4,019	4,232	4,524	5,031	5,371
International reserves	1,746	3,664	4,462	4,964	5,637	5,835	6,325	7,002
Ratios								
External debt stocks to exports (%)	96.8	134.5	131.0	151.4	134.7	123.6	108.2	127.8
External debt stocks to GNI (%)	20.7	35.6	36.2	40.5	37.5	35.4	28.6	32.0
Debt service to exports (%)	9.7	14.8	15.3	18.0	14.4	15.7	11.7	9.5
Reserves to external debt stocks (%)	44.2	38.5	32.3	33.5	37.5	35.8	45.0	41.6

Notes:

Long-term private nonguaranteed debt data are World Bank staff estimates based on reports provided by the country. Short-term debt before 2012 is based on data from the BIS.

GUINEA

(US$ million, unless otherwise indicated)

	2000	2005	2008	2009	2010	2011	2012	2013
Summary external debt data								
External debt stocks	**3,083**	**2,968**	**3,165**	**3,128**	**3,127**	**3,139**	**1,097**	**1,198**
Long-term external debt	2,650	2,771	2,873	2,868	2,798	2,849	842	846
Short-term external debt	298	84	194	40	124	91	40	108
interest arrears on long-term	81	84	38	38	56	80	40	39
Use of IMF credit	136	113	98	220	205	199	215	243
Long-term external debt								
Debt outstanding and disbursed	**2,650**	**2,771**	**2,873**	**2,868**	**2,798**	**2,849**	**842**	**846**
Public and publicly guaranteed	2,650	2,771	2,873	2,868	2,798	2,849	842	846
Official creditors	2,621	2,740	2,855	2,850	2,780	2,831	830	834
Private creditors	29	31	18	19	18	18	12	12
of which: Bonds	0	0	0	0	0	0	0	0
Private nonguaranteed	..	..	..	..	..	..	..	..
of which: Bonds	..	..	..	..	..	..	..	..
Disbursements	**71**	**93**	**63**	**42**	**32**	**33**	**39**	**54**
Public and publicly guaranteed	71	93	63	42	32	33	39	54
Official creditors	71	92	63	42	32	33	39	54
Private creditors	0	1	0	0	0	0	0	0
of which: Bonds	0	0	0	0	0	0	0	0
Private nonguaranteed	..	..	..	..	..	..	..	..
of which: Bonds	..		..	..	..	..	..	..
Principal repayments	**91**	**84**	**78**	**77**	**45**	**133**	**90**	**50**
Public and publicly guaranteed	91	84	78	77	45	133	90	50
Official creditors	91	84	78	77	45	133	90	50
Private creditors	0	0	0	0	0	0	0	0
of which: Bonds	0	0	0	0	0	0	0	0
Private nonguaranteed	..	..	..	..	..	..	..	..
of which: Bonds	..	..	..	..	..	..	..	..
Interest payments	**41**	**45**	**27**	**24**	**17**	**31**	**17**	**9**
Public and publicly guaranteed	41	45	27	24	17	31	17	9
Official creditors	41	45	27	24	17	31	17	9
Private creditors	0	0	0	0	0	0	0	0
of which: Bonds	0	0	0	0	0	0	0	0
Private nonguaranteed	..	..	..	..	..	..	..	..
of which: Bonds	..	..	..	..	..	..	..	..
Net financial flows								
Net debt inflows	-41	-17	105	-202	42	-163	-47	100
Official creditors (incl. IMF)	-28	-18	-7	-48	-24	-106	-36	31
Private creditors	-13	1	112	-154	66	-57	-11	69
Long-term	0	1	..	..	..	..	..	..
Public and publicly guaranteed	0	1	..	..	..	..	..	..
Private nonguaranteed	..	..	..	..	..	..	..	..
Short-term	-12	..	112	-154	66	-57	-11	69
Net equity inflows								
Foreign direct investment	10	105	379	141	101	955	605	25
Portfolio equity	..	..	..	..	..	..	..	..
Major economic aggregates								
Gross national income (GNI)	2,922	2,658	3,993	4,108	4,302	4,625	5,220	5,745
Exports of goods, services & prim. income	758	929	1,455	1,144	1,549	1,528	2,118	..
Imports of goods, services & prim. income	973	1,079	1,911	1,581	1,892	2,829	3,289	..
Primary income on FDI	8	..	14	88	0	26	39	..
Personal transfers & comp. of employees	1	42	62	52	46	65	66	..
International reserves	148	95	3	129	116	103	..	..
Ratios								
External debt stocks to exports (%)	406.9	319.5	217.5	273.4	201.9	205.4	51.8	..
External debt stocks to GNI (%)	105.5	111.7	79.3	76.2	72.7	67.9	21.0	20.8
Debt service to exports (%)	20.7	16.8	8.8	10.1	4.7	11.2	7.0	..
Reserves to external debt stocks (%)	4.8	3.2	0.1	4.1	3.7	3.3	..	..

Notes:

Long-term public and publicly guaranteed debt data are World Bank staff estimates based on the original terms of the loans. Short-term debt is based on data from the BIS. Data include the effects of Paris Club debt restructuring agreement signed in 2010, 2012 and HIPC debt relief.

GUINEA-BISSAU

(US$ million, unless otherwise indicated)

	2000	2005	2008	2009	2010	2011	2012	2013
Summary external debt data								
External debt stocks	**947.8**	**1,021.7**	**1,098.3**	**1,149.0**	**1,128.6**	**283.7**	**279.5**	**277.4**
Long-term external debt	821.1	887.8	941.4	963.3	977.3	218.5	213.4	212.2
Short-term external debt	100.4	120.7	146.5	154.5	126.6	33.1	34.1	33.1
interest arrears on long-term	87.4	118.7	144.5	147.5	125.6	33.1	33.1	33.1
Use of IMF credit	26.3	13.2	10.5	31.3	24.7	32.0	32.0	32.1
Long-term external debt								
Debt outstanding and disbursed	**821.1**	**887.8**	**941.4**	**963.3**	**977.3**	**218.5**	**213.4**	**212.2**
Public and publicly guaranteed	821.1	887.8	941.4	963.3	977.3	218.5	213.4	212.2
Official creditors	821.1	887.8	941.4	963.3	977.3	218.5	213.4	212.2
Private creditors	0.0	0.0	0.0	0.0	0.0	0.0	0.0	0.0
of which: Bonds	0.0	0.0	0.0	0.0	0.0	0.0	0.0	0.0
Private nonguaranteed	..	..	..	..	..	..	..	..
of which: Bonds	..	..	..	..	..	..	..	..
Disbursements	**13.6**	**15.6**	**7.6**	**6.0**	**4.0**	**9.1**	**2.7**	**1.0**
Public and publicly guaranteed	13.6	15.6	7.6	6.0	4.0	9.1	2.7	1.0
Official creditors	13.6	15.6	7.6	6.0	4.0	9.1	2.7	1.0
Private creditors	0.0	0.0	0.0	0.0	0.0	0.0	0.0	0.0
of which: Bonds	0.0	0.0	0.0	0.0	0.0	0.0	0.0	0.0
Private nonguaranteed	..	..	..	..	..	..	..	..
of which: Bonds	..	..	..	..	..	..	..	..
Principal repayments	**2.6**	**1.0**	**4.1**	**4.7**	**5.8**	**4.5**	**6.3**	**1.1**
Public and publicly guaranteed	2.6	1.0	4.1	4.7	5.8	4.5	6.3	1.1
Official creditors	2.4	1.0	4.1	4.7	5.8	4.5	6.3	1.1
Private creditors	0.2	0.0	0.0	0.0	0.0	0.0	0.0	0.0
of which: Bonds	0.0	0.0	0.0	0.0	0.0	0.0	0.0	0.0
Private nonguaranteed	..	..	..	..	..	..	..	..
of which: Bonds	..	..	..	..	..	..	..	..
Interest payments	**1.6**	**2.0**	**3.4**	**3.7**	**3.3**	**0.5**	**0.6**	**0.4**
Public and publicly guaranteed	1.6	2.0	3.4	3.7	3.3	0.5	0.6	0.4
Official creditors	1.6	2.0	3.4	3.7	3.3	0.5	0.6	0.4
Private creditors	0.0	0.0	0.0	0.0	0.0	0.0	0.0	0.0
of which: Bonds	0.0	0.0	0.0	0.0	0.0	0.0	0.0	0.0
Private nonguaranteed	..	..	..	..	..	..	..	..
of which: Bonds	..	..	..	..	..	..	..	..
Net financial flows								
Net debt inflows	29.4	10.4	2.1	7.4	-0.2	11.2	-2.7	-1.1
Official creditors (incl. IMF)	19.6	11.4	7.1	2.4	5.8	12.2	-3.7	-0.1
Private creditors	9.8	-1.0	-5.0	5.0	-6.0	-1.0	1.0	-1.0
Long-term	-0.2	..	..	..	..	..	..	..
Public and publicly guaranteed	-0.2	..	..	..	..	..	..	..
Private nonguaranteed	..	..	..	..	..	..	..	..
Short-term	10.0	-1.0	-5.0	5.0	-6.0	-1.0	1.0	-1.0
Net equity inflows								
Foreign direct investment	0.7	5.9	5.1	17.5	33.2	25.0	6.6	14.5
Portfolio equity	..	..	..	-0.2	2.7	..	..	..
Major economic aggregates								
Gross national income (GNI)	203.1	561.4	829.4	822.4	834.5	967.1	821.5	857.8
Exports of goods, services & prim. income	..	95.2	172.1	163.4	183.8	297.9	156.3	..
Imports of goods, services & prim. income	..	156.9	298.9	308.9	314.6	373.7	290.5	..
Primary income on FDI	..	..	0.3	5.6	5.7	..	..	..
Personal transfers & comp. of employees	8.0	19.9	49.5	48.9	45.9	..	..	..
International reserves	66.8	79.8	124.6	168.6	156.4	220.0	164.6	186.3
Ratios								
External debt stocks to exports (%)	..	1072.9	638.2	703.2	614.0	95.2	178.8	..
External debt stocks to GNI (%)	466.8	182.0	132.4	139.7	135.2	29.3	34.0	32.3
Debt service to exports (%)	..	6.7	5.7	6.2	9.5	1.7	4.4	..
Reserves to external debt stocks (%)	7.0	7.8	11.3	14.7	13.9	77.6	58.9	67.1

Notes:

Long-term public and publicly guaranteed debt data are World Bank staff estimates. Short-term debt is based on data from the BIS. Data include the effects of Paris Club debt restructuring agreement and HIPC and MDRI debt relief.

GUYANA

(US$ million, unless otherwise indicated)

	2000	2005	2008	2009	2010	2011	2012	2013
Summary external debt data								
External debt stocks	**1,384**	**1,237**	**850**	**1,172**	**1,485**	**1,846**	**1,974**	**2,303**
Long-term external debt	1,129	1,043	675	781	885	1,054	1,215	1,116
Short-term external debt	119	82	96	196	410	609	588	1,027
interest arrears on long-term	67	82	96	97	103	107	111	111
Use of IMF credit	136	112	79	195	190	182	171	160
Long-term external debt								
Debt outstanding and disbursed	**1,129**	**1,043**	**675**	**781**	**885**	**1,054**	**1,215**	**1,116**
Public and publicly guaranteed	1,125	1,041	675	779	885	1,054	1,215	1,116
Official creditors	1,080	1,033	654	758	864	1,034	1,194	1,095
Private creditors	45	9	21	21	21	21	21	21
of which: Bonds	27	0	0	0	0	0	0	0
Private nonguaranteed	4	2	0	2	0	0	..	0
of which: Bonds	..	..	..	..	..	..	..	..
Disbursements	**64**	**104**	**138**	**105**	**123**	**188**	**279**	**200**
Public and publicly guaranteed	64	104	138	105	123	188	279	200
Official creditors	64	104	138	105	123	188	279	200
Private creditors	0	0	0	0	0	0	0	0
of which: Bonds	0	0	0	0	0	0	0	0
Private nonguaranteed	..	..	..	..	0	0	..	..
of which: Bonds	..	..	..	..	..	..	..	..
Principal repayments	**23**	**16**	**16**	**8**	**16**	**20**	**119**	**21**
Public and publicly guaranteed	22	15	16	8	16	20	119	21
Official creditors	22	15	16	8	16	20	119	21
Private creditors	0	0	0	0	0	0	0	0
of which: Bonds	0	0	0	0	0	0	0	0
Private nonguaranteed	0	0	..	0	..	..	..	..
of which: Bonds	..	..	..	..	..	..	..	..
Interest payments	**26**	**10**	**10**	**11**	**11**	**13**	**13**	**14**
Public and publicly guaranteed	26	10	10	10	11	13	13	14
Official creditors	26	10	10	10	11	13	13	14
Private creditors	0	0	0	0	0	0	0	0
of which: Bonds	0	0	0	0	0	0	0	0
Private nonguaranteed	0	0	..	0	..	..	..	..
of which: Bonds	..	..	..	..	..	..	..	..
Net financial flows								
Net debt inflows	21	76	122	195	314	355	124	607
Official creditors (incl. IMF)	34	108	122	96	106	160	149	168
Private creditors	-14	-32	..	99	208	195	-25	439
Long-term	0	-1	..	0	0	0	..	0
Public and publicly guaranteed	0	0	..	..	..	..	..	0
Private nonguaranteed	0	0	..	0	0	0	..	..
Short-term	-13	-31	..	99	208	195	-25	439
Net equity inflows								
Foreign direct investment	67	18	34	31	39	46	42	29
Portfolio equity	..	..	..	..	..	..	..	..
Major economic aggregates								
Gross national income (GNI)	661	804	1,908	2,009	2,272	2,567	2,850	3,074
Exports of goods, services & prim. income	684	697	1,055	978	1,183	1,479	1,764	1,594
Imports of goods, services & prim. income	813	960	1,705	1,509	1,709	2,265	2,550	2,364
Primary income on FDI	6	7	12	13	13	18	10	5
Personal transfers & comp. of employees	27	201	274	262	368	412	469	..
International reserves	305	252	356	631	782	802	864	784
Ratios								
External debt stocks to exports (%)	202.4	177.5	80.6	119.8	125.5	124.8	111.9	144.5
External debt stocks to GNI (%)	209.5	153.7	44.6	58.3	65.4	71.9	69.3	74.9
Debt service to exports (%)	10.2	5.0	2.5	2.1	2.7	3.1	8.6	4.9
Reserves to external debt stocks (%)	22.0	20.4	41.9	53.9	52.7	43.4	43.8	34.0

Notes:

Principal payment shown from 2012 include rice for oil deal. Data include the effects of HIPC and MDRI debt relief. Short-term debt is based on data from the BIS.

HAITI

(US$ million, unless otherwise indicated)

	2000	2005	2008	2009	2010	2011	2012	2013
Summary external debt data								
External debt stocks	**1,203**	**1,347**	**1,964**	**1,448**	**953**	**750**	**1,122**	**1,271**
Long-term external debt	1,056	1,278	1,838	1,158	818	602	953	1,092
Short-term external debt	90	28	0	0	0	0	0	0
interest arrears on long-term	1	15	0	0	0	0	0	0
Use of IMF credit	57	41	126	291	135	148	169	178
Long-term external debt								
Debt outstanding and disbursed	**1,056**	**1,278**	**1,838**	**1,158**	**818**	**602**	**953**	**1,092**
Public and publicly guaranteed	1,056	1,278	1,838	1,158	818	602	953	1,092
Official creditors	1,056	1,278	1,838	1,158	818	602	953	1,092
Private creditors	0	0	0	0	0	0	0	0
of which: Bonds	0	0	0	0	0	0	0	0
Private nonguaranteed	..	..	..	..	..	..	..	..
of which: Bonds	..	..	..	..	..	..	..	..
Disbursements	**51**	**77**	**348**	**212**	**284**	**341**	**347**	**145**
Public and publicly guaranteed	51	77	348	212	284	341	347	145
Official creditors	51	77	348	212	284	341	347	145
Private creditors	0	0	0	0	0	0	0	0
of which: Bonds	0	0	0	0	0	0	0	0
Private nonguaranteed	..	..	..	..	..	..	..	..
of which: Bonds	..	..	..	..	..	..	..	..
Principal repayments	**19**	**34**	**34**	**26**	**122**	**2**	**0**	**5**
Public and publicly guaranteed	19	34	34	26	122	2	0	5
Official creditors	19	34	34	26	122	2	0	5
Private creditors	0	0	0	0	0	0	0	0
of which: Bonds	0	0	0	0	0	0	0	0
Private nonguaranteed	..	..	..	..	..	..	..	..
of which: Bonds	..	..	..	..	..	..	..	..
Interest payments	**15**	**17**	**23**	**15**	**8**	**3**	**3**	**4**
Public and publicly guaranteed	15	17	23	15	8	3	3	4
Official creditors	15	17	23	15	8	3	3	4
Private creditors	0	0	0	0	.0	0	0	0
of which: Bonds	0	0	0	0	0	0	0	0
Private nonguaranteed	..	..	..	..	..	..	..	..
of which: Bonds	..	..	..	..	..	..	..	..
Net financial flows								
Net debt inflows	20	21	364	243	286	351	369	150
Official creditors (incl. IMF)	26	55	364	243	286	351	369	150
Private creditors	-6	-34	..	..	..	..	..	..
Long-term	..	..	..	..	..	..	..	..
Public and publicly guaranteed	..	..	..	..	..	..	..	..
Private nonguaranteed	..	..	..	..	..	..	..	..
Short-term	-6	-34	..	..	..	..	..	..
Net equity inflows								
Foreign direct investment	13	26	30	55	178	119	156	186
Portfolio equity	..	..	..	..	..	..	..	..
Major economic aggregates								
Gross national income (GNI)	..	4,228	6,554	6,597	6,645	7,558	7,959	8,521
Exports of goods, services & prim. income	504	605	945	1,065	1,049	1,356	1,400	1,608
Imports of goods, services & prim. income	1,378	1,888	2,876	2,823	4,298	4,437	4,199	4,435
Primary income on FDI	..	..	..	..	..	..	..	..
Personal transfers & comp. of employees	578	986	1,370	1,376	1,474	1,571	..	..
International reserves	182	133	541	789	1,335	1,195	1,284	1,736
Ratios								
External debt stocks to exports (%)	238.9	222.6	207.8	136.0	90.8	55.3	80.1	79.0
External debt stocks to GNI (%)	..	31.9	30.0	22.0	14.3	9.9	14.1	14.9
Debt service to exports (%)	9.2	9.5	6.1	4.2	12.5	0.4	0.3	0.6
Reserves to external debt stocks (%)	15.1	9.9	27.6	54.4	140.1	159.2	114.5	136.6

Notes:

Short-term debt before 2007 is based on data from the BIS. Short-term debt since 2007 is based on reports provided by the country. Data include the effects of Paris Club restructuring agreements signed in 2006 and 2009, and HIPC and MDRI debt relief.

HONDURAS

(US$ million, unless otherwise indicated)

	2000	2005	2008	2009	2010	2011	2012	2013
Summary external debt data								
External debt stocks	**5,478**	**5,170**	**3,489**	**3,806**	**3,977**	**4,388**	**5,055**	**6,831**
Long-term external debt	4,863	4,654	2,963	3,330	3,382	3,905	4,444	6,116
Short-term external debt	374	321	466	249	374	267	402	512
interest arrears on long-term	35	12	3	10	11	6	6	4
Use of IMF credit	241	195	61	226	220	215	209	203
Long-term external debt								
Debt outstanding and disbursed	**4,863**	**4,654**	**2,963**	**3,330**	**3,382**	**3,905**	**4,444**	**6,116**
Public and publicly guaranteed	4,303	4,145	2,306	2,451	2,803	3,186	3,646	5,170
Official creditors	4,201	4,090	2,269	2,364	2,719	3,106	3,544	3,983
Private creditors	102	55	37	87	84	81	102	1,187
of which: Bonds	0	0	0	50	50	50	50	1,051
Private nonguaranteed	560	509	657	880	579	719	798	946
of which: Bonds	..	..	..	..	..	..	..	..
Disbursements	**347**	**481**	**649**	**703**	**904**	**1,554**	**1,348**	**2,444**
Public and publicly guaranteed	163	302	431	246	452	558	513	1,602
Official creditors	159	297	430	196	452	558	493	521
Private creditors	4	4	1	50	0	0	20	1,082
of which: Bonds	0	0	0	50	0	0	0	1,001
Private nonguaranteed	184	179	218	457	452	996	835	841
of which: Bonds	..	..	..	..	..	..		..
Principal repayments	**259**	**265**	**277**	**341**	**452**	**922**	**824**	**783**
Public and publicly guaranteed	93	139	54	107	62	65	58	82
Official creditors	91	138	53	106	61	63	58	81
Private creditors	1	1	1	1	1	2	0	0
of which: Bonds	0	0	0	0	0	0	0	0
Private nonguaranteed	166	126	223	234	390	856	766	701
of which: Bonds	..	..	..	..	..	..	..	..
Interest payments	**108**	**83**	**77**	**68**	**56**	**77**	**89**	**130**
Public and publicly guaranteed	77	64	49	41	46	59	70	111
Official creditors	76	63	49	41	46	58	70	81
Private creditors	0	0	0	0	0	0	0	30
of which: Bonds	0	0	0	0	0	0	0	29
Private nonguaranteed	31	20	27	27	10	19	19	19
of which: Bonds	..	..	..	..	..	..	..	..
Net financial flows								
Net debt inflows	42	155	523	139	575	526	652	1,768
Official creditors (incl. IMF)	84	159	377	90	389	490	428	433
Private creditors	-42	-4	146	49	185	36	223	1,335
Long-term	20	57	-5	272	62	138	89	1,222
Public and publicly guaranteed	3	4	0	49	-1	-2	20	1,081
Private nonguaranteed	18	54	-6	223	62	140	69	141
Short-term	-63	-61	151	-223	124	-102	134	113
Net equity inflows								
Foreign direct investment	382	537	1,046	443	469	958	1,006	820
Portfolio equity	..	..	..	..	..	..	..	..
Major economic aggregates								
Gross national income (GNI)	6,885	9,219	13,385	14,299	15,110	16,769	17,279	17,239
Exports of goods, services & prim. income	4,001	3,817	5,013	4,318	4,993	6,290	6,747	6,433
Imports of goods, services & prim. income	5,047	6,016	10,116	7,514	8,557	10,836	11,568	11,431
Primary income on FDI	160	479	534	602	681	910	1,220	1,169
Personal transfers & comp. of employees	484	1,805	2,821	2,477	2,618	2,811	2,920	3,136
International reserves	1,313	2,327	2,473	2,086	2,671	2,750	2,495	2,982
Ratios								
External debt stocks to exports (%)	136.9	135.5	69.6	88.1	79.6	69.8	74.9	106.2
External debt stocks to GNI (%)	79.6	56.1	26.1	26.6	26.3	26.2	29.3	39.6
Debt service to exports (%)	9.9	10.0	7.4	9.6	10.3	16.0	13.7	14.4
Reserves to external debt stocks (%)	24.0	45.0	70.9	54.8	67.2	62.7	49.4	43.7

Notes:

Data include the effects of HIPC and MDRI debt relief.

HUNGARY

(US$ million, unless otherwise indicated)

	2000	2005	2008	2009	2010	2011	2012	2013
Summary external debt data								
External debt stocks	**30,754**	**86,226**	**222,899**	**239,941**	**215,935**	**210,824**	**201,380**	**196,739**
Long-term external debt	25,310	66,184	186,755	197,704	169,850	165,937	170,323	172,268
Short-term external debt	4,152	18,626	28,125	28,711	32,798	31,641	22,745	22,945
interest arrears on long-term	0	0	0	0	0	0	0	0
Use of IMF credit	1,291	1,416	8,019	13,526	13,287	13,246	8,311	1,526
Long-term external debt								
Debt outstanding and disbursed	**25,310**	**66,184**	**186,755**	**197,704**	**169,850**	**165,937**	**170,323**	**172,268**
Public and publicly guaranteed	14,296	33,675	50,026	54,802	53,981	52,739	63,100	65,306
Official creditors	1,860	2,401	8,640	16,155	17,523	15,085	16,053	16,152
Private creditors	12,437	31,274	41,386	38,647	36,458	37,654	47,046	49,154
of which: Bonds	10,680	28,727	38,454	36,254	34,387	36,111	45,529	47,764
Private nonguaranteed	11,014	32,509	136,729	142,902	115,870	113,198	107,224	106,962
of which: Bonds	188	1,388	10,655	9,095	6,535	3,650	3,751	3,750
Disbursements	**6,283**	**26,467**	**112,009**	**105,860**	**67,426**	**113,914**	**95,194**	**128,543**
Public and publicly guaranteed	1,115	6,254	8,346	8,947	4,770	7,871	12,694	5,891
Official creditors	133	623	6,582	7,221	2,926	1,407	1,000	1,083
Private creditors	982	5,631	1,764	1,726	1,844	6,464	11,694	4,808
of which: Bonds	670	4,961	0	1,710	1,060	6,320	11,692	4,537
Private nonguaranteed	5,168	20,213	103,663	96,913	62,656	106,043	82,500	122,652
of which: Bonds	..	997	2,155	..	..	..	..	1,460
Principal repayments	**6,443**	**21,833**	**66,568**	**101,707**	**94,173**	**110,944**	**94,619**	**113,075**
Public and publicly guaranteed	2,512	4,209	9,605	5,612	3,060	8,213	2,867	4,856
Official creditors	343	214	952	226	374	3,360	382	1,590
Private creditors	2,169	3,995	8,653	5,386	2,686	4,854	2,485	3,266
of which: Bonds	1,847	3,679	6,733	4,762	1,701	4,212	2,429	2,810
Private nonguaranteed	3,931	17,624	56,964	96,095	91,113	102,731	91,752	108,220
of which: Bonds	..	..	..	1,560	2,560	2,886	..	1,461
Interest payments	**1,319**	**1,942**	**6,662**	**7,088**	**6,964**	**6,264**	**5,550**	**6,271**
Public and publicly guaranteed	937	893	1,497	1,468	1,531	1,830	1,700	1,919
Official creditors	126	87	291	343	437	567	480	377
Private creditors	811	806	1,207	1,124	1,094	1,263	1,220	1,542
of which: Bonds	727	736	1,034	1,049	1,047	1,206	1,185	1,518
Private nonguaranteed	382	1,049	5,165	5,620	5,433	4,434	3,850	4,352
of which: Bonds	18	46	319	399	412	402	39	99
Net financial flows								
Net debt inflows	449	6,114	46,895	10,017	-22,660	1,812	-13,240	8,929
Official creditors (incl. IMF)	-210	410	12,293	12,273	2,552	-1,953	-4,301	-7,245
Private creditors	660	5,704	34,602	-2,256	-25,212	3,765	-8,938	16,174
Long-term	50	4,224	39,810	-2,842	-29,299	4,922	-43	15,974
Public and publicly guaranteed	-1,187	1,636	-6,889	-3,660	-842	1,610	9,209	1,542
Private nonguaranteed	1,237	2,589	46,699	818	-28,457	3,312	-9,252	14,432
Short-term	609	1,480	-5,208	586	4,087	-1,157	-8,895	200
Net equity inflows								
Foreign direct investment	2,770	7,141	42,138	-5,848	198	-6,243	10,167	2,163
Portfolio equity	..	-16	-197	665	-206	-203	1,235	25
Major economic aggregates								
Gross national income (GNI)	44,085	104,367	144,332	121,138	121,473	130,231	117,908	..
Exports of goods, services & prim. income	..	74,311	139,525	113,546	122,322	134,601	124,322	131,647
Imports of goods, services & prim. income	..	82,180	149,801	114,299	122,527	134,646	123,866	129,156
Primary income on FDI	..	5,900	19,017	18,187	19,632	16,126	15,128	15,051
Personal transfers & comp. of employees	..	1,913	2,509	2,137	2,144	2,278	2,144	2,268
International reserves	11,190	18,552	33,788	44,074	44,849	48,681	44,506	46,389
Ratios								
External debt stocks to exports (%)	..	116.0	159.8	211.3	176.5	156.6	162.0	149.4
External debt stocks to GNI (%)	69.8	82.6	154.4	198.1	177.8	161.9	170.8	..
Debt service to exports (%)	..	32.9	54.3	97.8	85.3	89.4	86.4	97.4
Reserves to external debt stocks (%)	36.4	21.5	15.2	18.4	20.8	23.1	22.1	23.6

INDIA

(US$ million, unless otherwise indicated)

	2000	2005	2008	2009	2010	2011	2012	2013
Summary external debt data								
External debt stocks	**101,130**	**121,195**	**227,114**	**256,312**	**291,651**	**336,845**	**395,071**	**427,562**
Long-term external debt	96,781	111,406	182,243	203,473	229,076	252,686	295,608	328,728
Short-term external debt	3,462	8,816	43,821	46,603	56,448	78,052	93,349	92,707
interest arrears on long-term	0	0	0	0	0	0	0	0
Use of IMF credit	888	974	1,049	6,237	6,127	6,108	6,114	6,127
Long-term external debt								
Debt outstanding and disbursed	**96,781**	**111,406**	**182,243**	**203,473**	**229,076**	**252,686**	**295,608**	**328,728**
Public and publicly guaranteed	81,195	54,726	76,318	85,293	101,786	110,372	135,652	132,109
Official creditors	51,729	50,058	62,626	65,971	73,956	78,355	78,027	76,387
Private creditors	29,466	4,668	13,692	19,322	27,830	32,017	57,625	55,723
of which: Bonds	10,240	1,360	4,520	9,521	14,700	16,517	24,007	20,510
Private nonguaranteed	15,586	56,680	105,925	118,180	127,290	142,314	159,956	196,619
of which: Bonds	1,515	5,761	14,732	15,326	13,217	10,861	7,848	8,234
Disbursements	**10,556**	**19,380**	**38,712**	**26,646**	**44,629**	**44,073**	**49,929**	**68,894**
Public and publicly guaranteed	10,256	6,630	18,824	10,396	25,560	14,865	17,269	12,688
Official creditors	3,270	3,824	5,917	5,971	9,780	7,924	5,170	5,253
Private creditors	6,986	2,805	12,907	4,425	15,781	6,941	12,099	7,435
of which: Bonds	5,520	1,714	11,507	1,765	11,050	2,032	7,478	2,045
Private nonguaranteed	300	12,751	19,888	16,250	19,069	29,207	32,661	56,206
of which: Bonds	..	2,920	594	2,473	1,288	737	665	1,224
Principal repayments	**6,702**	**19,384**	**23,685**	**10,990**	**19,018**	**22,227**	**21,202**	**31,228**
Public and publicly guaranteed	6,454	12,469	13,447	5,336	5,164	6,823	6,183	13,052
Official creditors	3,494	2,701	3,001	2,923	3,159	3,907	3,695	4,004
Private creditors	2,959	9,769	10,446	2,413	2,005	2,915	2,488	9,049
of which: Bonds	0	8,457	9,468	588	148	200	0	5,553
Private nonguaranteed	249	6,914	10,238	5,654	13,854	15,405	15,019	18,176
of which: Bonds	35	117	880	1,679	1,851	2,847	3,678	833
Interest payments	**4,007**	**4,196**	**5,718**	**4,942**	**4,675**	**6,258**	**8,136**	**8,741**
Public and publicly guaranteed	3,378	3,022	1,524	1,322	1,063	1,262	1,758	1,558
Official creditors	1,436	1,062	1,164	1,012	798	926	1,265	916
Private creditors	1,941	1,960	360	310	265	335	493	642
of which: Bonds	143	1,799	61	60	39	51	121	158
Private nonguaranteed	630	1,174	4,194	3,620	3,612	4,996	6,378	7,183
of which: Bonds	224	141	278	290	421	848	516	518
Net financial flows								
Net debt inflows	3,358	1,949	22,755	18,437	35,456	43,449	44,025	37,024
Official creditors (incl. IMF)	-249	1,124	2,916	3,048	6,621	4,016	1,474	1,250
Private creditors	3,607	825	19,839	15,389	28,836	39,433	42,550	35,774
Long-term	4,078	-1,127	12,111	12,607	18,991	17,829	27,253	36,416
Public and publicly guaranteed	4,026	-6,964	2,461	2,011	13,776	4,026	9,611	-1,614
Private nonguaranteed	51	5,837	9,650	10,596	5,215	13,803	17,642	38,030
Short-term	-471	1,952	7,728	2,782	9,845	21,604	15,297	-642
Net equity inflows								
Foreign direct investment	3,584	7,269	42,690	34,111	27,357	34,643	23,172	26,713
Portfolio equity	2,481	12,151	-15,030	24,689	30,442	-4,048	22,809	19,892
Major economic aggregates								
Gross national income (GNI)	471,633	828,316	1,216,939	1,357,363	1,690,504	1,864,068	1,837,284	1,855,591
Exports of goods, services & prim. income	62,453	160,228	320,713	274,580	357,996	456,523	453,744	478,989
Imports of goods, services & prim. income	80,489	194,154	400,437	349,529	464,622	579,253	610,650	593,029
Primary income on FDI	..	5,244	11,989	12,279	21,763	23,760	16,389	12,555
Personal transfers & comp. of employees	12,883	22,125	49,977	49,204	53,480	62,499	68,821	69,970
International reserves	37,902	131,924	247,419	265,182	275,277	271,285	270,587	276,493
Ratios								
External debt stocks to exports (%)	161.9	75.6	70.8	93.3	81.5	73.8	87.1	89.3
External debt stocks to GNI (%)	21.4	14.6	18.7	18.9	17.3	18.1	21.5	23.0
Debt service to exports (%)	17.5	14.9	9.7	6.0	6.8	6.4	6.8	8.6
Reserves to external debt stocks (%)	37.5	108.9	108.9	103.5	94.4	80.5	68.5	64.7

Notes:

External debt data prior to 2003 are revised from fiscal year to calendar year. Long-term public and publicly guaranteed bonds include Foreign Institutional Investor debt (FII) as reported by the Reserve Bank of India.

INDONESIA

(US$ million, unless otherwise indicated)

	2000	2005	2008	2009	2010	2011	2012	2013
Summary external debt data								
External debt stocks	**143,655**	**141,820**	**157,906**	**179,394**	**198,268**	**219,619**	**245,821**	**259,069**
Long-term external debt	110,818	122,649	137,050	152,240	162,171	178,406	198,524	208,639
Short-term external debt	21,688	11,023	20,488	24,050	33,047	38,173	44,253	47,380
interest arrears on long-term	4,632	0	0	0	0	0	0	0
Use of IMF credit	11,149	8,148	368	3,105	3,050	3,041	3,044	3,050
Long-term external debt								
Debt outstanding and disbursed	**110,818**	**122,649**	**137,050**	**152,240**	**162,171**	**178,406**	**198,524**	**208,639**
Public and publicly guaranteed	69,649	77,405	87,753	97,447	103,388	108,786	112,150	114,074
Official creditors	54,883	59,945	63,184	63,259	66,487	66,503	61,538	55,780
Private creditors	14,766	17,460	24,569	34,188	36,901	42,283	50,612	58,294
of which: Bonds	971	7,192	18,451	25,833	29,348	35,501	44,637	52,506
Private nonguaranteed	41,169	45,244	49,297	54,793	58,783	69,620	86,374	94,565
of which: Bonds	6,337	7,858	6,592	7,856	7,787	14,112	14,037	16,121
Disbursements	**5,651**	**13,881**	**22,932**	**31,425**	**34,335**	**39,430**	**49,188**	**50,567**
Public and publicly guaranteed	3,301	5,015	9,065	12,729	14,345	9,820	12,428	13,330
Official creditors	3,038	2,581	4,602	6,142	6,587	3,782	3,202	3,883
Private creditors	263	2,434	4,463	6,587	7,758	6,038	9,226	9,447
of which: Bonds	0	2,095	4,080	3,893	5,640	5,775	9,022	8,647
Private nonguaranteed	2,350	8,866	13,867	18,695	19,990	29,609	36,761	37,237
of which: Bonds	350	194	368	1,808	195	295	1,470	2,590
Principal repayments	**9,268**	**15,746**	**16,704**	**20,432**	**23,975**	**25,164**	**29,508**	**32,047**
Public and publicly guaranteed	3,868	6,232	6,482	7,063	5,846	6,132	6,411	6,070
Official creditors	1,586	3,539	5,729	6,134	5,214	5,156	5,133	5,030
Private creditors	2,282	2,692	753	929	632	976	1,278	1,039
of which: Bonds	0	310	0	0	0	0	230	0
Private nonguaranteed	5,400	9,515	10,221	13,368	18,129	19,032	23,097	25,977
of which: Bonds	2,400	267	261	588	411	1,771	1,560	510
Interest payments	**5,673**	**2,933**	**4,461**	**4,301**	**4,944**	**5,532**	**5,951**	**7,721**
Public and publicly guaranteed	3,738	1,921	2,718	2,802	3,034	3,485	3,475	3,720
Official creditors	2,575	1,189	1,968	1,693	1,586	1,508	1,376	1,169
Private creditors	1,163	732	751	1,109	1,448	1,977	2,098	2,550
of which: Bonds	72	136	439	837	1,225	1,655	1,811	2,303
Private nonguaranteed	1,935	1,012	1,743	1,499	1,910	2,048	2,477	4,001
of which: Bonds	735	113	89	31	81	1,145	1,104	1,083
Net financial flows								
Net debt inflows	-1,967	-6,611	8,061	14,554	19,358	19,391	25,760	21,647
Official creditors (incl. IMF)	2,575	-2,103	-1,127	8	1,373	-1,374	-1,931	-1,147
Private creditors	-4,542	-4,508	9,189	14,546	17,985	20,765	27,691	22,794
Long-term	-5,069	-906	7,356	10,985	8,987	15,639	21,611	19,667
Public and publicly guaranteed	-2,019	-258	3,710	5,658	7,127	5,062	7,948	8,407
Private nonguaranteed	-3,050	-649	3,646	5,327	1,861	10,577	13,663	11,260
Short-term	527	-3,602	1,833	3,561	8,998	5,126	6,080	3,127
Net equity inflows								
Foreign direct investment	-4,550	7,812	9,105	4,982	12,468	14,350	15,887	19,938
Portfolio equity	-1,021	-165	322	787	2,132	-326	1,698	-1,827
Major economic aggregates								
Gross national income (GNI)	150,317	271,958	492,112	520,694	689,283	821,202	850,811	841,475
Exports of goods, services & prim. income	73,079	97,565	151,202	128,433	168,862	215,469	213,601	207,636
Imports of goods, services & prim. income	66,903	102,080	156,440	122,382	168,348	217,995	241,704	240,724
Primary income on FDI	3,574	9,525	10,675	8,848	12,844	17,975	17,366	..
Personal transfers & comp. of employees	1,190	5,420	6,794	6,793	6,916	6,924	7,212	7,614
International reserves	28,502	33,140	49,597	63,563	92,908	106,539	108,837	96,364
Ratios								
External debt stocks to exports (%)	196.6	145.4	104.4	139.7	117.4	101.9	115.1	124.8
External debt stocks to GNI (%)	95.6	52.1	32.1	34.5	28.8	26.7	28.9	30.8
Debt service to exports (%)	22.8	20.8	14.1	19.4	17.4	14.4	16.8	19.4
Reserves to external debt stocks (%)	19.8	23.4	31.4	35.4	46.9	48.5	44.3	37.2

IRAN, ISLAMIC REPUBLIC OF

(US$ million, unless otherwise indicated)

	2000	2005	2008	2009	2010	2011	2012	2013
Summary external debt data								
External debt stocks	**8,024**	**21,543**	**15,722**	**18,247**	**20,030**	**15,499**	**7,406**	**7,647**
Long-term external debt	4,709	10,506	8,758	7,295	6,156	4,814	4,271	3,842
Short-term external debt	3,008	10,686	6,599	8,787	11,613	8,475	943	1,600
interest arrears on long-term	0	0	0	0	0	0	0	0
Use of IMF credit	308	352	365	2,165	2,261	2,209	2,192	2,204
Long-term external debt								
Debt outstanding and disbursed	**4,709**	**10,506**	**8,758**	**7,295**	**6,156**	**4,814**	**4,271**	**3,842**
Public and publicly guaranteed	4,709	10,506	8,758	7,295	6,156	4,814	4,271	3,842
Official creditors	1,664	2,045	2,385	2,266	2,024	1,640	1,456	1,003
Private creditors	3,045	8,461	6,373	5,029	4,132	3,174	2,815	2,839
of which: Bonds	0	0	0	0	0	0	0	0
Private nonguaranteed	..	..	..	..	..	..	..	..
of which: Bonds	..	..	..	..	..	..	..	..
Disbursements	**1,469**	**2,740**	**787**	**400**	**252**	**216**	**18**	**22**
Public and publicly guaranteed	1,469	2,740	787	400	252	216	18	22
Official creditors	477	673	289	223	105	31	15	18
Private creditors	993	2,068	498	177	147	185	3	4
of which: Bonds	0	0	0	0	0	0	0	0
Private nonguaranteed	..	..	..	..	..	..	..	..
of which: Bonds	..	..	..	..	..	..	..	..
Principal repayments	**2,345**	**1,734**	**2,131**	**2,046**	**1,575**	**1,389**	**446**	**358**
Public and publicly guaranteed	2,345	1,734	2,131	2,046	1,575	1,389	446	358
Official creditors	1,785	329	328	379	321	420	183	224
Private creditors	561	1,405	1,802	1,667	1,255	970	263	133
of which: Bonds	0	0	0	0	0	0	0	0
Private nonguaranteed	..	..	..	..	..	..	..	..
of which: Bonds	..	..	..	..	..	..	..	..
Interest payments	**391**	**418**	**498**	**274**	**139**	**110**	**35**	**31**
Public and publicly guaranteed	391	418	498	274	139	110	35	31
Official creditors	190	103	89	73	53	46	17	22
Private creditors	202	316	410	201	86	64	19	8
of which: Bonds	0	0	0	0	0	0	0	0
Private nonguaranteed	..	..	..	..	..	..	..	..
of which: Bonds	..	..	..	..	..	..	..	..
Net financial flows								
Net debt inflows	-1,485	1,440	-4,636	542	1,502	-4,311	-7,960	321
Official creditors (incl. IMF)	-1,308	344	-40	-156	-216	-389	-168	-206
Private creditors	-177	1,096	-4,596	698	1,718	-3,922	-7,792	528
Long-term	432	663	-1,304	-1,490	-1,108	-784	-260	-129
Public and publicly guaranteed	432	663	-1,304	-1,490	-1,108	-784	-260	-129
Private nonguaranteed	..	..	..	..	..	..	..	..
Short-term	-609	433	-3,292	2,188	2,826	-3,138	-7,532	657
Net equity inflows								
Foreign direct investment	39	2,889	1,980	2,983	3,649	4,277	4,662	3,050
Portfolio equity	..	..	..	..	..	..	..	..
Major economic aggregates								
Gross national income (GNI)	101,335	188,503	335,654	328,593	..	..	503,156	369,272
Exports of goods, services & prim. income	30,131	50,757	107,760	112,334	98,191	123,593	155,666	107,189
Imports of goods, services & prim. income	18,107	50,115	75,808	89,859	88,815	96,224	96,707	81,468
Primary income on FDI	..	..	..	..	..	..	..	..
Personal transfers & comp. of employees	536	1,032	1,115	1,072	1,181	1,330	..	..
International reserves	..	..	..	..	..	..	..	..
Ratios								
External debt stocks to exports (%)	26.6	42.4	14.6	16.2	20.4	12.5	4.8	7.1
External debt stocks to GNI (%)	7.9	11.4	4.7	5.6	..	..	1.5	2.1
Debt service to exports (%)	9.7	5.5	2.6	2.2	1.9	1.3	0.4	0.4
Reserves to external debt stocks (%)	..	..	..	..	..	..	..	..

Notes:

Fiscal year-end for external debt data is March. Short-term debt is World Bank staff estimates based on Central Bank data.

JAMAICA

(US$ million, unless otherwise indicated)

	2000	2005	2008	2009	2010	2011	2012	2013
Summary external debt data								
External debt stocks	**4,716**	**6,466**	**10,308**	**11,026**	**14,099**	**14,264**	**14,219**	**13,790**
Long-term external debt	3,818	5,848	9,065	9,917	11,876	12,086	11,261	11,027
Short-term external debt	785	559	1,180	699	1,035	945	1,723	1,523
interest arrears on long-term	142	167	184	174	160	154	84	58
Use of IMF credit	113	58	63	410	1,188	1,234	1,235	1,239
Long-term external debt								
Debt outstanding and disbursed	**3,818**	**5,848**	**9,065**	**9,917**	**11,876**	**12,086**	**11,261**	**11,027**
Public and publicly guaranteed	3,715	5,458	6,901	6,676	7,569	7,743	7,366	7,422
Official creditors	2,396	2,078	2,273	2,387	3,243	3,201	3,164	3,318
Private creditors	1,320	3,380	4,628	4,289	4,326	4,541	4,202	4,104
of which: Bonds	1,004	3,043	4,218	3,890	3,786	4,027	3,724	3,686
Private nonguaranteed	103	390	2,164	3,241	4,307	4,343	3,895	3,605
of which: Bonds	..	300	2,130	3,215	4,290	4,290	3,840	3,550
Disbursements	**899**	**1,350**	**704**	**1,542**	**2,360**	**1,208**	**2,033**	**2,202**
Public and publicly guaranteed	899	1,043	704	457	1,285	1,170	265	401
Official creditors	306	91	278	353	1,075	418	225	375
Private creditors	593	953	426	103	210	753	39	26
of which: Bonds	553	875	350	0	0	694	0	0
Private nonguaranteed	..	307	..	1,085	1,075	37	1,768	1,801
of which: Bonds	..	300	..	1,085	1,075	..	1,750	1,800
Principal repayments	**420**	**540**	**455**	**727**	**339**	**713**	**1,077**	**346**
Public and publicly guaranteed	356	531	446	718	331	712	626	345
Official creditors	270	221	252	253	207	194	244	224
Private creditors	87	310	194	466	124	517	383	121
of which: Bonds	13	256	138	345	68	438	302	48
Private nonguaranteed	64	9	9	9	9	2	451	1
of which: Bonds	55	..	..	..	..	..	450	..
Interest payments	**205**	**386**	**673**	**746**	**828**	**899**	**687**	**561**
Public and publicly guaranteed	192	360	480	521	488	491	458	415
Official creditors	117	83	81	96	100	108	66	68
Private creditors	75	277	400	426	388	383	393	347
of which: Bonds	50	265	392	404	375	368	379	333
Private nonguaranteed	13	26	193	225	341	408	228	146
of which: Bonds	2	21	191	224	340	406	226	141
Net financial flows								
Net debt inflows	439	331	-10	344	3,149	461	1,804	1,685
Official creditors (incl. IMF)	17	-131	26	101	1,647	274	-18	153
Private creditors	421	462	-35	243	1,502	187	1,822	1,531
Long-term	443	941	224	714	1,152	271	974	1,705
Public and publicly guaranteed	506	642	232	-362	86	235	-343	-95
Private nonguaranteed	-64	298	-9	1,076	1,066	36	1,317	1,800
Short-term	-21	-479	-259	-471	350	-84	848	-174
Net equity inflows								
Foreign direct investment	468	660	1,322	440	183	199	490	577
Portfolio equity	..	..	..	..	..	..	83	149
Major economic aggregates								
Gross national income (GNI)	8,662	10,407	13,114	11,457	12,736	13,896	14,360	13,708
Exports of goods, services & prim. income	3,782	4,322	6,027	4,273	4,248	4,508	4,727	4,472
Imports of goods, services & prim. income	4,970	6,972	10,970	7,259	7,192	8,567	8,518	8,239
Primary income on FDI	290	454	376	232	127	112	136	258
Personal transfers & comp. of employees	892	1,762	2,157	1,889	2,026	2,106	2,145	2,161
International reserves	1,054	2,170	1,773	2,076	2,501	2,282	1,996	1,818
Ratios								
External debt stocks to exports (%)	124.7	149.6	171.0	258.0	331.9	316.4	300.8	308.3
External debt stocks to GNI (%)	54.4	62.1	78.6	96.2	110.7	102.6	99.0	100.6
Debt service to exports (%)	18.5	22.2	19.2	34.7	27.9	36.3	38.0	26.9
Reserves to external debt stocks (%)	22.3	33.6	17.2	18.8	17.7	16.0	14.0	13.2

Notes:

Short-term debt is based on data from the BIS.

JORDAN

(US$ million, unless otherwise indicated)

	2000	2005	2008	2009	2010	2011	2012	2013
Summary external debt data								
External debt stocks	**11,063**	**12,904**	**13,969**	**14,427**	**17,215**	**17,795**	**18,846**	**23,970**
Long-term external debt	6,183	6,901	5,319	5,643	7,908	7,844	8,468	11,356
Short-term external debt	4,396	5,742	8,596	8,518	9,049	9,694	9,737	11,314
interest arrears on long-term	102	0	0	0	1	1	1	1
Use of IMF credit	484	260	54	266	257	257	642	1,300
Long-term external debt								
Debt outstanding and disbursed	**6,183**	**6,901**	**5,319**	**5,643**	**7,908**	**7,844**	**8,468**	**11,356**
Public and publicly guaranteed	6,183	6,878	5,126	5,445	6,502	6,317	6,302	8,855
Official creditors	5,243	6,483	4,815	5,137	5,452	5,291	5,308	5,494
Private creditors	940	395	311	308	1,050	1,026	994	3,361
of which: Bonds	583	145	145	145	881	866	852	3,237
Private nonguaranteed	..	24	193	198	1,406	1,528	2,165	2,501
of which: Bonds	..	..	..	..	..	..	..	..
Disbursements	**176**	**434**	**330**	**787**	**1,538**	**475**	**1,010**	**3,644**
Public and publicly guaranteed	176	434	230	762	1,388	325	711	3,308
Official creditors	176	269	224	756	626	325	711	908
Private creditors	0	165	6	6	762	0	0	2,400
of which: Bonds	0	145	0	0	750	0	0	2,400
Private nonguaranteed	..	..	100	25	150	150	299	336
of which: Bonds	..	..	..	..	..	..	..	..
Principal repayments	**308**	**366**	**2,430**	**425**	**513**	**599**	**615**	**606**
Public and publicly guaranteed	308	341	2,412	405	487	574	585	566
Official creditors	238	323	2,341	396	463	548	557	538
Private creditors	70	19	71	9	25	26	28	28
of which: Bonds	10	10	0	0	15	15	15	15
Private nonguaranteed	..	25	19	20	26	25	30	40
of which: Bonds	..	..	..	..	..	..	..	..
Interest payments	**239**	**161**	**207**	**155**	**162**	**191**	**190**	**206**
Public and publicly guaranteed	239	160	200	147	147	171	165	162
Official creditors	162	157	185	134	124	130	126	113
Private creditors	77	4	15	12	22	41	39	49
of which: Bonds	43	0	9	9	19	39	37	48
Private nonguaranteed	..	1	7	8	15	20	25	44
of which: Bonds	..	..	..	..	..	..	..	..
Net financial flows								
Net debt inflows	3,371	325	-1,007	268	1,551	520	821	5,265
Official creditors (incl. IMF)	-73	-131	-2,176	344	159	-223	537	1,020
Private creditors	3,445	456	1,169	-76	1,392	744	284	4,245
Long-term	-70	121	16	2	862	99	241	2,667
Public and publicly guaranteed	-70	146	-65	-3	738	-26	-28	2,372
Private nonguaranteed	..	-25	82	5	124	125	269	296
Short-term	3,515	335	1,152	-78	530	645	44	1,577
Net equity inflows								
Foreign direct investment	913	1,984	2,827	2,413	1,651	1,474	1,497	1,798
Portfolio equity	-17	169	521	-30	-21	109	53	158
Major economic aggregates								
Gross national income (GNI)	8,558	12,920	22,667	24,326	26,218	28,576	30,626	33,339
Exports of goods, services & prim. income	4,207	7,426	13,751	12,022	13,639	14,454	14,997	15,062
Imports of goods, services & prim. income	6,363	12,314	19,869	17,044	19,343	22,276	24,053	25,088
Primary income on FDI	33	72	256	313	813	713	821	845
Personal transfers & comp. of employees	1,845	2,421	3,510	3,465	3,517	3,368	3,490	3,643
International reserves	3,331	5,250	8,562	11,689	13,057	11,467	8,090	13,224
Ratios								
External debt stocks to exports (%)	263.0	173.8	101.6	120.0	126.2	123.1	125.7	159.1
External debt stocks to GNI (%)	129.3	99.9	61.6	59.3	65.7	62.3	61.5	71.9
Debt service to exports (%)	20.1	11.9	20.9	6.0	5.8	6.6	6.5	6.7
Reserves to external debt stocks (%)	30.1	40.7	61.3	81.0	75.8	64.4	42.9	55.2

Notes:

Long-term private nonguaranteed debt data from 2001 are based on reports provided by the country. Short-term debt before 1999 is based on data from the BIS.

KAZAKHSTAN

(US$ million, unless otherwise indicated)

	2000	2005	2008	2009	2010	2011	2012	2013
Summary external debt data								
External debt stocks	**12,890**	**43,857**	**106,731**	**109,734**	**119,145**	**124,317**	**135,502**	**148,456**
Long-term external debt	11,481	35,263	96,715	102,210	109,751	115,033	125,883	138,526
Short-term external debt	961	8,102	9,487	6,985	8,864	8,756	9,091	9,401
interest arrears on long-term	0	0	0	0	0	0	0	0
Use of IMF credit	448	491	529	539	529	528	528	529
Long-term external debt								
Debt outstanding and disbursed	**11,481**	**35,263**	**96,715**	**102,210**	**109,751**	**115,033**	**125,883**	**138,526**
Public and publicly guaranteed	3,623	2,177	1,915	2,487	3,845	4,675	7,375	12,246
Official creditors	2,239	1,780	1,912	2,486	3,845	4,675	5,065	5,312
Private creditors	1,384	396	3	1	0	0	2,310	6,935
of which: Bonds	1,000	350	0	0	0	0	2,300	6,925
Private nonguaranteed	7,859	33,087	94,800	99,724	105,905	110,358	118,508	126,280
of which: Bonds	100	7,550	24,125	22,097	21,044	17,995	15,098	11,790
Disbursements	**3,063**	**17,207**	**40,803**	**30,471**	**45,054**	**32,740**	**31,396**	**45,750**
Public and publicly guaranteed	623	197	145	717	1,522	920	3,050	5,421
Official creditors	168	197	145	717	1,522	920	740	796
Private creditors	455	0	0	0	0	0	2,310	4,625
of which: Bonds	350	0	0	0	0	0	2,300	4,625
Private nonguaranteed	2,440	17,010	40,658	29,754	43,532	31,821	28,346	40,329
of which: Bonds	..	3,050	540	..	450	800	560	6,684
Principal repayments	**2,155**	**11,417**	**29,011**	**20,032**	**34,639**	**26,226**	**20,862**	**28,336**
Public and publicly guaranteed	216	1,090	131	131	278	134	254	404
Official creditors	133	1,018	120	130	278	134	254	404
Private creditors	83	72	11	2	1	0	0	0
of which: Bonds	0	0	0	0	0	0	0	0
Private nonguaranteed	1,939	10,327	28,881	19,901	34,360	26,092	20,607	27,932
of which: Bonds	..	..	850	2,108	1,503	3,789	3,457	4,210
Interest payments	**713**	**1,521**	**4,105**	**5,365**	**4,517**	**5,921**	**2,033**	**2,254**
Public and publicly guaranteed	235	146	67	58	54	61	75	144
Official creditors	124	102	66	58	54	61	75	65
Private creditors	112	44	1	0	0	0	0	79
of which: Bonds	90	39	0	0	0	0	0	78
Private nonguaranteed	478	1,376	4,039	5,307	4,463	5,860	1,957	2,110
of which: Bonds	11	543	1,802	1,706	1,525	1,343	1,115	655
Net financial flows								
Net debt inflows	1,061	9,950	9,749	7,937	12,295	6,406	10,869	17,724
Official creditors (incl. IMF)	-407	-820	26	587	1,244	786	486	392
Private creditors	1,469	10,770	9,723	7,350	11,050	5,620	10,383	17,332
Long-term	873	6,610	11,766	9,851	9,171	5,729	10,048	17,022
Public and publicly guaranteed	373	-72	-11	-2	-1	..	2,310	4,625
Private nonguaranteed	501	6,683	11,777	9,853	9,172	5,729	7,738	12,397
Short-term	595	4,160	-2,043	-2,502	1,879	-109	335	310
Net equity inflows								
Foreign direct investment	1,283	237	6,949	4,183	4,162	5,907	7,266	5,157
Portfolio equity	19	150	-1,280	38	134	8	-418	65
Major economic aggregates								
Gross national income (GNI)	17,038	51,568	114,115	102,688	128,676	160,325	175,377	198,930
Exports of goods, services & prim. income	10,480	31,380	79,997	51,205	68,212	91,764	93,845	90,998
Imports of goods, services & prim. income	10,362	32,008	72,687	54,597	66,337	81,301	91,756	89,528
Primary income on FDI	1,046	4,805	17,316	10,961	17,997	25,213	24,740	22,722
Personal transfers & comp. of employees	122	62	126	198	226	180	171	207
International reserves	1,594	6,084	17,871	20,720	25,223	25,179	22,132	19,127
Ratios								
External debt stocks to exports (%)	123.0	139.8	133.4	214.3	174.7	135.5	144.4	163.1
External debt stocks to GNI (%)	75.7	85.0	93.5	106.9	92.6	77.5	77.3	74.6
Debt service to exports (%)	32.4	41.9	41.7	50.2	57.9	35.4	24.7	34.0
Reserves to external debt stocks (%)	12.4	13.9	16.7	18.9	21.2	20.3	16.3	12.9

KENYA

(US$ million, unless otherwise indicated)

	2000	2005	2008	2009	2010	2011	2012	2013
Summary external debt data								
External debt stocks	**6,189**	**6,483**	**7,607**	**8,589**	**8,801**	**10,287**	**11,569**	**13,471**
Long-term external debt	5,216	5,772	6,388	6,720	6,979	7,566	8,835	9,647
Short-term external debt	798	499	910	1,012	1,005	1,622	1,442	2,353
interest arrears on long-term	47	21	66	73	80	100	93	111
Use of IMF credit	175	212	309	858	817	1,100	1,293	1,471
Long-term external debt								
Debt outstanding and disbursed	**5,216**	**5,772**	**6,388**	**6,720**	**6,979**	**7,566**	**8,835**	**9,647**
Public and publicly guaranteed	5,041	5,772	6,388	6,720	6,979	7,566	8,835	9,647
Official creditors	4,559	5,409	6,070	6,369	6,668	7,246	7,896	8,702
Private creditors	482	363	319	352	311	320	938	946
of which: Bonds	0	0	0	0	0	0	0	0
Private nonguaranteed	175	..	..	..	..	..	..	..
of which: Bonds	..	..	..	..	..	..	..	..
Disbursements	**333**	**168**	**350**	**538**	**530**	**865**	**1,680**	**1,228**
Public and publicly guaranteed	333	168	350	538	530	865	1,680	1,228
Official creditors	248	140	343	510	518	841	1,003	1,214
Private creditors	85	28	7	27	12	23	677	14
of which: Bonds	0	0	0	0	0	0	0	0
Private nonguaranteed	..	..	..	..	..	..	..	..
of which: Bonds	..	..	..	..	..	..	..	..
Principal repayments	**407**	**439**	**288**	**258**	**259**	**289**	**337**	**317**
Public and publicly guaranteed	362	429	288	258	259	289	337	317
Official creditors	241	356	273	255	255	282	328	300
Private creditors	121	74	15	3	4	7	10	17
of which: Bonds	0	0	0	0	0	0	0	0
Private nonguaranteed	45	10	..	..	..	..	..	..
of which: Bonds	..	..	..	..	..	..	..	..
Interest payments	**100**	**72**	**91**	**85**	**90**	**93**	**171**	**225**
Public and publicly guaranteed	81	72	91	85	90	93	171	225
Official creditors	55	66	90	84	90	92	144	189
Private creditors	27	6	1	1	1	1	26	36
of which: Bonds	0	0	0	0	0	0	0	0
Private nonguaranteed	19	0	..	..	..	..	..	..
of which: Bonds	..	..	..	..	..	..	..	..
Net financial flows								
Net debt inflows	-31	-459	-12	566	232	1,466	1,361	1,977
Official creditors (incl. IMF)	9	-149	60	446	238	853	867	1,088
Private creditors	-40	-310	-71	119	-6	614	495	889
Long-term	-81	-56	-8	24	8	17	668	-4
Public and publicly guaranteed	-36	-46	-8	24	8	17	668	-4
Private nonguaranteed	-45	-10	..	..	..	..	..	..
Short-term	41	-254	-63	95	-14	597	-173	893
Net equity inflows								
Foreign direct investment	111	6	23	32	89	40	49	79
Portfolio equity	-6	3	5	3	22	20	26	..
Major economic aggregates								
Gross national income (GNI)	12,576	18,732	30,419	30,679	32,293	34,254	40,094	43,762
Exports of goods, services & prim. income	2,821	5,416	8,467	7,567	9,127	10,130	11,205	10,903
Imports of goods, services & prim. income	3,941	6,921	12,781	11,514	13,823	16,631	18,270	18,828
Primary income on FDI	29	35	52	60	60	105	111	..
Personal transfers & comp. of employees	538	425	667	631	686	934	1,214	..
International reserves	898	1,799	2,879	3,849	4,320	4,264	5,711	6,598
Ratios								
External debt stocks to exports (%)	219.4	119.7	89.8	113.5	96.4	101.6	103.2	123.6
External debt stocks to GNI (%)	49.2	34.6	25.0	28.0	27.3	30.0	28.9	30.8
Debt service to exports (%)	21.0	10.0	4.9	5.1	4.4	4.3	5.1	5.7
Reserves to external debt stocks (%)	14.5	27.7	37.8	44.8	49.1	41.5	49.4	49.0

Notes:

Short-term debt is based on data from the BIS.

KOSOVO

(US$ million, unless otherwise indicated)

	2000	2005	2008	2009	2010	2011	2012	2013
Summary external debt data								
External debt stocks	..	..	**710**	**1,726**	**1,456**	**1,700**	**2,002**	**2,199**
Long-term external debt	..	..	430	818	886	1,130	1,116	1,293
Short-term external debt	..	..	194	821	455	456	652	675
interest arrears on long-term	..	..	0	0	0	0	0	0
Use of IMF credit	..	..	85	87	114	114	234	231
Long-term external debt								
Debt outstanding and disbursed	..	..	**430**	**818**	**886**	**1,130**	**1,116**	**1,293**
Public and publicly guaranteed	..	..	0	359	319	299	295	299
Official creditors	..	..	0	359	319	299	295	299
Private creditors	..	..	0	0	0	0	0	0
of which: Bonds	..	..	0	0	0	0	0	0
Private nonguaranteed	..	..	430	459	567	830	822	995
of which: Bonds	..	..	..	..	..	..	..	..
Disbursements	..	..	**161**	**90**	**169**	**158**	**93**	**123**
Public and publicly guaranteed	..	..	0	0	0	7	5	7
Official creditors	..	..	0	0	0	7	5	7
Private creditors	..	..	0	0	0	0	0	0
of which: Bonds	..	..	0	0	0	0	0	0
Private nonguaranteed	..	..	161	90	169	152	89	116
of which: Bonds	..	..	..	..	..	..	..	..
Principal repayments	..	..	**37**	**269**	**76**	**85**	**96**	**38**
Public and publicly guaranteed	..	..	0	208	14	17	15	15
Official creditors	..	..	0	208	14	17	15	15
Private creditors	..	..	0	0	0	0	0	0
of which: Bonds	..	..	0	0	0	0	0	0
Private nonguaranteed	..	..	37	61	61	68	82	23
of which: Bonds	..	..	..	..	..	..	..	..
Interest payments	..	..	**15**	**44**	**34**	**38**	**33**	**13**
Public and publicly guaranteed	..	..	0	23	11	12	11	12
Official creditors	..	..	0	23	11	12	11	12
Private creditors	..	..	0	0	0	0	0	0
of which: Bonds	..	..	0	0	0	0	0	0
Private nonguaranteed	..	..	15	22	23	26	22	1
of which: Bonds	..	..	..	..	..	..	..	..
Net financial flows								
Net debt inflows	..	..	177	448	-244	75	312	105
Official creditors (incl. IMF)	..	..	..	-208	14	-10	109	-12
Private creditors	..	..	177	656	-258	85	203	116
Long-term	..	..	124	29	108	84	7	93
Public and publicly guaranteed	..	..	..	..	..	..	..	..
Private nonguaranteed	..	..	124	29	108	84	7	93
Short-term	..	..	54	627	-366	1	196	23
Net equity inflows								
Foreign direct investment	..	..	408	376	439	478	260	223
Portfolio equity	..	..	..	..	..	..	1	-1
Major economic aggregates								
Gross national income (GNI)	..	..	6,011	5,707	5,829	6,789	6,644	7,122
Exports of goods, services & prim. income	..	..	1,138	1,170	1,333	1,670	1,477	1,520
Imports of goods, services & prim. income	..	..	3,222	3,101	3,377	4,018	3,495	3,596
Primary income on FDI	..	..	88	102	130	148	65	97
Personal transfers & comp. of employees	..	..	1,042	1,055	997	1,122	1,059	1,122
International reserves	..	..	892	830	846	742	1,108	1,103
Ratios								
External debt stocks to exports (%)	..	..	62.4	147.5	109.2	101.8	135.6	144.7
External debt stocks to GNI (%)	..	..	11.8	30.2	25.0	25.0	30.1	30.9
Debt service to exports (%)	..	..	4.6	26.8	8.3	7.4	8.8	3.7
Reserves to external debt stocks (%)	..	..	125.7	48.1	58.2	43.6	55.3	50.1

KYRGYZ REPUBLIC

(US$ million, unless otherwise indicated)

	2000	2005	2008	2009	2010	2011	2012	2013
Summary external debt data								
External debt stocks	**1,938**	**2,257**	**3,628**	**4,119**	**4,114**	**5,486**	**6,026**	**6,804**
Long-term external debt	1,510	1,825	2,942	3,395	3,612	4,986	5,492	6,163
Short-term external debt	129	132	391	424	195	188	214	308
interest arrears on long-term	10	3	6	2	12	3	4	1
Use of IMF credit	298	299	295	300	307	312	321	333
Long-term external debt								
Debt outstanding and disbursed	**1,510**	**1,825**	**2,942**	**3,395**	**3,612**	**4,986**	**5,492**	**6,163**
Public and publicly guaranteed	1,220	1,665	1,963	2,320	2,442	2,618	2,840	2,945
Official creditors	1,184	1,665	1,963	2,320	2,442	2,618	2,840	2,945
Private creditors	37	0	0	0	0	0	0	0
of which: Bonds	0	0	0	0	0	0	0	0
Private nonguaranteed	290	161	980	1,076	1,171	2,368	2,652	3,218
of which: Bonds	..	..	..	..	..	..	..	..
Disbursements	**161**	**132**	**878**	**635**	**668**	**746**	**853**	**916**
Public and publicly guaranteed	153	76	51	378	147	211	344	386
Official creditors	149	76	51	378	147	211	344	386
Private creditors	4	0	0	0	0	0	0	0
of which: Bonds	0	0	0	0	0	0	0	0
Private nonguaranteed	8	56	827	257	521	535	510	530
of which: Bonds	..	..	..	..	..	..	..	..
Principal repayments	**86**	**73**	**261**	**200**	**462**	**314**	**266**	**305**
Public and publicly guaranteed	17	16	35	38	38	44	41	44
Official creditors	13	16	35	38	38	44	41	44
Private creditors	4	0	0	0	0	0	0	0
of which: Bonds	0	0	0	0	0	0	0	0
Private nonguaranteed	69	57	225	162	424	270	226	261
of which: Bonds	..	..	..	..	..	..	..	..
Interest payments	**69**	**21**	**42**	**37**	**69**	**70**	**58**	**63**
Public and publicly guaranteed	23	12	17	19	23	40	32	34
Official creditors	20	12	17	19	23	40	32	34
Private creditors	2	0	0	0	0	0	0	0
of which: Bonds	0	0	0	0	0	0	0	0
Private nonguaranteed	47	9	24	18	46	29	25	29
of which: Bonds	..	..	..	..	..	..	..	..
Net financial flows								
Net debt inflows	152	-150	709	472	-20	439	620	719
Official creditors (incl. IMF)	143	47	35	339	121	173	311	354
Private creditors	9	-196	674	132	-141	266	309	365
Long-term	-60	-1	601	96	97	265	284	269
Public and publicly guaranteed	0	..	..	..	..	..	..	..
Private nonguaranteed	-60	-1	601	96	97	265	284	269
Short-term	69	-195	73	37	-238	1	25	97
Net equity inflows								
Foreign direct investment	-2	47	178	178	231	547	112	228
Portfolio equity	..	0	6	1	-18	5	0	-2
Major economic aggregates								
Gross national income (GNI)	1,288	2,372	4,960	4,500	4,489	5,668	6,461	6,911
Exports of goods, services & prim. income	590	963	2,723	2,354	2,408	3,159	2,951	3,131
Imports of goods, services & prim. income	753	1,501	4,912	3,763	4,117	5,591	6,687	7,053
Primary income on FDI	37	36	178	118	248	611	111	227
Personal transfers & comp. of employees	9	313	1,223	982	1,266	1,709	2,031	..
International reserves	239	570	1,153	1,494	1,604	1,703	1,903	2,099
Ratios								
External debt stocks to exports (%)	328.5	234.4	133.3	175.0	170.8	173.7	204.2	217.3
External debt stocks to GNI (%)	150.5	95.1	73.2	91.5	91.7	96.8	93.3	98.4
Debt service to exports (%)	30.2	14.8	12.3	11.4	23.1	13.0	11.8	12.4
Reserves to external debt stocks (%)	12.3	25.2	31.8	36.3	39.0	31.0	31.6	30.8

Notes:

Long-term private nonguaranteed debt data are World Bank staff estimates based on reports provided by the country. Short-term debt is based on data from the National Statistical Committee of Kyrgyz Republic.

LAO PEOPLE'S DEMOCRATIC REPUBLIC

(US$ million, unless otherwise indicated)

	2000	2005	2008	2009	2010	2011	2012	2013
Summary external debt data								
External debt stocks	**2,520**	**2,912**	**5,181**	**5,792**	**5,723**	**6,720**	**7,344**	**8,615**
Long-term external debt	2,459	2,815	4,980	5,498	5,617	6,575	7,218	7,733
Short-term external debt	6	55	166	199	18	62	47	804
interest arrears on long-term	0	0	0	0	0	0	0	0
Use of IMF credit	55	43	35	95	88	83	79	78
Long-term external debt								
Debt outstanding and disbursed	**2,459**	**2,815**	**4,980**	**5,498**	**5,617**	**6,575**	**7,218**	**7,733**
Public and publicly guaranteed	2,459	1,989	2,713	2,873	3,007	3,450	3,718	4,335
Official creditors	2,459	1,989	2,713	2,873	3,004	3,445	3,711	4,185
Private creditors	0	0	0	0	3	5	7	150
of which: Bonds	0	0	0	0	0	0	0	143
Private nonguaranteed	..	825	2,267	2,625	2,610	3,125	3,500	3,398
of which: Bonds	..	..	..	..	..	..	..	..
Disbursements	**77**	**472**	**746**	**648**	**294**	**1,036**	**848**	**1,602**
Public and publicly guaranteed	77	150	165	201	150	422	398	792
Official creditors	77	150	165	201	147	419	397	649
Private creditors	0	0	0	0	3	3	1	143
of which: Bonds	0	0	0	0	0	0	0	143
Private nonguaranteed	..	321	581	447	144	615	450	810
of which: Bonds	..	..	..	..	..	..	..	..
Principal repayments	**23**	**79**	**143**	**146**	**221**	**199**	**157**	**186**
Public and publicly guaranteed	23	39	44	57	62	99	82	95
Official creditors	23	39	44	57	62	99	82	95
Private creditors	0	0	0	0	0	0	0	0
of which: Bonds	0	0	0	0	0	0	0	0
Private nonguaranteed	..	40	100	89	159	100	75	92
of which: Bonds	..	..	..	..	..	..	..	..
Interest payments	**9**	**47**	**60**	**69**	**79**	**86**	**72**	**115**
Public and publicly guaranteed	9	14	23	25	29	36	42	57
Official creditors	9	14	23	25	29	35	42	56
Private creditors	0	0	0	0	0	0	0	1
of which: Bonds	0	0	0	0	0	0	0	1
Private nonguaranteed	..	32	37	43	50	50	30	58
of which: Bonds	..	..	..	..	..	..	..	..
Net financial flows								
Net debt inflows	53	441	562	530	-113	876	672	2,171
Official creditors (incl. IMF)	47	105	117	139	79	314	311	553
Private creditors	6	336	445	391	-193	562	361	1,619
Long-term	..	281	482	358	-12	518	376	862
Public and publicly guaranteed	..	..	..	..	3	3	1	143
Private nonguaranteed	..	281	482	358	-14	515	375	718
Short-term	6	55	-37	33	-181	44	-15	757
Net equity inflows								
Foreign direct investment	34	28	228	319	279	301	294	296
Portfolio equity	..	..	..	..	54	11	6	..
Major economic aggregates								
Gross national income (GNI)	1,660	2,670	5,188	5,668	6,713	7,663	8,766	10,590
Exports of goods, services & prim. income	513	762	1,526	1,492	2,308	2,452	2,917	..
Imports of goods, services & prim. income	638	1,003	1,589	1,685	2,457	2,881	3,584	..
Primary income on FDI	..	25	26	43	44	16	52	..
Personal transfers & comp. of employees	1	1	18	38	42	110	59	..
International reserves	139	234	629	609	703	741	799	722
Ratios								
External debt stocks to exports (%)	490.9	382.0	339.6	388.3	248.0	274.1	251.8	..
External debt stocks to GNI (%)	151.7	109.1	99.9	102.2	85.2	87.7	83.8	81.4
Debt service to exports (%)	8.0	17.4	13.6	14.7	13.2	11.8	8.0	..
Reserves to external debt stocks (%)	5.5	8.0	12.1	10.5	12.3	11.0	10.9	8.4

Notes:

Long-term private nonguaranteed debt data are World Bank staff estimates. Short-term debt is based on data from the BIS.

LEBANON

(US$ million, unless otherwise indicated)

	2000	2005	2008	2009	2010	2011	2012	2013
Summary external debt data								
External debt stocks	**10,250**	**23,334**	**24,328**	**24,803**	**24,591**	**24,767**	**28,951**	**30,947**
Long-term external debt	7,704	19,877	21,066	21,285	20,713	21,101	24,691	26,124
Short-term external debt	2,541	3,450	3,138	3,096	3,482	3,311	3,943	4,525
interest arrears on long-term	0	0	0	0	0	0	0	0
Use of IMF credit	6	6	124	422	395	355	317	298
Long-term external debt								
Debt outstanding and disbursed	**7,704**	**19,877**	**21,066**	**21,285**	**20,713**	**21,101**	**24,691**	**26,124**
Public and publicly guaranteed	6,968	18,866	20,596	20,615	20,213	20,601	23,991	25,424
Official creditors	1,290	2,172	2,432	2,356	2,226	2,088	1,997	1,734
Private creditors	5,677	16,694	18,165	18,259	17,987	18,513	21,994	23,690
of which: Bonds	5,260	16,142	17,490	17,704	17,422	17,966	21,489	23,298
Private nonguaranteed	736	1,011	470	670	500	500	700	700
of which: Bonds	736	1,011	470	670	500	500	700	700
Disbursements	**2,445**	**3,179**	**2,709**	**3,332**	**2,143**	**4,174**	**6,221**	**3,185**
Public and publicly guaranteed	2,330	2,649	2,709	3,132	2,143	4,174	5,721	3,185
Official creditors	238	106	421	223	199	206	226	136
Private creditors	2,092	2,543	2,288	2,909	1,943	3,968	5,495	3,049
of which: Bonds	2,031	2,500	2,257	2,894	1,925	3,954	5,478	2,992
Private nonguaranteed	115	530	..	200	..	..	500	..
of which: Bonds	115	530	..	200	..	..	500	..
Principal repayments	**884**	**2,172**	**2,905**	**3,096**	**2,632**	**3,743**	**2,642**	**1,801**
Public and publicly guaranteed	834	1,907	2,845	3,096	2,462	3,743	2,342	1,801
Official creditors	74	143	375	334	298	328	318	415
Private creditors	760	1,764	2,470	2,762	2,164	3,415	2,024	1,386
of which: Bonds	400	1,695	2,430	2,706	2,151	3,385	1,965	1,209
Private nonguaranteed	50	265	60	..	170	..	300	..
of which: Bonds	50	265	60	..	170	..	300	..
Interest payments	**475**	**1,287**	**1,442**	**1,475**	**1,454**	**1,491**	**1,484**	**1,618**
Public and publicly guaranteed	418	1,197	1,402	1,431	1,403	1,453	1,446	1,577
Official creditors	57	92	105	88	100	82	75	72
Private creditors	361	1,106	1,297	1,344	1,303	1,372	1,371	1,505
of which: Bonds	300	1,087	1,279	1,328	1,289	1,359	1,359	1,495
Private nonguaranteed	57	90	40	43	51	38	38	42
of which: Bonds	57	90	40	43	51	38	38	42
Net financial flows								
Net debt inflows	1,900	486	-1,136	195	-122	220	4,173	1,947
Official creditors (incl. IMF)	164	-37	87	-111	-117	-161	-130	-298
Private creditors	1,735	524	-1,222	305	-5	382	4,303	2,245
Long-term	1,397	1,045	-242	347	-391	553	3,671	1,663
Public and publicly guaranteed	1,332	780	-182	147	-221	553	3,471	1,663
Private nonguaranteed	65	265	-60	200	-170	..	200	..
Short-term	339	-521	-980	-42	386	-171	632	582
Net equity inflows								
Foreign direct investment	..	2,624	4,333	4,804	4,280	3,490	3,678	2,833
Portfolio equity	..	1,436	466	929	154	-145	-239	..
Major economic aggregates								
Gross national income (GNI)	17,581	21,101	29,267	34,912	37,501	39,905	43,596	44,926
Exports of goods, services & prim. income	..	14,958	24,813	23,137	22,177	26,687	29,639	..
Imports of goods, services & prim. income	..	18,768	31,276	31,705	32,179	34,071	33,969	..
Primary income on FDI	..	95	121	95	209	184	213	..
Personal transfers & comp. of employees	..	4,924	7,181	7,558	6,914	6,913	6,918	..
International reserves	5,944	11,887	20,244	29,103	31,514	33,741	37,186	36,748
Ratios								
External debt stocks to exports (%)	..	156.0	98.0	107.2	110.9	92.8	97.7	..
External debt stocks to GNI (%)	58.3	110.6	83.1	71.0	65.6	62.1	66.4	68.9
Debt service to exports (%)	..	24.3	17.8	19.9	18.7	20.0	14.2	..
Reserves to external debt stocks (%)	58.0	50.9	83.2	117.3	128.2	136.2	128.4	118.7

Notes:

Long-term private nonguaranteed debt only cover Bonds. Short-term debt is based on data from the BIS.

LESOTHO

(US$ million, unless otherwise indicated)

	2000	2005	2008	2009	2010	2011	2012	2013
Summary external debt data								
External debt stocks	**676.7**	**667.3**	**694.6**	**756.3**	**778.0**	**797.6**	**860.2**	**885.2**
Long-term external debt	656.7	618.9	659.2	680.6	699.2	717.2	745.1	755.0
Short-term external debt	4.0	8.0	0.0	0.0	0.0	0.0	0.0	0.0
interest arrears on long-term	0.0	0.0	0.0	0.0	0.0	0.0	0.0	0.0
Use of IMF credit	16.0	40.4	35.4	75.7	78.8	80.3	115.2	130.2
Long-term external debt								
Debt outstanding and disbursed	**656.7**	**618.9**	**659.2**	**680.6**	**699.2**	**717.2**	**745.1**	**755.0**
Public and publicly guaranteed	656.7	618.9	659.2	680.6	699.2	717.2	745.1	755.0
Official creditors	580.9	590.6	646.6	667.1	685.6	705.6	733.9	745.0
Private creditors	75.8	28.4	12.5	13.6	13.6	11.7	11.2	10.0
of which: Bonds	0.0	0.0	0.0	0.0	0.0	0.0	0.0	0.0
Private nonguaranteed	..	..	..	..	..	..	..	..
of which: Bonds	..	..	..	..	..	..	..	..
Disbursements	**69.4**	**21.1**	**45.8**	**37.4**	**42.1**	**44.0**	**54.8**	**39.7**
Public and publicly guaranteed	69.4	21.1	45.8	37.4	42.1	44.0	54.8	39.7
Official creditors	67.4	21.1	45.8	37.4	42.1	44.0	54.8	39.7
Private creditors	2.0	0.0	0.0	0.0	0.0	0.0	0.0	0.0
of which: Bonds	0.0	0.0	0.0	0.0	0.0	0.0	0.0	0.0
Private nonguaranteed	..	..	..	..	..	..	..	..
of which: Bonds	..	..	..	..	..	..	..	..
Principal repayments	**33.2**	**65.3**	**24.5**	**24.6**	**19.4**	**23.3**	**24.3**	**27.6**
Public and publicly guaranteed	33.2	65.3	24.5	24.6	19.4	23.3	24.3	27.6
Official creditors	26.4	32.0	21.3	23.9	19.1	23.0	24.0	27.3
Private creditors	6.8	33.3	3.2	0.7	0.3	0.3	0.3	0.3
of which: Bonds	0.0	0.0	0.0	0.0	0.0	0.0	0.0	0.0
Private nonguaranteed	..	..	..	..	..	..	..	..
of which: Bonds	..	..	..	..	..	..	..	..
Interest payments	**22.9**	**13.7**	**7.8**	**7.4**	**7.5**	**8.8**	**9.2**	**9.9**
Public and publicly guaranteed	22.9	13.7	7.8	7.4	7.5	8.8	9.2	9.9
Official creditors	16.0	7.7	6.7	6.9	6.4	7.8	8.3	9.1
Private creditors	7.0	6.0	1.1	0.5	1.0	1.0	0.9	0.7
of which: Bonds	0.0	0.0	0.0	0.0	0.0	0.0	0.0	0.0
Private nonguaranteed	..	..	..	..	..	..	..	..
of which: Bonds	..	..	..	..	..	..	..	..
Net financial flows								
Net debt inflows	31.0	-43.2	16.3	6.8	27.1	22.5	65.1	26.7
Official creditors (incl. IMF)	35.9	-10.9	19.5	7.5	27.4	22.8	65.3	27.0
Private creditors	-4.9	-32.3	-3.2	-0.7	-0.3	-0.3	-0.3	-0.3
Long-term	-4.9	-33.3	-3.2	-0.7	-0.3	-0.3	-0.3	-0.3
Public and publicly guaranteed	-4.9	-33.3	-3.2	-0.7	-0.3	-0.3	-0.3	-0.3
Private nonguaranteed	..	..	..	..	..	..	..	..
Short-term	..	1.0	..	..	..	..	..	..
Net equity inflows								
Foreign direct investment	32.4	71.1	62.5	171.2	170.2	192.3	190.3	44.1
Portfolio equity	..	0.0	..	..	..	..	..	..
Major economic aggregates								
Gross national income (GNI)	1,014.4	1,869.6	2,030.3	2,108.1	2,594.0	2,819.4	2,861.5	2,861.5
Exports of goods, services & prim. income	824.4	1,391.2	1,680.9	1,473.7	1,669.3	1,952.7	1,658.4	..
Imports of goods, services & prim. income	1,132.8	1,891.8	2,034.9	2,138.5	2,740.8	3,027.8	3,111.0	..
Primary income on FDI	68.3	196.2	91.4	116.6	317.8	386.4	406.8	..
Personal transfers & comp. of employees	478.1	599.4	575.9	547.9	610.1	649.3	554.0	..
International reserves	417.9	519.1	971.5	1,179.8	1,071.0	919.1	1,027.9	1,055.2
Ratios								
External debt stocks to exports (%)	82.1	48.0	41.3	51.3	46.6	40.8	51.9	..
External debt stocks to GNI (%)	66.7	35.7	34.2	35.9	30.0	28.3	30.1	30.9
Debt service to exports (%)	7.5	5.7	2.2	2.6	2.1	2.0	2.3	..
Reserves to external debt stocks (%)	61.8	77.8	139.9	156.0	137.6	115.2	119.5	119.2

Notes:

Large interest payment was made during 2007 to a creditor country to settle a long standing claim. Short-term debt is based on data from the BIS.

LIBERIA

(US$ million, unless otherwise indicated)

	2000	2005	2008	2009	2010	2011	2012	2013
Summary external debt data								
External debt stocks	**2,836.3**	**3,950.6**	**3,160.8**	**1,850.3**	**418.9**	**448.4**	**487.1**	**541.5**
Long-term external debt	1,104.0	1,179.1	865.0	673.1	183.1	188.0	208.5	240.2
Short-term external debt	1,412.6	2,421.8	1,405.5	91.6	0.4	12.2	12.0	11.4
interest arrears on long-term	1,412.6	2,421.8	1,405.5	91.6	0.4	12.2	12.0	11.4
Use of IMF credit	319.7	349.7	890.3	1,085.5	235.3	248.2	266.7	289.9
Long-term external debt								
Debt outstanding and disbursed	**1,104.0**	**1,179.1**	**865.0**	**673.1**	**183.1**	**188.0**	**208.5**	**240.2**
Public and publicly guaranteed	1,104.0	1,179.1	865.0	673.1	183.1	188.0	208.5	240.2
Official creditors	907.3	981.3	669.8	652.6	183.1	188.0	208.5	240.2
Private creditors	196.8	197.7	195.2	20.5	0.0	0.0	0.0	0.0
of which: Bonds	0.0	0.0	0.0	0.0	0.0	0.0	0.0	0.0
Private nonguaranteed	..	..	..	..	..	..	..	..
of which: Bonds	..	..	..	..	..	..	..	..
Disbursements	**0.0**	**0.0**	**0.0**	**0.0**	**0.0**	**20.3**	**23.1**	**35.1**
Public and publicly guaranteed	0.0	0.0	0.0	0.0	0.0	20.3	23.1	35.1
Official creditors	0.0	0.0	0.0	0.0	0.0	20.3	23.1	35.1
Private creditors	0.0	0.0	0.0	0.0	0.0	0.0	0.0	0.0
of which: Bonds	0.0	0.0	0.0	0.0	0.0	0.0	0.0	0.0
Private nonguaranteed	..	..	..	..	..	..	..	..
of which: Bonds		..	..	..	..	..	..	..
Principal repayments	**0.0**	**0.0**	**37.5**	**4.3**	**3.7**	**2.6**	**3.5**	**4.0**
Public and publicly guaranteed	0.0	0.0	37.5	4.3	3.7	2.6	3.5	4.0
Official creditors	0.0	0.0	37.5	4.3	3.7	2.6	3.5	4.0
Private creditors	0.0	0.0	0.0	0.0	0.0	0.0	0.0	0.0
of which: Bonds	0.0	0.0	0.0	0.0	0.0	0.0	0.0	0.0
Private nonguaranteed	..	..	..	..	..	..	..	..
of which: Bonds	..	..	..	..	..	..	..	..
Interest payments	**0.0**	**0.0**	**69.0**	**11.8**	**0.6**	**0.4**	**1.1**	**1.5**
Public and publicly guaranteed	0.0	0.0	69.0	11.8	0.6	0.4	1.1	1.5
Official creditors	0.0	0.0	69.0	11.8	0.6	0.4	1.1	1.5
Private creditors	0.0	0.0	0.0	0.0	0.0	0.0	0.0	0.0
of which: Bonds	0.0	0.0	0.0	0.0	0.0	0.0	0.0	0.0
Private nonguaranteed	..	..	..	..	..	..	..	..
of which: Bonds	..	..	..	..	..	..	..	..
Net financial flows								
Net debt inflows	-0.6	-0.1	491.1	13.3	9.8	31.8	37.7	53.6
Official creditors (incl. IMF)	-0.6	-0.1	491.1	13.3	9.8	31.8	37.7	53.6
Private creditors	..	..	..	..	..	..	..	..
Long-term	..	..	..	..	..	..	..	..
Public and publicly guaranteed	..	..	..	..	..	..	..	..
Private nonguaranteed	..	..	..	..	..	..	..	..
Short-term	..	..	..	..	..	..	..	..
Net equity inflows								
Foreign direct investment	20.8	3.5	11.3	2.9	0.0	30.5	..	..
Portfolio equity	..	..	..	..	..	..	..	..
Major economic aggregates								
Gross national income (GNI)	514.1	394.4	690.4	1,010.5	1,113.3	1,420.6	1,581.5	1,751.0
Exports of goods, services & prim. income	..	354.7	781.0	472.2	430.4	1,351.8	..	..
Imports of goods, services & prim. income	..	1,317.7	2,310.7	1,850.0	1,804.7	3,325.3	..	..
Primary income on FDI	..	7.1	22.5	5.8	0.1	11.7	..	..
Personal transfers & comp. of employees	..	31.9	58.1	25.1	31.4	360.0	..	..
International reserves	0.3	25.4	160.9	372.5	465.9	512.8	497.2	493.1
Ratios								
External debt stocks to exports (%)	..	1113.7	404.7	391.9	97.3	33.2	..	..
External debt stocks to GNI (%)	551.7	1001.7	457.8	183.1	37.6	31.6	30.8	30.9
Debt service to exports (%)	..	0.5	119.7	13.6	1.4	0.2	..	..
Reserves to external debt stocks (%)	0.0	0.6	5.1	20.1	111.2	114.4	102.1	91.1

Notes:

Historical long-term public and publicly guaranteed debt data before 2011 are revised based on reports provided by the country. Data include the effects of Paris Club rescheduling agreement signed in 2008 and 2010, and HIPC and MDRI debt relief.

MACEDONIA, FYR

(US$ million, unless otherwise indicated)

	2000	2005	2008	2009	2010	2011	2012	2013
Summary external debt data								
External debt stocks	**1,480**	**2,981**	**4,457**	**5,247**	**5,344**	**6,304**	**6,650**	**6,934**
Long-term external debt	1,333	2,108	3,013	3,731	3,840	4,132	4,376	4,928
Short-term external debt	55	800	1,432	1,413	1,403	1,769	1,870	1,602
interest arrears on long-term	4	9	29	30	64	80	109	129
Use of IMF credit	92	74	13	103	101	403	404	404
Long-term external debt								
Debt outstanding and disbursed	**1,333**	**2,108**	**3,013**	**3,731**	**3,840**	**4,132**	**4,376**	**4,928**
Public and publicly guaranteed	1,206	1,637	1,574	1,874	1,880	2,110	2,270	2,572
Official creditors	921	1,202	1,277	1,321	1,369	1,392	1,453	1,596
Private creditors	284	435	297	552	512	717	817	976
of which: Bonds	0	177	209	468	434	421	429	207
Private nonguaranteed	127	471	1,438	1,858	1,959	2,022	2,106	2,355
of which: Bonds	..	..	..	..	..	..	..	..
Disbursements	**151**	**318**	**789**	**1,012**	**596**	**968**	**637**	**1,063**
Public and publicly guaranteed	98	293	174	347	197	414	303	694
Official creditors	96	104	137	103	190	155	176	305
Private creditors	1	189	37	244	7	259	127	389
of which: Bonds	0	187	0	244	0	0	0	0
Private nonguaranteed	54	25	615	665	399	555	334	369
of which: Bonds	..	..	..	..	..	..	..	..
Principal repayments	**74**	**171**	**293**	**375**	**443**	**739**	**479**	**734**
Public and publicly guaranteed	25	81	78	88	98	126	168	462
Official creditors	23	67	74	81	90	103	124	192
Private creditors	2	14	5	7	9	23	44	270
of which: Bonds	0	0	0	0	0	0	0	235
Private nonguaranteed	49	90	215	287	344	614	310	272
of which: Bonds	..	..	..	..	..	..	..	..
Interest payments	**37**	**54**	**104**	**93**	**128**	**129**	**125**	**117**
Public and publicly guaranteed	30	41	54	47	56	60	64	64
Official creditors	20	32	41	33	22	24	23	19
Private creditors	10	9	14	15	35	36	41	45
of which: Bonds	0	0	10	10	32	33	31	21
Private nonguaranteed	7	13	50	46	71	70	60	54
of which: Bonds	..	..	..	..	..	..	..	..
Net financial flows								
Net debt inflows	59	117	329	617	109	890	230	41
Official creditors (incl. IMF)	58	42	64	22	101	362	51	113
Private creditors	2	75	265	595	9	528	179	-72
Long-term	5	109	432	615	53	177	108	216
Public and publicly guaranteed	0	174	32	237	-2	236	83	119
Private nonguaranteed	5	-65	400	378	55	-59	24	97
Short-term	-3	-34	-167	-20	-44	350	72	-288
Net equity inflows								
Foreign direct investment	215	155	324	57	202	572	140	196
Portfolio equity	..	54	-49	-14	-4	-8	-6	-1
Major economic aggregates								
Gross national income (GNI)	3,517	5,877	9,714	9,231	9,207	10,252	9,548	9,978
Exports of goods, services & prim. income	1,679	2,196	4,540	3,186	3,825	5,031	4,544	4,893
Imports of goods, services & prim. income	2,391	3,408	7,234	5,397	5,828	7,367	6,939	7,136
Primary income on FDI	31	142	253	138	232	276	268	324
Personal transfers & comp. of employees	81	227	407	381	388	434	394	376
International reserves	429	1,229	1,920	2,051	1,970	2,331	2,528	2,485
Ratios								
External debt stocks to exports (%)	88.1	135.8	98.2	164.7	139.7	125.3	146.4	141.7
External debt stocks to GNI (%)	42.1	50.7	45.9	56.8	58.0	61.5	69.6	69.5
Debt service to exports (%)	8.3	12.5	10.2	16.7	16.5	18.9	15.1	18.8
Reserves to external debt stocks (%)	29.0	41.2	43.1	39.1	36.9	37.0	38.0	35.8

MADAGASCAR

(US$ million, unless otherwise indicated)

	2000	2005	2008	2009	2010	2011	2012	2013
Summary external debt data								
External debt stocks	**4,716**	**3,521**	**2,480**	**2,788**	**2,699**	**2,769**	**2,896**	**2,849**
Long-term external debt	4,286	3,182	1,738	1,855	1,997	2,066	2,167	2,247
Short-term external debt	301	99	613	649	425	430	463	345
interest arrears on long-term	203	72	188	189	188	188	192	52
Use of IMF credit	129	240	129	284	278	273	267	256
Long-term external debt								
Debt outstanding and disbursed	**4,286**	**3,182**	**1,738**	**1,855**	**1,997**	**2,066**	**2,167**	**2,247**
Public and publicly guaranteed	4,286	3,182	1,717	1,836	1,982	2,053	2,157	2,240
Official creditors	4,247	3,173	1,710	1,829	1,975	2,046	2,147	2,205
Private creditors	39	9	7	7	7	7	10	34
of which: Bonds	0	0	0	0	0	0	0	0
Private nonguaranteed	..	..	21	19	15	12	10	8
of which: Bonds	..	..	..	..	..	..	..	..
Disbursements	**150**	**249**	**345**	**126**	**198**	**90**	**138**	**149**
Public and publicly guaranteed	150	249	342	124	198	90	138	149
Official creditors	150	249	342	124	197	90	135	146
Private creditors	0	0	0	0	0	0	3	3
of which: Bonds	0	0	0	0	0	0	0	0
Private nonguaranteed	..	..	3	2	..	..	..	..
of which: Bonds	..	..	..	..	..	..	..	
Principal repayments	**74**	**38**	**20**	**34**	**37**	**18**	**37**	**38**
Public and publicly guaranteed	74	38	20	32	36	18	35	38
Official creditors	73	37	20	32	36	18	35	38
Private creditors	0	1	0	0	0	0	0	0
of which: Bonds	0	0	0	0	0	0	0	0
Private nonguaranteed	..	..	1	1	1	1	2	1
of which: Bonds	..	..	..	..	..	..	..	..
Interest payments	**28**	**28**	**11**	**15**	**16**	**16**	**17**	**17**
Public and publicly guaranteed	28	28	11	15	16	16	17	17
Official creditors	28	28	11	15	16	16	17	17
Private creditors	0	0	0	0	0	0	0	0
of which: Bonds	0	0	0	0	0	0	0	0
Private nonguaranteed	..	..	0	0	0	0	0	0
of which: Bonds	..	..	..	..	..	..	..	..
Net financial flows								
Net debt inflows	45	244	198	127	-65	74	123	122
Official creditors (incl. IMF)	122	218	381	92	160	69	94	97
Private creditors	-77	26	-183	35	-225	5	29	24
Long-term	0	-1	3	0	-1	-1	1	2
Public and publicly guaranteed	0	-1	0	0	..	0	3	3
Private nonguaranteed	..	..	3	0	-1	-1	-2	-1
Short-term	-76	27	-186	35	-224	6	29	22
Net equity inflows								
Foreign direct investment	83	85	1,169	1,066	808	810	812	838
Portfolio equity	..	..	..	..	..	..	..	..
Major economic aggregates								
Gross national income (GNI)	3,807	4,960	9,335	8,404	8,621	9,699	9,560	10,453
Exports of goods, services & prim. income	1,210	954	2,614	1,982	1,653	1,965	..	..
Imports of goods, services & prim. income	1,584	1,743	4,805	4,134	2,744	3,003	..	..
Primary income on FDI	4	38	..	..	..	..	..	..
Personal transfers & comp. of employees	11	11	..	..	..	..	..	..
International reserves	285	481	982	982	1,023	1,135	1,053	776
Ratios								
External debt stocks to exports (%)	389.7	369.2	94.9	140.7	163.3	140.9	..	..
External debt stocks to GNI (%)	123.9	71.0	26.6	33.2	31.3	28.6	30.3	27.3
Debt service to exports (%)	9.7	8.3	1.7	2.8	3.7	2.1	..	..
Reserves to external debt stocks (%)	6.0	13.7	39.6	35.2	37.9	41.0	36.3	27.2

Notes:

Data include the effects of HIPC and MDRI debt relief.

MALAWI

(US$ million, unless otherwise indicated)

	2000	2005	2008	2009	2010	2011	2012	2013
Summary external debt data								
External debt stocks	**2,719**	**3,196**	**996**	**1,144**	**1,039**	**1,205**	**1,316**	**1,558**
Long-term external debt	2,544	3,062	769	846	729	929	1,025	1,244
Short-term external debt	78	43	85	67	61	30	8	19
interest arrears on long-term	37	34	0	0	0	0	0	0
Use of IMF credit	97	91	142	231	248	247	283	295
Long-term external debt								
Debt outstanding and disbursed	**2,544**	**3,062**	**769**	**846**	**729**	**929**	**1,025**	**1,244**
Public and publicly guaranteed	2,544	3,062	769	846	729	929	1,025	1,244
Official creditors	2,526	3,043	763	841	724	923	1,019	1,238
Private creditors	18	18	6	6	5	5	5	6
of which: Bonds	0	0	0	0	0	0	0	0
Private nonguaranteed	..	..	..	..	..	..	..	..
of which: Bonds	..	..	..	..	..	..	..	..
Disbursements	**119**	**89**	**66**	**107**	**81**	**208**	**109**	**230**
Public and publicly guaranteed	119	89	66	107	81	208	109	230
Official creditors	119	89	66	107	81	208	109	230
Private creditors	0	0	0	0	0	0	0	0
of which: Bonds	0	0	0	0	0	0	0	0
Private nonguaranteed	..	..	..	..	..	..	..	..
of which: Bonds	..	..	..	..	..	..	..	..
Principal repayments	**33**	**38**	**17**	**22**	**13**	**14**	**15**	**22**
Public and publicly guaranteed	33	38	17	22	13	14	15	22
Official creditors	33	35	17	22	13	14	15	22
Private creditors	0	3	0	0	0	0	0	0
of which: Bonds	0	0	0	0	0	0	0	0
Private nonguaranteed	..	..	..	..	..	..	..	..
of which: Bonds	..	..	..	..	..	..	..	..
Interest payments	**18**	**22**	**15**	**15**	**7**	**7**	**9**	**14**
Public and publicly guaranteed	18	22	15	15	7	7	9	14
Official creditors	18	22	15	15	7	7	9	14
Private creditors	0	0	0	0	0	0	0	0
of which: Bonds	0	0	0	0	0	0	0	0
Private nonguaranteed	..	..	..	..	..	..	..	..
of which: Bonds	..	..	..	..	..	..	..	..
Net financial flows								
Net debt inflows	83	42	170	67	83	162	108	231
Official creditors (incl. IMF)	85	47	146	85	89	193	130	220
Private creditors	-2	-5	24	-18	-6	-31	-22	11
Long-term	..	-3	0	..	..	..	..	..
Public and publicly guaranteed	..	-3	0	..	..	..	..	..
Private nonguaranteed	..	..	..	..	..	..	..	..
Short-term	-2	-2	24	-18	-6	-31	-22	11
Net equity inflows								
Foreign direct investment	26	88	146	69	133	89	89	118
Portfolio equity	..	-4	-1	0	1	1	1	..
Major economic aggregates								
Gross national income (GNI)	1,707	2,715	4,254	4,972	5,290	5,512	4,104	3,574
Exports of goods, services & prim. income	471	609	1,026	1,348	1,224	1,632	1,397	..
Imports of goods, services & prim. income	680	1,390	2,127	2,298	2,650	2,917	2,646	..
Primary income on FDI	15	52	139	103	173	92	93	..
Personal transfers & comp. of employees	1	23	17	17	22	25	28	..
International reserves	243	159	243	149	307	197	223	413
Ratios								
External debt stocks to exports (%)	577.7	524.5	97.0	84.9	84.9	73.9	94.2	..
External debt stocks to GNI (%)	159.3	117.7	23.4	23.0	19.6	21.9	32.1	43.6
Debt service to exports (%)	13.5	12.5	3.1	2.9	1.7	1.4	2.0	..
Reserves to external debt stocks (%)	8.9	5.0	24.4	13.1	29.6	16.4	17.0	26.5

Notes:

Short-term debt is based on data from the BIS. Data include the effects of Paris Club rescheduling agreement signed in 2006 and HIPC and MDRI debt relief.

MALAYSIA

(US$ million, unless otherwise indicated)

	2000	2005	2008	2009	2010	2011	2012	2013
Summary external debt data								
External debt stocks	**41,946**	**64,911**	**106,896**	**119,611**	**135,800**	**146,898**	**195,064**	**213,129**
Long-term external debt	37,192	51,537	67,882	73,806	82,450	80,128	100,201	107,226
Short-term external debt	4,573	13,176	38,800	43,695	51,276	64,704	92,794	103,830
interest arrears on long-term	0	0	0	0	0	0	0	0
Use of IMF credit	181	199	214	2,110	2,073	2,067	2,069	2,073
Long-term external debt								
Debt outstanding and disbursed	**37,192**	**51,537**	**67,882**	**73,806**	**82,450**	**80,128**	**100,201**	**107,226**
Public and publicly guaranteed	19,125	34,387	49,070	53,717	61,858	60,647	67,392	70,365
Official creditors	4,950	6,542	5,164	4,092	3,750	3,263	2,980	2,463
Private creditors	14,175	27,845	43,906	49,626	58,108	57,384	64,412	67,901
of which: Bonds	9,836	24,585	39,374	45,670	51,638	52,735	61,762	66,044
Private nonguaranteed	18,067	17,150	18,812	20,089	20,593	19,481	32,809	36,861
of which: Bonds	3,402	7,623	6,568	5,927	4,893	5,509	9,408	10,378
Disbursements	**5,921**	**10,378**	**9,100**	**12,554**	**10,938**	**10,982**	**21,901**	**17,426**
Public and publicly guaranteed	3,460	6,195	6,508	9,634	6,014	3,311	8,870	7,887
Official creditors	1,446	981	98	47	18	10	514	56
Private creditors	2,015	5,215	6,410	9,587	5,996	3,301	8,356	7,831
of which: Bonds	1,061	5,164	4,566	8,815	2,339	2,892	8,033	7,227
Private nonguaranteed	2,461	4,183	2,592	2,920	4,923	7,671	13,031	9,538
of which: Bonds	361	1,615	..	..	400	1,293	3,988	1,783
Principal repayments	**4,146**	**7,192**	**3,258**	**7,750**	**3,564**	**4,681**	**4,100**	**6,728**
Public and publicly guaranteed	2,017	4,752	1,503	5,351	1,863	3,608	3,304	1,681
Official creditors	840	1,218	820	1,053	688	625	604	300
Private creditors	1,176	3,534	683	4,298	1,176	2,983	2,701	1,381
of which: Bonds	200	2,036	0	2,959	0	750	380	9
Private nonguaranteed	2,129	2,440	1,755	2,399	1,701	1,073	796	5,046
of which: Bonds	745	237	250	1,398	715	420	100	300
Interest payments	**2,021**	**1,858**	**2,112**	**1,746**	**1,708**	**1,563**	**2,053**	**2,451**
Public and publicly guaranteed	1,159	1,208	1,058	876	1,024	1,017	1,293	1,251
Official creditors	259	314	129	124	97	86	79	69
Private creditors	900	894	929	752	927	931	1,214	1,182
of which: Bonds	599	746	802	652	771	853	1,084	1,117
Private nonguaranteed	862	650	1,053	870	684	545	760	1,200
of which: Bonds	159	363	373	339	295	266	354	424
Net financial flows								
Net debt inflows	337	4,929	21,542	9,698	14,955	19,728	45,890	21,734
Official creditors (incl. IMF)	606	-238	-722	-1,006	-669	-614	-90	-245
Private creditors	-269	5,167	22,264	10,705	15,625	20,343	45,980	21,979
Long-term	1,170	3,424	6,564	5,810	8,043	6,915	17,890	10,943
Public and publicly guaranteed	838	1,681	5,726	5,289	4,821	317	5,656	6,450
Private nonguaranteed	331	1,743	837	521	3,223	6,598	12,235	4,492
Short-term	-1,439	1,744	15,700	4,895	7,581	13,428	28,090	11,036
Net equity inflows								
Foreign direct investment	3,788	4,232	5,167	706	10,886	15,119	9,734	11,583
Portfolio equity	..	-1,200	-10,716	-449	..	..	..	..
Major economic aggregates								
Gross national income (GNI)	86,182	137,211	224,078	198,218	239,358	282,128	293,358	301,268
Exports of goods, services & prim. income	114,356	166,725	242,055	197,562	243,301	281,911	279,255	274,038
Imports of goods, services & prim. income	103,944	142,268	197,879	160,181	209,534	241,520	254,714	257,485
Primary income on FDI	7,173	8,330	13,838	11,119	15,298	18,105	18,385	18,408
Personal transfers & comp. of employees	342	1,117	1,329	1,131	1,103	1,211	1,320	1,396
International reserves	28,330	69,858	91,149	95,432	104,884	131,780	137,784	133,444
Ratios								
External debt stocks to exports (%)	36.7	38.9	44.2	60.5	55.8	52.1	69.9	77.8
External debt stocks to GNI (%)	48.7	47.3	47.7	60.3	56.7	52.1	66.5	70.7
Debt service to exports (%)	5.6	5.6	2.4	5.1	2.3	2.3	2.3	3.5
Reserves to external debt stocks (%)	67.5	107.6	85.3	79.8	77.2	89.7	70.6	62.6

Notes:

Long-term public and publicly guaranteed, long-term private nonguaranteed, and short-term debt data are World Bank staff estimates based on reports provided by the country.

MALDIVES

(US$ million, unless otherwise indicated)

	2000	2005	2008	2009	2010	2011	2012	2013
Summary external debt data								
External debt stocks	**206.4**	**362.3**	**898.6**	**965.1**	**994.3**	**973.8**	**844.8**	**820.5**
Long-term external debt	184.7	299.8	678.4	758.5	743.1	717.1	721.1	748.0
Short-term external debt	21.4	56.3	215.9	185.6	223.6	229.2	96.1	50.4
interest arrears on long-term	0.0	0.3	1.6	1.0	2.9	1.3	3.0	5.6
Use of IMF credit	0.4	6.3	4.4	20.9	27.6	27.5	27.6	22.1
Long-term external debt								
Debt outstanding and disbursed	**184.7**	**299.8**	**678.4**	**758.5**	**743.1**	**717.1**	**721.1**	**748.0**
Public and publicly guaranteed	184.7	299.8	469.9	542.7	627.8	675.2	721.1	748.0
Official creditors	154.8	250.2	355.7	445.2	522.3	565.3	633.8	668.9
Private creditors	29.9	49.6	114.2	97.5	105.5	109.9	87.3	79.1
of which: Bonds	0.0	0.0	0.0	0.0	0.0	0.0	0.0	0.0
Private nonguaranteed	..	..	208.5	215.8	115.2	41.9	..	..
of which: Bonds	..	..	..	..	..	..	..	..
Disbursements	**13.6**	**45.9**	**144.9**	**156.8**	**168.5**	**124.5**	**113.3**	**77.0**
Public and publicly guaranteed	13.6	45.9	100.2	112.0	142.4	115.9	113.3	77.0
Official creditors	6.3	29.5	52.8	107.3	108.4	82.9	111.7	70.4
Private creditors	7.3	16.3	47.4	4.6	34.0	33.0	1.6	6.6
of which: Bonds	0.0	0.0	0.0	0.0	0.0	0.0	0.0	0.0
Private nonguaranteed	..	..	44.7	44.8	26.1	8.6	..	..
of which: Bonds	..	..	..	..	..	..	..	..
Principal repayments	**13.9**	**22.1**	**62.0**	**64.7**	**59.8**	**70.3**	**66.1**	**55.0**
Public and publicly guaranteed	13.9	22.1	38.1	44.4	50.9	66.3	66.1	55.0
Official creditors	6.7	13.1	22.8	21.5	27.1	40.9	40.8	37.4
Private creditors	7.3	9.0	15.4	22.9	23.9	25.4	25.2	17.7
of which: Bonds	0.0	0.0	0.0	0.0	0.0	0.0	0.0	0.0
Private nonguaranteed	..	..	23.9	20.3	8.9	3.9	..	..
of which: Bonds	..	..	..	..	..	..	..	..
Interest payments	**4.7**	**7.1**	**19.2**	**16.4**	**10.6**	**11.0**	**10.1**	**9.1**
Public and publicly guaranteed	4.7	7.1	12.3	12.1	9.2	10.4	10.1	9.1
Official creditors	2.6	4.8	7.3	6.8	5.4	6.2	6.9	7.4
Private creditors	2.2	2.2	5.0	5.3	3.7	4.2	3.2	1.7
of which: Bonds	0.0	0.0	0.0	0.0	0.0	0.0	0.0	0.0
Private nonguaranteed	..	..	6.9	4.2	1.5	0.5	..	..
of which: Bonds	..	..	..	..	..	..	..	..
Net financial flows								
Net debt inflows	-3.8	53.8	104.9	67.2	151.8	61.4	-87.5	-31.8
Official creditors (incl. IMF)	-0.4	22.5	27.6	90.6	88.3	42.0	70.9	27.6
Private creditors	-3.4	31.3	77.3	-23.4	63.5	19.4	-158.4	-59.4
Long-term	0.0	7.3	52.9	6.2	27.4	12.2	-23.6	-11.1
Public and publicly guaranteed	0.0	7.3	32.1	-18.2	10.2	7.6	-23.6	-11.1
Private nonguaranteed	..	..	20.8	24.5	17.2	4.7	..	..
Short-term	-3.5	24.0	24.5	-29.6	36.1	7.2	-134.8	-48.3
Net equity inflows								
Foreign direct investment	22.3	53.0	181.3	158.0	216.5	256.5	284.0	325.3
Portfolio equity	..	..	13.9	-14.5	-10.4	0.0	0.0	..
Major economic aggregates								
Gross national income (GNI)	594.3	961.6	1,601.8	1,712.2	1,822.8	1,804.3	1,742.9	1,952.5
Exports of goods, services & prim. income	467.5	495.4	1,983.8	1,718.0	2,011.5	2,358.3	2,351.2	..
Imports of goods, services & prim. income	492.0	910.4	2,380.8	1,758.2	2,008.5	2,594.9	2,709.5	..
Primary income on FDI	34.4	31.0	248.8	235.9	271.9	280.2	281.0	..
Personal transfers & comp. of employees	2.2	2.3	6.3	4.5	3.2	3.0	3.1	..
International reserves	122.8	189.0	243.6	275.6	364.3	348.7	318.3	381.9
Ratios								
External debt stocks to exports (%)	44.1	73.1	45.3	56.2	49.4	41.3	35.9	..
External debt stocks to GNI (%)	34.7	37.7	56.1	56.4	54.5	54.0	48.5	42.0
Debt service to exports (%)	4.2	6.3	4.7	5.2	4.0	3.8	3.4	..
Reserves to external debt stocks (%)	59.5	52.2	27.1	28.6	36.6	35.8	37.7	46.5

Notes:

Long-term private nonguaranteed and short-term debt data from 2006 are World Bank staff estimates based on reports provided by the country.

MALI

(US$ million, unless otherwise indicated)

	2000	2005	2008	2009	2010	2011	2012	2013
Summary external debt data								
External debt stocks	**2,981**	**3,224**	**2,055**	**2,210**	**2,456**	**2,923**	**3,064**	**3,423**
Long-term external debt	2,671	3,036	1,984	2,002	2,263	2,500	2,787	3,078
Short-term external debt	114	55	7	25	6	193	39	68
interest arrears on long-term	42	6	7	1	0	18	26	29
Use of IMF credit	196	132	65	184	187	230	237	277
Long-term external debt								
Debt outstanding and disbursed	**2,671**	**3,036**	**1,984**	**2,002**	**2,263**	**2,500**	**2,787**	**3,078**
Public and publicly guaranteed	2,671	3,036	1,984	2,002	2,263	2,500	2,787	3,078
Official creditors	2,671	3,032	1,979	1,995	2,258	2,497	2,784	3,075
Private creditors	0	5	5	7	5	4	3	3
of which: Bonds	0	0	0	0	0	0	0	0
Private nonguaranteed	..	..	..	..	..	..	..	..
of which: Bonds	..	..	..	..	..	..	..	..
Disbursements	**100**	**280**	**234**	**494**	**304**	**292**	**275**	**321**
Public and publicly guaranteed	100	280	234	494	304	292	275	321
Official creditors	100	277	234	491	304	292	275	321
Private creditors	0	3	0	3	0	0	0	0
of which: Bonds	0	0	0	0	0	0	0	0
Private nonguaranteed	..	..	..	..	..	..	..	..
of which: Bonds	..	..	..	..	..	..	..	..
Principal repayments	**50**	**52**	**44**	**46**	**39**	**39**	**28**	**64**
Public and publicly guaranteed	50	52	44	46	39	39	28	64
Official creditors	50	52	43	45	38	38	27	63
Private creditors	0	0	1	1	1	1	0	1
of which: Bonds	0	0	0	0	0	0	0	0
Private nonguaranteed	..	..	..	..	..	..	..	..
of which: Bonds	..	..	..	..	..	..	..	..
Interest payments	**18**	**27**	**24**	**22**	**21**	**25**	**24**	**27**
Public and publicly guaranteed	18	27	24	22	21	25	24	27
Official creditors	18	27	24	21	21	25	24	27
Private creditors	0	0	0	0	0	0	0	0
of which: Bonds	0	0	0	0	0	0	0	0
Private nonguaranteed	..	..	..	..	..	..	..	..
of which: Bonds	..	..	..	..	..	..	..	..
Net financial flows								
Net debt inflows	-31	219	218	475	253	467	92	321
Official creditors (incl. IMF)	42	210	220	449	272	299	255	296
Private creditors	-73	8	-1	25	-19	168	-162	25
Long-term	..	3	-1	1	-1	-1	0	-1
Public and publicly guaranteed	..	3	-1	1	-1	-1	0	-1
Private nonguaranteed	..	..	..	..	..	..	..	..
Short-term	-73	5	..	24	-18	169	-162	26
Net equity inflows								
Foreign direct investment	82	160	268	796	504	393	398	410
Portfolio equity	0	9	-3	-3	1	2	..	..
Major economic aggregates								
Gross national income (GNI)	2,392	5,099	8,425	8,508	9,003	10,195	9,808	10,273
Exports of goods, services & prim. income	665	1,443	2,653	2,210	2,508	2,859	3,519	..
Imports of goods, services & prim. income	1,046	2,108	4,171	3,351	4,236	4,371	4,616	..
Primary income on FDI	76	190	326	459	402	407	..	..
Personal transfers & comp. of employees	73	177	431	454	473	784	..	..
International reserves	382	854	1,072	1,604	1,344	1,379	1,341	1,306
Ratios								
External debt stocks to exports (%)	448.5	223.4	77.5	100.0	97.9	102.3	87.0	..
External debt stocks to GNI (%)	124.6	63.2	24.4	26.0	27.3	28.7	31.2	33.3
Debt service to exports (%)	14.1	6.9	2.6	3.1	2.5	2.3	1.5	..
Reserves to external debt stocks (%)	12.8	26.5	52.1	72.6	54.7	47.2	43.8	38.1

Notes:

Short-term debt is based on data from the BIS. The data for Principal Arrears on long-term are revised from 2001. Data include the effects of HIPC and MDRI debt relief.

MAURITANIA

(US$ million, unless otherwise indicated)

	2000	2005	2008	2009	2010	2011	2012	2013
Summary external debt data								
External debt stocks	**2,390**	**2,322**	**2,001**	**2,289**	**2,705**	**2,867**	**3,352**	**3,570**
Long-term external debt	2,029	2,072	1,669	1,984	2,323	2,538	2,945	3,142
Short-term external debt	251	167	301	192	237	151	196	202
interest arrears on long-term	112	109	135	134	76	77	76	76
Use of IMF credit	111	83	31	113	145	178	211	226
Long-term external debt								
Debt outstanding and disbursed	**2,029**	**2,072**	**1,669**	**1,984**	**2,323**	**2,538**	**2,945**	**3,142**
Public and publicly guaranteed	2,029	2,072	1,669	1,984	2,323	2,538	2,945	3,142
Official creditors	2,009	2,048	1,655	1,972	2,322	2,538	2,945	3,142
Private creditors	19	23	14	12	1	0	0	0
of which: Bonds	0	0	0	0	0	0	0	0
Private nonguaranteed	..	..	..	..	..	..	..	..
of which: Bonds	..	..	..	..	..	..	..	..
Disbursements	**115**	**143**	**294**	**407**	**412**	**287**	**444**	**292**
Public and publicly guaranteed	115	143	294	407	412	287	444	292
Official creditors	115	128	294	407	412	287	444	292
Private creditors	0	15	0	0	0	0	0	0
of which: Bonds	0	0	0	0	0	0	0	0
Private nonguaranteed	..	..	..	..	..	..	..	..
of which: Bonds	..	..	..	..	..	..	..	..
Principal repayments	**46**	**33**	**38**	**53**	**76**	**79**	**85**	**106**
Public and publicly guaranteed	46	33	38	53	76	79	85	106
Official creditors	43	31	31	52	65	78	85	106
Private creditors	2	1	6	1	11	1	0	0
of which: Bonds	0	0	0	0	0	0	0	0
Private nonguaranteed	..	..	..	..	..	..	..	..
of which: Bonds	..	..	..	..	..	..	..	..
Interest payments	**20**	**20**	**21**	**23**	**35**	**41**	**55**	**54**
Public and publicly guaranteed	20	20	21	23	35	41	55	54
Official creditors	18	19	21	23	34	41	55	54
Private creditors	2	1	0	0	1	0	0	0
of which: Bonds	0	0	0	0	0	0	0	0
Private nonguaranteed	..	..	..	..	..	..	..	..
of which: Bonds	..	..	..	..	..	..	..	..
Net financial flows								
Net debt inflows	62	92	300	246	473	156	437	206
Official creditors (incl. IMF)	74	87	266	355	381	244	391	200
Private creditors	-11	5	34	-109	92	-88	46	6
Long-term	-2	14	-6	-1	-11	-1	..	..
Public and publicly guaranteed	-2	14	-6	-1	-11	-1	..	..
Private nonguaranteed	..	..	..	..	..	..	..	..
Short-term	-9	-9	40	-108	103	-87	46	6
Net equity inflows								
Foreign direct investment	40	814	343	-3	131	589	1,383	1,154
Portfolio equity	..	..	..	..	..	..	..	..
Major economic aggregates								
Gross national income (GNI)	1,304	2,249	3,821	3,079	3,445	3,980	3,768	3,892
Exports of goods, services & prim. income	..	..	2,056	1,641	2,306	3,124	2,914	..
Imports of goods, services & prim. income	..	..	2,776	2,176	2,787	3,522	4,497	..
Primary income on FDI	..	..	..	..	..	..	..	..
Personal transfers & comp. of employees	..	..	..	..	..	..	..	..
International reserves	46	64	189	225	272	485	949	..
Ratios								
External debt stocks to exports (%)	..	..	97.3	139.5	117.3	91.8	115.0	..
External debt stocks to GNI (%)	183.3	103.2	52.4	74.3	78.5	72.0	89.0	91.7
Debt service to exports (%)	..	..	3.1	4.7	4.9	3.9	4.9	..
Reserves to external debt stocks (%)	1.9	2.8	9.4	9.8	10.0	16.9	28.3	..

Notes:

Short-term debt is based on data from the BIS. Data include the effects of MDRI debt relief.

MAURITIUS

(US$ million, unless otherwise indicated)

	2000	2005	2008	2009	2010	2011	2012	2013
Summary external debt data								
External debt stocks	**967**	**805**	**671**	**2,265**	**2,734**	**9,574**	**10,221**	**10,919**
Long-term external debt	946	782	647	821	1,107	7,720	7,164	7,912
Short-term external debt	..	..	..	1,292	1,478	1,706	2,908	2,858
interest arrears on long-term	0	0	0	0	0	0	1	0
Use of IMF credit	21	23	24	152	149	149	149	149
Long-term external debt								
Debt outstanding and disbursed	**946**	**782**	**647**	**821**	**1,107**	**7,720**	**7,164**	**7,912**
Public and publicly guaranteed	828	716	597	740	1,007	1,215	1,412	1,777
Official creditors	494	504	501	655	888	1,099	1,301	1,682
Private creditors	334	213	96	85	119	116	110	95
of which: Bonds	0	0	0	0	0	0	0	0
Private nonguaranteed	118	66	49	81	100	6,505	5,752	6,135
of which: Bonds	..	..	..	..	..	..	..	..
Disbursements	**128**	**138**	**116**	**287**	**425**	**4,629**	**3,723**	**3,936**
Public and publicly guaranteed	119	126	88	218	356	300	254	409
Official creditors	43	62	88	199	293	271	243	409
Private creditors	76	64	0	19	63	29	11	0
of which: Bonds	0	0	0	0	0	0	0	0
Private nonguaranteed	9	11	28	69	69	4,329	3,469	3,528
of which: Bonds	..	..	..	..	..	..	..	
Principal repayments	**401**	**197**	**145**	**122**	**118**	**3,343**	**3,032**	**3,278**
Public and publicly guaranteed	385	176	111	85	69	79	66	68
Official creditors	55	87	83	52	45	51	47	48
Private creditors	330	89	27	33	24	28	19	20
of which: Bonds	150	0	0	0	0	0	0	0
Private nonguaranteed	16	21	35	37	49	3,264	2,966	3,210
of which: Bonds	..	..	..	..	..	..	..	..
Interest payments	**52**	**30**	**26**	**21**	**18**	**79**	**73**	**76**
Public and publicly guaranteed	51	30	25	20	17	23	27	26
Official creditors	23	19	18	16	15	20	24	24
Private creditors	29	10	7	4	2	4	3	2
of which: Bonds	5	0	0	0	0	0	0	0
Private nonguaranteed	1	0	0	1	1	55	46	50
of which: Bonds	..	..	..	..	..	..	..	..
Net financial flows								
Net debt inflows	-273	-59	-30	165	492	1,514	1,893	609
Official creditors (incl. IMF)	-12	-24	5	147	249	220	196	361
Private creditors	-261	-35	-34	18	243	1,294	1,697	248
Long-term	-261	-35	-34	18	58	1,066	495	297
Public and publicly guaranteed	-254	-25	-27	-14	38	1	-8	-20
Private nonguaranteed	-6	-10	-7	32	20	1,065	503	317
Short-term	..	..	..	..	185	228	1,202	-49
Net equity inflows								
Foreign direct investment	266	42	378	257	430	433	589	259
Portfolio equity	-4	36	34	206	..	..	..	..
Major economic aggregates								
Gross national income (GNI)	4,553	6,276	9,714	8,793	9,835	11,282	11,479	11,952
Exports of goods, services & prim. income	2,671	3,899	5,748	4,635	10,189	6,983	8,048	8,085
Imports of goods, services & prim. income	2,772	4,284	6,948	5,514	11,378	8,664	9,017	9,355
Primary income on FDI	8	34	163	195	4,639	601	1,074	773
Personal transfers & comp. of employees	177	1	1	1	1	1	1	1
International reserves	897	1,340	1,743	2,179	2,442	2,583	2,837	3,340
Ratios								
External debt stocks to exports (%)	36.2	20.6	11.7	48.9	26.8	137.1	127.0	135.1
External debt stocks to GNI (%)	21.2	12.8	6.9	25.8	27.8	84.9	89.0	91.4
Debt service to exports (%)	17.0	5.8	3.0	3.4	1.5	49.4	39.1	42.0
Reserves to external debt stocks (%)	92.8	166.4	259.8	96.2	89.3	27.0	27.8	30.6

Notes:

Long-term private nonguaranteed debt data from 2009 are based on reports provided by the country and do not include offshore liabilities and 2011-2013 are World Bank staff estimates based on reports provided by the country. Short-term debt data are based on reports provided by the country and include offshore liabilities.

MEXICO

(US$ million, unless otherwise indicated)

	2000	2005	2008	2009	2010	2011	2012	2013
Summary external debt data								
External debt stocks	**152,260**	**175,918**	**206,190**	**201,911**	**262,022**	**302,173**	**375,830**	**443,012**
Long-term external debt	132,951	153,302	177,884	167,747	200,231	231,088	278,204	330,844
Short-term external debt	18,932	22,201	27,860	29,695	57,400	66,707	93,245	107,778
interest arrears on long-term	0	0	0	0	0	0	0	0
Use of IMF credit	378	415	447	4,470	4,391	4,377	4,382	4,391
Long-term external debt								
Debt outstanding and disbursed	**132,951**	**153,302**	**177,884**	**167,747**	**200,231**	**231,088**	**278,204**	**330,844**
Public and publicly guaranteed	82,470	118,145	133,102	123,226	150,603	171,586	208,649	228,364
Official creditors	20,892	18,789	12,424	21,082	25,973	28,161	29,848	31,092
Private creditors	61,577	99,356	120,679	102,144	124,630	143,426	178,801	197,272
of which: Bonds	53,693	78,193	97,385	82,872	102,336	122,879	160,560	166,843
Private nonguaranteed	50,481	35,158	44,782	44,521	49,628	59,502	69,555	102,480
of which: Bonds	20,644	19,442	19,958	21,525	29,997	36,223	50,016	82,624
Disbursements	**32,830**	**28,801**	**33,704**	**36,695**	**54,986**	**59,712**	**98,408**	**85,269**
Public and publicly guaranteed	11,483	17,995	24,746	26,616	42,142	34,063	47,826	35,481
Official creditors	2,855	2,309	2,761	8,572	6,166	4,518	3,099	2,886
Private creditors	8,628	15,686	21,985	18,044	35,976	29,546	44,727	32,594
of which: Bonds	7,368	12,949	18,224	15,735	26,819	26,845	41,687	13,225
Private nonguaranteed	21,346	10,806	8,958	10,079	12,844	25,649	50,582	49,789
of which: Bonds	3,346	6,669	931	5,067	11,298	18,065	31,005	43,355
Principal repayments	**38,967**	**25,101**	**24,565**	**22,318**	**21,683**	**28,708**	**35,413**	**20,200**
Public and publicly guaranteed	16,337	15,686	14,831	11,872	13,941	12,383	8,501	12,209
Official creditors	3,386	2,530	1,463	1,795	1,679	1,947	1,490	1,426
Private creditors	12,950	13,155	13,368	10,077	12,263	10,436	7,011	10,783
of which: Bonds	9,256	9,989	10,642	4,965	7,118	5,851	1,703	3,630
Private nonguaranteed	22,630	9,416	9,735	10,446	7,742	16,325	26,912	7,991
of which: Bonds	3,552	2,645	3,247	3,500	2,826	2,216	3,723	2,190
Interest payments	**12,174**	**9,398**	**9,975**	**8,792**	**8,345**	**10,887**	**32,204**	**16,668**
Public and publicly guaranteed	7,923	7,532	7,176	6,019	5,859	7,318	28,709	10,288
Official creditors	1,554	848	458	551	627	730	756	764
Private creditors	6,368	6,685	6,718	5,468	5,232	6,587	27,954	9,524
of which: Bonds	4,897	6,247	6,381	4,856	4,927	6,258	27,633	9,197
Private nonguaranteed	4,251	1,866	2,799	2,773	2,486	3,570	3,495	6,381
of which: Bonds	1,620	957	1,310	1,583	1,379	1,761	1,849	4,606
Net financial flows								
Net debt inflows	-15,566	5,588	9,636	16,212	61,009	40,311	89,533	79,603
Official creditors (incl. IMF)	-4,830	-221	1,298	6,777	4,487	2,570	1,609	1,460
Private creditors	-10,736	5,809	8,338	9,435	56,521	37,740	87,924	78,143
Long-term	-5,606	3,920	7,840	7,600	28,816	28,433	61,387	63,609
Public and publicly guaranteed	-4,322	2,530	8,617	7,966	23,713	19,110	37,717	21,811
Private nonguaranteed	-1,284	1,390	-777	-367	5,103	9,324	23,670	41,798
Short-term	-5,130	1,889	498	1,835	27,705	9,307	26,537	14,534
Net equity inflows								
Foreign direct investment	18,110	17,334	21,021	13,676	19,123	18,292	11,878	30,783
Portfolio equity	447	3,353	-3,503	4,155	373	-6,566	9,877	-943
Major economic aggregates								
Gross national income (GNI)	668,631	850,654	1,080,519	884,093	1,042,120	1,152,678	1,166,799	1,234,127
Exports of goods, services & prim. income	185,853	235,187	318,089	251,597	324,906	376,155	400,742	410,515
Imports of goods, services & prim. income	211,589	266,281	363,752	281,476	350,510	411,884	438,563	458,909
Primary income on FDI	6,076	8,486	11,838	8,647	8,755	12,612	16,408	21,860
Personal transfers & comp. of employees	7,525	22,742	26,041	22,076	22,080	23,588	23,366	23,022
International reserves	35,509	74,054	95,126	99,589	120,265	143,991	160,413	175,432
Ratios								
External debt stocks to exports (%)	81.9	74.8	64.8	80.3	80.6	80.3	93.8	107.9
External debt stocks to GNI (%)	22.8	20.7	19.1	22.8	25.1	26.2	32.2	35.9
Debt service to exports (%)	31.6	15.5	11.1	12.7	10.4	11.4	17.9	10.3
Reserves to external debt stocks (%)	23.3	42.1	46.1	49.3	45.9	47.7	42.7	39.6

MOLDOVA

(US$ million, unless otherwise indicated)

	2000	2005	2008	2009	2010	2011	2012	2013
Summary external debt data								
External debt stocks	**1,843**	**2,219**	**3,655**	**3,753**	**4,837**	**5,322**	**5,877**	**6,613**
Long-term external debt	1,047	1,238	2,019	2,011	2,745	2,899	3,205	3,579
Short-term external debt	489	718	1,289	1,403	1,583	1,769	1,879	2,262
interest arrears on long-term	22	56	22	38	37	42	52	56
Use of IMF credit	308	264	347	338	509	655	793	773
Long-term external debt								
Debt outstanding and disbursed	**1,047**	**1,238**	**2,019**	**2,011**	**2,745**	**2,899**	**3,205**	**3,579**
Public and publicly guaranteed	850	698	805	809	839	857	942	973
Official creditors	743	664	790	790	823	836	913	944
Private creditors	107	34	15	19	16	21	29	29
of which: Bonds	75	25	6	0	0	0	0	0
Private nonguaranteed	197	540	1,214	1,203	1,906	2,042	2,263	2,606
of which: Bonds	..	..	..	..	..	..	..	..
Disbursements	**164**	**237**	**484**	**284**	**464**	**530**	**648**	**683**
Public and publicly guaranteed	54	26	53	54	94	94	142	109
Official creditors	52	26	53	41	89	80	121	94
Private creditors	2	0	0	13	5	14	21	15
of which: Bonds	0	0	0	0	0	0	0	0
Private nonguaranteed	110	211	432	230	370	436	505	574
of which: Bonds	..	..	..	..	..	..	..	..
Principal repayments	**57**	**163**	**391**	**303**	**306**	**368**	**467**	**543**
Public and publicly guaranteed	30	42	44	55	55	71	65	84
Official creditors	27	35	35	46	47	63	51	67
Private creditors	3	7	8	9	8	8	14	16
of which: Bonds	0	6	6	6	0	0	0	0
Private nonguaranteed	28	120	347	248	251	297	402	459
of which: Bonds	..	..	..	..	..	..	..	..
Interest payments	**46**	**42**	**56**	**54**	**49**	**58**	**54**	**65**
Public and publicly guaranteed	39	22	17	22	16	16	16	16
Official creditors	28	20	15	21	16	16	15	15
Private creditors	11	2	1	1	1	0	1	1
of which: Bonds	7	2	1	0	0	0	0	0
Private nonguaranteed	7	20	39	32	33	42	38	49
of which: Bonds	..	..	..	..	..	..	..	..
Net financial flows								
Net debt inflows	560	157	313	65	514	495	417	497
Official creditors (incl. IMF)	13	-31	28	-21	217	169	207	5
Private creditors	547	188	285	86	297	327	211	492
Long-term	82	84	76	-13	117	145	111	113
Public and publicly guaranteed	0	-7	-8	4	-3	6	7	-1
Private nonguaranteed	82	91	85	-18	119	140	104	114
Short-term	465	104	208	99	180	181	100	378
Net equity inflows								
Foreign direct investment	128	107	540	150	172	231	134	171
Portfolio equity	3	1	11	2	6	5	14	10
Major economic aggregates								
Gross national income (GNI)	1,310	3,347	6,660	5,761	6,316	7,588	8,125	8,812
Exports of goods, services & prim. income	780	1,871	3,056	2,308	2,745	3,656	3,818	4,244
Imports of goods, services & prim. income	1,089	2,673	5,670	3,975	4,523	5,957	5,923	6,337
Primary income on FDI	3	45	151	141	152	257	118	155
Personal transfers & comp. of employees	179	915	1,888	1,199	1,351	1,600	1,786	1,976
International reserves	222	597	1,672	1,480	1,718	1,965	2,511	2,818
Ratios								
External debt stocks to exports (%)	236.2	118.6	119.6	162.6	176.2	145.6	154.0	155.8
External debt stocks to GNI (%)	140.7	66.3	54.9	65.1	76.6	70.1	72.3	75.0
Debt service to exports (%)	20.0	13.6	16.5	16.9	14.5	12.8	15.1	15.9
Reserves to external debt stocks (%)	12.1	26.9	45.8	39.4	35.5	36.9	42.7	42.6

MONGOLIA

(US$ million, unless otherwise indicated)

	2000	2005	2008	2009	2010	2011	2012	2013
Summary external debt data								
External debt stocks	**960**	**1,396**	**2,184**	**2,986**	**5,928**	**9,627**	**15,385**	**18,921**
Long-term external debt	833	1,267	2,019	2,479	5,290	8,775	14,248	17,217
Short-term external debt	13	25	70	248	365	583	903	1,563
interest arrears on long-term	2	0	0	0	0	0	0	4
Use of IMF credit	114	105	95	258	273	268	234	140
Long-term external debt								
Debt outstanding and disbursed	**833**	**1,267**	**2,019**	**2,479**	**5,290**	**8,775**	**14,248**	**17,217**
Public and publicly guaranteed	833	1,267	1,657	1,817	1,782	1,826	3,243	3,568
Official creditors	831	1,266	1,571	1,733	1,775	1,814	1,734	2,062
Private creditors	3	0	86	84	7	12	1,508	1,505
of which: Bonds	0	0	75	75	0	0	1,500	1,500
Private nonguaranteed	..	..	362	662	3,508	6,949	11,006	13,650
of which: Bonds	..	..	..	..	..	..	900	900
Disbursements	**75**	**91**	**435**	**520**	**2,929**	**3,554**	**6,422**	**3,895**
Public and publicly guaranteed	75	91	75	212	66	87	1,558	453
Official creditors	75	91	75	212	66	83	58	453
Private creditors	0	0	0	0	0	5	1,500	0
of which: Bonds	0	0	0	0	0	0	1,500	0
Private nonguaranteed	..	..	360	308	2,863	3,466	4,864	3,442
of which: Bonds	..	..	..	..	..	..	900	..
Principal repayments	**22**	**17**	**41**	**70**	**139**	**78**	**898**	**885**
Public and publicly guaranteed	22	17	40	62	122	54	84	71
Official creditors	19	17	37	59	44	54	80	68
Private creditors	3	0	3	2	77	0	4	3
of which: Bonds	0	0	0	0	75	0	0	0
Private nonguaranteed	..	..	1	8	18	24	814	814
of which: Bonds	..	..	..	..	..	..	..	..
Interest payments	**9**	**15**	**30**	**41**	**89**	**155**	**258**	**396**
Public and publicly guaranteed	9	15	24	26	20	20	21	60
Official creditors	9	15	18	19	19	20	21	22
Private creditors	0	0	7	7	1	0	0	38
of which: Bonds	0	0	6	6	1	0	0	38
Private nonguaranteed	..	..	6	15	70	134	236	337
of which: Bonds	..	..	..	..	..	..	27	79
Net financial flows								
Net debt inflows	45	-73	401	787	2,925	3,689	5,808	3,574
Official creditors (incl. IMF)	58	69	33	312	40	24	-58	292
Private creditors	-12	-142	368	475	2,885	3,665	5,866	3,282
Long-term	-3	0	357	297	2,768	3,447	5,547	2,625
Public and publicly guaranteed	-3	0	-3	-2	-77	5	1,496	-3
Private nonguaranteed	..	..	359	299	2,845	3,442	4,050	2,628
Short-term	-9	-142	12	179	117	218	319	657
Net equity inflows								
Foreign direct investment	54	185	828	488	1,331	1,501	1,487	377
Portfolio equity	..	..	13	4	680	9	15	3
Major economic aggregates								
Gross national income (GNI)	1,132	2,472	5,450	4,388	5,640	7,918	9,373	10,751
Exports of goods, services & prim. income	627	1,494	3,045	2,322	3,423	5,481	5,402	5,030
Imports of goods, services & prim. income	791	1,635	3,956	2,850	4,496	8,480	9,004	8,364
Primary income on FDI	9	41	109	121	464	632	594	282
Personal transfers & comp. of employees	12	180	225	200	266	279	320	256
International reserves	179	333	561	1,294	2,197	2,275	3,930	2,096
Ratios								
External debt stocks to exports (%)	153.2	93.5	71.7	128.6	173.2	175.6	284.8	376.1
External debt stocks to GNI (%)	84.8	56.5	40.1	68.0	105.1	121.6	164.1	176.0
Debt service to exports (%)	6.6	3.0	2.6	5.3	7.0	4.6	22.4	27.9
Reserves to external debt stocks (%)	18.6	23.9	25.7	43.4	37.1	23.6	25.5	11.1

Notes:

Long-term private nonguaranteed debt data from 2008 are World Bank staff estimates based on reports provided by the country. Short-term debt before 2008 is based on data from the BIS.

MONTENEGRO

(US$ million, unless otherwise indicated)

	2000	2005	2008	2009	2010	2011	2012	2013
Summary external debt data								
External debt stocks	..	..	**1,502**	**2,357**	**1,603**	**2,354**	**2,830**	**2,956**
Long-term external debt	..	..	860	1,109	1,378	1,859	2,252	2,449
Short-term external debt	..	..	602	1,207	186	455	538	467
interest arrears on long-term	..	..	0	0	0	0	0	0
Use of IMF credit	..	..	40	40	40	40	40	40
Long-term external debt								
Debt outstanding and disbursed	..	..	**860**	**1,109**	**1,378**	**1,859**	**2,252**	**2,449**
Public and publicly guaranteed	..	..	851	1,094	1,359	1,805	2,184	2,372
Official creditors	..	..	836	894	846	1,012	1,168	1,210
Private creditors	..	..	15	201	512	792	1,016	1,162
of which: Bonds	..	..	0	0	267	492	501	634
Private nonguaranteed	..	..	9	15	19	54	68	77
of which: Bonds	..	..	..	..	..	..	..	..
Disbursements	..	..	**64**	**248**	**395**	**659**	**526**	**364**
Public and publicly guaranteed	..	..	60	242	383	619	506	344
Official creditors	..	..	60	61	35	258	187	76
Private creditors	..	..	0	181	348	361	319	268
of which: Bonds	..	..	0	0	265	248	0	107
Private nonguaranteed	..	..	4	7	12	40	21	20
of which: Bonds	..	..	..	..	..	..	..	..
Principal repayments	..	..	**28**	**25**	**61**	**127**	**174**	**262**
Public and publicly guaranteed	..	..	25	23	60	124	166	248
Official creditors	..	..	24	22	33	43	48	78
Private creditors	..	..	1	1	27	81	118	170
of which: Bonds	..	..	0	0	0	0	0	0
Private nonguaranteed	..	..	3	2	2	2	8	14
of which: Bonds	..	..	..	..	..	..	..	..
Interest payments	..	..	**28**	**28**	**34**	**79**	**87**	**97**
Public and publicly guaranteed	..	..	27	28	33	78	86	96
Official creditors	..	..	27	26	20	24	24	31
Private creditors	..	..	0	2	13	55	63	65
of which: Bonds	..	..	0	0	0	22	37	39
Private nonguaranteed	..	..	0	0	1	1	1	1
of which: Bonds	..	..	..	..	..	..	..	..
Net financial flows								
Net debt inflows	..	..	233	829	-687	802	435	30
Official creditors (incl. IMF)	..	..	36	38	2	214	139	-2
Private creditors	..	..	197	790	-689	587	297	32
Long-term	..	..	0	185	332	318	214	103
Public and publicly guaranteed	..	..	-1	180	322	280	201	98
Private nonguaranteed	..	..	1	5	11	38	13	5
Short-term	..	..	197	605	-1,021	269	83	-71
Net equity inflows								
Foreign direct investment	..	..	623	1,359	566	438	535	330
Portfolio equity	..	..	-6	-5	-8	-15	0	14
Major economic aggregates								
Gross national income (GNI)	..	..	4,606	4,166	4,086	4,538	4,115	4,515
Exports of goods, services & prim. income	..	..	2,064	1,663	1,722	2,198	1,975	2,129
Imports of goods, services & prim. income	..	..	4,428	2,933	2,826	3,152	2,918	2,952
Primary income on FDI	..	..	43	91	99	45	33	28
Personal transfers & comp. of employees	..	..	298	303	301	343	333	365
International reserves	..	..	436	573	556	393	459	584
Ratios								
External debt stocks to exports (%)	..	..	72.8	141.7	93.1	107.1	143.3	138.8
External debt stocks to GNI (%)	..	..	32.6	56.6	39.2	51.9	68.8	65.5
Debt service to exports (%)	..	..	3.4	4.1	5.7	9.7	13.6	17.2
Reserves to external debt stocks (%)	..	..	29.0	24.3	34.7	16.7	16.2	19.8

Notes:

Long-term private nonguaranteed debt data (excluding bonds) only cover European Bank for Reconstruction and Development lending. Short-term debt is based on data from the BIS. Montenegro became independent in 2006 and started to report data in 2007.

MOROCCO

(US$ million, unless otherwise indicated)

	2000	2005	2008	2009	2010	2011	2012	2013
Summary external debt data								
External debt stocks	**20,790**	**16,297**	**20,957**	**24,662**	**27,250**	**29,903**	**33,815**	**39,261**
Long-term external debt	19,106	15,493	19,194	21,572	23,638	25,204	28,785	33,046
Short-term external debt	1,573	682	1,631	2,210	2,747	3,837	4,167	5,351
interest arrears on long-term	122	0	0	0	0	0	0	0
Use of IMF credit	112	122	132	880	865	862	863	865
Long-term external debt								
Debt outstanding and disbursed	**19,106**	**15,493**	**19,194**	**21,572**	**23,638**	**25,204**	**28,785**	**33,046**
Public and publicly guaranteed	17,244	12,442	16,538	19,218	21,049	22,371	25,086	28,278
Official creditors	12,759	10,119	14,543	16,713	17,269	18,628	19,814	21,945
Private creditors	4,485	2,323	1,994	2,504	3,780	3,743	5,271	6,333
of which: Bonds	152	472	0	0	1,336	1,294	2,819	3,629
Private nonguaranteed	1,862	3,051	2,656	2,354	2,589	2,833	3,699	4,768
of which: Bonds	..	..	..	..	..	..	..	..
Disbursements	**1,638**	**2,456**	**4,554**	**4,551**	**4,999**	**4,506**	**6,122**	**7,504**
Public and publicly guaranteed	980	1,658	3,093	3,468	3,882	3,285	4,114	4,425
Official creditors	631	1,562	2,800	2,868	2,258	2,995	2,477	3,259
Private creditors	349	97	292	600	1,625	290	1,636	1,166
of which: Bonds	0	0	0	0	1,327	0	1,500	750
Private nonguaranteed	658	798	1,461	1,083	1,116	1,222	2,008	3,079
of which: Bonds	..	..	..	..	..	..	..	..
Principal repayments	**1,632**	**2,139**	**3,452**	**2,709**	**2,428**	**2,436**	**2,769**	**3,998**
Public and publicly guaranteed	1,593	1,881	1,795	1,138	1,274	1,481	1,572	1,821
Official creditors	928	1,303	1,043	966	1,090	1,277	1,392	1,557
Private creditors	666	578	753	172	184	205	179	264
of which: Bonds	30	41	589	0	0	0	0	0
Private nonguaranteed	39	258	1,656	1,572	1,154	955	1,198	2,177
of which: Bonds	..	..	..	..	..	..	..	..
Interest payments	**949**	**569**	**709**	**678**	**850**	**757**	**785**	**1,014**
Public and publicly guaranteed	877	501	655	612	819	722	750	907
Official creditors	548	388	536	523	731	571	587	661
Private creditors	329	113	120	89	88	152	163	246
of which: Bonds	14	25	29	0	0	62	57	130
Private nonguaranteed	71	68	54	66	31	35	35	107
of which: Bonds	..	..	..	..	..	..	..	..
Net financial flows								
Net debt inflows	-449	831	814	2,421	3,108	3,160	3,683	4,690
Official creditors (incl. IMF)	-296	259	1,758	1,902	1,168	1,718	1,085	1,702
Private creditors	-153	573	-944	519	1,940	1,442	2,598	2,988
Long-term	302	59	-656	-61	1,403	352	2,268	1,804
Public and publicly guaranteed	-317	-481	-460	428	1,441	85	1,457	902
Private nonguaranteed	619	540	-195	-489	-37	267	810	902
Short-term	-455	514	-288	579	537	1,090	330	1,183
Net equity inflows								
Foreign direct investment	221	950	2,423	2,456	1,369	2,076	2,092	3,213
Portfolio equity	18	64	148	-4	132	166	-108	43
Major economic aggregates								
Gross national income (GNI)	36,053	58,760	87,411	88,520	88,544	96,120	92,704	101,519
Exports of goods, services & prim. income	10,729	17,281	31,613	24,924	27,913	32,649	32,954	33,086
Imports of goods, services & prim. income	13,686	21,616	44,910	37,346	39,109	48,764	49,913	49,667
Primary income on FDI	268	594	835	1,753	1,445	2,086	2,092	1,279
Personal transfers & comp. of employees	2,161	4,589	6,894	6,269	6,423	7,256	6,508	6,882
International reserves	4,823	16,187	22,104	22,797	22,613	19,526	16,356	18,404
Ratios								
External debt stocks to exports (%)	193.8	94.3	66.3	98.9	97.6	91.6	102.6	118.7
External debt stocks to GNI (%)	57.7	27.7	24.0	27.9	30.8	31.1	36.5	38.7
Debt service to exports (%)	25.3	15.8	13.3	13.7	11.8	9.9	10.9	15.3
Reserves to external debt stocks (%)	23.2	99.3	105.5	92.4	83.0	65.3	48.4	46.9

Notes:

Short-term debt before 2009 is based on data from the BIS.

MOZAMBIQUE

(US$ million, unless otherwise indicated)

	2000	2005	2008	2009	2010	2011	2012	2013
Summary external debt data								
External debt stocks	**5,613**	**4,393**	**3,489**	**4,138**	**3,747**	**4,091**	**4,878**	**6,890**
Long-term external debt	4,693	3,367	2,726	3,165	2,909	3,602	4,324	6,229
Short-term external debt	560	714	580	632	480	134	201	311
interest arrears on long-term	404	525	449	465	381	5	31	36
Use of IMF credit	361	312	183	342	357	355	353	351
Long-term external debt								
Debt outstanding and disbursed	**4,693**	**3,367**	**2,726**	**3,165**	**2,909**	**3,602**	**4,324**	**6,229**
Public and publicly guaranteed	4,693	3,367	2,726	3,165	2,909	3,602	4,324	6,229
Official creditors	4,682	3,365	2,719	3,136	2,811	3,372	4,062	5,098
Private creditors	11	2	7	28	98	230	262	1,130
of which: Bonds	0	0	0	0	0	0	0	850
Private nonguaranteed	..	..	..	..	..	..	..	..
of which: Bonds	..	..	..	..	..	..	..	..
Disbursements	**131**	**326**	**399**	**446**	**373**	**497**	**745**	**1,960**
Public and publicly guaranteed	131	326	399	446	373	497	745	1,960
Official creditors	131	326	397	422	294	346	714	1,088
Private creditors	0	0	2	23	79	151	31	872
of which: Bonds	0	0	0	0	0	0	0	850
Private nonguaranteed	..	..	..	..	..	..	..	..
of which: Bonds								
Principal repayments	**34**	**18**	**14**	**15**	**38**	**28**	**40**	**84**
Public and publicly guaranteed	34	18	14	15	38	28	40	84
Official creditors	33	18	11	12	30	22	36	69
Private creditors	1	0	3	3	8	6	4	15
of which: Bonds	0	0	0	0	0	0	0	0
Private nonguaranteed	..	..	..	..	..	..	..	..
of which: Bonds	..	..	..	..	..	..	..	..
Interest payments	**20**	**22**	**19**	**23**	**47**	**26**	**29**	**52**
Public and publicly guaranteed	20	22	19	23	47	26	29	52
Official creditors	20	22	19	23	46	26	29	50
Private creditors	0	0	0	0	0	0	0	2
of which: Bonds	0	0	0	0	0	0	0	0
Private nonguaranteed	..	..	..	..	..	..	..	..
of which: Bonds	..	..	..	..	..	..	..	..
Net financial flows								
Net debt inflows	83	125	387	620	289	497	744	1,978
Official creditors (incl. IMF)	157	297	386	564	286	322	676	1,016
Private creditors	-74	-172	1	56	3	174	68	963
Long-term	-1	..	-1	20	71	144	27	858
Public and publicly guaranteed	-1	..	-1	20	71	144	27	858
Private nonguaranteed	..	..	..	..	..	..	..	..
Short-term	-73	-172	2	36	-68	30	41	105
Net equity inflows								
Foreign direct investment	139	60	254	242	410	1,383	216	929
Portfolio equity	..	0	0	0	0	0	..	0
Major economic aggregates								
Gross national income (GNI)	4,075	6,219	9,158	9,430	9,192	12,358	14,341	15,313
Exports of goods, services & prim. income	769	2,186	3,270	2,909	3,102	4,002	5,105	5,442
Imports of goods, services & prim. income	1,763	3,350	5,325	4,893	5,245	7,891	12,305	12,568
Primary income on FDI	0	284	544	240	214	234	54	78
Personal transfers & comp. of employees	37	59	116	111	139	157	220	217
International reserves	723	1,054	1,578	2,099	2,159	2,469	2,770	3,142
Ratios								
External debt stocks to exports (%)	730.3	201.0	106.7	142.3	120.8	102.2	95.6	126.6
External debt stocks to GNI (%)	137.7	70.6	38.1	43.9	40.8	33.1	34.0	45.0
Debt service to exports (%)	9.4	3.2	1.1	1.4	2.8	1.5	1.4	2.6
Reserves to external debt stocks (%)	12.9	24.0	45.2	50.7	57.6	60.4	56.8	45.6

Notes:

Short-term debt is based on data from the BIS. Data include HIPC and MDRI debt relief.

MYANMAR

(US$ million, unless otherwise indicated)

	2000	2005	2008	2009	2010	2011	2012	2013
Summary external debt data								
External debt stocks	**5,916**	**6,888**	**7,454**	**7,625**	**8,189**	**8,371**	**8,271**	**7,367**
Long-term external debt	5,347	6,033	6,404	6,545	6,757	6,771	6,697	6,095
Short-term external debt	511	792	979	1,013	1,069	1,207	1,201	902
interest arrears on long-term	511	792	979	1,013	1,069	1,207	1,201	902
Use of IMF credit	58	63	71	67	363	393	373	370
Long-term external debt								
Debt outstanding and disbursed	**5,347**	**6,033**	**6,404**	**6,545**	**6,757**	**6,771**	**6,697**	**6,095**
Public and publicly guaranteed	5,347	6,033	6,404	6,545	6,757	6,771	6,697	6,095
Official creditors	4,814	4,931	5,256	5,417	5,631	6,151	6,095	5,519
Private creditors	533	1,102	1,148	1,127	1,126	619	602	576
of which: Bonds	0	0	0	0	0	0	0	0
Private nonguaranteed	..	..	..	..	..	..	..	..
of which: Bonds	..	..	..	..	..	..	..	..
Disbursements	**64**	**2**	**1**	**1**	**0**	**0**	**0**	**931**
Public and publicly guaranteed	64	2	1	1	0	0	0	931
Official creditors	34	2	1	1	0	0	0	931
Private creditors	29	0	0	0	0	0	0	0
of which: Bonds	0	0	0	0	0	0	0	0
Private nonguaranteed	..	..	..	..	..	..	..	..
of which: Bonds	..	..	..	..	..	..	..	..
Principal repayments	**64**	**3**	**5**	**4**	**4**	**2**	**1**	**764**
Public and publicly guaranteed	64	3	5	4	4	2	1	764
Official creditors	22	3	5	4	4	2	1	764
Private creditors	42	0	0	0	0	0	0	0
of which: Bonds	0	0	0	0	0	0	0	0
Private nonguaranteed	..	..	..	..	..	..	..	..
of which: Bonds	..	..	..	..	..	..	..	..
Interest payments	**24**	**0**	**1**	**1**	**1**	**1**	**1**	**179**
Public and publicly guaranteed	24	0	1	1	1	1	1	179
Official creditors	20	0	1	1	1	1	1	179
Private creditors	4	0	0	0	0	0	0	0
of which: Bonds	0	0	0	0	0	0	0	0
Private nonguaranteed	..	..	..	..	..	..	..	..
of which: Bonds	..	..	..	..	..	..	..	..
Net financial flows								
Net debt inflows	0	-1	-4	-4	-4	-2	-1	167
Official creditors (incl. IMF)	13	-1	-4	-4	-4	-2	-1	167
Private creditors	-13	0	..	..	..	..	..	..
Long-term	-13	0	..	..	..	..	..	..
Public and publicly guaranteed	-13	0	..	..	..	..	..	..
Private nonguaranteed	..	..	..	..	..	..	..	..
Short-term	..	..	..	..	..	..	..	..
Net equity inflows								
Foreign direct investment	258	235	864	1,079	901	1,001	2,243	2,621
Portfolio equity	..	..	..	..	..	..	..	..
Major economic aggregates								
Gross national income (GNI)	..	..	..	..	..	..	..	..
Exports of goods, services & prim. income	2,145	3,838	6,439	6,347	7,851	8,566	..	..
Imports of goods, services & prim. income	2,627	3,429	5,500	5,794	6,516	10,379	..	..
Primary income on FDI	135	1,388	1,884	1,811	1,816	1,721	..	..
Personal transfers & comp. of employees	104	129	55	54	115	127	..	..
International reserves	223	771	3,717	5,252	5,717	7,004	6,964	..
Ratios								
External debt stocks to exports (%)	275.8	179.5	115.8	120.1	104.3	97.7	..	..
External debt stocks to GNI (%)	..	..	..	..	..	..	..	..
Debt service to exports (%)	4.2	0.1	0.1	0.1	0.1	6.5	..	..
Reserves to external debt stocks (%)	3.8	11.2	49.9	68.9	69.8	83.7	84.2	..

Notes:

Fiscal year-end for external debt data is March. Long-term public and publicly guaranteed and short-term debt data are World Bank staff estimates based on the original terms of the loans. Country is expected to resume DRS reporting in 2015.

NEPAL

(US$ million, unless otherwise indicated)

	2000	2005	2008	2009	2010	2011	2012	2013
Summary external debt data								
External debt stocks	**2,878**	**3,191**	**3,698**	**3,778**	**3,789**	**3,828**	**3,812**	**3,833**
Long-term external debt	2,826	3,112	3,551	3,552	3,509	3,530	3,495	3,572
Short-term external debt	29	47	57	44	61	84	113	72
interest arrears on long-term	0	0	0	0	0	0	0	0
Use of IMF credit	23	32	89	183	219	214	204	189
Long-term external debt								
Debt outstanding and disbursed	**2,826**	**3,112**	**3,551**	**3,552**	**3,509**	**3,530**	**3,495**	**3,572**
Public and publicly guaranteed	2,826	3,112	3,551	3,552	3,509	3,530	3,495	3,572
Official creditors	2,821	3,108	3,547	3,548	3,506	3,528	3,493	3,570
Private creditors	5	5	4	4	3	2	2	2
of which: Bonds	0	0	0	0	0	0	0	0
Private nonguaranteed	..	..	..	..	..	..	..	..
of which: Bonds	..	..	..	..	..	..	..	..
Disbursements	**154**	**192**	**103**	**116**	**126**	**174**	**159**	**264**
Public and publicly guaranteed	154	192	103	116	126	174	159	264
Official creditors	154	192	103	116	126	174	159	264
Private creditors	0	0	0	0	0	0	0	0
of which: Bonds	0	0	0	0	0	0	0	0
Private nonguaranteed	..	..	..	..	..	..	..	..
of which: Bonds		..	..	..	..	..	..	..
Principal repayments	**67**	**85**	**127**	**140**	**149**	**154**	**175**	**165**
Public and publicly guaranteed	67	85	127	140	149	154	175	165
Official creditors	59	85	126	140	149	153	175	164
Private creditors	7	1	1	1	0	1	0	1
of which: Bonds	0	0	0	0	0	0	0	0
Private nonguaranteed	..	..	..	..	..	..	..	..
of which: Bonds	..	..	..	..	..	..	..	..
Interest payments	**28**	**30**	**34**	**32**	**33**	**35**	**33**	**34**
Public and publicly guaranteed	28	30	34	32	33	35	33	34
Official creditors	27	30	34	32	32	35	33	34
Private creditors	1	0	0	0	0	0	0	0
of which: Bonds	0	0	0	0	0	0	0	0
Private nonguaranteed	..	..	..	..	..	..	..	..
of which: Bonds	..	..	..	..	..	..	..	..
Net financial flows								
Net debt inflows	69	118	-21	-40	33	39	3	43
Official creditors (incl. IMF)	90	108	-23	-27	16	16	-26	84
Private creditors	-21	10	1	-14	17	22	29	-42
Long-term	-7	-1	-1	-1	0	-1	0	-1
Public and publicly guaranteed	-7	-1	-1	-1	0	-1	0	-1
Private nonguaranteed	..	..	..	..	..	..	..	..
Short-term	-14	11	2	-13	17	23	29	-41
Net equity inflows								
Foreign direct investment	0	2	-5	38	88	94	92	74
Portfolio equity	..	..	..	..	..	..	..	..
Major economic aggregates								
Gross national income (GNI)	5,514	8,153	12,668	13,053	16,116	18,954	19,361	19,443
Exports of goods, services & prim. income	1,354	1,423	1,946	1,753	1,783	2,150	2,177	2,500
Imports of goods, services & prim. income	1,825	2,803	4,456	5,160	6,004	6,588	6,969	7,570
Primary income on FDI	..	57	44	9	50	59	34	25
Personal transfers & comp. of employees	111	1,212	2,727	2,985	3,469	4,217	4,793	5,552
International reserves	945	1,499	2,458	2,769	2,937	3,631	4,307	5,293
Ratios								
External debt stocks to exports (%)	212.5	224.2	190.0	215.6	212.4	178.0	175.1	153.3
External debt stocks to GNI (%)	52.2	39.1	29.2	28.9	23.5	20.2	19.7	19.7
Debt service to exports (%)	7.5	8.4	8.5	10.1	10.6	9.2	10.3	8.7
Reserves to external debt stocks (%)	32.9	47.0	66.5	73.3	77.5	94.8	113.0	138.1

Notes:

Short-term debt is based on data from the BIS.

NICARAGUA

(US$ million, unless otherwise indicated)

	2000	2005	2008	2009	2010	2011	2012	2013
Summary external debt data								
External debt stocks	**6,823**	**5,000**	**4,715**	**5,685**	**6,957**	**7,772**	**8,911**	**9,601**
Long-term external debt	5,717	4,231	3,421	4,346	5,206	5,956	6,856	7,598
Short-term external debt	912	540	1,153	993	1,392	1,443	1,695	1,658
interest arrears on long-term	791	364	472	484	495	506	518	528
Use of IMF credit	194	229	141	346	359	373	361	345
Long-term external debt								
Debt outstanding and disbursed	**5,717**	**4,231**	**3,421**	**4,346**	**5,206**	**5,956**	**6,856**	**7,598**
Public and publicly guaranteed	5,435	3,939	2,253	2,505	2,683	2,846	3,055	3,295
Official creditors	5,220	3,867	2,249	2,502	2,680	2,843	3,051	3,291
Private creditors	216	72	4	4	3	3	3	3
of which: Bonds	0	0	0	0	0	0	0	0
Private nonguaranteed	281	292	1,168	1,841	2,522	3,109	3,801	4,304
of which: Bonds	..	..	..	..	..	..	..	..
Disbursements	**511**	**287**	**946**	**827**	**1,185**	**1,378**	**1,216**	**1,146**
Public and publicly guaranteed	226	226	183	291	267	239	258	287
Official creditors	220	226	183	291	267	239	258	287
Private creditors	6	0	0	0	0	0	0	0
of which: Bonds	0	0	0	0	0	0	0	0
Private nonguaranteed	285	61	763	536	919	1,138	958	859
of which: Bonds	..	..	..	..	..	..	..	..
Principal repayments	**184**	**110**	**309**	**365**	**456**	**500**	**445**	**433**
Public and publicly guaranteed	71	64	52	62	56	63	53	54
Official creditors	62	64	52	62	56	63	53	53
Private creditors	8	0	0	0	0	0	0	0
of which: Bonds	0	0	0	0	0	0	0	0
Private nonguaranteed	114	47	257	302	400	437	392	380
of which: Bonds	..	..	..	..	..	..	..	..
Interest payments	**91**	**46**	**98**	**121**	**104**	**118**	**144**	**147**
Public and publicly guaranteed	79	44	39	37	33	39	39	44
Official creditors	76	44	39	37	33	39	39	44
Private creditors	3	0	0	0	0	0	0	0
of which: Bonds	0	0	0	0	0	0	0	0
Private nonguaranteed	12	2	59	84	70	79	105	104
of which: Bonds	..	..	..	..	..	..	..	..
Net financial flows								
Net debt inflows	350	210	657	326	1,138	932	998	649
Official creditors (incl. IMF)	179	153	160	265	230	191	192	217
Private creditors	172	57	497	61	907	741	806	433
Long-term	169	14	506	233	518	701	566	479
Public and publicly guaranteed	-2	0	0	0	0	0	0	0
Private nonguaranteed	171	14	506	233	518	701	566	480
Short-term	3	43	-8	-173	389	40	240	-47
Net equity inflows								
Foreign direct investment	267	241	626	434	508	968	805	845
Portfolio equity	..	..	..	..	..	..	0	..
Major economic aggregates								
Gross national income (GNI)	4,906	6,173	8,268	8,128	8,699	9,649	10,344	10,942
Exports of goods, services & prim. income	1,133	1,434	2,833	2,765	3,455	4,460	5,033	5,022
Imports of goods, services & prim. income	2,479	3,075	5,473	4,658	5,473	6,956	7,690	7,671
Primary income on FDI	69	82	113	121	135	146	157	169
Personal transfers & comp. of employees	320	616	820	770	825	914	1,016	1,081
International reserves	488	728	1,141	1,573	1,799	1,892	1,887	1,993
Ratios								
External debt stocks to exports (%)	602.4	348.7	166.5	205.6	201.4	174.3	177.1	191.2
External debt stocks to GNI (%)	139.1	81.0	57.0	69.9	80.0	80.5	86.1	87.7
Debt service to exports (%)	25.6	12.1	15.2	18.3	16.9	14.8	12.7	12.6
Reserves to external debt stocks (%)	7.2	14.6	24.2	27.7	25.9	24.3	21.2	20.8

Notes:

Short-term debt before 2006 is based on data from the BIS. Data include the effects of HIPC and MDRI debt relief.

NIGER

(US$ million, unless otherwise indicated)

	2000	2005	2008	2009	2010	2011	2012	2013
Summary external debt data								
External debt stocks	**1,721**	**1,967**	**961**	**1,258**	**1,550**	**2,237**	**2,320**	**2,656**
Long-term external debt	1,563	1,785	803	972	1,221	1,930	2,059	2,319
Short-term external debt	72	41	93	131	171	154	97	164
interest arrears on long-term	60	38	19	17	22	19	22	117
Use of IMF credit	86	141	65	155	158	153	164	173
Long-term external debt								
Debt outstanding and disbursed	**1,563**	**1,785**	**803**	**972**	**1,221**	**1,930**	**2,059**	**2,319**
Public and publicly guaranteed	1,495	1,753	790	965	1,221	1,930	2,059	2,319
Official creditors	1,495	1,753	790	965	1,221	1,930	2,059	2,319
Private creditors	0	0	0	0	0	0	0	0
of which: Bonds	0	0	0	0	0	0	0	0
Private nonguaranteed	68	33	13	7	..	..	..	..
of which: Bonds	..	..	..	..	..	..	..	..
Disbursements	**76**	**122**	**96**	**211**	**283**	**747**	**144**	**276**
Public and publicly guaranteed	76	122	96	211	283	747	144	276
Official creditors	76	122	96	211	283	747	144	276
Private creditors	0	0	0	0	0	0	0	0
of which: Bonds	0	0	0	0	0	0	0	0
Private nonguaranteed	..	..	..	..	..	..	..	..
of which: Bonds	..	..	..	..	..	..	..	..
Principal repayments	**14**	**22**	**16**	**32**	**14**	**18**	**18**	**25**
Public and publicly guaranteed	12	15	10	25	7	18	18	25
Official creditors	12	15	10	25	7	18	18	25
Private creditors	0	0	0	0	0	0	0	0
of which: Bonds	0	0	0	0	0	0	0	0
Private nonguaranteed	2	7	7	7	7	..	..	..
of which: Bonds	..	..	..	..	..	..	..	..
Interest payments	**8**	**13**	**7**	**8**	**8**	**10**	**10**	**11**
Public and publicly guaranteed	8	11	6	8	8	10	10	11
Official creditors	8	11	6	8	8	10	10	11
Private creditors	0	0	0	0	0	0	0	0
of which: Bonds	0	0	0	0	0	0	0	0
Private nonguaranteed	0	2	1	0	0	..	..	..
of which: Bonds	..	..	..	..	..	..	..	..
Net financial flows								
Net debt inflows	52	109	-57	224	309	711	77	232
Official creditors (incl. IMF)	73	119	98	191	281	725	137	260
Private creditors	-22	-10	-156	33	28	-14	-60	-28
Long-term	-2	-7	-7	-7	-7	..	..	..
Public and publicly guaranteed	..	..	..	..	..	..	..	..
Private nonguaranteed	-2	-7	-7	-7	-7	..	..	..
Short-term	-20	-3	-149	40	35	-14	-60	-28
Net equity inflows								
Foreign direct investment	8	23	-48	-6	0	1,066	841	631
Portfolio equity	0	1	1	9	6	..	..	..
Major economic aggregates								
Gross national income (GNI)	1,782	3,396	5,384	5,362	5,674	6,362	6,656	7,317
Exports of goods, services & prim. income	334	602	1,124	1,186	1,332	1,433	..	..
Imports of goods, services & prim. income	485	1,095	2,006	2,657	2,916	3,208	..	..
Primary income on FDI	2	21	23	84	17	..	..	..
Personal transfers & comp. of employees	14	66	94	102	134	..	..	..
International reserves	81	251	705	656	760	673	1,015	1,167
Ratios								
External debt stocks to exports (%)	515.7	326.6	85.5	106.1	116.4	156.1	..	..
External debt stocks to GNI (%)	96.6	57.9	17.9	23.5	27.3	35.2	34.9	36.3
Debt service to exports (%)	8.0	6.8	2.4	3.5	1.8	2.4	..	..
Reserves to external debt stocks (%)	4.7	12.7	73.3	52.1	49.1	30.1	43.7	43.9

Notes:
Short-term debt is based on data from the BIS. Data include the effects of HIPC and MDRI debt relief.

NIGERIA

(US$ million, unless otherwise indicated)

	2000	2005	2008	2009	2010	2011	2012	2013
Summary external debt data								
External debt stocks	**31,582**	**20,476**	**4,043**	**6,765**	**7,207**	**8,963**	**10,059**	**13,792**
Long-term external debt	30,257	20,248	3,801	4,139	4,627	6,391	7,484	11,211
Short-term external debt	1,120	3	0	0	0	0	0	1
interest arrears on long-term	43	3	0	0	0	0	0	1
Use of IMF credit	205	225	242	2,626	2,580	2,572	2,575	2,580
Long-term external debt								
Debt outstanding and disbursed	**30,257**	**20,248**	**3,801**	**4,139**	**4,627**	**6,391**	**7,484**	**11,211**
Public and publicly guaranteed	30,042	20,248	3,801	4,139	4,627	5,891	6,634	8,786
Official creditors	26,596	18,039	3,688	4,052	4,627	5,391	6,134	7,286
Private creditors	3,446	2,209	112	87	0	500	500	1,500
of which: Bonds	2,051	1,442	0	0	0	500	500	1,500
Private nonguaranteed	215	..	..	..	..	500	850	2,425
of which: Bonds	..	..	..	..	..	500	850	2,425
Disbursements	**153**	**379**	**409**	**519**	**1,057**	**2,087**	**1,183**	**3,945**
Public and publicly guaranteed	153	379	409	519	1,057	1,587	833	2,370
Official creditors	153	345	385	519	1,057	1,087	833	1,370
Private creditors	0	34	24	0	0	500	0	1,000
of which: Bonds	0	0	0	0	0	500	0	1,000
Private nonguaranteed	..	..	..	..	..	500	350	1,575
of which: Bonds	..	..	..	..	..	500	350	1,575
Principal repayments	**1,092**	**3,863**	**326**	**323**	**229**	**256**	**158**	**203**
Public and publicly guaranteed	1,057	3,863	326	323	229	256	158	203
Official creditors	915	3,685	319	297	225	256	158	203
Private creditors	142	179	8	26	4	0	0	0
of which: Bonds	0	0	0	0	0	0	0	0
Private nonguaranteed	35	..	..	..	..	..	..	..
of which: Bonds	..	..	..	..	..	..	..	..
Interest payments	**690**	**4,937**	**85**	**79**	**55**	**93**	**144**	**281**
Public and publicly guaranteed	673	4,937	85	79	55	74	94	182
Official creditors	516	4,717	84	73	54	57	60	68
Private creditors	157	220	1	6	0	17	34	113
of which: Bonds	128	170	0	0	0	17	34	113
Private nonguaranteed	18	..	..	..	..	19	50	99
of which: Bonds	..	..	..	..	..	19	50	99
Net financial flows								
Net debt inflows	-697	-3,484	82	196	827	1,831	1,025	3,742
Official creditors (incl. IMF)	-762	-3,340	66	222	831	831	675	1,167
Private creditors	64	-145	16	-26	-4	1,000	350	2,575
Long-term	-177	-145	16	-26	-4	1,000	350	2,575
Public and publicly guaranteed	-142	-145	16	-26	-4	500	..	1,000
Private nonguaranteed	-35	..	..	..	..	500	350	1,575
Short-term	241	..	..	..	..	..	0	..
Net equity inflows								
Foreign direct investment	1,140	4,983	8,133	8,534	5,988	8,590	7,033	5,609
Portfolio equity	..	751	-954	487	2,161	2,571	10,003	5,577
Major economic aggregates								
Gross national income (GNI)	40,238	98,881	192,910	154,918	349,388	388,771	440,674	499,041
Exports of goods, services & prim. income	21,183	57,149	90,388	59,321	81,976	100,653	99,048	98,465
Imports of goods, services & prim. income	15,383	35,773	81,632	64,815	88,299	109,908	100,602	99,974
Primary income on FDI	2,279	2,603	17,000	15,042	20,032	23,072	22,430	..
Personal transfers & comp. of employees	1,392	14,640	19,206	18,368	19,818	20,619	20,633	..
International reserves	9,911	28,280	53,002	44,763	34,919	35,212	46,405	..
Ratios								
External debt stocks to exports (%)	149.1	35.8	4.5	11.4	8.8	8.9	10.2	14.0
External debt stocks to GNI (%)	78.5	20.7	2.1	4.4	2.1	2.3	2.3	2.8
Debt service to exports (%)	8.8	15.4	0.5	0.7	0.4	0.3	0.3	0.5
Reserves to external debt stocks (%)	31.4	138.1	1,311.0	661.7	484.5	392.9	461.3	..

Notes:

Long-term private nonguaranteed debt only cover Bonds. Short-term debt is revised from 2001 based on reports provided by the country.

PAKISTAN

(US$ million, unless otherwise indicated)

	2000	2005	2008	2009	2010	2011	2012	2013
Summary external debt data								
External debt stocks	**32,954**	**34,018**	**49,524**	**56,340**	**61,960**	**63,989**	**60,938**	**56,461**
Long-term external debt	29,684	31,053	43,540	45,829	49,411	51,492	50,656	49,426
Short-term external debt	1,519	1,230	1,370	1,466	2,291	2,535	2,598	1,922
interest arrears on long-term	0	0	0	0	0	0	0	0
Use of IMF credit	1,751	1,735	4,614	9,045	10,258	9,962	7,684	5,113
Long-term external debt								
Debt outstanding and disbursed	**29,684**	**31,053**	**43,540**	**45,829**	**49,411**	**51,492**	**50,656**	**49,426**
Public and publicly guaranteed	27,124	30,089	40,356	42,564	43,402	45,127	44,736	43,303
Official creditors	25,074	28,907	37,270	40,059	41,603	43,360	43,007	41,613
Private creditors	2,051	1,182	3,086	2,505	1,799	1,768	1,729	1,690
of which: Bonds	623	1,100	2,650	2,150	1,550	1,550	1,550	1,550
Private nonguaranteed	2,560	964	3,184	3,265	6,009	6,365	5,920	6,123
of which: Bonds	45	600	850	850	250	250	250	..
Disbursements	**1,644**	**2,831**	**3,596**	**4,414**	**5,477**	**3,210**	**2,312**	**4,150**
Public and publicly guaranteed	1,527	2,231	2,684	3,732	1,857	2,572	2,312	2,417
Official creditors	1,522	1,619	2,557	3,731	1,856	2,572	2,312	2,417
Private creditors	4	612	127	1	1	0	0	0
of which: Bonds	0	600	0	0	0	0	0	0
Private nonguaranteed	117	600	912	681	3,620	638	..	1,734
of which: Bonds	..	600	..	..	..	..	..	..
Principal repayments	**1,587**	**1,463**	**1,764**	**2,243**	**3,010**	**1,665**	**1,527**	**3,361**
Public and publicly guaranteed	1,143	1,136	1,307	1,637	2,134	1,383	1,395	1,830
Official creditors	1,105	993	1,272	1,055	1,427	1,351	1,356	1,791
Private creditors	37	143	35	582	707	32	39	39
of which: Bonds	0	108	0	500	600	0	0	0
Private nonguaranteed	445	327	456	606	876	282	132	1,531
of which: Bonds	..	..	..	..	600	..	..	250
Interest payments	**857**	**674**	**1,028**	**917**	**845**	**784**	**752**	**914**
Public and publicly guaranteed	641	598	880	812	786	711	686	666
Official creditors	527	548	683	643	654	594	583	582
Private creditors	114	50	197	169	131	117	103	84
of which: Bonds	61	47	184	156	120	111	99	81
Private nonguaranteed	217	76	147	105	59	73	65	248
of which: Bonds	2	3	60	50	30	22	22	11
Net financial flows								
Net debt inflows	-343	1,116	3,995	5,350	4,661	1,518	-1,427	-2,449
Official creditors (incl. IMF)	330	389	4,306	5,760	1,798	950	-1,319	-1,937
Private creditors	-672	727	-311	-410	2,863	568	-108	-512
Long-term	-361	742	547	-506	2,038	324	-171	164
Public and publicly guaranteed	-33	469	92	-581	-706	-32	-39	-39
Private nonguaranteed	-328	273	455	75	2,744	356	-132	203
Short-term	-311	-15	-858	96	825	244	63	-676
Net equity inflows								
Foreign direct investment	308	2,201	5,438	2,338	2,016	1,309	958	1,510
Portfolio equity	35	451	-270	-37	524	-37	178	118
Major economic aggregates								
Gross national income (GNI)	73,025	111,767	173,418	172,279	183,913	223,271	236,473	248,002
Exports of goods, services & prim. income	10,237	19,760	26,756	22,921	28,738	32,173	31,962	30,573
Imports of goods, services & prim. income	14,484	32,445	53,546	39,373	43,885	50,838	52,875	53,503
Primary income on FDI	429	1,871	3,203	2,548	2,140	2,102	2,372	2,906
Personal transfers & comp. of employees	1,075	4,280	7,039	8,717	9,690	12,263	14,006	14,626
International reserves	1,513	10,033	7,194	11,318	14,346	14,528	10,242	5,156
Ratios								
External debt stocks to exports (%)	321.9	172.2	185.1	245.8	215.6	198.9	190.7	184.7
External debt stocks to GNI (%)	45.1	30.4	28.6	32.7	33.7	28.7	25.8	22.8
Debt service to exports (%)	28.0	12.4	11.3	15.2	14.9	9.1	14.8	26.3
Reserves to external debt stocks (%)	4.6	29.5	14.5	20.1	23.2	22.7	16.8	9.1

Notes:

Long-term private nonguaranteed debt data from 2006 are World Bank staff estimates based on the reports provided by the country. Short-term debt is based on data from the BIS.

PANAMA

(US$ million, unless otherwise indicated)

	2000	2005	2008	2009	2010	2011	2012	2013
Summary external debt data								
External debt stocks	**6,606**	**8,108**	**9,280**	**11,243**	**11,382**	**12,583**	**13,247**	**16,471**
Long-term external debt	6,481	8,047	9,240	10,934	11,078	12,281	12,944	16,168
Short-term external debt	1	0	0	0	0	0	0	0
interest arrears on long-term	1	0	0	0	0	0	0	0
Use of IMF credit	124	61	41	309	303	302	303	303
Long-term external debt								
Debt outstanding and disbursed	**6,481**	**8,047**	**9,240**	**10,934**	**11,078**	**12,281**	**12,944**	**16,168**
Public and publicly guaranteed	5,700	6,305	8,129	9,798	10,087	10,890	10,676	11,973
Official creditors	1,289	1,306	1,529	1,833	2,126	2,399	2,733	3,199
Private creditors	4,411	4,999	6,600	7,965	7,961	8,491	7,943	8,773
of which: Bonds	4,141	4,920	6,415	7,738	7,738	8,272	7,725	8,306
Private nonguaranteed	780	1,742	1,111	1,136	991	1,391	2,268	4,195
of which: Bonds	266	635	1,061	1,061	911	1,261	2,061	3,671
Disbursements	**724**	**1,595**	**704**	**1,890**	**445**	**1,377**	**1,453**	**2,806**
Public and publicly guaranteed	486	1,325	654	1,865	440	973	537	2,191
Official creditors	97	94	254	461	440	438	537	691
Private creditors	388	1,231	400	1,404	0	535	0	1,500
of which: Bonds	370	1,230	235	1,323	0	535	0	1,250
Private nonguaranteed	238	270	50	25	5	404	915	615
of which: Bonds	..	150	..	..	..	350	800	270
Principal repayments	**411**	**1,207**	**659**	**190**	**320**	**185**	**955**	**792**
Public and publicly guaranteed	386	955	659	190	170	178	917	764
Official creditors	109	139	160	154	165	175	174	179
Private creditors	277	817	499	36	5	3	742	584
of which: Bonds	120	799	490	0	0	0	741	584
Private nonguaranteed	25	251	..	..	150	7	38	28
of which: Bonds	..	..	..	..	150	..	..	..
Interest payments	**418**	**541**	**641**	**684**	**726**	**745**	**736**	**875**
Public and publicly guaranteed	365	454	578	596	638	668	689	662
Official creditors	79	59	71	72	75	76	77	85
Private creditors	286	394	506	524	563	592	612	577
of which: Bonds	264	390	501	514	560	589	606	567
Private nonguaranteed	53	87	64	88	87	77	47	213
of which: Bonds	24	44	63	83	83	73	42	205
Net financial flows								
Net debt inflows	261	378	41	1,700	125	1,192	498	2,014
Official creditors (incl. IMF)	-63	-55	89	307	275	263	363	512
Private creditors	324	433	-48	1,393	-150	929	135	1,503
Long-term	324	433	-48	1,393	-150	929	135	1,503
Public and publicly guaranteed	112	414	-98	1,368	-5	531	-742	916
Private nonguaranteed	213	19	50	25	-145	397	877	587
Short-term	..	..	..	..	..	..	..	..
Net equity inflows								
Foreign direct investment	624	470	2,057	1,155	1,967	1,909	2,195	4,111
Portfolio equity	..	..	..	..	..	..	..	..
Major economic aggregates								
Gross national income (GNI)	11,007	14,340	26,297	27,326	30,229	31,301	35,175	42,387
Exports of goods, services & prim. income	9,408	11,619	18,313	19,024	20,534	26,799	29,935	29,533
Imports of goods, services & prim. income	10,258	12,882	21,216	19,314	23,748	31,994	33,846	34,314
Primary income on FDI	562	1,048	1,743	1,310	2,176	2,046	2,538	3,514
Personal transfers & comp. of employees	16	130	245	337	410	384	402	418
International reserves	723	1,211	2,424	3,028	2,714	2,304	2,466	2,848
Ratios								
External debt stocks to exports (%)	70.2	69.8	50.7	59.1	55.4	47.0	44.3	55.8
External debt stocks to GNI (%)	60.0	56.5	35.3	41.1	37.7	40.2	37.7	38.9
Debt service to exports (%)	9.4	15.1	7.1	4.6	5.1	3.5	5.6	5.6
Reserves to external debt stocks (%)	10.9	14.9	26.1	26.9	23.8	18.3	18.6	17.3

Notes:

Long-term private nonguaranteed debt data only cover Inter-American Development Bank and Bonds.

PAPUA NEW GUINEA

(US$ million, unless otherwise indicated)

	2000	2005	2008	2009	2010	2011	2012	2013
Summary external debt data								
External debt stocks	**2,305**	**1,896**	**1,435**	**1,787**	**5,965**	**12,584**	**23,128**	**21,733**
Long-term external debt	2,204	1,651	1,412	1,460	5,380	12,268	22,651	21,231
Short-term external debt	49	232	9	130	392	123	284	309
interest arrears on long-term	0	0	0	0	0	0	0	0
Use of IMF credit	51	13	14	197	193	193	193	193
Long-term external debt								
Debt outstanding and disbursed	**2,204**	**1,651**	**1,412**	**1,460**	**5,380**	**12,268**	**22,651**	**21,231**
Public and publicly guaranteed	1,454	1,264	1,067	1,045	1,042	1,069	1,130	2,733
Official creditors	1,394	1,213	1,023	1,008	1,009	1,043	1,114	2,725
Private creditors	60	51	44	36	33	26	16	8
of which: Bonds	0	0	0	0	0	0	0	0
Private nonguaranteed	750	387	345	415	4,337	11,199	21,521	18,498
of which: Bonds	..	..	..	..	..	..	..	..
Disbursements	**254**	**335**	**951**	**516**	**3,153**	**8,158**	**10,896**	**2,808**
Public and publicly guaranteed	219	45	26	33	37	94	161	1,708
Official creditors	206	44	26	33	37	94	161	1,708
Private creditors	13	1	0	0	0	0	0	0
of which: Bonds	0	0	0	0	0	0	0	0
Private nonguaranteed	35	290	925	483	3,116	8,064	10,735	1,100
of which: Bonds	..	..	..	..	..	..	..	..
Principal repayments	**196**	**183**	**932**	**513**	**758**	**1,076**	**349**	**4,198**
Public and publicly guaranteed	115	114	163	62	67	79	78	75
Official creditors	96	93	157	55	60	71	70	69
Private creditors	19	21	6	7	7	8	8	7
of which: Bonds	0	0	0	0	0	0	0	0
Private nonguaranteed	80	69	769	451	691	997	271	4,123
of which: Bonds	..	..	..	..	..	..	..	..
Interest payments	**85**	**54**	**40**	**28**	**50**	**104**	**131**	**231**
Public and publicly guaranteed	54	38	32	21	16	19	18	18
Official creditors	50	36	31	20	16	19	18	17
Private creditors	5	2	1	1	1	1	0	0
of which: Bonds	0	0	0	0	0	0	0	0
Private nonguaranteed	31	16	8	7	33	85	113	213
of which: Bonds	..	..	..	..	..	..	..	..
Net financial flows								
Net debt inflows	30	214	-63	124	2,657	6,812	10,708	-1,365
Official creditors (incl. IMF)	128	-110	-131	-22	-23	23	91	1,639
Private creditors	-99	323	67	146	2,680	6,790	10,617	-3,005
Long-term	-51	200	149	25	2,418	7,059	10,456	-3,030
Public and publicly guaranteed	-5	-20	-6	-7	-7	-8	-8	-7
Private nonguaranteed	-45	221	156	32	2,426	7,067	10,464	-3,023
Short-term	-48	123	-82	121	262	-269	161	25
Net equity inflows								
Foreign direct investment	96	31	-26	419	28	-309	-64	18
Portfolio equity	..	..	..	..	..	..	..	..
Major economic aggregates								
Gross national income (GNI)	3,303	4,531	7,931	7,855	9,262	12,003	15,024	14,642
Exports of goods, services & prim. income	2,369	3,649	6,259	4,624	6,097	7,380	6,855	..
Imports of goods, services & prim. income	2,013	3,368	5,713	5,382	6,920	7,796	9,274	..
Primary income on FDI	198	511	611	537	466	350	588	..
Personal transfers & comp. of employees	7	7	7	5	3	17	14	..
International reserves	287	718	1,953	2,561	3,033	4,256	3,930	2,775
Ratios								
External debt stocks to exports (%)	97.3	52.0	22.9	38.6	97.8	170.5	337.4	..
External debt stocks to GNI (%)	69.8	41.8	18.1	22.8	64.4	104.8	153.9	148.4
Debt service to exports (%)	12.9	8.4	15.6	11.7	13.3	16.0	7.0	..
Reserves to external debt stocks (%)	12.4	37.9	136.1	143.3	50.8	33.8	17.0	12.8

Notes:

Short-term debt is based on data from the BIS.

PARAGUAY

(US$ million, unless otherwise indicated)

	2000	2005	2008	2009	2010	2011	2012	2013
Summary external debt data								
External debt stocks	**3,135**	**5,412**	**9,590**	**10,624**	**12,652**	**13,078**	**12,880**	**13,430**
Long-term external debt	2,537	4,879	8,423	9,723	11,358	11,029	11,216	11,251
Short-term external debt	580	513	1,146	752	1,147	1,903	1,517	2,032
interest arrears on long-term	11	0	0	0	0	0	0	0
Use of IMF credit	18	20	21	149	147	146	146	147
Long-term external debt								
Debt outstanding and disbursed	**2,537**	**4,879**	**8,423**	**9,723**	**11,358**	**11,029**	**11,216**	**11,251**
Public and publicly guaranteed	2,087	2,266	2,263	2,261	2,366	2,305	2,245	2,696
Official creditors	1,639	1,845	1,940	1,979	2,099	2,072	2,051	2,041
Private creditors	449	421	323	282	267	233	194	655
of which: Bonds	0	0	0	0	0	0	0	500
Private nonguaranteed	450	2,614	6,159	7,462	8,992	8,724	8,971	8,555
of which: Bonds	..	..	..	..	..	..	500	500
Disbursements	**192**	**1,292**	**1,480**	**1,571**	**1,912**	**512**	**1,670**	**1,647**
Public and publicly guaranteed	192	144	196	248	308	163	227	725
Official creditors	192	141	196	248	308	163	227	225
Private creditors	0	3	0	0	0	0	0	500
of which: Bonds	0	0	0	0	0	0	0	500
Private nonguaranteed	..	1,147	1,284	1,323	1,605	349	1,443	922
of which: Bonds	..	..	..	..	..	..	500	..
Principal repayments	**207**	**332**	**296**	**308**	**313**	**711**	**1,738**	**1,550**
Public and publicly guaranteed	114	205	237	262	239	244	240	208
Official creditors	107	176	208	221	224	211	201	169
Private creditors	7	29	29	41	15	34	39	39
of which: Bonds	0	0	0	0	0	0	0	0
Private nonguaranteed	93	126	59	46	75	467	1,497	1,342
of which: Bonds	..	..	..	..	..	..	..	..
Interest payments	**116**	**115**	**136**	**122**	**131**	**140**	**179**	**236**
Public and publicly guaranteed	100	94	96	97	65	66	59	65
Official creditors	70	77	78	83	63	61	55	51
Private creditors	30	17	18	14	2	4	4	15
of which: Bonds	0	0	0	0	0	0	0	12
Private nonguaranteed	16	21	40	25	66	75	120	170
of which: Bonds	..	..	..	..	..	..	38	38
Net financial flows								
Net debt inflows	-187	807	1,527	868	1,994	557	-454	613
Official creditors (incl. IMF)	85	-35	-11	27	84	-47	26	56
Private creditors	-272	842	1,538	841	1,910	605	-480	557
Long-term	-100	995	1,195	1,235	1,515	-151	-94	42
Public and publicly guaranteed	-7	-26	-29	-41	-15	-34	-39	461
Private nonguaranteed	-93	1,021	1,224	1,277	1,530	-118	-54	-420
Short-term	-173	-153	343	-394	395	756	-386	515
Net equity inflows								
Foreign direct investment	104	32	77	197	87	277	300	263
Portfolio equity	..	..	..	..	..	..	..	..
Major economic aggregates								
Gross national income (GNI)	7,085	7,360	17,378	14,729	18,618	23,793	23,230	28,447
Exports of goods, services & prim. income	3,185	5,182	10,278	8,386	11,135	13,336	12,384	14,408
Imports of goods, services & prim. income	3,524	5,473	10,509	8,423	11,749	13,940	13,374	14,475
Primary income on FDI	84	158	505	555	759	641	800	896
Personal transfers & comp. of employees	278	161	363	377	410	541	634	591
International reserves	763	1,297	2,845	3,839	4,137	4,950	4,557	5,556
Ratios								
External debt stocks to exports (%)	98.4	104.4	93.3	126.7	113.6	98.1	104.0	93.2
External debt stocks to GNI (%)	44.2	73.5	55.2	72.1	68.0	55.0	55.4	47.2
Debt service to exports (%)	11.2	9.2	4.5	5.3	4.1	6.5	15.7	12.9
Reserves to external debt stocks (%)	24.3	24.0	29.7	36.1	32.7	37.9	35.4	41.4

Notes:

Long-term private nonguaranteed debt data are estimates based on Central Bank data. Short-term debt is based on data from the BIS.

PERU

(US$ million, unless otherwise indicated)

	2000	2005	2008	2009	2010	2011	2012	2013
Summary external debt data								
External debt stocks	**28,813**	**29,508**	**34,720**	**37,390**	**42,154**	**45,012**	**54,150**	**56,661**
Long-term external debt	24,208	26,109	29,159	31,649	34,822	37,751	44,680	49,272
Short-term external debt	3,928	3,212	5,420	4,784	6,393	6,325	8,532	6,450
interest arrears on long-term	14	4	22	1	1	0	0	0
Use of IMF credit	677	188	141	956	939	936	937	939
Long-term external debt								
Debt outstanding and disbursed	**24,208**	**26,109**	**29,159**	**31,649**	**34,822**	**37,751**	**44,680**	**49,272**
Public and publicly guaranteed	19,270	22,537	19,415	20,788	20,009	20,142	19,966	17,077
Official creditors	14,439	13,830	12,358	11,727	10,555	10,721	9,982	7,505
Private creditors	4,830	8,706	7,056	9,061	9,454	9,422	9,984	9,573
of which: Bonds	3,727	8,390	6,879	8,911	9,311	9,299	9,894	9,511
Private nonguaranteed	4,938	3,572	9,744	10,862	14,813	17,608	24,714	32,195
of which: Bonds	150	1,230	3,599	4,428	727	1,705	4,665	9,885
Disbursements	**2,066**	**3,721**	**4,630**	**4,772**	**5,425**	**3,386**	**6,865**	**5,787**
Public and publicly guaranteed	1,489	2,635	1,165	3,232	3,862	1,003	1,347	370
Official creditors	1,454	985	1,165	1,232	1,601	1,003	447	370
Private creditors	35	1,650	0	2,000	2,261	0	900	0
of which: Bonds	0	1,650	0	2,000	2,261	0	900	0
Private nonguaranteed	577	1,086	3,466	1,539	1,563	2,382	5,518	5,417
of which: Bonds	..	1,080	..	878	..	1,705	2,960	5,220
Principal repayments	**1,003**	**4,189**	**3,265**	**2,221**	**4,060**	**2,128**	**2,758**	**5,130**
Public and publicly guaranteed	986	3,033	2,618	1,833	3,490	892	1,348	2,846
Official creditors	840	2,918	1,255	1,808	2,971	867	1,013	2,431
Private creditors	146	114	1,363	25	518	25	335	415
of which: Bonds	0	90	1,338	0	497	0	312	400
Private nonguaranteed	17	1,156	647	389	570	1,236	1,410	2,284
of which: Bonds	..	..	150	50	..	727	..	..
Interest payments	**1,174**	**1,718**	**1,808**	**1,976**	**2,550**	**1,789**	**3,007**	**1,571**
Public and publicly guaranteed	1,105	1,403	1,185	1,084	1,096	1,001	969	940
Official creditors	917	807	572	452	346	288	275	233
Private creditors	188	596	613	632	750	712	694	708
of which: Bonds	179	568	603	623	742	705	688	704
Private nonguaranteed	69	314	623	892	1,454	788	2,038	630
of which: Bonds	11	56	213	223	284	463	176	392
Net financial flows								
Net debt inflows	283	-46	1,447	1,935	2,974	1,191	6,314	-1,425
Official creditors (incl. IMF)	473	-1,972	-91	-575	-1,370	136	-566	-2,061
Private creditors	-190	1,927	1,538	2,511	4,344	1,055	6,880	636
Long-term	448	1,465	1,457	3,126	2,735	1,121	4,673	2,718
Public and publicly guaranteed	-111	1,536	-1,363	1,975	1,742	-25	565	-415
Private nonguaranteed	560	-70	2,819	1,151	993	1,147	4,108	3,133
Short-term	-638	461	81	-615	1,608	-67	2,207	-2,082
Net equity inflows								
Foreign direct investment	810	2,579	6,267	7,213	7,762	5,948	12,904	10,172
Portfolio equity	123	769	85	47	87	147	-32	..
Major economic aggregates								
Gross national income (GNI)	49,268	69,733	118,081	118,547	142,562	162,801	186,844	195,232
Exports of goods, services & prim. income	9,247	20,006	36,144	31,801	39,986	51,046	51,509	49,213
Imports of goods, services & prim. income	11,794	20,631	44,404	35,411	46,794	57,586	61,647	61,685
Primary income on FDI	344	4,030	8,346	8,172	10,714	12,866	11,748	..
Personal transfers & comp. of employees	718	1,440	2,444	2,409	2,534	2,697	2,788	2,707
International reserves	8,374	13,599	30,271	32,013	42,648	47,206	62,300	64,423
Ratios								
External debt stocks to exports (%)	311.6	147.5	96.1	117.6	105.4	88.2	105.1	115.1
External debt stocks to GNI (%)	58.5	42.3	29.4	31.5	29.6	27.6	29.0	29.0
Debt service to exports (%)	27.9	30.3	14.6	13.4	16.7	7.9	11.4	13.8
Reserves to external debt stocks (%)	29.1	46.1	87.2	85.6	101.2	104.9	115.1	113.7

Notes:

Long-term private nonguaranteed debt data are World Bank staff estimates based on reports provided by the country.

PHILIPPINES

(US$ million, unless otherwise indicated)

	2000	2005	2008	2009	2010	2011	2012	2013
Summary external debt data								
External debt stocks	**58,456**	**58,693**	**58,206**	**55,711**	**60,775**	**61,023**	**61,390**	**60,609**
Long-term external debt	50,777	51,742	51,026	50,395	53,189	52,723	51,619	48,106
Short-term external debt	5,495	6,395	7,001	4,002	6,295	7,013	8,483	11,212
interest arrears on long-term	0	0	0	0	0	0	0	0
Use of IMF credit	2,183	555	180	1,314	1,290	1,287	1,288	1,290
Long-term external debt								
Debt outstanding and disbursed	**50,777**	**51,742**	**51,026**	**50,395**	**53,189**	**52,723**	**51,619**	**48,106**
Public and publicly guaranteed	33,744	35,364	39,195	41,923	44,727	44,579	43,037	38,697
Official creditors	19,890	18,580	21,599	22,054	23,210	23,587	21,934	18,665
Private creditors	13,855	16,784	17,596	19,870	21,517	20,992	21,103	20,032
of which: Bonds	10,466	14,290	16,144	18,627	20,221	19,722	19,954	19,124
Private nonguaranteed	17,033	16,378	11,831	8,472	8,462	8,144	8,582	9,410
of which: Bonds	2,856	2,975	1,314	956	1,651	1,579	2,600	6,250
Disbursements	**5,747**	**5,544**	**4,293**	**8,767**	**10,928**	**7,954**	**5,761**	**4,755**
Public and publicly guaranteed	5,228	3,874	2,130	8,124	8,251	4,999	3,828	962
Official creditors	1,528	1,144	1,454	2,349	1,370	1,709	1,436	910
Private creditors	3,701	2,730	677	5,776	6,881	3,290	2,392	52
of which: Bonds	2,630	2,384	576	5,510	6,680	3,121	2,241	0
Private nonguaranteed	519	1,670	2,163	642	2,677	2,954	1,933	3,793
of which: Bonds	5	250	..	..	..	1,075	1,525	3,650
Principal repayments	**4,047**	**5,748**	**6,995**	**5,675**	**8,341**	**6,311**	**2,725**	**2,918**
Public and publicly guaranteed	2,515	3,353	3,592	3,841	6,813	4,887	2,629	2,767
Official creditors	1,572	1,788	2,322	1,722	1,818	2,007	1,756	2,184
Private creditors	943	1,566	1,270	2,120	4,996	2,880	873	583
of which: Bonds	395	1,209	844	1,644	4,807	2,669	655	366
Private nonguaranteed	1,533	2,395	3,402	1,833	1,527	1,424	96	151
of which: Bonds	445	333	572	339	174	158	..	..
Interest payments	**2,469**	**3,152**	**3,376**	**3,266**	**3,112**	**3,195**	**2,973**	**2,922**
Public and publicly guaranteed	1,882	2,409	2,865	2,841	2,977	2,850	2,844	2,660
Official creditors	841	584	612	542	498	489	431	341
Private creditors	1,041	1,825	2,253	2,299	2,479	2,361	2,414	2,319
of which: Bonds	880	1,725	2,198	2,257	2,441	2,323	2,379	2,289
Private nonguaranteed	586	743	511	425	135	345	129	261
of which: Bonds	479	283	103	88	25	147	107	243
Net financial flows								
Net debt inflows	2,551	828	-2,785	93	4,880	2,360	4,505	4,566
Official creditors (incl. IMF)	261	-961	-868	627	-447	-298	-320	-1,275
Private creditors	2,290	1,788	-1,917	-534	5,328	2,658	4,826	5,840
Long-term	1,744	439	-1,834	2,465	3,035	1,941	3,356	3,111
Public and publicly guaranteed	2,758	1,164	-594	3,656	1,885	410	1,520	-531
Private nonguaranteed	-1,014	-725	-1,240	-1,191	1,149	1,530	1,836	3,642
Short-term	546	1,349	-83	-2,998	2,293	718	1,470	2,729
Net equity inflows								
Foreign direct investment	2,240	1,321	1,288	1,886	-214	1,531	2,824	1,364
Portfolio equity	-202	420	-462	308	833	1,040	1,753	-34
Major economic aggregates								
Gross national income (GNI)	94,969	129,797	219,815	223,416	265,929	267,776	298,581	325,828
Exports of goods, services & prim. income	44,060	38,514	54,738	49,632	61,241	64,792	75,080	74,534
Imports of goods, services & prim. income	51,931	48,158	70,313	57,753	71,658	77,716	87,631	86,491
Primary income on FDI	230	1,382	2,163	2,202	2,417	2,910	3,955	3,908
Personal transfers & comp. of employees	6,961	13,733	18,851	19,960	21,557	23,054	24,610	26,700
International reserves	13,090	15,926	33,193	38,783	55,363	67,290	73,478	75,689
Ratios								
External debt stocks to exports (%)	132.7	152.4	106.3	112.2	99.2	94.2	81.8	81.3
External debt stocks to GNI (%)	61.6	45.2	26.5	24.9	22.9	22.8	20.6	18.6
Debt service to exports (%)	16.0	24.7	19.0	18.1	18.7	14.7	7.6	7.8
Reserves to external debt stocks (%)	22.4	27.1	57.0	69.6	91.1	110.3	119.7	124.9

Notes:

Long-term private nonguaranteed debt data no longer include unregistered debt and are revised from 2005 based on the reports provided by the country.

ROMANIA

(US$ million, unless otherwise indicated)

	2000	2005	2008	2009	2010	2011	2012	2013
Summary external debt data								
External debt stocks	**11,252**	**38,626**	**102,305**	**119,865**	**124,136**	**129,633**	**130,419**	**133,996**
Long-term external debt	9,937	30,844	73,528	86,319	81,404	82,142	88,639	98,649
Short-term external debt	763	7,413	28,660	22,459	26,122	29,752	26,032	25,807
interest arrears on long-term	12	13	2	1	1	1	1	1
Use of IMF credit	552	369	117	11,088	16,609	17,738	15,748	9,540
Long-term external debt								
Debt outstanding and disbursed	**9,937**	**30,844**	**73,528**	**86,319**	**81,404**	**82,142**	**88,639**	**98,649**
Public and publicly guaranteed	6,575	13,071	15,022	18,022	20,578	24,646	29,379	35,574
Official creditors	4,149	5,930	7,820	11,099	14,058	16,665	17,284	19,177
Private creditors	2,426	7,141	7,203	6,922	6,520	7,981	12,095	16,397
of which: Bonds	736	2,123	2,714	2,809	3,006	4,852	10,166	14,783
Private nonguaranteed	3,362	17,773	58,505	68,297	60,826	57,496	59,260	63,075
of which: Bonds	..	..	..	..	..	117	288	4,707
Disbursements	**3,144**	**12,908**	**32,747**	**23,270**	**17,434**	**17,847**	**20,955**	**21,721**
Public and publicly guaranteed	1,937	2,637	3,059	3,937	5,622	6,177	6,504	6,379
Official creditors	1,083	1,016	1,543	3,735	4,128	3,900	1,263	2,154
Private creditors	854	1,620	1,516	202	1,494	2,277	5,241	4,225
of which: Bonds	139	623	1,104	0	1,327	2,070	5,117	4,186
Private nonguaranteed	1,207	10,272	29,688	19,332	11,812	11,670	14,451	15,342
of which: Bonds	..	..		..	..	83	38	135
Principal repayments	**1,705**	**5,159**	**14,464**	**13,161**	**15,779**	**15,729**	**15,888**	**19,562**
Public and publicly guaranteed	984	1,686	2,533	1,414	2,146	1,274	2,080	1,225
Official creditors	493	590	685	671	668	767	742	826
Private creditors	490	1,096	1,847	743	1,478	507	1,338	399
of which: Bonds	0	374	883	0	929	0	0	0
Private nonguaranteed	721	3,473	11,932	11,746	13,633	14,454	13,808	18,338
of which: Bonds	75	..	..	..	..	..	4	..
Interest payments	**631**	**1,245**	**2,925**	**2,775**	**2,180**	**2,454**	**2,313**	**2,230**
Public and publicly guaranteed	438	670	900	740	617	751	971	1,155
Official creditors	269	229	347	328	297	421	471	464
Private creditors	170	442	552	412	320	330	500	691
of which: Bonds	45	184	199	156	156	171	362	648
Private nonguaranteed	193	575	2,025	2,034	1,563	1,703	1,342	1,076
of which: Bonds	7	..	..	..	..	3	6	6
Net financial flows								
Net debt inflows	1,843	10,629	17,621	13,299	10,982	6,961	-650	-4,247
Official creditors (incl. IMF)	608	275	857	12,454	9,124	4,346	-1,475	-4,853
Private creditors	1,235	10,354	16,764	845	1,858	2,616	825	606
Long-term	850	7,322	17,425	7,046	-1,805	-1,015	4,545	831
Public and publicly guaranteed	364	524	-331	-540	16	1,770	3,903	3,827
Private nonguaranteed	486	6,799	17,757	7,586	-1,821	-2,784	643	-2,996
Short-term	386	3,032	-662	-6,200	3,663	3,630	-3,720	-225
Net equity inflows								
Foreign direct investment	1,037	4,790	7,124	2,402	2,419	2,100	1,022	2,512
Portfolio equity	58	229	23	7	4	-37	403	83
Major economic aggregates								
Gross national income (GNI)	37,024	96,279	198,922	161,691	162,255	179,539	165,510	183,821
Exports of goods, services & prim. income	12,438	25,693	59,740	47,150	54,951	69,695	65,765	76,921
Imports of goods, services & prim. income	14,653	38,645	92,343	59,813	66,966	82,665	77,678	83,959
Primary income on FDI	72	2,926	4,362	1,212	717	674	1,687	4,105
Personal transfers & comp. of employees	96	4,708	9,285	4,881	3,879	3,889	3,674	3,515
International reserves	2,470	19,872	36,868	40,757	43,361	42,939	41,162	44,811
Ratios								
External debt stocks to exports (%)	90.5	150.3	171.3	254.2	225.9	186.0	198.3	174.2
External debt stocks to GNI (%)	30.4	40.1	51.4	74.1	76.5	72.2	78.8	72.9
Debt service to exports (%)	20.1	26.8	30.3	34.6	33.8	27.4	33.7	39.7
Reserves to external debt stocks (%)	21.9	51.4	36.0	34.0	34.9	33.1	31.6	33.4

RWANDA

(US$ million, unless otherwise indicated)

	2000	2005	2008	2009	2010	2011	2012	2013
Summary external debt data								
External debt stocks	**1,289**	**1,528**	**684**	**869**	**913**	**1,103**	**1,268**	**1,690**
Long-term external debt	1,148	1,415	646	724	765	971	1,048	1,553
Short-term external debt	38	17	6	10	14	0	89	8
interest arrears on long-term	16	13	1	0	0	0	0	0
Use of IMF credit	104	97	33	136	133	132	131	130
Long-term external debt								
Debt outstanding and disbursed	**1,148**	**1,415**	**646**	**724**	**765**	**971**	**1,048**	**1,553**
Public and publicly guaranteed	1,148	1,415	646	724	765	971	1,048	1,553
Official creditors	1,147	1,415	646	724	765	971	1,048	1,153
Private creditors	1	0	0	0	0	0	0	400
of which: Bonds	0	0	0	0	0	0	0	400
Private nonguaranteed	..	..	..	..	..	..	..	..
of which: Bonds	..	..	..	..	..	..	..	..
Disbursements	**40**	**85**	**111**	**85**	**61**	**223**	**97**	**524**
Public and publicly guaranteed	40	85	111	85	61	223	97	524
Official creditors	40	85	111	85	61	223	97	124
Private creditors	0	0	0	0	0	0	0	400
of which: Bonds	0	0	0	0	0	0	0	400
Private nonguaranteed	..	..	..	..	..	..	..	..
of which: Bonds	..	..	..	..	..	..	..	..
Principal repayments	**13**	**13**	**9**	**5**	**8**	**12**	**13**	**14**
Public and publicly guaranteed	13	13	9	5	8	12	13	14
Official creditors	13	13	9	5	8	12	13	14
Private creditors	0	0	0	0	0	0	0	0
of which: Bonds	0	0	0	0	0	0	0	0
Private nonguaranteed	..	..	..	..	..	..	..	..
of which: Bonds	..	..	..	..	..	..	..	..
Interest payments	**8**	**10**	**6**	**6**	**6**	**7**	**8**	**25**
Public and publicly guaranteed	8	10	6	6	6	7	8	25
Official creditors	8	10	6	6	6	7	8	11
Private creditors	0	0	0	0	0	0	0	14
of which: Bonds	0	0	0	0	0	0	0	14
Private nonguaranteed	..	..	..	..	..	..	..	..
of which: Bonds	..	..	..	..	..	..	..	..
Net financial flows								
Net debt inflows	24	67	111	88	57	197	172	427
Official creditors (incl. IMF)	41	70	106	83	53	211	83	108
Private creditors	-16	-3	5	5	4	-14	89	319
Long-term	..	..	..	..	..	..	..	400
Public and publicly guaranteed	..	..	..	..	..	..	..	400
Private nonguaranteed	..	..	..	..	..	..	..	..
Short-term	-16	-3	5	5	4	-14	89	-81
Net equity inflows								
Foreign direct investment	8	8	103	119	42	106	160	111
Portfolio equity	..	..	..	..	21	31	7	0
Major economic aggregates								
Gross national income (GNI)	1,719	2,554	4,639	5,172	5,582	6,355	7,060	7,337
Exports of goods, services & prim. income	142	260	726	611	639	933	1,027	1,217
Imports of goods, services & prim. income	452	693	1,487	1,594	1,710	2,291	2,570	2,615
Primary income on FDI	3	5	16	5	4	12	1	..
Personal transfers & comp. of employees	7	9	68	93	106	174	182	170
International reserves	191	406	596	743	813	1,050	848	1,070
Ratios								
External debt stocks to exports (%)	911.2	587.3	94.2	142.2	142.9	118.3	123.5	138.9
External debt stocks to GNI (%)	75.0	59.8	14.7	16.8	16.4	17.4	18.0	23.0
Debt service to exports (%)	25.7	10.8	2.0	1.9	2.3	2.1	2.2	3.5
Reserves to external debt stocks (%)	14.8	26.5	87.2	85.4	89.0	95.2	66.8	63.3

Notes:

Short-term debt is based on data from the BIS. Data include the effects of HIPC and MDRI debt relief.

SAMOA

(US$ million, unless otherwise indicated)

	2000	2005	2008	2009	2010	2011	2012	2013
Summary external debt data								
External debt stocks	**139.2**	**169.1**	**207.4**	**252.9**	**325.1**	**368.3**	**422.9**	**447.2**
Long-term external debt	137.7	167.5	205.6	226.4	299.1	342.4	396.9	412.3
Short-term external debt	0.0	0.0	0.0	0.0	0.0	0.0	0.0	0.0
interest arrears on long-term	0.0	0.0	0.0	0.0	0.0	0.0	0.0	0.0
Use of IMF credit	1.5	1.6	1.8	26.5	26.0	25.9	26.0	34.9
Long-term external debt								
Debt outstanding and disbursed	**137.7**	**167.5**	**205.6**	**226.4**	**299.1**	**342.4**	**396.9**	**412.3**
Public and publicly guaranteed	137.7	167.5	205.6	226.4	299.1	342.4	396.9	412.3
Official creditors	137.7	167.5	205.6	226.4	299.1	342.4	396.9	412.3
Private creditors	0.0	0.0	0.0	0.0	0.0	0.0	0.0	0.0
of which: Bonds	0.0	0.0	0.0	0.0	0.0	0.0	0.0	0.0
Private nonguaranteed	..	..	..	..	..	..	..	..
of which: Bonds	..	..	..	..	..	..	..	..
Disbursements	**6.7**	**10.4**	**25.5**	**25.2**	**78.9**	**47.6**	**64.3**	**26.0**
Public and publicly guaranteed	6.7	10.4	25.5	25.2	78.9	47.6	64.3	26.0
Official creditors	6.7	10.4	25.5	25.2	78.9	47.6	64.3	26.0
Private creditors	0.0	0.0	0.0	0.0	0.0	0.0	0.0	0.0
of which: Bonds	0.0	0.0	0.0	0.0	0.0	0.0	0.0	0.0
Private nonguaranteed	..	..	..	..	..	..	..	..
of which: Bonds	..	..	..	..	..	..	..	..
Principal repayments	**4.2**	**4.3**	**6.0**	**6.0**	**7.2**	**7.7**	**8.6**	**9.7**
Public and publicly guaranteed	4.2	4.3	6.0	6.0	7.2	7.7	8.6	9.7
Official creditors	4.2	4.3	6.0	6.0	7.2	7.7	8.6	9.7
Private creditors	0.0	0.0	0.0	0.0	0.0	0.0	0.0	0.0
of which: Bonds	0.0	0.0	0.0	0.0	0.0	0.0	0.0	0.0
Private nonguaranteed	..	..	..	..	..	..	..	..
of which: Bonds	..	..	..	..	..	..	..	..
Interest payments	**1.3**	**1.5**	**2.1**	**2.5**	**3.3**	**4.1**	**4.7**	**5.2**
Public and publicly guaranteed	1.3	1.5	2.1	2.5	3.3	4.1	4.7	5.2
Official creditors	1.3	1.5	2.1	2.5	3.3	4.1	4.7	5.2
Private creditors	0.0	0.0	0.0	0.0	0.0	0.0	0.0	0.0
of which: Bonds	0.0	0.0	0.0	0.0	0.0	0.0	0.0	0.0
Private nonguaranteed	..	..	..	..	..	..	..	..
of which: Bonds	..	..	..	..	..	..	..	..
Net financial flows								
Net debt inflows	2.5	6.1	19.6	28.1	71.6	39.8	55.7	25.2
Official creditors (incl. IMF)	2.5	6.1	19.6	28.1	71.6	39.8	55.7	25.2
Private creditors	..	..	..	..	..	..	..	..
Long-term	..	..	..	..	..	..	..	..
Public and publicly guaranteed	..	..	..	..	..	..	..	..
Private nonguaranteed	..	..	..	..	..	..	..	..
Short-term	..	..	..	..	..	..	..	..
Net equity inflows								
Foreign direct investment	-1.5	3.8	45.9	9.9	1.0	15.2	23.5	28.0
Portfolio equity	..	..	..	..	..	..	..	..
Major economic aggregates								
Gross national income (GNI)	239.7	388.2	531.6	470.3	552.4	605.3	647.6	665.1
Exports of goods, services & prim. income	..	147.3	193.5	181.4	210.4	217.6	250.8	..
Imports of goods, services & prim. income	..	300.2	376.8	319.8	386.4	434.2	456.6	..
Primary income on FDI	..	30.0	50.5	27.4	17.8	29.2	36.0	..
Personal transfers & comp. of employees	45.0	81.6	109.0	119.5	122.1	139.1	158.8	..
International reserves	63.7	81.8	87.1	165.8	209.4	166.8	168.7	170.9
Ratios								
External debt stocks to exports (%)	..	114.8	107.2	139.4	154.5	169.3	168.6	..
External debt stocks to GNI (%)	58.1	43.6	39.0	53.8	58.9	60.8	65.3	67.2
Debt service to exports (%)	..	3.9	4.2	4.7	5.0	5.5	5.3	..
Reserves to external debt stocks (%)	45.7	48.4	42.0	65.6	64.4	45.3	39.9	38.2

Notes:

Short-term debt data are excluded since BIS data include debt liabilities of offshore centers located in the country. BIS short-term debt data for 2011, 2012, and 2013 are $2.5 billion, $3.0 billion, and $3.3 billion respectively.

SAO TOME AND PRINCIPE

(US$ million, unless otherwise indicated)

	2000	2005	2008	2009	2010	2011	2012	2013
Summary external debt data								
External debt stocks	**303.8**	**335.0**	**131.4**	**159.6**	**180.9**	**230.8**	**201.6**	**214.4**
Long-term external debt	277.3	316.5	108.4	124.7	145.1	189.1	169.3	183.3
Short-term external debt	23.3	14.4	18.2	19.4	19.9	25.9	15.9	14.1
interest arrears on long-term	11.3	14.4	8.2	8.4	5.9	5.9	7.9	8.1
Use of IMF credit	3.3	4.1	4.8	15.6	15.9	15.8	16.4	17.0
Long-term external debt								
Debt outstanding and disbursed	**277.3**	**316.5**	**108.4**	**124.7**	**145.1**	**189.1**	**169.3**	**183.3**
Public and publicly guaranteed	277.3	316.5	108.4	124.7	145.1	189.1	169.3	183.3
Official creditors	277.3	316.5	108.4	124.7	145.1	189.1	169.3	183.3
Private creditors	0.0	0.0	0.0	0.0	0.0	0.0	0.0	0.0
of which: Bonds	0.0	0.0	0.0	0.0	0.0	0.0	0.0	0.0
Private nonguaranteed	..	..	..	..	..	..	..	..
of which: Bonds	..	..	..	..	..	..	..	..
Disbursements	**9.4**	**5.4**	**5.2**	**18.8**	**19.8**	**47.6**	**1.7**	**16.0**
Public and publicly guaranteed	9.4	5.4	5.2	18.8	19.8	47.6	1.7	16.0
Official creditors	9.4	5.4	5.2	18.8	19.8	47.6	1.7	16.0
Private creditors	0.0	0.0	0.0	0.0	0.0	0.0	0.0	0.0
of which: Bonds	0.0	0.0	0.0	0.0	0.0	0.0	0.0	0.0
Private nonguaranteed	..	..	..	..	..	..	..	..
of which: Bonds	..	..	..	..	..	..	..	..
Principal repayments	**2.2**	**4.3**	**1.6**	**1.7**	**1.1**	**1.0**	**10.6**	**4.8**
Public and publicly guaranteed	2.2	4.3	1.6	1.7	1.1	1.0	10.6	4.8
Official creditors	2.2	4.3	1.6	1.7	1.1	1.0	10.6	4.8
Private creditors	0.0	0.0	0.0	0.0	0.0	0.0	0.0	0.0
of which: Bonds	0.0	0.0	0.0	0.0	0.0	0.0	0.0	0.0
Private nonguaranteed	..	..	..	..	..	..	..	..
of which: Bonds	..	..	..	..	..	..	..	..
Interest payments	**1.2**	**2.0**	**0.3**	**0.3**	**0.3**	**0.3**	**0.5**	**0.5**
Public and publicly guaranteed	1.2	2.0	0.3	0.3	0.3	0.3	0.5	0.5
Official creditors	1.2	2.0	0.3	0.3	0.3	0.3	0.5	0.5
Private creditors	0.0	0.0	0.0	0.0	0.0	0.0	0.0	0.0
of which: Bonds	0.0	0.0	0.0	0.0	0.0	0.0	0.0	0.0
Private nonguaranteed	..	..	..	..	..	..	..	..
of which: Bonds	..	..	..	..	..	..	..	..
Net financial flows								
Net debt inflows	9.7	1.6	3.9	18.7	22.2	52.6	-20.3	9.8
Official creditors (incl. IMF)	9.7	1.6	4.9	17.7	19.2	46.6	-8.3	11.8
Private creditors	..	..	-1.0	1.0	3.0	6.0	-12.0	-2.0
Long-term	..	..	..	..	..	..	..	..
Public and publicly guaranteed	..	..	..	..	..	..	..	..
Private nonguaranteed	..	..	..	..	..	..	..	..
Short-term	..	..	-1.0	1.0	3.0	6.0	-12.0	-2.0
Net equity inflows								
Foreign direct investment	3.8	15.7	79.1	15.5	50.6	32.2	22.5	30.0
Portfolio equity	..	..	..	..	..	..	..	..
Major economic aggregates								
Gross national income (GNI)	..	120.3	183.4	196.2	200.7	247.9	261.1	308.2
Exports of goods, services & prim. income	17.1	18.1	19.4	21.3	26.2	31.2	30.8	36.6
Imports of goods, services & prim. income	42.0	57.8	115.6	104.7	122.8	149.4	144.4	159.4
Primary income on FDI	..	..	..	..	..	..	..	..
Personal transfers & comp. of employees	0.5	1.5	3.0	2.0	6.4	6.9	6.4	..
International reserves	11.6	26.7	61.3	66.7	48.2	52.3	51.6	63.8
Ratios								
External debt stocks to exports (%)	1772.0	1853.8	675.6	751.0	690.1	739.7	654.8	586.0
External debt stocks to GNI (%)	..	278.4	71.6	81.4	90.1	93.1	77.2	69.6
Debt service to exports (%)	25.4	36.3	11.5	9.4	6.0	5.0	36.5	16.3
Reserves to external debt stocks (%)	3.8	8.0	46.6	41.8	26.6	22.7	25.6	29.8

Notes:

Short-term debt is based on data from the BIS. Data include HIPC and MDRI debt relief.

SENEGAL

(US$ million, unless otherwise indicated)

	2000	2005	2008	2009	2010	2011	2012	2013
Summary external debt data								
External debt stocks	**3,653**	**3,862**	**2,851**	**3,721**	**3,908**	**4,324**	**4,904**	**5,223**
Long-term external debt	3,221	3,643	2,552	3,312	3,457	3,877	4,462	4,785
Short-term external debt	146	36	197	0	0	0	0	0
interest arrears on long-term	1	0	0	0	0	0	0	0
Use of IMF credit	286	183	102	409	451	447	442	438
Long-term external debt								
Debt outstanding and disbursed	**3,221**	**3,643**	**2,552**	**3,312**	**3,457**	**3,877**	**4,462**	**4,785**
Public and publicly guaranteed	3,208	3,501	2,372	2,954	3,149	3,612	4,197	4,514
Official creditors	3,203	3,492	2,367	2,752	2,949	3,112	3,695	4,012
Private creditors	5	9	4	202	200	500	502	502
of which: Bonds	0	0	0	200	200	500	500	500
Private nonguaranteed	13	141	180	357	308	265	266	271
of which: Bonds	..	..	..	..	..	..	..	..
Disbursements	**137**	**382**	**522**	**837**	**434**	**1,009**	**746**	**533**
Public and publicly guaranteed	136	333	518	628	352	928	672	407
Official creditors	131	333	518	428	352	428	670	407
Private creditors	5	0	0	200	0	500	2	0
of which: Bonds	0	0	0	200	0	500	0	0
Private nonguaranteed	1	49	4	208	83	81	74	126
of which: Bonds		..	..	..	..	..	..	..
Principal repayments	**127**	**112**	**126**	**146**	**229**	**236**	**211**	**267**
Public and publicly guaranteed	125	83	87	97	84	140	138	147
Official creditors	124	81	85	94	83	140	138	147
Private creditors	0	2	3	3	2	0	0	0
of which: Bonds	0	0	0	0	0	0	0	0
Private nonguaranteed	3	29	39	49	144	96	73	121
of which: Bonds	..	..	..	..	..	..	..	..
Interest payments	**58**	**55**	**49**	**50**	**75**	**122**	**102**	**128**
Public and publicly guaranteed	58	45	36	41	64	108	85	107
Official creditors	58	44	36	41	46	57	48	61
Private creditors	0	1	0	0	18	51	37	46
of which: Bonds	0	0	0	0	18	51	37	46
Private nonguaranteed	0	10	13	9	11	15	17	21
of which: Bonds	..	..	..	..	..	..	..	..
Net financial flows								
Net debt inflows	-153	242	299	594	254	770	530	261
Official creditors (incl. IMF)	5	224	471	434	318	285	527	255
Private creditors	-158	18	-172	160	-63	485	3	5
Long-term	3	18	-37	357	-63	485	3	5
Public and publicly guaranteed	5	-2	-3	197	-2	500	2	..
Private nonguaranteed	-1	20	-34	159	-62	-15	2	5
Short-term	-161	..	-135	-197	..	..	..	..
Net equity inflows								
Foreign direct investment	63	152	442	244	267	296	276	298
Portfolio equity	-2	-6	-93	-2	23	14	..	..
Major economic aggregates								
Gross national income (GNI)	4,589	8,551	13,339	12,634	12,799	14,274	13,865	14,974
Exports of goods, services & prim. income	1,383	2,562	3,785	3,286	3,418	4,055	4,323	..
Imports of goods, services & prim. income	1,929	3,991	7,353	5,613	5,557	6,969	7,697	..
Primary income on FDI	75	173	178	147	135	209	..	..
Personal transfers & comp. of employees	233	789	1,476	1,350	1,478	1,614	..	..
International reserves	388	1,186	1,602	2,123	2,047	1,946	2,082	2,253
Ratios								
External debt stocks to exports (%)	264.2	150.8	75.3	113.2	114.3	106.6	113.4	..
External debt stocks to GNI (%)	79.6	45.2	21.4	29.5	30.5	30.3	35.4	34.9
Debt service to exports (%)	16.3	7.9	4.8	6.0	8.9	8.9	7.4	..
Reserves to external debt stocks (%)	10.6	30.7	56.2	57.1	52.4	45.0	42.4	43.1

Notes:

Short-term debt before 2009 is based on data from the BIS.

SERBIA

(US$ million, unless otherwise indicated)

	2000	2005	2008	2009	2010	2011	2012	2013
Summary external debt data								
External debt stocks	**11,573**	**16,159**	**30,493**	**33,814**	**32,935**	**31,724**	**34,444**	**36,397**
Long-term external debt	6,789	12,970	26,719	27,915	27,417	27,779	30,910	34,180
Short-term external debt	4,558	2,242	3,687	3,600	2,798	1,162	1,018	571
interest arrears on long-term	3,668	728	704	712	352	324	367	279
Use of IMF credit	226	947	87	2,299	2,720	2,783	2,517	1,647
Long-term external debt								
Debt outstanding and disbursed	**6,789**	**12,970**	**26,719**	**27,915**	**27,417**	**27,779**	**30,910**	**34,180**
Public and publicly guaranteed	6,178	7,756	8,399	8,839	9,504	11,339	13,701	16,722
Official creditors	4,243	6,679	7,223	7,664	8,172	8,738	9,324	10,085
Private creditors	1,935	1,077	1,175	1,175	1,332	2,601	4,378	6,637
of which: Bonds	0	0	0	0	0	1,000	2,750	5,250
Private nonguaranteed	611	5,214	18,320	19,076	17,912	16,440	17,208	17,457
of which: Bonds	..	..	165	165	165	165	..	641
Disbursements	**222**	**2,904**	**6,996**	**4,533**	**4,617**	**6,280**	**6,382**	**8,973**
Public and publicly guaranteed	222	311	294	971	1,388	2,541	2,854	3,789
Official creditors	187	311	291	971	1,149	1,137	965	999
Private creditors	35	0	3	0	239	1,404	1,889	2,789
of which: Bonds	0	0	0	0	0	1,000	1,750	2,500
Private nonguaranteed	..	2,593	6,703	3,562	3,230	3,739	3,528	5,184
of which: Bonds	..	..	..	..	..	..	..	641
Principal repayments	**0**	**570**	**3,486**	**3,613**	**3,431**	**4,257**	**4,756**	**6,296**
Public and publicly guaranteed	0	48	181	158	351	451	623	1,149
Official creditors	0	48	180	154	275	350	494	580
Private creditors	0	0	1	4	76	101	129	568
of which: Bonds	0	0	0	0	0	0	0	0
Private nonguaranteed	..	522	3,305	3,454	3,081	3,806	4,133	5,147
of which: Bonds	..	..	..	..	..	..	165	..
Interest payments	**0**	**367**	**1,136**	**916**	**759**	**905**	**978**	**1,269**
Public and publicly guaranteed	0	237	354	348	321	348	430	617
Official creditors	0	194	328	303	241	257	268	313
Private creditors	0	44	26	45	80	91	162	303
of which: Bonds	0	0	0	0	0	0	73	221
Private nonguaranteed	..	129	782	568	438	557	548	652
of which: Bonds	..	..	10	10	10	10	5	..
Net financial flows								
Net debt inflows	51	2,827	4,948	2,401	1,201	489	1,171	1,452
Official creditors (incl. IMF)	268	241	111	2,392	1,332	861	204	-448
Private creditors	-217	2,586	4,837	9	-130	-372	968	1,900
Long-term	35	2,071	3,400	104	312	1,235	1,155	2,258
Public and publicly guaranteed	35	0	1	-4	163	1,303	1,760	2,221
Private nonguaranteed	..	2,071	3,398	108	149	-68	-605	37
Short-term	-252	515	1,437	-95	-442	-1,607	-188	-358
Net equity inflows								
Foreign direct investment	52	..	2,211	1,397	815	2,213	-711	1,377
Portfolio equity	..	..	-57	22	84	69	-24	..
Major economic aggregates								
Gross national income (GNI)	6,082	24,910	46,395	39,560	36,099	42,238	36,940	41,315
Exports of goods, services & prim. income	..	..	15,792	12,544	13,916	16,561	16,012	19,376
Imports of goods, services & prim. income	..	..	29,927	20,348	20,884	24,773	23,788	26,348
Primary income on FDI	..	..	890	451	552	531	602	..
Personal transfers & comp. of employees	..	..	2,708	3,933	3,349	3,271	2,763	..
International reserves	392	5,628	11,123	14,769	12,715	14,877	13,585	14,803
Ratios								
External debt stocks to exports (%)	..	..	193.1	269.6	236.7	191.6	215.1	187.8
External debt stocks to GNI (%)	190.3	64.9	65.7	85.5	91.2	75.1	93.2	88.1
Debt service to exports (%)	..	..	30.0	37.0	30.9	31.5	37.7	43.6
Reserves to external debt stocks (%)	3.4	34.8	36.5	43.7	38.6	46.9	39.4	40.7

Notes:

Beginning 2006, the data for Serbia exclude Montenegro.

SEYCHELLES

(US$ million, unless otherwise indicated)

	2000	2005	2008	2009	2010	2011	2012	2013
Summary external debt data								
External debt stocks	**304**	**672**	**1,502**	**1,707**	**1,487**	**1,778**	**2,024**	**2,714**
Long-term external debt	220	398	650	708	463	457	475	485
Short-term external debt	84	273	842	968	980	1,272	1,494	2,173
interest arrears on long-term	5	57	78	110	24	16	13	13
Use of IMF credit	1	1	10	32	44	49	54	56
Long-term external debt								
Debt outstanding and disbursed	**220**	**398**	**650**	**708**	**463**	**457**	**475**	**485**
Public and publicly guaranteed	220	398	650	708	463	457	475	485
Official creditors	159	224	196	271	213	209	228	245
Private creditors	61	175	453	436	250	249	247	240
of which: Bonds	0	0	305	307	169	169	169	169
Private nonguaranteed	..	..	..	..	..	..	..	..
of which: Bonds	..	..	..	..	..	..	..	..
Disbursements	**38**	**59**	**84**	**34**	**49**	**7**	**23**	**24**
Public and publicly guaranteed	38	59	84	34	49	7	23	24
Official creditors	19	8	4	25	33	6	20	24
Private creditors	19	51	80	9	16	1	3	0
of which: Bonds	0	0	0	0	0	0	0	0
Private nonguaranteed	..	..	..	..	..	..	..	..
of which: Bonds	..	..	..	..	..	..	..	..
Principal repayments	**10**	**41**	**53**	**43**	**9**	**8**	**9**	**18**
Public and publicly guaranteed	10	41	53	43	9	8	9	18
Official creditors	5	11	15	18	6	7	5	10
Private creditors	5	30	38	25	3	1	5	8
of which: Bonds	0	0	2	0	0	0	0	0
Private nonguaranteed	..	..	..	..	..	..	..	..
of which: Bonds	..	..	..	..	..	..	..	..
Interest payments	**7**	**11**	**21**	**8**	**28**	**9**	**12**	**14**
Public and publicly guaranteed	7	11	21	8	28	9	12	14
Official creditors	2	3	4	4	2	3	4	5
Private creditors	5	8	18	4	26	6	8	9
of which: Bonds	0	0	10	0	20	5	7	8
Private nonguaranteed	..	..	..	..	..	..	..	..
of which: Bonds	..	..	..	..	..	..	..	..
Net financial flows								
Net debt inflows	71	180	81	93	151	305	244	687
Official creditors (incl. IMF)	14	-3	-1	15	40	4	20	16
Private creditors	57	183	82	78	111	300	224	671
Long-term	15	21	42	-16	13	0	-1	-8
Public and publicly guaranteed	15	21	42	-16	13	0	-1	-8
Private nonguaranteed	..	..	..	..	..	..	..	..
Short-term	42	162	40	94	98	300	225	679
Net equity inflows								
Foreign direct investment	24	86	130	118	119	68	58	178
Portfolio equity	..	..	..	..	..	..	..	..
Major economic aggregates								
Gross national income (GNI)	582	879	894	801	926	1,008	987	1,220
Exports of goods, services & prim. income	492	729	907	853	850	957	951	1,108
Imports of goods, services & prim. income	545	935	1,164	1,050	1,069	1,247	1,254	1,321
Primary income on FDI	8	20	22	8	-13	50	45	..
Personal transfers & comp. of employees	3	12	3	16	17	25	18	..
International reserves	44	56	64	191	256	279	308	426
Ratios								
External debt stocks to exports (%)	61.9	92.1	165.6	200.1	174.9	185.7	212.8	245.0
External debt stocks to GNI (%)	52.3	76.4	167.9	213.0	160.6	176.4	205.2	222.4
Debt service to exports (%)	4.2	8.1	10.2	7.2	5.7	3.6	4.7	5.6
Reserves to external debt stocks (%)	14.4	8.4	4.2	11.2	17.2	15.7	15.2	15.7

Notes:

Short-term debt is based on data from the BIS.

SIERRA LEONE

(US$ million, unless otherwise indicated)

	2000	2005	2008	2009	2010	2011	2012	2013
Summary external debt data								
External debt stocks	**1,213**	**1,776**	**634**	**857**	**931**	**1,050**	**1,125**	**1,395**
Long-term external debt	973	1,538	545	605	661	741	837	900
Short-term external debt	44	21	9	23	4	35	14	214
interest arrears on long-term	36	11	0	0	0	0	0	0
Use of IMF credit	196	217	80	229	266	274	274	281
Long-term external debt								
Debt outstanding and disbursed	**973**	**1,538**	**545**	**605**	**661**	**741**	**837**	**900**
Public and publicly guaranteed	973	1,538	545	605	661	741	837	900
Official creditors	967	1,325	334	394	450	533	627	705
Private creditors	5	213	211	211	211	208	210	195
of which: Bonds	0	0	0	0	0	0	0	0
Private nonguaranteed	..	..	..	..	..	..	..	..
of which: Bonds	..	..	..	..	..	..	..	..
Disbursements	**77**	**51**	**69**	**62**	**66**	**95**	**106**	**89**
Public and publicly guaranteed	77	51	69	62	66	95	106	89
Official creditors	77	51	69	62	66	95	106	89
Private creditors	0	0	0	0	0	0	0	0
of which: Bonds	0	0	0	0	0	0	0	0
Private nonguaranteed	..	..	..	..	..	..	..	..
of which: Bonds	..	..	..	..	..	..	..	..
Principal repayments	**10**	**5**	**2**	**3**	**5**	**7**	**8**	**10**
Public and publicly guaranteed	10	5	2	3	5	7	8	10
Official creditors	10	5	2	3	5	7	8	10
Private creditors	0	0	0	0	0	0	0	0
of which: Bonds	0	0	0	0	0	0	0	0
Private nonguaranteed	..	..	..	..	..	..	..	..
of which: Bonds	..	..	..	..	..	..	..	..
Interest payments	**9**	**9**	**3**	**4**	**4**	**6**	**6**	**7**
Public and publicly guaranteed	9	9	3	4	4	6	6	7
Official creditors	9	9	3	4	4	6	6	7
Private creditors	0	0	0	0	0	0	0	0
of which: Bonds	0	0	0	0	0	0	0	0
Private nonguaranteed	..	..	..	..	..	..	..	..
of which: Bonds	..	..	..	..	..	..	..	..
Net financial flows								
Net debt inflows	57	54	89	92	83	128	77	285
Official creditors (incl. IMF)	55	64	85	78	102	97	98	85
Private creditors	1	-10	4	14	-19	31	-21	200
Long-term	..	..	..	..	..	..	..	..
Public and publicly guaranteed	..	..	..	..	..	..	..	..
Private nonguaranteed	..	..	..	..	..	..	..	..
Short-term	1	-10	4	14	-19	31	-21	200
Net equity inflows								
Foreign direct investment	39	53	74	85	225	770	529	579
Portfolio equity	..	..	..	6	0	0	7	..
Major economic aggregates								
Gross national income (GNI)	616	1,590	2,701	2,665	2,607	3,039	3,438	4,483
Exports of goods, services & prim. income	62	267	348	380	427	548	1,350	..
Imports of goods, services & prim. income	262	509	685	797	1,191	2,711	2,689	..
Primary income on FDI	2	41	76	39	46	219	130	..
Personal transfers & comp. of employees	7	2	23	36	44	59	61	..
International reserves	49	171	220	405	409	439	478	533
Ratios								
External debt stocks to exports (%)	1,941.0	664.7	182.1	225.7	218.3	191.8	83.3	..
External debt stocks to GNI (%)	196.8	111.7	23.5	32.2	35.7	34.6	32.7	31.1
Debt service to exports (%)	76.4	6.9	1.7	2.1	2.7	3.4	1.5	..
Reserves to external debt stocks (%)	4.1	9.6	34.7	47.3	43.9	41.8	42.5	38.2

Notes:

Short-term debt before 2013 is based on data from the BIS.

SOLOMON ISLANDS

(US$ million, unless otherwise indicated)

	2000	2005	2008	2009	2010	2011	2012	2013
Summary external debt data								
External debt stocks	**156.2**	**167.4**	**166.9**	**172.4**	**230.8**	**257.5**	**228.1**	**204.0**
Long-term external debt	152.1	151.2	162.8	154.4	201.9	210.3	191.5	166.0
Short-term external debt	3.2	15.3	3.1	2.5	4.0	12.9	2.0	3.0
interest arrears on long-term	1.8	12.3	3.1	1.5	4.0	8.9	0.0	0.0
Use of IMF credit	0.9	0.9	1.0	15.5	24.9	34.4	34.6	34.9
Long-term external debt								
Debt outstanding and disbursed	**152.1**	**151.2**	**162.8**	**154.4**	**201.9**	**210.3**	**191.5**	**166.0**
Public and publicly guaranteed	120.7	144.2	137.1	132.9	125.3	117.8	110.2	101.1
Official creditors	117.3	143.8	136.6	132.7	125.2	117.8	110.2	101.1
Private creditors	3.4	0.4	0.4	0.2	0.1	0.0	0.0	0.0
of which: Bonds	0.0	0.0	0.0	0.0	0.0	0.0	0.0	0.0
Private nonguaranteed	31.5	7.0	25.8	21.5	76.6	92.4	81.3	64.9
of which: Bonds	..	..	..	..	..	..	..	..
Disbursements	**3.4**	**5.7**	**1.1**	**13.7**	**36.8**	**27.3**	**2.2**	**5.5**
Public and publicly guaranteed	3.4	5.7	0.1	0.0	0.0	0.0	0.0	0.0
Official creditors	3.4	5.3	0.1	0.0	0.0	0.0	0.0	0.0
Private creditors	0.0	0.4	0.0	0.0	0.0	0.0	0.0	0.0
of which: Bonds	0.0	0.0	0.0	0.0	0.0	0.0	0.0	0.0
Private nonguaranteed	..	..	1.0	13.7	36.8	27.3	2.2	5.5
of which: Bonds	..	..	..	..	..	..	..	..
Principal repayments	**6.2**	**10.0**	**10.8**	**7.6**	**17.5**	**12.6**	**21.8**	**38.9**
Public and publicly guaranteed	2.7	5.8	10.8	6.5	8.6	6.6	6.5	6.4
Official creditors	2.7	3.2	10.7	6.3	8.4	6.5	6.5	6.4
Private creditors	0.0	2.6	0.1	0.2	0.2	0.1	0.0	0.0
of which: Bonds	0.0	0.0	0.0	0.0	0.0	0.0	0.0	0.0
Private nonguaranteed	3.5	4.2	..	1.1	8.9	6.0	15.3	32.5
of which: Bonds	..	..	..	..	..	..	..	..
Interest payments	**2.7**	**3.9**	**4.3**	**2.4**	**3.2**	**2.6**	**8.1**	**5.3**
Public and publicly guaranteed	0.8	1.7	4.3	1.8	1.7	1.7	1.5	1.4
Official creditors	0.8	1.7	4.3	1.8	1.7	1.7	1.5	1.4
Private creditors	0.0	0.0	0.0	0.0	0.0	0.0	0.0	0.0
of which: Bonds	0.0	0.0	0.0	0.0	0.0	0.0	0.0	0.0
Private nonguaranteed	1.9	2.3	0.0	0.5	1.5	0.9	6.5	3.9
of which: Bonds	..	..	..	..	..	..	..	..
Net financial flows								
Net debt inflows	-4.4	-2.3	-9.7	7.1	27.9	28.5	-21.3	-32.2
Official creditors (incl. IMF)	0.6	2.1	-10.6	-6.3	1.1	3.3	-6.3	-6.1
Private creditors	-5.0	-4.4	0.9	13.4	26.8	25.2	-15.1	-26.0
Long-term	-3.5	-6.4	0.9	12.4	27.8	21.2	-13.1	-27.0
Public and publicly guaranteed	..	-2.1	-0.1	-0.2	-0.2	-0.1	..	..
Private nonguaranteed	-3.5	-4.2	1.0	12.6	28.0	21.3	-13.1	-27.0
Short-term	-1.5	2.0	..	1.0	-1.0	4.0	-2.0	1.0
Net equity inflows								
Foreign direct investment	13.0	0.3	82.8	109.9	113.0	104.5	64.6	105.3
Portfolio equity	..	..	..	..	..	..	..	..
Major economic aggregates								
Gross national income (GNI)	435.5	415.5	514.0	432.9	508.3	690.2	897.6	960.5
Exports of goods, services & prim. income	128.8	154.9	289.7	247.5	347.8	582.9	665.1	..
Imports of goods, services & prim. income	176.4	250.1	524.0	492.5	690.3	771.9	761.3	..
Primary income on FDI	8.3	5.3	103.5	135.5	127.0	133.5	84.2	..
Personal transfers & comp. of employees	4.3	7.2	1.7	2.5	1.7	1.9	17.2	..
International reserves	32.0	94.8	88.8	146.0	265.8	412.3	469.5	491.5
Ratios								
External debt stocks to exports (%)	121.3	108.1	57.6	69.7	66.4	44.2	34.3	..
External debt stocks to GNI (%)	35.9	40.3	32.5	39.8	45.4	37.3	25.4	21.2
Debt service to exports (%)	7.1	9.1	5.2	4.0	6.0	2.6	4.5	..
Reserves to external debt stocks (%)	20.5	56.7	53.2	84.7	115.2	160.1	205.8	241.0

Notes:

Short-term debt is based on data from the BIS.

SOMALIA

(US$ million, unless otherwise indicated)

	2000	2005	2008	2009	2010	2011	2012	2013
Summary external debt data								
External debt stocks	**2,579**	**2,770**	**2,970**	**3,046**	**3,045**	**3,053**	**3,055**	**3,054**
Long-term external debt	1,825	1,882	1,983	1,987	1,990	1,992	1,985	1,977
Short-term external debt	591	709	793	810	811	818	827	834
interest arrears on long-term	569	709	793	810	811	818	827	834
Use of IMF credit	164	180	194	248	244	243	243	243
Long-term external debt								
Debt outstanding and disbursed	**1,825**	**1,882**	**1,983**	**1,987**	**1,990**	**1,992**	**1,985**	**1,977**
Public and publicly guaranteed	1,825	1,882	1,983	1,987	1,990	1,992	1,985	1,977
Official creditors	1,792	1,846	1,946	1,950	1,954	1,955	1,948	1,940
Private creditors	33	35	37	38	37	36	36	37
of which: Bonds	0	0	0	0	0	0	0	0
Private nonguaranteed	..	..	..	..	..	..	..	..
of which: Bonds	..	..	..	..	..	..	..	..
Disbursements	**0**	**0**	**0**	**0**	**0**	**0**	**0**	**0**
Public and publicly guaranteed	0	0	0	0	0	0	0	0
Official creditors	0	0	0	0	0	0	0	0
Private creditors	0	0	0	0	0	0	0	0
of which: Bonds	0	0	0	0	0	0	0	0
Private nonguaranteed	..	..	..	..	..	..	..	..
of which: Bonds	..	..	..	..	..	..	..	..
Principal repayments	**0**	**0**	**0**	**0**	**0**	**0**	**0**	**0**
Public and publicly guaranteed	0	0	0	0	0	0	0	0
Official creditors	0	0	0	0	0	0	0	0
Private creditors	0	0	0	0	0	0	0	0
of which: Bonds	0	0	0	0	0	0	0	0
Private nonguaranteed	..	..	..	..	..	..	..	..
of which: Bonds	..	..	..	..	..	..	..	..
Interest payments	**0**	**0**	**0**	**0**	**0**	**0**	**0**	**0**
Public and publicly guaranteed	0	0	0	0	0	0	0	0
Official creditors	0	0	0	0	0	0	0	0
Private creditors	0	0	0	0	0	0	0	0
of which: Bonds	0	0	0	0	0	0	0	0
Private nonguaranteed	..	..	..	..	..	..	..	..
of which: Bonds	..	..	..	..	..	..	..	..
Net financial flows								
Net debt inflows	-7	..	..	..	..	..	0	0
Official creditors (incl. IMF)	..	..	..	..	..	..	0	0
Private creditors	-7	..	..	..	..	..	..	..
Long-term	..	..	..	..	..	..	..	..
Public and publicly guaranteed	..	..	..	..	..	..	..	..
Private nonguaranteed	..	..	..	..	..	..	..	..
Short-term	-7	..	..	..	..	..	..	..
Net equity inflows								
Foreign direct investment	0	24	87	108	112	102	107	107
Portfolio equity	..	..	..	..	..	..	..	..
Major economic aggregates								
Gross national income (GNI)	..	..	..	..	..	..	..	..
Exports of goods, services & prim. income	..	..	..	..	..	..	..	..
Imports of goods, services & prim. income	..	..	..	..	..	..	..	..
Primary income on FDI	..	..	..	..	..	..	..	..
Personal transfers & comp. of employees	..	..	..	..	..	..	..	..
International reserves	..	..	..	..	..	..	..	..
Ratios								
External debt stocks to exports (%)	..	..	..	..	..	..	..	..
External debt stocks to GNI (%)	..	..	..	..	..	..	..	..
Debt service to exports (%)	..	..	..	..	..	..	..	..
Reserves to external debt stocks (%)	..	..	..	..	..	..	..	..

Notes:

Long-term public and publicly guaranteed debt data are World Bank staff estimates based on the original terms of the loans.

SOUTH AFRICA

(US$ million, unless otherwise indicated)

	2000	2005	2008	2009	2010	2011	2012	2013
Summary external debt data								
External debt stocks	**25,435**	**44,737**	**70,696**	**81,360**	**107,131**	**116,119**	**144,871**	**139,845**
Long-term external debt	15,595	30,146	44,895	57,275	82,651	92,844	114,259	109,846
Short-term external debt	9,553	14,276	25,462	21,286	21,730	20,534	27,868	27,249
interest arrears on long-term	0	0	0	0	0	0	0	0
Use of IMF credit	287	315	339	2,799	2,750	2,741	2,744	2,750
Long-term external debt								
Debt outstanding and disbursed	**15,595**	**30,146**	**44,895**	**57,275**	**82,651**	**92,844**	**114,259**	**109,846**
Public and publicly guaranteed	9,088	20,743	20,016	24,658	39,017	46,669	62,471	60,793
Official creditors	145	286	259	227	1,139	1,449	2,782	3,046
Private creditors	8,943	20,457	19,757	24,430	37,878	45,220	59,689	57,747
of which: Bonds	4,749	12,242	13,663	18,508	32,329	38,548	53,133	50,242
Private nonguaranteed	6,507	9,403	24,879	32,617	43,634	46,175	51,788	49,053
of which: Bonds	1,110	3,196	8,322	8,485	8,786	12,638	14,069	13,152
Disbursements	**3,611**	**2,678**	**1,871**	**4,502**	**6,833**	**10,655**	**10,126**	**9,434**
Public and publicly guaranteed	1,597	2,678	1,219	2,332	3,777	5,050	4,729	5,231
Official creditors	91	58	3	32	913	490	1,415	526
Private creditors	1,506	2,620	1,216	2,300	2,864	4,560	3,314	4,705
of which: Bonds	765	0	0	2,000	2,000	3,500	2,500	3,000
Private nonguaranteed	2,014	..	652	2,170	3,056	5,605	5,397	4,202
of which: Bonds	712	..	..	163	1,135	3,852	2,738	3,543
Principal repayments	**2,631**	**2,870**	**4,492**	**2,127**	**2,864**	**2,382**	**5,255**	**5,518**
Public and publicly guaranteed	1,649	2,870	2,353	1,419	1,278	1,165	2,637	2,319
Official creditors	0	27	26	38	40	42	37	25
Private creditors	1,649	2,844	2,327	1,381	1,238	1,123	2,600	2,294
of which: Bonds	306	1,091	888	250	0	104	1,670	1,535
Private nonguaranteed	982	..	2,139	708	1,586	1,217	2,618	3,199
of which: Bonds	..	..	1,513	..	834	..	1,307	2,083
Interest payments	**746**	**1,269**	**1,931**	**1,749**	**2,382**	**2,975**	**3,574**	**3,282**
Public and publicly guaranteed	549	1,058	1,192	1,097	1,573	2,061	2,627	2,413
Official creditors	1	12	16	10	20	40	62	70
Private creditors	548	1,046	1,176	1,087	1,553	2,021	2,565	2,342
of which: Bonds	278	771	894	953	1,488	1,968	2,475	2,278
Private nonguaranteed	196	212	739	652	810	914	948	869
of which: Bonds	27	212	549	432	460	664	776	602
Net financial flows								
Net debt inflows	-282	2,888	-1,203	-1,801	4,413	7,077	12,205	3,297
Official creditors (incl. IMF)	91	31	-23	-6	873	448	1,378	502
Private creditors	-373	2,857	-1,180	-1,795	3,540	6,629	10,827	2,795
Long-term	889	-224	-2,598	2,381	3,096	7,825	3,493	3,414
Public and publicly guaranteed	-143	-224	-1,111	919	1,626	3,437	714	2,411
Private nonguaranteed	1,032	..	-1,487	1,462	1,470	4,388	2,779	1,003
Short-term	-1,262	3,081	1,418	-4,176	444	-1,196	7,334	-619
Net equity inflows								
Foreign direct investment	969	6,192	6,729	4,957	-4,194	2,903	1,671	2,699
Portfolio equity	4,169	7,230	-4,707	9,364	5,826	-3,769	-679	1,011
Major economic aggregates								
Gross national income (GNI)	129,702	242,112	264,189	277,840	357,981	394,726	373,455	343,243
Exports of goods, services & prim. income	39,507	72,202	104,867	82,551	108,665	128,925	120,378	115,817
Imports of goods, services & prim. income	38,771	78,267	122,644	91,219	113,410	136,432	136,593	133,129
Primary income on FDI	2,329	4,320	8,031	5,279	6,165	8,375	8,486	8,049
Personal transfers & comp. of employees	344	614	783	862	1,070	1,158	1,085	971
International reserves	6,083	18,579	30,584	35,237	38,175	42,595	43,995	44,864
Ratios								
External debt stocks to exports (%)	64.4	62.0	67.4	98.6	98.6	90.1	120.3	120.7
External debt stocks to GNI (%)	19.6	18.5	26.8	29.3	29.9	29.4	38.8	40.7
Debt service to exports (%)	9.9	6.5	6.8	5.6	5.5	4.6	8.1	8.3
Reserves to external debt stocks (%)	23.9	41.5	43.3	43.3	35.6	36.7	30.4	32.1

Notes:

Long-term public and publicly guaranteed and long-term private nonguaranteed debt data are World Bank staff estimates based on reports provided by the country.

SRI LANKA

(US$ million, unless otherwise indicated)

	2000	2005	2008	2009	2010	2011	2012	2013
Summary external debt data								
External debt stocks	**9,173**	**11,472**	**15,710**	**16,244**	**19,898**	**22,072**	**23,520**	**25,168**
Long-term external debt	8,236	9,997	13,345	14,642	17,392	19,747	20,377	22,497
Short-term external debt	685	992	2,087	261	586	0	25	6
interest arrears on long-term	112	0	0	0	0	0	0	6
Use of IMF credit	253	483	278	1,341	1,920	2,325	3,118	2,665
Long-term external debt								
Debt outstanding and disbursed	**8,236**	**9,997**	**13,345**	**14,642**	**17,392**	**19,747**	**20,377**	**22,497**
Public and publicly guaranteed	7,868	9,609	12,611	13,676	16,473	18,734	20,374	22,397
Official creditors	6,928	8,982	11,285	11,933	13,603	14,793	15,878	16,619
Private creditors	940	627	1,327	1,743	2,870	3,941	4,497	5,778
of which: Bonds	65	65	500	1,000	2,000	3,000	3,500	4,750
Private nonguaranteed	368	388	734	967	919	1,013	3	100
of which: Bonds	..	100	100	..	..	..	..	100
Disbursements	**732**	**929**	**1,238**	**2,209**	**3,086**	**2,990**	**3,312**	**3,592**
Public and publicly guaranteed	563	818	1,083	1,822	2,989	2,746	3,312	3,492
Official creditors	348	670	789	1,160	1,805	1,607	2,143	2,063
Private creditors	215	149	293	662	1,183	1,138	1,169	1,429
of which: Bonds	0	0	0	500	1,000	1,000	1,000	1,250
Private nonguaranteed	169	111	156	387	97	244	0	100
of which: Bonds	..	..	..	..	..	..	..	100
Principal repayments	**453**	**228**	**804**	**967**	**715**	**805**	**1,200**	**743**
Public and publicly guaranteed	439	209	743	812	570	651	1,199	743
Official creditors	216	123	518	555	507	587	604	613
Private creditors	223	86	224	257	64	64	595	130
of which: Bonds	50	0	65	0	0	0	500	0
Private nonguaranteed	14	19	61	154	145	154	0	..
of which: Bonds	..	..	..	100	..	..	..	..
Interest payments	**213**	**106**	**286**	**325**	**616**	**448**	**515**	**571**
Public and publicly guaranteed	178	84	251	285	596	405	515	571
Official creditors	125	65	178	227	308	268	292	326
Private creditors	54	19	73	58	288	137	223	245
of which: Bonds	6	4	46	43	72	124	207	220
Private nonguaranteed	35	22	35	40	20	43	0	..
of which: Bonds	..	7	7	7	..	..	..	..
Net financial flows								
Net debt inflows	-25	1,160	811	-43	3,293	2,021	2,923	2,369
Official creditors (incl. IMF)	45	661	193	1,145	1,895	1,443	2,325	995
Private creditors	-70	499	619	-1,189	1,397	578	599	1,374
Long-term	148	155	164	637	1,072	1,165	574	1,399
Public and publicly guaranteed	-7	63	69	405	1,120	1,075	574	1,299
Private nonguaranteed	155	92	95	233	-48	90	0	100
Short-term	-218	344	455	-1,826	325	-586	25	-25
Net equity inflows								
Foreign direct investment	173	272	542	173	240	251	360	373
Portfolio equity	..	-216	-488	-382	-1,049	-171	272	263
Major economic aggregates								
Gross national income (GNI)	16,016	24,107	39,746	41,583	48,950	58,526	58,179	65,363
Exports of goods, services & prim. income	6,527	7,963	10,338	9,099	11,423	14,109	13,716	15,227
Imports of goods, services & prim. income	8,554	10,441	16,889	12,318	16,159	23,368	23,152	23,531
Primary income on FDI	109	115	470	230	303	385	449	772
Personal transfers & comp. of employees	1,166	1,976	2,925	3,337	4,123	5,153	6,000	6,422
International reserves	1,039	2,650	2,469	4,616	6,710	6,248	6,378	6,611
Ratios								
External debt stocks to exports (%)	140.5	144.1	152.0	178.5	174.2	156.4	171.5	165.3
External debt stocks to GNI (%)	57.3	47.6	39.5	39.1	40.6	37.7	40.4	38.5
Debt service to exports (%)	12.1	5.3	11.9	15.5	12.2	9.2	13.1	11.9
Reserves to external debt stocks (%)	11.3	23.1	15.7	28.4	33.7	28.3	27.1	26.3

Notes:

Long-term private nonguaranteed debt data for 2013 are World Bank staff estimates based on reports provided by the country. Short-term debt before 2009 is based on data from the BIS.

ST. LUCIA

(US$ million, unless otherwise indicated)

	2000	2005	2008	2009	2010	2011	2012	2013
Summary external debt data								
External debt stocks	**222.2**	**415.7**	**832.4**	**433.1**	**579.6**	**451.2**	**432.3**	**486.3**
Long-term external debt	153.5	238.6	316.3	314.9	321.3	310.1	345.4	342.2
Short-term external debt	67.8	176.0	514.9	84.6	225.3	99.9	45.7	102.7
interest arrears on long-term	0.0	0.0	0.9	2.6	5.3	3.9	1.6	2.2
Use of IMF credit	1.0	1.1	1.1	33.6	33.0	41.2	41.2	41.3
Long-term external debt								
Debt outstanding and disbursed	**153.5**	**238.6**	**316.3**	**314.9**	**321.3**	**310.1**	**345.4**	**342.2**
Public and publicly guaranteed	153.5	238.6	316.3	314.9	321.3	310.1	345.4	342.2
Official creditors	120.7	164.6	232.7	239.8	258.0	258.7	249.7	246.3
Private creditors	32.8	74.0	83.6	75.1	63.3	51.4	95.7	95.9
of which: Bonds	23.5	70.9	83.6	75.1	63.3	51.4	95.7	95.9
Private nonguaranteed	..	..	..	..	..	..	..	..
of which: Bonds	..	..	..	..	..	..	..	..
Disbursements	**48.7**	**12.6**	**13.0**	**25.8**	**36.4**	**20.0**	**6.9**	**12.0**
Public and publicly guaranteed	48.7	12.6	13.0	25.8	36.4	20.0	6.9	12.0
Official creditors	16.8	12.6	13.0	22.4	36.4	20.0	6.9	12.0
Private creditors	31.9	0.0	0.0	3.4	0.0	0.0	0.0	0.0
of which: Bonds	23.5	0.0	0.0	3.4	0.0	0.0	0.0	0.0
Private nonguaranteed	..	..	..	..	..	..	..	..
of which: Bonds	..	..	..	..	..	..	..	..
Principal repayments	**20.9**	**14.2**	**32.4**	**27.8**	**29.9**	**31.3**	**28.0**	**20.8**
Public and publicly guaranteed	20.9	14.2	32.4	27.8	29.9	31.3	28.0	20.8
Official creditors	11.7	9.5	17.5	16.0	18.0	19.4	16.1	15.9
Private creditors	9.2	4.7	15.0	11.9	11.9	11.9	11.9	4.9
of which: Bonds	0.0	4.7	11.9	11.9	11.9	11.9	11.9	4.9
Private nonguaranteed	..	..	..	..	..	..	..	..
of which: Bonds	..	..	..	..	..	..	..	..
Interest payments	**6.4**	**12.8**	**15.1**	**13.4**	**10.6**	**11.3**	**14.4**	**13.6**
Public and publicly guaranteed	6.4	12.8	15.1	13.4	10.6	11.3	14.4	13.6
Official creditors	5.2	6.3	8.3	7.4	7.4	6.7	6.4	6.1
Private creditors	1.2	6.5	6.9	6.1	3.2	4.6	8.0	7.5
of which: Bonds	1.0	6.3	6.6	6.1	3.2	4.6	8.0	7.5
Private nonguaranteed	..	..	..	..	..	..	..	..
of which: Bonds	..	..	..	..	..	..	..	..
Net financial flows								
Net debt inflows	40.3	65.4	321.6	-423.4	144.5	-126.8	-73.0	47.7
Official creditors (incl. IMF)	5.1	3.1	-4.5	17.1	18.4	9.1	-9.2	-3.9
Private creditors	35.2	62.3	326.0	-440.5	126.1	-135.9	-63.8	51.5
Long-term	22.7	-4.7	-15.0	-8.5	-11.9	-11.9	-11.9	-4.9
Public and publicly guaranteed	22.7	-4.7	-15.0	-8.5	-11.9	-11.9	-11.9	-4.9
Private nonguaranteed	..	..	..	..	..	..	..	..
Short-term	12.5	67.0	341.0	-432.0	138.0	-124.0	-51.9	56.4
Net equity inflows								
Foreign direct investment	53.7	75.3	108.5	72.6	67.9	44.8	45.2	52.4
Portfolio equity	..				..	..	..	..
Major economic aggregates								
Gross national income (GNI)	719.9	836.0	1,112.2	1,134.8	1,212.6	1,276.3	1,283.7	1,306.3
Exports of goods, services & prim. income	380.6	533.0	544.3	560.5	626.6	589.1	621.7	631.7
Imports of goods, services & prim. income	494.2	675.5	900.4	709.6	844.7	852.3	811.7	739.3
Primary income on FDI	33.4	51.1	52.5	35.3	31.7	12.0	23.3	19.8
Personal transfers & comp. of employees	26.4	27.1	28.9	28.0	29.0	29.4	29.8	30.1
International reserves	78.8	116.4	142.8	174.8	206.3	213.4	232.0	192.2
Ratios								
External debt stocks to exports (%)	58.4	78.0	152.9	77.3	92.5	76.6	69.5	77.0
External debt stocks to GNI (%)	30.9	49.7	74.8	38.2	47.8	35.4	33.7	37.2
Debt service to exports (%)	7.9	6.0	10.6	7.7	7.4	7.6	7.4	5.9
Reserves to external debt stocks (%)	35.5	28.0	17.2	40.4	35.6	47.3	53.7	39.5

Notes:

Short-term debt before 2012 is based on data from the BIS.

ST. VINCENT AND THE GRENADINES

(US$ million, unless otherwise indicated)

	2000	2005	2008	2009	2010	2011	2012	2013
Summary external debt data								
External debt stocks	**195.1**	**252.6**	**204.6**	**222.0**	**273.4**	**282.8**	**268.4**	**292.8**
Long-term external debt	163.3	247.8	203.9	203.2	255.5	259.8	245.4	269.7
Short-term external debt	31.4	4.3	0.2	0.5	0.0	0.0	0.0	0.0
interest arrears on long-term	0.4	4.3	0.2	0.5	0.0	0.0	0.0	0.0
Use of IMF credit	0.5	0.5	0.5	18.3	17.9	23.0	23.0	23.0
Long-term external debt								
Debt outstanding and disbursed	**163.3**	**247.8**	**203.9**	**203.2**	**255.5**	**259.8**	**245.4**	**269.7**
Public and publicly guaranteed	163.3	247.8	203.9	203.2	255.5	259.8	245.4	269.7
Official creditors	104.8	114.8	133.3	143.3	206.7	222.0	220.0	252.2
Private creditors	58.5	133.0	70.6	59.8	48.7	37.8	25.4	17.5
of which: Bonds	0.0	0.0	0.0	0.0	0.0	0.0	0.0	0.0
Private nonguaranteed	..	..	..	..	..	..	..	..
of which: Bonds	..	..	..	..	..	..	..	..
Disbursements	**8.5**	**42.4**	**23.4**	**20.2**	**76.2**	**25.9**	**9.9**	**45.0**
Public and publicly guaranteed	8.5	42.4	23.4	20.2	76.2	25.9	9.9	45.0
Official creditors	8.5	12.4	7.4	20.2	76.2	25.9	9.9	44.1
Private creditors	0.0	30.0	16.0	0.0	0.0	0.0	0.0	1.0
of which: Bonds	0.0	0.0	0.0	0.0	0.0	0.0	0.0	0.0
Private nonguaranteed	..	..	..	..	..	..	..	..
of which: Bonds	..	..	..	..	..	..	..	..
Principal repayments	**6.1**	**15.5**	**18.7**	**21.4**	**22.7**	**21.4**	**24.6**	**21.0**
Public and publicly guaranteed	6.1	15.5	18.7	21.4	22.7	21.4	24.6	21.0
Official creditors	5.7	7.7	8.6	10.6	11.6	10.5	12.2	12.1
Private creditors	0.4	7.7	10.1	10.7	11.1	10.9	12.4	8.9
of which: Bonds	0.0	0.0	0.0	0.0	0.0	0.0	0.0	0.0
Private nonguaranteed	..	..	..	..	..	..	..	..
of which: Bonds	..	..	..	..	..	..	..	..
Interest payments	**5.1**	**8.2**	**10.7**	**9.7**	**8.7**	**8.9**	**7.4**	**7.2**
Public and publicly guaranteed	5.1	8.2	10.7	9.7	8.7	8.9	7.4	7.2
Official creditors	3.3	3.5	5.6	4.4	4.4	5.4	4.6	5.3
Private creditors	1.8	4.7	5.1	5.4	4.3	3.4	2.8	1.9
of which: Bonds	0.0	0.0	0.0	0.0	0.0	0.0	0.0	0.0
Private nonguaranteed	..	..	..	..	..	..	..	..
of which: Bonds	..	..	..	..	..	..	..	..
Net financial flows								
Net debt inflows	1.6	26.9	4.7	4.6	53.5	9.8	-14.7	24.0
Official creditors (incl. IMF)	2.8	4.6	-1.2	15.4	64.6	20.7	-2.2	31.9
Private creditors	-1.2	22.3	5.9	-10.7	-11.1	-10.9	-12.4	-7.9
Long-term	-0.4	22.3	5.9	-10.7	-11.1	-10.9	-12.4	-7.9
Public and publicly guaranteed	-0.4	22.3	5.9	-10.7	-11.1	-10.9	-12.4	-7.9
Private nonguaranteed	..	..	..	..	..	..	..	..
Short-term	-0.8	..	..	..	..	..	..	..
Net equity inflows								
Foreign direct investment	37.7	23.7	75.2	60.2	63.1	74.6	88.3	89.5
Portfolio equity	..	..	..	..	..	..	..	..
Major economic aggregates								
Gross national income (GNI)	378.3	521.8	672.6	661.9	669.3	664.4	690.7	721.9
Exports of goods, services & prim. income	182.6	208.9	220.3	206.0	195.9	192.3	202.4	208.6
Imports of goods, services & prim. income	222.8	329.2	463.8	414.7	414.1	399.1	420.1	443.1
Primary income on FDI	12.7	22.1	18.1	12.4	11.0	7.4	5.6	5.8
Personal transfers & comp. of employees	22.5	22.4	26.8	29.1	29.1	29.2	31.1	31.6
International reserves	55.2	69.5	83.7	87.8	112.7	89.6	111.0	135.1
Ratios								
External debt stocks to exports (%)	106.9	120.9	92.9	107.7	139.6	147.0	132.6	140.3
External debt stocks to GNI (%)	51.6	48.4	30.4	33.5	40.9	42.6	38.9	40.6
Debt service to exports (%)	7.2	11.3	13.4	15.1	16.1	15.8	15.8	13.5
Reserves to external debt stocks (%)	28.3	27.5	40.9	39.6	41.2	31.7	41.4	46.1

Notes:

Short-term debt data are excluded since BIS data include debt liabilities of offshore centers located in the country. BIS short-term debt data for 2011, 2012, and 2013 are $393 million, $361 million, and $464 million respectively.

SUDAN

(US$ million, unless otherwise indicated)

	2000	2005	2008	2009	2010	2011	2012	2013
Summary external debt data								
External debt stocks	**16,085**	**17,613**	**20,280**	**21,128**	**22,233**	**21,146**	**21,793**	**22,416**
Long-term external debt	10,647	11,232	13,120	13,707	14,444	15,093	15,697	16,395
Short-term external debt	4,745	5,788	6,673	6,740	7,126	5,402	5,452	5,382
interest arrears on long-term	4,474	5,377	6,197	6,523	6,772	4,891	5,090	5,147
Use of IMF credit	693	593	486	682	664	651	645	639
Long-term external debt								
Debt outstanding and disbursed	**10,647**	**11,232**	**13,120**	**13,707**	**14,444**	**15,093**	**15,697**	**16,395**
Public and publicly guaranteed	10,151	11,232	13,120	13,707	14,444	15,093	15,697	16,395
Official creditors	8,393	9,145	10,730	11,258	11,815	11,350	11,366	11,611
Private creditors	1,758	2,087	2,390	2,449	2,629	3,743	4,331	4,785
of which: Bonds	0	0	0	0	0	0	0	0
Private nonguaranteed	496	..	..	..	..	..	..	..
of which: Bonds	..	..	..	..	..	..	..	..
Disbursements	**861**	**387**	**673**	**971**	**935**	**793**	**319**	**415**
Public and publicly guaranteed	861	387	673	971	935	793	319	415
Official creditors	318	387	673	971	935	793	319	415
Private creditors	543	0	0	0	0	0	0	0
of which: Bonds	0	0	0	0	0	0	0	0
Private nonguaranteed	..	..	..	..	..	..	..	..
of which: Bonds	..	..	..	..	..	..	..	..
Principal repayments	**143**	**291**	**219**	**362**	**397**	**416**	**274**	**211**
Public and publicly guaranteed	143	291	219	362	397	416	274	211
Official creditors	143	291	219	362	397	416	274	211
Private creditors	0	0	0	0	0	0	0	0
of which: Bonds	0	0	0	0	0	0	0	0
Private nonguaranteed	..	..	..	..	..	..	..	..
of which: Bonds	..	..	..	..	..	..	..	..
Interest payments	**42**	**67**	**68**	**111**	**83**	**100**	**76**	**73**
Public and publicly guaranteed	42	67	68	111	83	100	76	73
Official creditors	42	67	68	111	83	100	76	73
Private creditors	0	0	0	0	0	0	0	0
of which: Bonds	0	0	0	0	0	0	0	0
Private nonguaranteed	..	..	..	..	..	..	..	..
of which: Bonds	..	..	..	..	..	..	..	..
Net financial flows								
Net debt inflows	625	76	591	339	669	524	-111	70
Official creditors (incl. IMF)	121	67	389	598	532	367	38	197
Private creditors	504	9	202	-259	137	157	-149	-127
Long-term	543	..	..	..	..	..	..	..
Public and publicly guaranteed	543	..	..	..	..	..	..	..
Private nonguaranteed	..	..	..	..	..	..	..	..
Short-term	-39	9	202	-259	137	157	-149	-127
Net equity inflows								
Foreign direct investment	392	-676	-947	-846	-831	-378	2,313	2,179
Portfolio equity	..	78	72	0	7	13	2	0
Major economic aggregates								
Gross national income (GNI)	11,548	24,587	50,398	48,824	59,712	61,232	56,347	46,768
Exports of goods, services & prim. income	1,839	5,051	12,248	8,686	11,797	10,508	5,140	8,357
Imports of goods, services & prim. income	2,594	8,836	16,119	14,567	15,466	12,788	12,253	14,551
Primary income on FDI	..	699	4,314	2,112	2,393	1,011	529	2,749
Personal transfers & comp. of employees	641	704	1,591	1,394	1,100	442	401	424
International reserves	138	1,869	1,399	1,094	1,036	193	193	193
Ratios								
External debt stocks to exports (%)	874.8	348.7	165.6	243.2	188.5	201.2	424.0	268.2
External debt stocks to GNI (%)	139.3	71.6	40.2	43.3	37.2	34.5	38.7	47.9
Debt service to exports (%)	13.5	7.9	3.0	5.6	4.2	5.1	7.0	3.5
Reserves to external debt stocks (%)	0.9	10.6	6.9	5.2	4.7	0.9	0.9	0.9

Notes:

Long-term public and publicly guaranteed debt data exclude penalty interest. Short-term debt is based on data from the BIS.

SWAZILAND

(US$ million, unless otherwise indicated)

	2000	2005	2008	2009	2010	2011	2012	2013
Summary external debt data								
External debt stocks	**273.2**	**459.3**	**447.4**	**507.9**	**707.1**	**653.7**	**481.8**	**463.6**
Long-term external debt	262.9	370.0	365.5	405.3	402.1	378.6	340.2	316.5
Short-term external debt	1.8	80.1	72.0	27.0	230.7	201.0	67.4	72.7
interest arrears on long-term	0.0	15.1	15.0	25.0	35.7	48.0	42.4	41.7
Use of IMF credit	8.4	9.2	9.9	75.7	74.4	74.1	74.2	74.4
Long-term external debt								
Debt outstanding and disbursed	**262.9**	**370.0**	**365.5**	**405.3**	**402.1**	**378.6**	**340.2**	**316.5**
Public and publicly guaranteed	262.9	370.0	365.5	405.3	402.1	378.6	340.2	316.5
Official creditors	243.1	338.6	345.6	380.8	375.5	357.5	320.5	300.7
Private creditors	19.8	31.4	19.9	24.5	26.6	21.1	19.7	15.8
of which: Bonds	0.0	0.0	0.0	0.0	0.0	0.0	0.0	0.0
Private nonguaranteed	..	..	..	..	..	..	..	..
of which: Bonds	..	..	..	..	..	..	..	..
Disbursements	**15.8**	**51.7**	**56.3**	**36.5**	**11.5**	**32.1**	**5.2**	**18.2**
Public and publicly guaranteed	15.8	51.7	56.3	36.5	11.5	32.1	5.2	18.2
Official creditors	15.8	51.1	56.3	36.5	11.5	32.1	5.2	18.2
Private creditors	0.0	0.6	0.0	0.0	0.0	0.0	0.0	0.0
of which: Bonds	0.0	0.0	0.0	0.0	0.0	0.0	0.0	0.0
Private nonguaranteed	..	..	..	..	..	..	..	..
of which: Bonds	..	..	..	..	..	..	..	..
Principal repayments	**12.4**	**18.8**	**34.2**	**28.9**	**27.9**	**26.7**	**35.4**	**19.4**
Public and publicly guaranteed	12.4	18.8	34.2	28.9	27.9	26.7	35.4	19.4
Official creditors	12.4	18.1	33.6	28.4	27.3	26.1	34.9	19.2
Private creditors	0.0	0.7	0.5	0.5	0.6	0.6	0.5	0.2
of which: Bonds	0.0	0.0	0.0	0.0	0.0	0.0	0.0	0.0
Private nonguaranteed	..	..	..	..	..	..	..	..
of which: Bonds	..	..	..	..	..	..	..	..
Interest payments	**16.1**	**14.7**	**19.4**	**16.4**	**13.5**	**14.4**	**15.7**	**10.2**
Public and publicly guaranteed	16.1	14.7	19.4	16.4	13.5	14.4	15.7	10.2
Official creditors	10.2	10.5	16.3	14.6	13.0	14.0	13.0	9.0
Private creditors	5.9	4.2	3.1	1.7	0.5	0.4	2.7	1.2
of which: Bonds	0.0	0.0	0.0	0.0	0.0	0.0	0.0	0.0
Private nonguaranteed	..	..	..	..	..	..	..	..
of which: Bonds	..	..	..	..	..	..	..	..
Net financial flows								
Net debt inflows	-47.5	54.0	49.1	-47.4	176.6	-36.6	-158.2	4.8
Official creditors (incl. IMF)	3.4	33.1	22.7	8.2	-15.7	6.0	-29.7	-0.9
Private creditors	-50.9	20.9	26.5	-55.5	192.4	-42.6	-128.5	5.8
Long-term	..	-0.1	-0.5	-0.5	-0.6	-0.6	-0.5	-0.2
Public and publicly guaranteed	..	-0.1	-0.5	-0.5	-0.6	-0.6	-0.5	-0.2
Private nonguaranteed	..	..	..	..	..	..	..	..
Short-term	-50.9	21.0	27.0	-55.0	193.0	-42.0	-128.0	6.0
Net equity inflows								
Foreign direct investment	90.7	-15.8	90.6	53.1	49.3	50.3	2.7	67.0
Portfolio equity	1.4	0.8	43.9	-6.6	4.7	..	..	..
Major economic aggregates								
Gross national income (GNI)	1,558.7	2,762.4	3,014.6	3,069.1	3,802.1	3,890.1	3,748.3	3,530.3
Exports of goods, services & prim. income	1,376.4	2,075.9	2,042.3	2,066.2	2,275.3	2,397.6	2,361.1	2,316.1
Imports of goods, services & prim. income	1,522.9	2,276.0	2,483.4	2,672.4	3,063.4	3,265.8	3,181.5	2,978.2
Primary income on FDI	65.9	44.0	252.7	352.5	401.6	397.6	466.1	..
Personal transfers & comp. of employees	56.9	95.4	89.6	93.5	54.7	38.1	31.3	..
International reserves	351.8	243.9	751.9	958.9	756.3	600.5	741.0	762.5
Ratios								
External debt stocks to exports (%)	19.8	22.1	21.9	24.6	31.1	27.3	20.4	20.0
External debt stocks to GNI (%)	17.5	16.6	14.8	16.6	18.6	16.8	12.9	13.1
Debt service to exports (%)	2.2	1.8	2.7	2.2	1.9	1.8	2.2	1.3
Reserves to external debt stocks (%)	128.8	53.1	168.1	188.8	107.0	91.9	153.8	164.5

Notes:

Short-term debt is based on data from the BIS.

SYRIAN ARAB REPUBLIC

(US$ million, unless otherwise indicated)

	2000	2005	2008	2009	2010	2011	2012	2013
Summary external debt data								
External debt stocks	**22,203**	**5,583**	**5,374**	**5,674**	**5,263**	**4,968**	**4,736**	**4,753**
Long-term external debt	16,464	5,025	4,737	4,480	4,276	3,998	3,948	3,898
Short-term external debt	5,692	506	581	756	558	542	359	425
interest arrears on long-term	2,372	193	145	206	217	218	316	401
Use of IMF credit	48	52	56	438	430	429	429	430
Long-term external debt								
Debt outstanding and disbursed	**16,464**	**5,025**	**4,737**	**4,480**	**4,276**	**3,998**	**3,948**	**3,898**
Public and publicly guaranteed	16,464	5,025	4,737	4,480	4,276	3,998	3,948	3,898
Official creditors	15,502	5,025	4,737	4,480	4,276	3,998	3,948	3,898
Private creditors	962	0	0	0	0	0	0	0
of which: Bonds	0	0	0	0	0	0	0	0
Private nonguaranteed	..	..	..	..	..	..	..	..
of which: Bonds	..	..	..	..	..	..	..	..
Disbursements	**18**	**189**	**282**	**281**	**286**	**222**	**0**	**0**
Public and publicly guaranteed	18	189	282	281	286	222	0	0
Official creditors	18	189	282	281	286	222	0	0
Private creditors	0	0	0	0	0	0	0	0
of which: Bonds	0	0	0	0	0	0	0	0
Private nonguaranteed	..	..	..	..	..	..	..	..
of which: Bonds	..	..	..	..	..	..	..	..
Principal repayments	**239**	**439**	**560**	**499**	**508**	**509**	**0**	**0**
Public and publicly guaranteed	239	439	560	499	508	509	0	0
Official creditors	224	428	560	499	508	509	0	0
Private creditors	16	11	0	0	0	0	0	0
of which: Bonds	0	0	0	0	0	0	0	0
Private nonguaranteed	..	..	..	..	..	..	..	..
of which: Bonds	..	..	..	..	..	..	..	..
Interest payments	**127**	**110**	**125**	**119**	**111**	**109**	**0**	**0**
Public and publicly guaranteed	127	110	125	119	111	109	0	0
Official creditors	126	110	125	119	111	109	0	0
Private creditors	1	0	0	0	0	0	0	0
of which: Bonds	0	0	0	0	0	0	0	0
Private nonguaranteed	..	..	..	..	..	..	..	..
of which: Bonds	..	..	..	..	..	..	..	..
Net financial flows								
Net debt inflows	-826	-357	-350	-104	-430	-304	-281	-19
Official creditors (incl. IMF)	-205	-239	-279	-218	-221	-287	..	..
Private creditors	-621	-118	-71	114	-209	-17	-281	-19
Long-term	-16	-11	..	..	..	..	..	..
Public and publicly guaranteed	-16	-11	..	..	..	..	..	..
Private nonguaranteed	..	..	..	..	..	..	..	..
Short-term	-605	-107	-71	114	-209	-17	-281	-19
Net equity inflows								
Foreign direct investment	270	500	1,466	2,570	1,469	..	..	..
Portfolio equity	..	..	..	..	..	..	..	..
Major economic aggregates								
Gross national income (GNI)	18,446	27,980	..	..	..	..	..	..
Exports of goods, services & prim. income	7,190	11,907	20,289	16,026	19,919	..	..	..
Imports of goods, services & prim. income	6,614	12,359	20,967	18,118	21,235	..	..	..
Primary income on FDI	..	1,220	1,527	1,301	1,684	..	..	..
Personal transfers & comp. of employees	180	823	1,325	1,350	1,623	..	..	..
International reserves	126	17,347	17,062	17,398	19,465	..	..	..
Ratios								
External debt stocks to exports (%)	308.8	46.9	26.5	35.4	26.4	..	..	..
External debt stocks to GNI (%)	120.4	20.0	..	..	..	..	..	..
Debt service to exports (%)	6.8	4.8	3.4	3.9	3.1	..	..	..
Reserves to external debt stocks (%)	0.6	310.7	317.5	306.6	369.8	..	..	..

Notes:

Long-term public and publicly guaranteed debt data are World Bank staff estimates. Short-term debt is based on data from the BIS.

TAJIKISTAN

(US$ million, unless otherwise indicated)

	2000	2005	2008	2009	2010	2011	2012	2013
Summary external debt data								
External debt stocks	**1,141**	**1,121**	**2,493**	**2,666**	**3,082**	**3,322**	**3,643**	**3,538**
Long-term external debt	846	850	2,261	2,423	2,734	2,946	3,340	3,126
Short-term external debt	77	27	90	74	122	129	16	125
interest arrears on long-term	45	2	0	0	0	0	16	17
Use of IMF credit	218	244	142	170	227	246	287	287
Long-term external debt								
Debt outstanding and disbursed	**846**	**850**	**2,261**	**2,423**	**2,734**	**2,946**	**3,340**	**3,126**
Public and publicly guaranteed	755	826	1,374	1,606	1,806	1,968	2,001	2,016
Official creditors	704	817	1,374	1,606	1,806	1,968	2,001	2,016
Private creditors	51	8	0	0	0	0	0	0
of which: Bonds	0	0	0	0	0	0	0	0
Private nonguaranteed	91	24	887	816	927	979	1,339	1,110
of which: Bonds	..	..	..	..	..	..	..	..
Disbursements	**37**	**108**	**379**	**518**	**924**	**723**	**556**	**105**
Public and publicly guaranteed	36	105	356	211	251	200	105	105
Official creditors	36	105	356	211	251	200	105	105
Private creditors	0	0	0	0	0	0	0	0
of which: Bonds	0	0	0	0	0	0	0	0
Private nonguaranteed	1	2	24	307	673	523	451	..
of which: Bonds	..	..	..	..	..	..	..	..
Principal repayments	**28**	**42**	**64**	**409**	**630**	**513**	**334**	**320**
Public and publicly guaranteed	15	37	52	35	37	34	74	93
Official creditors	15	37	52	35	37	34	74	93
Private creditors	0	0	0	0	0	0	0	0
of which: Bonds	0	0	0	0	0	0	0	0
Private nonguaranteed	12	5	12	374	593	479	261	227
of which: Bonds	..	..	..	..	..	..	..	..
Interest payments	**21**	**10**	**28**	**41**	**54**	**64**	**94**	**104**
Public and publicly guaranteed	7	9	26	24	23	28	30	30
Official creditors	4	9	26	24	23	28	30	30
Private creditors	4	0	0	0	0	0	0	0
of which: Bonds	0	0	0	0	0	0	0	0
Private nonguaranteed	14	1	2	17	31	36	63	74
of which: Bonds	..	..	..	..	..	..	..	..
Net financial flows								
Net debt inflows	-4	23	302	119	401	238	132	-107
Official creditors (incl. IMF)	36	84	273	202	274	187	71	12
Private creditors	-40	-61	29	-83	127	52	61	-119
Long-term	-11	-3	12	-67	80	44	190	-227
Public and publicly guaranteed	..	..	..	..	..	..	..	..
Private nonguaranteed	-11	-3	12	-67	80	44	190	-227
Short-term	-29	-58	18	-16	47	7	-129	108
Net equity inflows								
Foreign direct investment	24	54	376	16	29	20	41	108
Portfolio equity	..	..	..	..	..	..	..	..
Major economic aggregates								
Gross national income (GNI)	824	2,234	5,108	4,908	5,563	6,483	7,581	8,458
Exports of goods, services & prim. income	..	1,264	1,776	1,225	899	1,198	1,684	..
Imports of goods, services & prim. income	..	1,733	4,227	3,141	3,458	4,319	5,383	..
Primary income on FDI	..	2	4	5	9	7	33	..
Personal transfers & comp. of employees	..	467	2,544	1,748	2,306	3,060	3,626	..
International reserves	93	168	104	175	324	289	298	461
Ratios								
External debt stocks to exports (%)	..	88.7	140.3	217.6	342.8	277.3	216.2	..
External debt stocks to GNI (%)	138.4	50.2	48.8	54.3	55.4	51.2	48.0	41.8
Debt service to exports (%)	..	5.8	7.1	38.0	76.3	48.3	25.5	..
Reserves to external debt stocks (%)	8.1	15.0	4.2	6.5	10.5	8.7	8.2	13.0

Notes:

Long-term private nonguaranteed debt data for 2013 are World Bank staff estimates based on reports provided by the country. Short-term debt is based on data from the BIS. Data include MDRI debt relief.

TANZANIA

(US$ million, unless otherwise indicated)

	2000	2005	2008	2009	2010	2011	2012	2013
Summary external debt data								
External debt stocks	**7,183**	**8,400**	**6,012**	**7,624**	**8,987**	**9,940**	**11,581**	**13,024**
Long-term external debt	5,970	7,006	4,600	5,656	6,825	7,686	8,830	10,624
Short-term external debt	849	1,006	1,346	1,341	1,515	1,611	2,110	1,647
interest arrears on long-term	647	615	763	836	908	989	1,054	1,108
Use of IMF credit	364	387	66	628	647	643	641	753
Long-term external debt								
Debt outstanding and disbursed	**5,970**	**7,006**	**4,600**	**5,656**	**6,825**	**7,686**	**8,830**	**10,624**
Public and publicly guaranteed	5,970	6,446	3,711	4,640	5,601	6,438	7,366	9,107
Official creditors	5,776	6,341	3,613	4,522	5,488	6,030	6,761	7,739
Private creditors	194	105	98	118	113	408	604	1,368
of which: Bonds	0	0	0	0	0	0	0	600
Private nonguaranteed	..	560	889	1,016	1,224	1,248	1,465	1,517
of which: Bonds	..	..	..	..	..	..	..	..
Disbursements	**211**	**466**	**523**	**1,065**	**1,254**	**1,179**	**978**	**2,007**
Public and publicly guaranteed	211	466	523	919	1,038	872	794	1,854
Official creditors	206	447	523	889	1,021	568	791	1,032
Private creditors	5	19	0	30	17	304	2	821
of which: Bonds	0	0	0	0	0	0	0	600
Private nonguaranteed	..	..	..	146	216	307	184	153
of which: Bonds	..	..	..	..	..	..	..	..
Principal repayments	**94**	**31**	**22**	**105**	**131**	**76**	**78**	**80**
Public and publicly guaranteed	94	31	13	26	52	33	35	61
Official creditors	77	31	13	13	35	26	27	29
Private creditors	17	0	0	13	17	7	7	32
of which: Bonds	0	0	0	0	0	0	0	0
Private nonguaranteed	..	..	9	79	79	44	43	19
of which: Bonds	..	..	..	..	..	..	..	..
Interest payments	**51**	**44**	**27**	**45**	**50**	**53**	**60**	**62**
Public and publicly guaranteed	51	42	21	27	32	39	43	58
Official creditors	49	42	21	24	31	36	39	46
Private creditors	2	0	0	3	2	3	4	13
of which: Bonds	0	0	0	0	0	0	0	0
Private nonguaranteed	..	2	6	18	17	14	17	3
of which: Bonds	..	..	..	..	..	..	..	..
Net financial flows								
Net debt inflows	205	459	647	1,188	1,255	1,116	1,331	1,520
Official creditors (incl. IMF)	172	378	510	1,182	1,016	540	761	1,114
Private creditors	33	81	137	6	239	576	569	406
Long-term	-12	19	-9	84	137	561	135	923
Public and publicly guaranteed	-12	19	..	17	0	297	-5	789
Private nonguaranteed	..	..	-9	67	137	264	140	134
Short-term	44	62	146	-78	102	15	434	-517
Net equity inflows								
Foreign direct investment	463	439	398	664	1,192	879	1,266	1,872
Portfolio equity	..	3	3	3	3	3	4	..
Major economic aggregates								
Gross national income (GNI)	10,114	13,836	20,425	21,093	22,607	23,609	27,682	32,817
Exports of goods, services & prim. income	1,411	3,053	5,700	5,314	6,530	7,582	8,675	8,662
Imports of goods, services & prim. income	2,230	4,641	9,111	8,015	9,541	12,477	13,106	14,094
Primary income on FDI	13	319	318	342	365	309	268	..
Personal transfers & comp. of employees	8	19	37	40	55	78	67	..
International reserves	974	2,049	2,863	3,470	3,905	3,726	4,052	4,674
Ratios								
External debt stocks to exports (%)	509.0	275.2	105.5	143.5	137.6	131.1	133.5	150.4
External debt stocks to GNI (%)	71.0	60.7	29.4	36.1	39.8	42.1	41.8	39.7
Debt service to exports (%)	11.9	4.4	1.1	3.1	3.0	1.9	1.9	1.8
Reserves to external debt stocks (%)	13.6	24.4	47.6	45.5	43.4	37.5	35.0	35.9

Notes:

Long-term public and publicly guaranteed debt data include debt liabilities of Zanzibar. Long-term private nonguaranteed debt data from 2004 to 2007 are World Bank staff estimates and from 2008 are reported by Central Bank. Short-term debt is based on data from the BIS. Data include the effects of HIPC and MDRI debt relief.

THAILAND

(US$ million, unless otherwise indicated)

	2000	2005	2008	2009	2010	2011	2012	2013
Summary external debt data								
External debt stocks	**79,830**	**58,600**	**66,583**	**80,787**	**106,323**	**109,910**	**134,222**	**135,379**
Long-term external debt	61,778	42,465	45,997	45,981	54,172	61,132	74,551	73,927
Short-term external debt	14,880	16,014	20,455	33,284	50,657	47,288	58,181	59,958
interest arrears on long-term	0	0	4	8	2	5	2	0
Use of IMF credit	3,172	121	130	1,521	1,494	1,490	1,491	1,494
Long-term external debt								
Debt outstanding and disbursed	**61,778**	**42,465**	**45,997**	**45,981**	**54,172**	**61,132**	**74,551**	**73,927**
Public and publicly guaranteed	29,463	17,585	14,659	14,707	21,172	26,445	34,731	34,014
Official creditors	20,820	7,862	6,947	6,468	6,843	6,865	6,327	6,001
Private creditors	8,643	9,723	7,711	8,239	14,329	19,580	28,403	28,013
of which: Bonds	2,630	3,836	2,304	3,074	8,004	12,894	21,894	21,854
Private nonguaranteed	32,316	24,880	31,338	31,274	33,000	34,687	39,820	39,913
of which: Bonds	8,414	4,685	5,068	5,125	4,265	3,618	6,040	5,575
Disbursements	**4,031**	**17,083**	**13,526**	**12,989**	**16,838**	**17,452**	**29,509**	**19,846**
Public and publicly guaranteed	3,031	2,521	1,638	1,716	6,442	6,128	9,735	1,552
Official creditors	2,156	434	74	76	160	493	735	1,552
Private creditors	876	2,086	1,564	1,640	6,282	5,635	9,000	0
of which: Bonds	0	936	1,564	970	5,080	4,890	9,000	0
Private nonguaranteed	1,000	14,562	11,888	11,273	10,396	11,324	19,775	18,294
of which: Bonds	..	1,600	437	198	..	700	1,500	..
Principal repayments	**8,945**	**16,464**	**15,417**	**11,313**	**9,386**	**8,815**	**13,316**	**11,054**
Public and publicly guaranteed	3,010	2,709	2,721	1,590	803	1,197	757	1,211
Official creditors	1,666	2,321	819	468	534	779	619	871
Private creditors	1,344	388	1,902	1,122	269	418	137	340
of which: Bonds	174	172	1,192	200	150	0	0	40
Private nonguaranteed	5,935	13,755	12,696	9,723	8,582	7,618	12,560	9,842
of which: Bonds	1,044	908	100	141	460	180	550	465
Interest payments	**3,776**	**1,074**	**1,091**	**1,085**	**1,075**	**1,176**	**1,354**	**1,213**
Public and publicly guaranteed	1,577	437	255	231	230	263	409	333
Official creditors	1,008	234	121	112	113	114	111	80
Private creditors	569	202	134	119	118	149	298	253
of which: Bonds	193	135	71	58	56	88	255	213
Private nonguaranteed	2,199	637	836	855	845	913	944	880
of which: Bonds	476	286	244	251	234	311	339	353
Net financial flows								
Net debt inflows	-13,649	5,145	265	14,501	24,831	5,266	27,088	10,572
Official creditors (incl. IMF)	292	-1,886	-744	-392	-374	-285	115	681
Private creditors	-13,942	7,031	1,009	14,893	25,205	5,552	26,972	9,891
Long-term	-5,404	2,505	-1,147	2,068	7,826	8,923	16,078	8,111
Public and publicly guaranteed	-469	1,698	-339	518	6,012	5,217	8,863	-340
Private nonguaranteed	-4,935	807	-808	1,550	1,813	3,706	7,215	8,452
Short-term	-8,538	4,526	2,156	12,825	17,379	-3,371	10,895	1,780
Net equity inflows								
Foreign direct investment	3,366	7,000	8,733	5,634	9,839	2,486	8,613	10,114
Portfolio equity	900	5,121	-3,802	1,695	3,215	-406	2,663	-6,487
Major economic aggregates								
Gross national income (GNI)	120,809	167,799	262,864	253,430	305,181	333,324	351,389	363,545
Exports of goods, services & prim. income	85,997	131,744	214,536	186,028	231,029	267,630	283,282	291,554
Imports of goods, services & prim. income	77,269	143,591	218,993	169,485	227,130	269,549	296,929	304,723
Primary income on FDI	..	10,812	15,171	13,283	18,845	13,876	22,596	..
Personal transfers & comp. of employees	1,697	1,187	1,898	2,776	3,580	4,554	4,713	5,690
International reserves	32,016	50,691	108,661	135,483	167,530	167,389	173,328	161,328
Ratios								
External debt stocks to exports (%)	92.8	44.5	31.0	43.4	46.0	41.1	47.4	46.4
External debt stocks to GNI (%)	66.1	34.9	25.3	31.9	34.8	33.0	38.2	37.2
Debt service to exports (%)	16.3	13.7	7.9	6.8	4.7	3.9	5.4	4.4
Reserves to external debt stocks (%)	40.1	86.5	163.2	167.7	157.6	152.3	129.1	119.2

TOGO

(US$ million, unless otherwise indicated)

	2000	2005	2008	2009	2010	2011	2012	2013
Summary external debt data								
External debt stocks	**1,446.0**	**1,686.9**	**1,641.7**	**1,730.1**	**1,284.6**	**629.4**	**754.1**	**903.4**
Long-term external debt	1,229.6	1,439.5	1,468.8	1,481.9	1,004.2	369.4	450.0	563.2
Short-term external debt	132.5	217.7	107.8	47.0	38.9	5.8	49.6	86.9
interest arrears on long-term	62.6	166.7	23.8	30.0	9.9	2.8	3.6	2.9
Use of IMF credit	83.8	29.7	65.0	201.2	241.5	254.2	254.5	253.2
Long-term external debt								
Debt outstanding and disbursed	**1,229.6**	**1,439.5**	**1,468.8**	**1,481.9**	**1,004.2**	**369.4**	**450.0**	**563.2**
Public and publicly guaranteed	1,229.6	1,439.5	1,468.8	1,481.9	1,004.2	369.4	450.0	563.2
Official creditors	1,229.6	1,439.5	1,468.8	1,481.9	1,004.2	369.4	450.0	513.6
Private creditors	0.0	0.0	0.0	0.0	0.0	0.0	0.0	49.6
of which: Bonds	0.0	0.0	0.0	0.0	0.0	0.0	0.0	0.0
Private nonguaranteed	..	..	..	..	..	..	..	..
of which: Bonds	..	..	..	..	..	..	..	..
Disbursements	**24.4**	**9.9**	**2.2**	**34.6**	**82.8**	**30.0**	**126.6**	**183.7**
Public and publicly guaranteed	24.4	9.9	2.2	34.6	82.8	30.0	126.6	183.7
Official creditors	24.4	9.9	2.2	34.6	82.8	30.0	126.6	123.2
Private creditors	0.0	0.0	0.0	0.0	0.0	0.0	0.0	60.4
of which: Bonds	0.0	0.0	0.0	0.0	0.0	0.0	0.0	0.0
Private nonguaranteed	..	..	..	..	..	..	..	..
of which: Bonds	..	..	..	..	..	..	..	..
Principal repayments	**9.9**	**7.9**	**140.1**	**39.5**	**28.3**	**10.0**	**13.0**	**37.8**
Public and publicly guaranteed	9.9	7.9	140.1	39.5	28.3	10.0	13.0	37.8
Official creditors	9.9	7.9	140.1	39.5	28.3	10.0	13.0	25.7
Private creditors	0.0	0.0	0.0	0.0	0.0	0.0	0.0	12.1
of which: Bonds	0.0	0.0	0.0	0.0	0.0	0.0	0.0	0.0
Private nonguaranteed	..	..	..	..	..	..	..	..
of which: Bonds	..	..	..	..	..	..	..	..
Interest payments	**4.6**	**0.3**	**51.3**	**13.1**	**8.0**	**4.6**	**9.3**	**11.4**
Public and publicly guaranteed	4.6	0.3	51.3	13.1	8.0	4.6	9.3	11.4
Official creditors	4.6	0.3	51.3	13.1	8.0	4.6	9.3	11.4
Private creditors	0.0	0.0	0.0	0.0	0.0	0.0	0.0	0.0
of which: Bonds	0.0	0.0	0.0	0.0	0.0	0.0	0.0	0.0
Private nonguaranteed	..	..	..	..	..	..	..	..
of which: Bonds	..	..	..	..	..	..	..	..
Net financial flows								
Net debt inflows	-44.3	15.8	-82.2	-30.6	110.2	7.9	156.7	182.1
Official creditors (incl. IMF)	5.1	-9.2	-90.2	36.4	98.2	33.9	113.7	95.8
Private creditors	-49.4	25.0	8.0	-67.0	12.0	-26.0	43.0	86.3
Long-term	..	..	..	..	..	..	..	48.3
Public and publicly guaranteed	..	..	..	..	..	..	..	48.3
Private nonguaranteed	..	..	..	..	..	..	..	..
Short-term	-49.4	25.0	8.0	-67.0	12.0	-26.0	43.0	38.0
Net equity inflows								
Foreign direct investment	41.9	54.4	19.6	32.6	78.0	171.0	93.8	84.2
Portfolio equity	6.1	16.0	1.4	2.1	4.5	..	..	..
Major economic aggregates								
Gross national income (GNI)	1,265.3	2,079.9	2,794.2	2,803.4	2,761.6	3,197.5	3,331.3	3,696.3
Exports of goods, services & prim. income	456.5	857.3	1,216.8	1,265.0	1,395.8	2,079.0	..	..
Imports of goods, services & prim. income	664.1	1,249.0	1,762.6	1,777.3	1,951.3	2,651.3	..	..
Primary income on FDI	17.2	47.2	51.5	41.5	67.0	..	..	..
Personal transfers & comp. of employees	34.2	192.5	337.1	334.5	336.6	..	..	..
International reserves	140.9	191.5	581.8	703.2	714.9	774.3	441.6	507.1
Ratios								
External debt stocks to exports (%)	316.7	196.8	134.9	136.8	92.0	30.3	..	..
External debt stocks to GNI (%)	114.3	81.1	58.8	61.7	46.5	19.7	22.6	24.4
Debt service to exports (%)	6.6	2.5	16.0	4.3	2.6	0.7	..	..
Reserves to external debt stocks (%)	9.7	11.4	35.4	40.6	55.7	123.0	58.6	56.1

Notes:

Short-term debt is based on data from the BIS. Data include the effects of Paris Club debt restructuring agreement and HIPC and MDRI debt relief.

TONGA

(US$ million, unless otherwise indicated)

	2000	2005	2008	2009	2010	2011	2012	2013
Summary external debt data								
External debt stocks	**73.8**	**89.0**	**99.0**	**114.9**	**153.7**	**190.6**	**197.4**	**199.1**
Long-term external debt	65.0	79.5	88.8	104.6	143.5	180.5	187.2	188.9
Short-term external debt	0.2	0.1	0.0	0.0	0.0	0.0	0.0	0.0
interest arrears on long-term	0.2	0.1	0.0	0.0	0.0	0.0	0.0	0.0
Use of IMF credit	8.6	9.4	10.1	10.3	10.1	10.1	10.1	10.1
Long-term external debt								
Debt outstanding and disbursed	**65.0**	**79.5**	**88.8**	**104.6**	**143.5**	**180.5**	**187.2**	**188.9**
Public and publicly guaranteed	65.0	79.5	88.8	104.6	143.5	180.5	187.2	188.9
Official creditors	65.0	79.5	88.8	103.7	142.4	180.0	187.0	188.8
Private creditors	0.0	0.0	0.0	0.9	1.1	0.4	0.3	0.2
of which: Bonds	0.0	0.0	0.0	0.0	0.0	0.0	0.0	0.0
Private nonguaranteed	..	..	..	..	..	..	..	..
of which: Bonds	..	..	..	..	..	..	..	..
Disbursements	**5.4**	**4.5**	**8.5**	**17.4**	**40.9**	**36.9**	**9.9**	**1.3**
Public and publicly guaranteed	5.4	4.5	8.5	17.4	40.9	36.9	9.9.	1.3
Official creditors	5.4	4.5	8.5	16.5	40.7	36.9	9.9	1.3
Private creditors	0.0	0.0	0.0	0.8	0.2	0.0	0.0	0.0
of which: Bonds	0.0	0.0	0.0	0.0	0.0	0.0	0.0	0.0
Private nonguaranteed	..	..	..	..	..	..	..	..
of which: Bonds	..	..	..	..	..	..	..	..
Principal repayments	**3.7**	**3.7**	**3.7**	**2.4**	**2.7**	**3.3**	**3.4**	**3.4**
Public and publicly guaranteed	3.7	3.7	3.7	2.4	2.7	3.3	3.4	3.4
Official creditors	2.4	3.7	3.7	2.4	2.6	3.3	3.3	3.3
Private creditors	1.3	0.0	0.0	0.0	0.1	0.0	0.2	0.1
of which: Bonds	0.0	0.0	0.0	0.0	0.0	0.0	0.0	0.0
Private nonguaranteed	..	..	..	..	..	..	..	..
of which: Bonds	..	..	..	..	..	..	..	..
Interest payments	**0.9**	**1.2**	**1.7**	**1.4**	**2.4**	**2.6**	**2.9**	**3.1**
Public and publicly guaranteed	0.9	1.2	1.7	1.4	2.4	2.6	2.9	3.1
Official creditors	0.8	1.2	1.7	1.4	2.3	2.6	2.9	3.1
Private creditors	0.1	0.0	0.0	0.0	0.1	0.0	0.0	0.0
of which: Bonds	0.0	0.0	0.0	0.0	0.0	0.0	0.0	0.0
Private nonguaranteed	..	..	..	..	..	..	..	..
of which: Bonds	..	..	..	..	..	..	..	..
Net financial flows								
Net debt inflows	1.8	0.9	4.8	14.9	38.2	33.6	6.5	-2.1
Official creditors (incl. IMF)	3.0	0.9	4.8	14.2	38.1	33.7	6.6	-2.0
Private creditors	-1.3	..	..	0.8	0.1	0.0	-0.2	-0.1
Long-term	-1.3	..	..	0.8	0.1	0.0	-0.2	-0.1
Public and publicly guaranteed	-1.3	..	..	0.8	0.1	0.0	-0.2	-0.1
Private nonguaranteed	..	..	..	..	..	..	..	..
Short-term	..	..	..	..	..	..	..	..
Net equity inflows								
Foreign direct investment	4.8	7.2	0.2	0.0	7.3	27.7	8.1	11.6
Portfolio equity	..	..	..	..	..	..	..	..
Major economic aggregates								
Gross national income (GNI)	191.0	264.7	354.4	324.9	373.2	432.0	485.3	479.0
Exports of goods, services & prim. income	..	59.0	60.1	53.6	69.7	96.3	111.6	..
Imports of goods, services & prim. income	..	156.8	251.2	245.4	232.6	282.0	274.7	..
Primary income on FDI	..	..	0.0	0.0	..	..	0.6	..
Personal transfers & comp. of employees	..	68.6	93.9	72.1	76.0	69.9	59.6	..
International reserves	24.6	46.9	69.8	95.7	104.5	143.3	152.4	155.5
Ratios								
External debt stocks to exports (%)	..	151.0	164.7	214.5	220.6	197.9	176.8	..
External debt stocks to GNI (%)	38.6	33.6	27.9	35.4	41.2	44.1	40.7	41.6
Debt service to exports (%)	..	8.8	9.2	7.2	7.2	6.1	5.7	..
Reserves to external debt stocks (%)	33.4	52.6	70.5	83.3	68.0	75.2	77.2	78.1

TUNISIA

(US$ million, unless otherwise indicated)

	2000	2005	2008	2009	2010	2011	2012	2013
Summary external debt data								
External debt stocks	**11,355**	**17,926**	**21,378**	**22,688**	**22,472**	**22,642**	**25,261**	**25,827**
Long-term external debt	9,688	14,742	16,998	17,459	17,073	17,274	18,613	18,976
Short-term external debt	1,590	3,135	4,327	4,801	4,979	4,949	6,230	6,279
interest arrears on long-term	0	0	0	0	0	0	0	0
Use of IMF credit	77	49	53	428	420	419	419	572
Long-term external debt								
Debt outstanding and disbursed	**9,688**	**14,742**	**16,998**	**17,459**	**17,073**	**17,274**	**18,613**	**18,976**
Public and publicly guaranteed	8,888	13,001	14,451	14,852	14,671	14,931	16,569	17,337
Official creditors	6,093	8,421	9,286	9,979	10,220	11,295	12,500	13,794
Private creditors	2,795	4,580	5,165	4,873	4,451	3,636	4,068	3,543
of which: Bonds	1,327	3,510	4,050	3,776	3,819	3,063	3,571	3,110
Private nonguaranteed	800	1,741	2,547	2,607	2,402	2,343	2,044	1,638
of which: Bonds	..	..	..	..	..	..	..	..
Disbursements	**1,542**	**1,256**	**1,225**	**1,548**	**1,642**	**2,244**	**3,417**	**1,525**
Public and publicly guaranteed	1,242	1,126	915	1,371	1,545	2,157	3,361	1,505
Official creditors	709	843	831	1,315	1,507	2,131	2,047	1,271
Private creditors	533	283	84	56	39	26	1,314	234
of which: Bonds	0	249	0	0	0	0	1,298	225
Private nonguaranteed	300	130	310	177	97	87	56	20
of which: Bonds	..	..	..	..	..	..	..	..
Principal repayments	**1,296**	**1,187**	**1,170**	**1,350**	**1,617**	**1,905**	**1,899**	**1,799**
Public and publicly guaranteed	1,264	1,129	1,057	1,233	1,397	1,759	1,609	1,373
Official creditors	662	873	958	837	887	860	880	874
Private creditors	602	255	99	396	510	899	729	499
of which: Bonds	371	136	0	313	0	814	650	443
Private nonguaranteed	32	58	112	117	220	146	290	426
of which: Bonds	..	..	..	..	..	..	..	..
Interest payments	**489**	**686**	**745**	**700**	**670**	**678**	**610**	**572**
Public and publicly guaranteed	479	584	630	598	546	559	500	489
Official creditors	297	334	366	335	309	330	342	318
Private creditors	182	249	264	263	237	230	158	171
of which: Bonds	99	200	217	217	193	203	135	155
Private nonguaranteed	10	102	115	102	124	119	110	83
of which: Bonds	..	..	..	..	..	..	..	..
Net financial flows								
Net debt inflows	258	-141	399	673	203	310	2,797	-73
Official creditors (incl. IMF)	7	-31	-126	478	619	1,270	1,167	548
Private creditors	251	-111	525	195	-417	-961	1,631	-621
Long-term	199	99	182	-280	-594	-931	351	-670
Public and publicly guaranteed	-69	27	-16	-340	-471	-872	585	-264
Private nonguaranteed	268	72	198	60	-123	-59	-234	-406
Short-term	52	-210	343	474	177	-29	1,280	49
Net equity inflows								
Foreign direct investment	752	716	2,609	1,529	1,339	439	1,560	1,071
Portfolio equity	-18	12	-39	-89	-26	-44	-15	80
Major economic aggregates								
Gross national income (GNI)	20,525	30,645	42,244	41,370	41,798	43,633	44,139	46,566
Exports of goods, services & prim. income	8,701	14,884	25,602	20,133	22,556	22,950	22,600	22,513
Imports of goods, services & prim. income	10,347	16,495	29,235	23,318	26,595	28,235	28,471	28,642
Primary income on FDI	468	962	1,958	1,588	1,658	1,716	1,533	1,756
Personal transfers & comp. of employees	796	1,393	1,977	1,964	2,063	2,004	2,266	2,291
International reserves	1,811	4,437	8,849	11,057	9,459	7,454	8,357	7,287
Ratios								
External debt stocks to exports (%)	130.5	120.4	83.5	112.7	99.6	98.7	111.8	114.7
External debt stocks to GNI (%)	55.3	58.5	50.6	54.8	53.8	51.9	57.2	55.5
Debt service to exports (%)	21.9	13.7	7.9	10.5	10.4	11.5	11.5	11.8
Reserves to external debt stocks (%)	15.9	24.8	41.4	48.7	42.1	32.9	33.1	28.2

Notes:

Long-term private nonguaranteed debt data from 2008 are World Bank staff estimates based on reports provided by the country.

TURKEY

(US$ million, unless otherwise indicated)

	2000	2005	2008	2009	2010	2011	2012	2013
Summary external debt data								
External debt stocks	**116,787**	**172,131**	**288,978**	**277,270**	**299,183**	**305,388**	**337,096**	**388,243**
Long-term external debt	83,552	118,408	227,759	218,639	214,580	219,026	234,045	257,486
Short-term external debt	28,912	38,916	52,522	48,993	77,326	81,841	100,540	129,107
interest arrears on long-term	0	0	0	0	0	0	0	0
Use of IMF credit	4,323	14,807	8,697	9,638	7,277	4,521	2,510	1,650
Long-term external debt								
Debt outstanding and disbursed	**83,552**	**118,408**	**227,759**	**218,639**	**214,580**	**219,026**	**234,045**	**257,486**
Public and publicly guaranteed	55,724	62,965	82,313	85,609	91,501	94,759	98,817	105,356
Official creditors	12,537	12,435	19,719	23,109	26,427	28,221	29,416	31,802
Private creditors	43,187	50,530	62,595	62,500	65,074	66,538	69,402	73,555
of which: Bonds	20,386	27,903	39,106	40,926	44,268	47,014	52,440	58,421
Private nonguaranteed	27,828	55,443	145,446	133,030	123,080	124,267	135,228	152,130
of which: Bonds	1,784	4,025	6,759	6,606	6,202	4,003	11,835	20,885
Disbursements	**22,949**	**41,260**	**65,149**	**39,688**	**48,617**	**54,358**	**64,378**	**77,921**
Public and publicly guaranteed	14,069	7,756	10,679	9,842	14,578	11,049	12,268	12,592
Official creditors	2,393	1,001	3,850	4,749	5,561	4,008	2,940	3,863
Private creditors	11,676	6,754	6,829	5,093	9,017	7,042	9,328	8,729
of which: Bonds	6,974	5,230	4,000	3,739	6,665	4,820	7,927	7,613
Private nonguaranteed	8,881	33,504	54,470	29,846	34,039	43,308	52,110	65,329
of which: Bonds	454	3,125	150	150	2,300	2,085	6,965	8,635
Principal repayments	**13,744**	**24,649**	**40,169**	**49,657**	**45,489**	**38,665**	**41,306**	**46,880**
Public and publicly guaranteed	6,268	7,957	7,736	6,469	6,013	5,010	5,671	5,034
Official creditors	1,745	1,653	1,570	1,650	1,788	1,714	1,739	1,794
Private creditors	4,523	6,303	6,166	4,819	4,225	3,296	3,932	3,240
of which: Bonds	1,858	3,886	3,790	2,275	2,575	1,785	2,274	1,500
Private nonguaranteed	7,476	16,693	32,433	43,188	39,476	33,654	35,635	41,846
of which: Bonds	..	1,150	..	350	420	523	404	1,965
Interest payments	**5,000**	**6,396**	**11,396**	**10,421**	**8,703**	**12,006**	**8,541**	**9,361**
Public and publicly guaranteed	3,467	4,471	5,169	4,785	4,526	4,594	4,752	4,524
Official creditors	659	596	703	650	488	580	611	536
Private creditors	2,807	3,875	4,466	4,135	4,038	4,014	4,141	3,988
of which: Bonds	1,479	2,673	3,252	3,100	3,203	3,268	3,507	3,443
Private nonguaranteed	1,533	1,925	6,227	5,635	4,177	7,412	3,789	4,837
of which: Bonds	126	338	371	288	228	385	266	813
Net financial flows								
Net debt inflows	18,017	19,346	35,941	-14,203	29,290	17,401	39,767	58,750
Official creditors (incl. IMF)	4,020	-5,972	3,868	2,392	1,602	-513	-803	1,212
Private creditors	13,997	25,317	32,073	-16,596	27,688	17,914	40,570	57,539
Long-term	8,557	17,262	22,700	-13,067	-645	13,399	21,871	28,972
Public and publicly guaranteed	7,152	451	663	274	4,792	3,745	5,396	5,489
Private nonguaranteed	1,405	16,811	22,037	-13,342	-5,437	9,654	16,475	23,483
Short-term	5,440	8,055	9,374	-3,529	28,333	4,515	18,699	28,567
Net equity inflows								
Foreign direct investment	982	9,975	17,650	7,966	8,715	16,158	12,760	12,725
Portfolio equity	489	5,669	716	2,827	3,468	-986	6,274	841
Major economic aggregates								
Gross national income (GNI)	262,146	477,153	722,029	606,262	723,966	766,923	781,716	810,860
Exports of goods, services & prim. income	53,189	109,975	184,904	150,712	161,919	188,423	211,686	215,002
Imports of goods, services & prim. income	67,873	132,878	227,408	165,245	208,862	265,263	261,616	281,293
Primary income on FDI	279	1,051	2,953	2,929	2,867	2,928	2,637	4,009
Personal transfers & comp. of employees	4,560	887	1,476	1,050	993	1,087	1,015	919
International reserves	22,488	50,579	70,428	70,874	80,713	78,322	99,943	110,927
Ratios								
External debt stocks to exports (%)	219.6	156.5	156.3	184.0	184.8	162.1	159.2	180.6
External debt stocks to GNI (%)	44.6	36.1	40.0	45.7	41.3	39.8	43.1	47.9
Debt service to exports (%)	38.9	37.4	30.2	41.6	36.6	29.9	26.2	28.7
Reserves to external debt stocks (%)	19.3	29.4	24.4	25.6	27.0	25.6	29.6	28.6

Notes:

Long-term public and publicly guaranteed debt data include nonresident deposits made under the Dresdner Bank scheme, amounting to $4.7 billion at end-2013.

TURKMENISTAN

(US$ million, unless otherwise indicated)

	2000	2005	2008	2009	2010	2011	2012	2013
Summary external debt data								
External debt stocks	**2,609.3**	**1,157.8**	**745.7**	**661.5**	**529.1**	**454.3**	**508.9**	**501.9**
Long-term external debt	2,288.1	911.0	587.4	477.2	366.8	299.3	309.8	328.6
Short-term external debt	230.3	147.0	50.8	74.8	54.8	47.8	91.8	65.8
interest arrears on long-term	5.0	5.0	0.8	0.8	0.8	0.8	0.8	0.8
Use of IMF credit	91.0	99.8	107.5	109.5	107.5	107.2	107.3	107.5
Long-term external debt								
Debt outstanding and disbursed	**2,288.1**	**911.0**	**587.4**	**477.2**	**366.8**	**299.3**	**309.8**	**328.6**
Public and publicly guaranteed	2,271.3	877.8	586.8	463.3	359.5	265.5	270.6	280.7
Official creditors	838.6	685.9	500.2	409.5	341.6	265.5	270.6	280.7
Private creditors	1,432.7	192.0	86.5	53.9	17.8	0.0	0.0	0.0
of which: Bonds	0.0	0.0	0.0	0.0	0.0	0.0	0.0	0.0
Private nonguaranteed	16.7	33.1	0.6	13.9	7.4	33.8	39.2	47.8
of which: Bonds	..	..	..	..	..	..	..	..
Disbursements	**430.1**	**89.0**	**25.9**	**35.2**	**25.5**	**44.4**	**54.7**	**58.0**
Public and publicly guaranteed	420.9	24.9	25.6	22.4	17.9	13.6	45.6	46.0
Official creditors	292.6	24.9	25.6	22.4	17.9	13.6	45.6	46.0
Private creditors	128.3	0.0	0.0	0.0	0.0	0.0	0.0	0.0
of which: Bonds	0.0	0.0	0.0	0.0	0.0	0.0	0.0	0.0
Private nonguaranteed	9.2	64.1	0.3	12.8	7.5	30.9	9.1	12.0
of which: Bonds	..	..		..	..	..	..	..
Principal repayments	**353.0**	**261.4**	**140.8**	**146.4**	**142.8**	**120.9**	**41.0**	**40.6**
Public and publicly guaranteed	347.4	189.1	139.3	146.4	129.8	118.4	37.1	35.3
Official creditors	44.0	112.6	104.3	112.4	96.7	100.0	37.1	35.3
Private creditors	303.4	76.5	35.0	34.0	33.1	18.4	0.0	0.0
of which: Bonds	0.0	0.0	0.0	0.0	0.0	0.0	0.0	0.0
Private nonguaranteed	5.5	72.3	1.5	..	13.0	2.5	3.9	5.3
of which: Bonds	..	..	..	..	..	..	..	..
Interest payments	**101.9**	**39.1**	**26.7**	**17.6**	**10.8**	**9.6**	**7.7**	**6.6**
Public and publicly guaranteed	101.2	37.3	26.6	17.1	10.3	9.0	7.1	6.2
Official creditors	27.8	23.9	20.1	14.3	9.6	8.7	7.1	6.2
Private creditors	73.4	13.4	6.6	2.8	0.8	0.3	0.0	0.0
of which: Bonds	0.0	0.0	0.0	0.0	0.0	0.0	0.0	0.0
Private nonguaranteed	0.7	1.8	0.1	0.4	0.4	0.6	0.6	0.4
of which: Bonds	..	..	..	..	..	..	..	..
Net financial flows								
Net debt inflows	-1.6	-280.4	-154.9	-87.2	-137.3	-83.5	57.6	-8.6
Official creditors (incl. IMF)	248.6	-87.7	-78.7	-90.0	-78.7	-86.4	8.5	10.7
Private creditors	-250.2	-192.7	-76.2	2.8	-58.6	3.0	49.2	-19.3
Long-term	-171.5	-84.7	-36.2	-21.2	-38.6	10.0	5.2	6.7
Public and publicly guaranteed	-175.2	-76.5	-35.0	-34.0	-33.1	-18.4	..	..
Private nonguaranteed	3.7	-8.1	-1.2	12.8	-5.5	28.4	5.2	6.7
Short-term	-78.8	-108.0	-40.0	24.0	-20.0	-7.0	44.0	-26.0
Net equity inflows								
Foreign direct investment	131.0	418.2	1,277.0	4,553.0	3,631.0	3,399.0	3,117.0	3,061.0
Portfolio equity	..	..	..	..	..	..	..	..
Major economic aggregates								
Gross national income (GNI)	2,727.4	7,541.4	18,235.7	18,957.5	20,254.0	25,874.7	30,628.4	38,617.5
Exports of goods, services & prim. income	..	..	..	..	..	..	..	..
Imports of goods, services & prim. income	..	..	..	..	..	..	..	..
Primary income on FDI	..	..	..	..	..	..	..	..
Personal transfers & comp. of employees	..	..	..	..	..	..	..	..
International reserves	..	..	..	..	..	..	..	..
Ratios								
External debt stocks to exports (%)	..	..	..	..	..	..	..	..
External debt stocks to GNI (%)	95.7	15.4	4.1	3.5	2.6	1.8	1.7	1.3
Debt service to exports (%)	..	..	..	..	..	..	..	..
Reserves to external debt stocks (%)	..	..	..	..	..	..	..	..

Notes:

Long-term public and publicly guaranteed debt from 2010 are World Bank staff estimates. Long-term private nonguaranteed debt data (excluding bonds) only cover European Bank for Reconstruction and Development lending.

UGANDA

(US$ million, unless otherwise indicated)

	2000	2005	2008	2009	2010	2011	2012	2013
Summary external debt data								
External debt stocks	**3,535**	**4,437**	**2,268**	**2,739**	**2,975**	**3,263**	**3,776**	**4,361**
Long-term external debt	3,051	4,184	1,756	2,223	2,673	2,963	3,478	4,064
Short-term external debt	129	79	458	235	26	26	26	27
interest arrears on long-term	58	29	26	26	26	26	26	27
Use of IMF credit	354	173	55	281	275	273	272	270
Long-term external debt								
Debt outstanding and disbursed	**3,051**	**4,184**	**1,756**	**2,223**	**2,673**	**2,963**	**3,478**	**4,064**
Public and publicly guaranteed	3,051	4,184	1,756	2,223	2,673	2,963	3,478	4,064
Official creditors	3,027	4,182	1,755	2,223	2,673	2,963	3,478	4,064
Private creditors	24	2	0	0	0	0	0	0
of which: Bonds	4	0	0	0	0	0	0	0
Private nonguaranteed	..	..	..	..	..	..	..	..
of which: Bonds	..	..	..	..	..	..	..	..
Disbursements	**219**	**224**	**277**	**494**	**486**	**335**	**559**	**630**
Public and publicly guaranteed	219	224	277	494	486	335	559	630
Official creditors	219	224	277	494	486	335	559	630
Private creditors	0	0	0	0	0	0	0	0
of which: Bonds	0	0	0	0	0	0	0	0
Private nonguaranteed	..	..	..	..	..	..	..	..
of which: Bonds	..	..	..	..	..	..	..	..
Principal repayments	**26**	**99**	**52**	**49**	**40**	**35**	**38**	**44**
Public and publicly guaranteed	26	99	52	49	40	35	38	44
Official creditors	25	98	52	49	40	35	38	44
Private creditors	1	1	1	0	0	0	0	0
of which: Bonds	0	0	0	0	0	0	0	0
Private nonguaranteed	..	..	..	..	..	..	..	..
of which: Bonds	..	..	..	..	..	..	..	..
Interest payments	**21**	**33**	**15**	**18**	**21**	**26**	**28**	**36**
Public and publicly guaranteed	21	33	15	18	21	26	28	36
Official creditors	20	32	15	18	21	26	28	36
Private creditors	0	0	0	0	0	0	0	0
of which: Bonds	0	0	0	0	0	0	0	0
Private nonguaranteed	..	..	..	..	..	..	..	..
of which: Bonds	..	..	..	..	..	..	..	..
Net financial flows								
Net debt inflows	177	85	657	222	237	298	520	584
Official creditors (incl. IMF)	184	95	226	445	447	298	520	584
Private creditors	-7	-10	431	-223	-209	..	..	..
Long-term	-1	-1	-1	0	0	..	..	..
Public and publicly guaranteed	-1	-1	-1	0	0	..	..	..
Private nonguaranteed	..	..	..	..	..	..	..	..
Short-term	-6	-10	432	-223	-209	..	..	..
Net equity inflows								
Foreign direct investment	161	381	578	771	248	573	922	826
Portfolio equity	..	..	13	131	-70	106	14	95
Major economic aggregates								
Gross national income (GNI)	6,086	8,748	13,981	14,534	15,713	15,180	19,542	20,806
Exports of goods, services & prim. income	716	1,592	3,170	3,398	3,491	4,324	5,022	5,222
Imports of goods, services & prim. income	1,574	2,641	5,680	5,638	6,500	7,855	8,255	8,438
Primary income on FDI	19	202	250	247	183	262	252	532
Personal transfers & comp. of employees	238	322	724	781	771	816	910	932
International reserves	808	1,344	2,301	2,994	2,706	2,617	3,169	3,338
Ratios								
External debt stocks to exports (%)	493.6	278.7	71.6	80.6	85.2	75.4	75.2	83.5
External debt stocks to GNI (%)	58.1	50.7	16.2	18.8	18.9	21.5	19.3	21.0
Debt service to exports (%)	10.6	10.8	2.3	2.1	1.8	1.5	1.4	1.6
Reserves to external debt stocks (%)	22.9	30.3	101.4	109.3	91.0	80.2	83.9	76.5

Notes:

Data include the effects of HIPC and MDRI debt relief.

UKRAINE

(US$ million, unless otherwise indicated)

	2000	2005	2008	2009	2010	2011	2012	2013
Summary external debt data								
External debt stocks	**13,890**	**33,721**	**98,326**	**104,402**	**125,173**	**135,501**	**135,872**	**147,712**
Long-term external debt	9,664	18,599	70,965	71,502	81,647	86,563	88,326	105,699
Short-term external debt	447	12,063	20,636	19,873	27,264	32,727	34,750	34,823
interest arrears on long-term	183	110	335	650	1,671	13	1,518	48
Use of IMF credit	3,779	3,059	6,726	13,027	16,262	16,212	12,795	7,190
Long-term external debt								
Debt outstanding and disbursed	**9,664**	**18,599**	**70,965**	**71,502**	**81,647**	**86,563**	**88,326**	**105,699**
Public and publicly guaranteed	8,123	9,069	14,708	18,107	24,967	25,473	32,081	32,859
Official creditors	5,000	5,021	5,859	11,093	14,731	12,528	14,436	11,656
Private creditors	3,123	4,048	8,848	7,014	10,236	12,945	17,645	21,203
of which: Bonds	2,366	2,850	7,705	5,907	9,148	11,873	16,588	21,163
Private nonguaranteed	1,541	9,530	56,257	53,395	56,681	61,090	56,245	72,840
of which: Bonds	..	550	4,964	5,114	5,319	5,794	5,294	9,269
Disbursements	**1,401**	**7,853**	**31,483**	**22,298**	**33,946**	**28,446**	**21,164**	**33,076**
Public and publicly guaranteed	173	1,411	990	5,581	7,944	3,352	8,561	7,030
Official creditors	141	563	985	5,581	4,259	600	3,109	430
Private creditors	32	847	4	0	3,685	2,753	5,453	6,600
of which: Bonds	0	747	0	0	3,685	2,750	5,450	6,600
Private nonguaranteed	1,228	6,442	30,493	16,717	26,002	25,094	12,602	26,046
of which: Bonds	..	450	1,230	846	1,730	1,550	..	3,975
Principal repayments	**2,114**	**4,018**	**13,595**	**17,855**	**23,058**	**24,054**	**21,178**	**26,415**
Public and publicly guaranteed	1,250	1,193	482	1,721	895	2,836	2,056	6,392
Official creditors	1,208	546	456	475	477	2,818	1,288	3,313
Private creditors	42	647	26	1,246	418	18	768	3,079
of which: Bonds	33	622	0	1,209	401	0	750	2,061
Private nonguaranteed	864	2,825	13,113	16,134	22,163	21,218	19,122	20,023
of which: Bonds	..	..	450	695	1,525	1,075	500	..
Interest payments	**447**	**894**	**3,200**	**4,171**	**3,494**	**4,302**	**4,472**	**5,315**
Public and publicly guaranteed	375	424	587	681	555	832	908	1,251
Official creditors	148	130	165	204	225	263	219	151
Private creditors	228	294	422	478	330	569	689	1,100
of which: Bonds	220	213	336	392	251	490	611	1,061
Private nonguaranteed	72	470	2,613	3,490	2,938	3,470	3,564	4,064
of which: Bonds	..	41	336	423	407	423	403	497
Net financial flows								
Net debt inflows	-1,285	5,234	19,875	9,446	20,691	11,513	-2,909	2,626
Official creditors (incl. IMF)	-1,666	-283	4,930	11,187	7,215	-2,218	-1,593	-8,460
Private creditors	380	5,516	14,945	-1,741	13,476	13,731	-1,317	11,086
Long-term	354	3,818	17,359	-663	7,106	6,610	-1,835	9,543
Public and publicly guaranteed	-10	201	-21	-1,246	3,267	2,735	4,685	3,521
Private nonguaranteed	364	3,617	17,380	583	3,839	3,876	-6,519	6,022
Short-term	26	1,698	-2,414	-1,078	6,370	7,121	518	1,543
Net equity inflows								
Foreign direct investment	595	7,493	9,612	4,456	5,550	6,121	6,248	3,668
Portfolio equity	146	82	388	105	290	519	516	1,180
Major economic aggregates								
Gross national income (GNI)	30,320	85,157	178,452	114,788	134,410	161,004	180,603	180,979
Exports of goods, services & prim. income	19,665	43,384	87,899	56,704	70,341	89,137	93,598	89,328
Imports of goods, services & prim. income	19,032	43,695	103,807	61,101	76,332	103,078	110,909	107,879
Primary income on FDI	43	268	2,506	2,542	2,218	4,084	4,775	5,005
Personal transfers & comp. of employees	33	2,408	6,782	5,941	6,535	7,822	8,449	9,667
International reserves	1,353	18,988	30,801	25,557	33,327	30,409	22,656	18,776
Ratios								
External debt stocks to exports (%)	70.6	77.7	111.9	184.1	178.0	152.0	145.2	165.4
External debt stocks to GNI (%)	45.8	39.6	55.1	91.0	93.1	84.2	75.2	81.6
Debt service to exports (%)	18.4	13.2	20.0	39.7	38.6	32.7	31.4	42.4
Reserves to external debt stocks (%)	9.7	56.3	31.3	24.5	26.6	22.4	16.7	12.7

UZBEKISTAN

(US$ million, unless otherwise indicated)

	2000	2005	2008	2009	2010	2011	2012	2013
Summary external debt data								
External debt stocks	**4,980**	**4,656**	**5,100**	**6,950**	**7,782**	**8,424**	**8,871**	**10,605**
Long-term external debt	4,228	4,168	4,474	6,375	7,140	7,655	8,131	9,781
Short-term external debt	282	112	221	163	238	366	337	419
interest arrears on long-term	3	8	10	19	70	70	0	0
Use of IMF credit	469	376	405	412	405	403	404	405
Long-term external debt								
Debt outstanding and disbursed	**4,228**	**4,168**	**4,474**	**6,375**	**7,140**	**7,655**	**8,131**	**9,781**
Public and publicly guaranteed	3,762	3,626	3,168	3,257	3,410	3,745	4,006	4,303
Official creditors	2,117	2,451	2,686	2,923	3,184	3,518	3,843	4,178
Private creditors	1,645	1,175	482	335	226	227	163	125
of which: Bonds	0	0	0	0	0	0	0	0
Private nonguaranteed	467	542	1,306	3,117	3,730	3,910	4,125	5,478
of which: Bonds	..	..	..	..	..	..	..	..
Disbursements	**770**	**404**	**1,003**	**2,610**	**1,188**	**949**	**1,062**	**2,279**
Public and publicly guaranteed	713	262	309	472	452	605	621	682
Official creditors	409	200	272	464	437	530	611	672
Private creditors	304	62	37	8	15	75	10	10
of which: Bonds	0	0	0	0	0	0	0	0
Private nonguaranteed	57	142	694	2,138	736	344	441	1,598
of which: Bonds	..	..	..	..	..	..	..	..
Principal repayments	**584**	**620**	**710**	**713**	**493**	**460**	**516**	**528**
Public and publicly guaranteed	443	510	460	386	370	295	293	284
Official creditors	148	177	242	225	256	226	217	232
Private creditors	295	333	219	161	114	69	76	52
of which: Bonds	0	0	0	0	0	0	0	0
Private nonguaranteed	141	110	250	327	123	165	224	244
of which: Bonds	..	..	..	..	..	..	..	..
Interest payments	**206**	**140**	**141**	**120**	**118**	**158**	**173**	**164**
Public and publicly guaranteed	182	117	114	82	63	68	75	67
Official creditors	75	63	84	71	59	62	66	65
Private creditors	108	53	30	12	4	6	9	2
of which: Bonds	0	0	0	0	0	0	0	0
Private nonguaranteed	24	23	26	38	55	90	97	97
of which: Bonds	..	..	..	..	..	..	..	..
Net financial flows								
Net debt inflows	-223	-301	308	1,830	719	617	587	1,833
Official creditors (incl. IMF)	196	5	31	238	181	304	394	440
Private creditors	-419	-305	278	1,591	538	313	193	1,393
Long-term	-75	-239	263	1,658	514	185	152	1,311
Public and publicly guaranteed	9	-271	-181	-153	-99	6	-66	-42
Private nonguaranteed	-84	32	444	1,811	613	179	218	1,353
Short-term	-344	-66	15	-67	24	128	41	82
Net equity inflows								
Foreign direct investment	75	192	711	842	1,628	1,651	674	1,077
Portfolio equity	..	..	..	..	..	..	..	..
Major economic aggregates								
Gross national income (GNI)	13,541	14,283	29,656	33,714	40,492	47,104	52,596	58,687
Exports of goods, services & prim. income	..	..	..	..	..	..	..	..
Imports of goods, services & prim. income	..	..	..	..	..	..	..	..
Primary income on FDI	..	..	..	..	..	..	..	..
Personal transfers & comp. of employees	..	..	..	..	..	..	..	..
International reserves	..	..	..	..	..	..	..	..
Ratios								
External debt stocks to exports (%)	..	..	..	..	..	..	..	..
External debt stocks to GNI (%)	36.8	32.6	17.2	20.6	19.2	17.9	16.9	18.1
Debt service to exports (%)	..	..	..	..	..	..	..	..
Reserves to external debt stocks (%)	..	..	..	..	..	..	..	..

VANUATU

(US$ million, unless otherwise indicated)

	2000	2005	2008	2009	2010	2011	2012	2013
Summary external debt data								
External debt stocks	**95.7**	**105.3**	**150.9**	**155.3**	**173.3**	**201.8**	**369.2**	**132.4**
Long-term external debt	73.1	71.9	89.7	98.8	99.3	98.8	92.2	84.3
Short-term external debt	1.4	10.2	36.1	31.0	49.0	78.0	252.0	23.0
interest arrears on long-term	0.0	0.2	0.1	0.0	0.0	0.0	0.0	0.0
Use of IMF credit	21.2	23.3	25.1	25.5	25.1	25.0	25.0	25.1
Long-term external debt								
Debt outstanding and disbursed	**73.1**	**71.9**	**89.7**	**98.8**	**99.3**	**98.8**	**92.2**	**84.3**
Public and publicly guaranteed	73.1	71.9	89.7	98.8	99.3	98.8	92.2	84.3
Official creditors	73.1	71.9	89.7	98.8	99.3	98.8	92.2	84.3
Private creditors	0.0	0.0	0.0	0.0	0.0	0.0	0.0	0.0
of which: Bonds	0.0	0.0	0.0	0.0	0.0	0.0	0.0	0.0
Private nonguaranteed	..	..	..	..	..	..	..	..
of which: Bonds	..	..	..	..	..	..	..	..
Disbursements	**14.2**	**0.0**	**10.1**	**11.7**	**0.0**	**0.0**	**0.0**	**0.0**
Public and publicly guaranteed	14.2	0.0	10.1	11.7	0.0	0.0	0.0	0.0
Official creditors	14.2	0.0	10.1	11.7	0.0	0.0	0.0	0.0
Private creditors	0.0	0.0	0.0	0.0	0.0	0.0	0.0	0.0
of which: Bonds	0.0	0.0	0.0	0.0	0.0	0.0	0.0	0.0
Private nonguaranteed	..	..	..	..	..	..	..	..
of which: Bonds	..	..	..	..	..	..	..	..
Principal repayments	**0.9**	**1.1**	**2.5**	**3.5**	**3.6**	**3.4**	**3.8**	**3.7**
Public and publicly guaranteed	0.9	1.1	2.5	3.5	3.6	3.4	3.8	3.7
Official creditors	0.9	1.1	2.5	3.5	3.6	3.4	3.8	3.7
Private creditors	0.0	0.0	0.0	0.0	0.0	0.0	0.0	0.0
of which: Bonds	0.0	0.0	0.0	0.0	0.0	0.0	0.0	0.0
Private nonguaranteed	..	..	..	..	..	..	..	..
of which: Bonds	..	..	..	..	..	..	..	..
Interest payments	**0.6**	**0.7**	**1.1**	**1.4**	**1.4**	**1.3**	**1.2**	**1.4**
Public and publicly guaranteed	0.6	0.7	1.1	1.4	1.4	1.3	1.2	1.4
Official creditors	0.6	0.7	1.1	1.4	1.4	1.3	1.2	1.4
Private creditors	0.0	0.0	0.0	0.0	0.0	0.0	0.0	0.0
of which: Bonds	0.0	0.0	0.0	0.0	0.0	0.0	0.0	0.0
Private nonguaranteed	..	..	..	..	..	..	..	..
of which: Bonds	..	..	..	..	..	..	..	..
Net financial flows								
Net debt inflows	13.6	-28.1	23.6	3.1	14.4	25.6	170.2	-232.7
Official creditors (incl. IMF)	13.4	-1.1	7.6	8.1	-3.6	-3.4	-3.8	-3.7
Private creditors	0.3	-27.0	16.0	-5.0	18.0	29.0	174.0	-229.0
Long-term	..	..	..	..	..	..	..	..
Public and publicly guaranteed	..	..	..	..	..	..	..	..
Private nonguaranteed	..	..	..	..	..	..	..	..
Short-term	0.3	-27.0	16.0	-5.0	18.0	29.0	174.0	-229.0
Net equity inflows								
Foreign direct investment	20.3	13.5	29.6	23.8	40.6	57.8	37.2	34.8
Portfolio equity	..	..	..	..	..	..	..	..
Major economic aggregates								
Gross national income (GNI)	259.0	369.0	603.2	586.8	679.1	765.7	746.6	793.9
Exports of goods, services & prim. income	175.7	204.6	313.7	330.9	365.5	395.7	413.8	..
Imports of goods, services & prim. income	178.8	258.6	492.8	345.5	422.7	465.8	480.9	..
Primary income on FDI	21.9	35.3	29.7	41.7	48.0	52.7	76.8	..
Personal transfers & comp. of employees	34.7	5.1	8.9	11.5	11.8	21.8	22.0	..
International reserves	38.9	67.2	115.2	148.6	161.4	173.8	..	..
Ratios								
External debt stocks to exports (%)	54.4	51.5	48.1	46.9	47.4	51.0	89.2	..
External debt stocks to GNI (%)	36.9	28.5	25.0	26.5	25.5	26.4	49.5	16.7
Debt service to exports (%)	1.6	1.6	1.5	1.7	1.6	1.6	2.1	..
Reserves to external debt stocks (%)	40.7	63.8	76.4	95.7	93.1	86.1	..	..

Notes:

Long-term public and publicly guaranteed debt data from 2010 are World Bank staff estimates. Short-term debt is based on data from the BIS.

VENEZUELA, REPUBLICA BOLIVARIANA de

(US$ million, unless otherwise indicated)

	2000	2005	2008	2009	2010	2011	2012	2013
Summary external debt data								
External debt stocks	**42,753**	**45,355**	**66,840**	**81,942**	**97,081**	**110,730**	**118,927**	**118,758**
Long-term external debt	33,952	34,794	46,168	59,039	72,504	87,715	95,625	90,742
Short-term external debt	8,186	10,108	20,184	18,915	20,660	19,110	19,393	24,100
interest arrears on long-term	59	5	0	7	7	7	1	1
Use of IMF credit	616	453	488	3,987	3,917	3,905	3,909	3,917
Long-term external debt								
Debt outstanding and disbursed	**33,952**	**34,794**	**46,168**	**59,039**	**72,504**	**87,715**	**95,625**	**90,742**
Public and publicly guaranteed	27,820	31,092	29,888	35,198	37,512	44,264	46,236	45,607
Official creditors	6,180	3,434	3,550	4,144	5,382	6,719	8,724	9,633
Private creditors	21,640	27,658	26,338	31,054	32,130	37,546	37,511	35,974
of which: Bonds	16,217	24,401	24,211	29,219	30,620	36,627	36,624	35,097
Private nonguaranteed	6,132	3,702	16,279	23,842	34,992	43,451	49,390	45,135
of which: Bonds	3,880	3,670	3,310	3,972	8,067	6,942	12,110	12,626
Disbursements	**2,343**	**7,250**	**5,490**	**6,068**	**4,729**	**9,266**	**2,661**	**1,564**
Public and publicly guaranteed	2,343	7,250	4,840	6,068	4,729	9,266	2,661	1,564
Official creditors	787	406	645	1,035	1,707	2,060	2,514	1,446
Private creditors	1,556	6,844	4,196	5,033	3,023	7,206	147	117
of which: Bonds	462	6,143	4,000	4,992	3,000	7,200	0	0
Private nonguaranteed	..	..	650	..	..	..	..	..
of which: Bonds	..	..	650	..	..	..	..	..
Principal repayments	**2,921**	**2,385**	**6,760**	**7,086**	**9,669**	**13,798**	**14,569**	**12,224**
Public and publicly guaranteed	2,265	1,698	2,445	812	885	2,515	690	2,258
Official creditors	613	739	527	450	479	726	504	529
Private creditors	1,652	959	1,918	362	406	1,790	186	1,729
of which: Bonds	1,119	226	1,295	0	119	1,186	0	1,585
Private nonguaranteed	655	687	4,315	6,274	8,784	11,283	13,879	9,966
of which: Bonds	..	..	300	..	659	..	2,365	..
Interest payments	**2,435**	**2,656**	**3,768**	**3,982**	**5,375**	**6,197**	**7,684**	**7,215**
Public and publicly guaranteed	1,867	2,308	2,525	2,441	2,789	3,119	4,002	3,945
Official creditors	343	204	235	186	177	205	207	227
Private creditors	1,524	2,103	2,290	2,255	2,612	2,914	3,795	3,718
of which: Bonds	1,298	1,840	2,098	2,117	2,503	2,812	3,613	3,615
Private nonguaranteed	568	349	1,243	1,541	2,586	3,077	3,682	3,269
of which: Bonds	304	296	274	337	708	582	1,213	1,055
Net financial flows								
Net debt inflows	-384	7,136	1,213	-2,294	-3,194	-6,082	-11,619	-5,953
Official creditors (incl. IMF)	-333	-333	118	585	1,228	1,334	2,010	918
Private creditors	-52	7,469	1,095	-2,879	-4,422	-7,417	-13,629	-6,871
Long-term	-752	5,198	-1,388	-1,603	-6,167	-5,867	-13,918	-11,578
Public and publicly guaranteed	-96	5,885	2,277	4,671	2,617	5,416	-39	-1,612
Private nonguaranteed	-655	-687	-3,665	-6,274	-8,784	-11,283	-13,879	-9,966
Short-term	700	2,271	2,483	-1,276	1,745	-1,550	289	4,707
Net equity inflows								
Foreign direct investment	4,701	2,588	1,631	-1,714	691	1,635	1,876	1,876
Portfolio equity	-574	28	1	118	10	..	-50	..
Major economic aggregates								
Gross national income (GNI)	115,760	143,311	316,085	325,885	387,497	309,358	371,238	431,080
Exports of goods, services & prim. income	37,760	61,208	106,204	62,445	69,584	97,042	101,543	..
Imports of goods, services & prim. income	25,737	36,093	73,145	59,517	59,879	71,865	89,549	..
Primary income on FDI	1,424	3,895	5,297	3,139	4,877	4,810	5,757	..
Personal transfers & comp. of employees	17	148	137	131	143	138	118	..
International reserves	13,088	23,919	33,098	21,703	13,137	9,930	9,900	6,038
Ratios								
External debt stocks to exports (%)	113.2	74.1	62.9	131.2	139.5	114.1	117.1	..
External debt stocks to GNI (%)	36.9	31.6	21.1	25.1	25.1	35.8	32.0	27.5
Debt service to exports (%)	16.9	8.7	10.4	18.1	22.0	20.9	22.2	..
Reserves to external debt stocks (%)	30.6	52.7	49.5	26.5	13.5	9.0	8.3	5.1

Notes:

Long-term private nonguaranteed debt data from 2004 are based on Central Bank data. Short-term debt from 1997 is based on Central Bank data.

VIETNAM

(US$ million, unless otherwise indicated)

	2000	2005	2008	2009	2010	2011	2012	2013
Summary external debt data								
External debt stocks	**12,859**	**19,039**	**26,488**	**33,084**	**44,923**	**53,072**	**59,119**	**65,461**
Long-term external debt	11,558	16,193	22,014	27,320	37,444	42,612	48,746	54,404
Short-term external debt	923	2,574	4,279	5,186	6,949	9,964	9,889	10,572
interest arrears on long-term	78	74	1	0	0	0	0	0
Use of IMF credit	378	272	195	578	529	496	484	485
Long-term external debt								
Debt outstanding and disbursed	**11,558**	**16,193**	**22,014**	**27,320**	**37,444**	**42,612**	**48,746**	**54,404**
Public and publicly guaranteed	11,558	16,193	22,014	27,320	32,764	36,750	39,940	42,918
Official creditors	8,680	14,259	19,370	23,938	27,435	31,077	33,465	34,748
Private creditors	2,878	1,934	2,644	3,382	5,329	5,673	6,475	8,170
of which: Bonds	534	1,145	1,033	1,301	2,020	2,001	1,982	2,586
Private nonguaranteed	..	..	..	..	4,680	5,862	8,806	11,486
of which: Bonds	..	..	..	..	..	90	90	290
Disbursements	**1,272**	**2,047**	**2,799**	**4,730**	**6,878**	**6,968**	**8,727**	**10,897**
Public and publicly guaranteed	1,272	2,047	2,799	4,730	5,593	4,751	5,958	7,010
Official creditors	1,176	1,261	2,202	4,104	3,675	4,001	4,711	4,798
Private creditors	96	786	597	627	1,918	750	1,247	2,212
of which: Bonds	0	750	0	0	1,000	0	0	627
Private nonguaranteed	..	..	..	..	1,285	2,217	2,769	3,887
of which: Bonds	..	..	..	..	..	90	..	200
Principal repayments	**937**	**480**	**770**	**915**	**1,048**	**3,082**	**3,276**	**3,851**
Public and publicly guaranteed	937	480	770	915	1,048	1,201	1,473	1,895
Official creditors	134	303	587	687	735	823	1,024	1,361
Private creditors	802	177	183	228	313	378	449	534
of which: Bonds	0	41	31	39	19	19	19	23
Private nonguaranteed	..	..	..	..	..	1,881	1,803	1,956
of which: Bonds	..	..	..	..	..	..	..	..
Interest payments	**296**	**317**	**464**	**476**	**707**	**902**	**1,012**	**1,074**
Public and publicly guaranteed	296	317	464	476	563	689	744	763
Official creditors	77	256	329	344	398	457	494	514
Private creditors	218	61	135	132	165	232	250	249
of which: Bonds	21	21	69	74	93	126	126	126
Private nonguaranteed	..	..	..	..	144	213	268	311
of which: Bonds	..	..	..	..	..	4	9	9
Net financial flows								
Net debt inflows	472	1,926	1,638	4,685	7,554	6,868	5,364	7,729
Official creditors (incl. IMF)	1,020	904	1,575	3,378	2,902	3,145	3,675	3,438
Private creditors	-548	1,022	62	1,307	4,652	3,722	1,689	4,291
Long-term	-706	609	414	399	2,889	707	1,764	3,609
Public and publicly guaranteed	-706	609	414	399	1,605	371	798	1,678
Private nonguaranteed	..	..	..	..	1,285	336	966	1,931
Short-term	158	413	-352	908	1,763	3,015	-75	683
Net equity inflows								
Foreign direct investment	1,298	1,204	8,960	6,369	7,101	5,941	6,943	6,202
Portfolio equity	..	115	-578	128	2,383	1,064	1,887	1,389
Major economic aggregates								
Gross national income (GNI)	33,194	56,575	96,181	101,448	111,513	129,698	148,961	162,820
Exports of goods, services & prim. income	17,481	36,987	71,048	63,615	80,153	106,180	124,468	142,916
Imports of goods, services & prim. income	18,107	40,927	89,182	76,671	92,314	114,629	123,618	142,922
Primary income on FDI	..	..	..	..	..	..	..	..
Personal transfers & comp. of employees	..	3,150	6,805	6,020	8,260	8,600	..	..
International reserves	3,417	9,051	23,890	16,447	12,467	13,539	25,573	25,893
Ratios								
External debt stocks to exports (%)	73.6	51.5	37.3	52.0	56.0	50.0	47.5	45.8
External debt stocks to GNI (%)	38.7	33.7	27.5	32.6	40.3	40.9	39.7	40.2
Debt service to exports (%)	7.5	2.6	2.0	2.3	2.3	3.9	3.6	3.5
Reserves to external debt stocks (%)	26.6	47.5	90.2	49.7	27.8	25.5	43.3	39.6

YEMEN, REPUBLIC OF

(US$ million, unless otherwise indicated)

	2000	2005	2008	2009	2010	2011	2012	2013
Summary external debt data								
External debt stocks	**5,162**	**5,501**	**6,319**	**6,734**	**6,682**	**6,418**	**7,556**	**7,671**
Long-term external debt	4,109	4,814	5,696	5,875	5,933	5,876	6,912	6,884
Short-term external debt	699	353	483	442	313	131	140	282
interest arrears on long-term	27	94	112	117	124	131	140	147
Use of IMF credit	355	333	140	417	436	410	504	505
Long-term external debt								
Debt outstanding and disbursed	**4,109**	**4,814**	**5,696**	**5,875**	**5,933**	**5,876**	**6,912**	**6,884**
Public and publicly guaranteed	4,109	4,814	5,696	5,875	5,933	5,876	6,912	6,884
Official creditors	4,046	4,807	5,690	5,871	5,930	5,874	6,911	6,883
Private creditors	63	7	6	5	3	2	1	1
of which: Bonds	0	0	0	0	0	0	0	0
Private nonguaranteed	..	..	..	..	..	..	..	..
of which: Bonds	..	..	..	..	..	..	..	..
Disbursements	**137**	**265**	**285**	**332**	**287**	**101**	**1,251**	**203**
Public and publicly guaranteed	137	265	285	332	287	101	1,251	203
Official creditors	137	265	285	332	287	101	1,251	203
Private creditors	0	0	0	0	0	0	0	0
of which: Bonds	0	0	0	0	0	0	0	0
Private nonguaranteed	..	..	..	..	..	..	..	..
of which: Bonds	..	..	..	..	..	..	..	..
Principal repayments	**81**	**94**	**134**	**140**	**155**	**175**	**181**	**194**
Public and publicly guaranteed	81	94	134	140	155	175	181	194
Official creditors	81	94	133	139	154	174	180	193
Private creditors	0	0	1	1	1	1	1	1
of which: Bonds	0	0	0	0	0	0	0	0
Private nonguaranteed	..	..	..	..	..	..	..	..
of which: Bonds	..	..	..	..	..	..	..	..
Interest payments	**45**	**55**	**70**	**72**	**74**	**75**	**73**	**75**
Public and publicly guaranteed	45	55	70	72	74	75	73	75
Official creditors	45	55	70	72	74	74	73	75
Private creditors	0	0	0	0	0	0	0	0
of which: Bonds	0	0	0	0	0	0	0	0
Private nonguaranteed	..	..	..	..	..	..	..	..
of which: Bonds	..	..	..	..	..	..	..	..
Net financial flows								
Net debt inflows	270	176	145	102	22	-288	1,163	237
Official creditors (incl. IMF)	-15	116	81	149	159	-98	1,164	103
Private creditors	285	61	64	-47	-137	-190	-1	134
Long-term	0	0	-1	-1	-1	-1	-1	-1
Public and publicly guaranteed	0	0	-1	-1	-1	-1	-1	-1
Private nonguaranteed	..	..	..	..	..	..	..	..
Short-term	285	61	65	-46	-136	-189	..	135
Net equity inflows								
Foreign direct investment	6	-302	40	129	43	44	30	-134
Portfolio equity	..	..	..	..	..	..	..	..
Major economic aggregates								
Gross national income (GNI)	8,863	15,139	28,590	26,781	29,984	27,111	30,815	34,721
Exports of goods, services & prim. income	4,158	6,963	10,504	7,233	9,325	10,437	9,415	9,592
Imports of goods, services & prim. income	4,221	7,745	13,918	11,276	12,503	13,099	15,207	14,747
Primary income on FDI	855	1,603	1,875	927	1,510	2,025	1,145	1,352
Personal transfers & comp. of employees	1,288	1,283	1,411	1,160	1,526	1,404	3,351	3,343
International reserves	2,900	6,115	8,111	6,936	5,868	4,449	6,068	5,284
Ratios								
External debt stocks to exports (%)	124.2	79.0	60.2	93.1	71.7	61.5	80.3	80.0
External debt stocks to GNI (%)	58.2	36.3	22.1	25.1	22.3	23.7	24.5	22.1
Debt service to exports (%)	5.9	3.1	2.7	3.6	2.8	2.6	2.7	2.8
Reserves to external debt stocks (%)	56.2	111.2	128.4	103.0	87.8	69.3	80.3	68.9

Notes:

Short-term debt is based on data from the BIS.

ZAMBIA

(US$ million, unless otherwise indicated)

	2000	2005	2008	2009	2010	2011	2012	2013
Summary external debt data								
External debt stocks	**5,811**	**5,461**	**3,080**	**3,774**	**4,419**	**4,944**	**5,385**	**5,596**
Long-term external debt	4,508	4,538	2,205	2,220	2,111	3,482	3,929	4,154
Short-term external debt	76	234	674	474	1,191	326	330	332
interest arrears on long-term	33	90	152	154	167	167	171	173
Use of IMF credit	1,227	689	201	1,080	1,117	1,137	1,126	1,110
Long-term external debt								
Debt outstanding and disbursed	**4,508**	**4,538**	**2,205**	**2,220**	**2,111**	**3,482**	**3,929**	**4,154**
Public and publicly guaranteed	4,444	3,942	1,157	1,200	1,317	1,964	3,166	3,392
Official creditors	4,412	3,646	1,108	1,158	1,284	1,857	2,347	2,579
Private creditors	31	295	48	42	33	108	820	813
of which: Bonds	0	0	0	0	0	0	734	750
Private nonguaranteed	65	596	1,049	1,020	794	1,517	763	763
of which: Bonds	..	..	..	..	..	..	..	..
Disbursements	**261**	**218**	**239**	**126**	**203**	**789**	**1,333**	**390**
Public and publicly guaranteed	251	114	118	91	176	696	1,300	357
Official creditors	251	114	108	91	176	605	566	341
Private creditors	0	0	10	0	0	91	734	16
of which: Bonds	0	0	0	0	0	0	734	16
Private nonguaranteed	10	105	121	35	27	93	33	33
of which: Bonds	..	..	..	..	..	..	..	..
Principal repayments	**98**	**136**	**114**	**122**	**86**	**139**	**143**	**192**
Public and publicly guaranteed	79	71	61	59	47	56	101	150
Official creditors	79	59	52	52	38	40	78	127
Private creditors	1	12	8	7	8	16	23	23
of which: Bonds	0	0	0	0	0	0	0	0
Private nonguaranteed	18	66	53	63	40	82	42	42
of which: Bonds	..	..	..	..	..	..	..	..
Interest payments	**80**	**58**	**39**	**36**	**29**	**48**	**59**	**99**
Public and publicly guaranteed	76	29	14	13	11	13	41	82
Official creditors	76	29	14	13	11	13	41	42
Private creditors	0	0	0	0	0	0	0	40
of which: Bonds	0	0	0	0	0	0	0	40
Private nonguaranteed	4	28	24	24	18	35	18	18
of which: Bonds	..	..	..	..	..	..	..	..
Net financial flows								
Net debt inflows	159	88	232	45	876	-192	1,179	180
Official creditors (incl. IMF)	198	-8	67	283	193	589	476	197
Private creditors	-39	96	166	-238	683	-780	702	-17
Long-term	-9	27	70	-36	-21	85	702	-17
Public and publicly guaranteed	-1	-12	2	-7	-8	75	712	-7
Private nonguaranteed	-8	39	68	-29	-13	10	-9	-9
Short-term	-30	69	96	-202	704	-865	..	..
Net equity inflows								
Foreign direct investment	122	329	603	472	1,228	941	1,044	1,811
Portfolio equity	6	5	-6	-13	101	25	26	..
Major economic aggregates								
Gross national income (GNI)	3,097	6,547	13,242	12,386	14,827	18,047	20,261	21,628
Exports of goods, services & prim. income	891	2,533	5,291	4,564	7,733	9,046	9,891	..
Imports of goods, services & prim. income	1,567	3,239	6,890	4,498	6,959	8,724	10,346	..
Primary income on FDI	71	461	1,346	265	1,303	1,093	1,033	..
Personal transfers & comp. of employees	..	53	68	41	44	46	73	..
International reserves	245	560	1,096	1,892	2,094	2,324	3,042	2,684
Ratios								
External debt stocks to exports (%)	652.0	215.6	58.2	82.7	57.1	54.7	54.4	..
External debt stocks to GNI (%)	187.6	83.4	23.3	30.5	29.8	27.4	26.6	25.9
Debt service to exports (%)	21.2	11.2	3.2	3.7	1.9	2.2	2.2	..
Reserves to external debt stocks (%)	4.2	10.3	35.6	50.1	47.4	47.0	56.5	48.0

Notes:

Long-term private nonguaranteed before 2011 are World Bank staff estimates based on reports provided by the country. Short-term debt data before 2011 are from the BIS. Short-term debt from 2011 only include private nonguaranteed short-term debt. Data include the effects of HIPC and MDRI debt relief.

ZIMBABWE

(US$ million, unless otherwise indicated)

	2000	2005	2008	2009	2010	2011	2012	2013
Summary external debt data								
External debt stocks	**3,843**	**4,445**	**5,711**	**6,000**	**6,605**	**7,310**	**8,653**	**8,193**
Long-term external debt	2,981	3,209	3,743	3,824	4,259	4,724	5,715	4,952
Short-term external debt	568	1,111	1,838	1,634	1,817	2,059	2,417	2,722
interest arrears on long-term	55	534	807	915	938	1,052	1,141	1,234
Use of IMF credit	294	125	129	542	529	527	520	519
Long-term external debt								
Debt outstanding and disbursed	**2,981**	**3,209**	**3,743**	**3,824**	**4,259**	**4,724**	**5,715**	**4,952**
Public and publicly guaranteed	2,776	3,177	3,654	3,734	3,663	3,820	3,884	3,951
Official creditors	2,439	2,771	3,227	3,287	3,230	3,389	3,447	3,506
Private creditors	337	406	427	448	433	431	437	445
of which: Bonds	0	0	0	0	0	0	0	0
Private nonguaranteed	205	32	89	89	596	904	1,831	1,001
of which: Bonds	..	..	..	..	..	..	..	..
Disbursements	**185**	**25**	**105**	**79**	**847**	**1,584**	**1,433**	**1,710**
Public and publicly guaranteed	139	24	39	13	4	186	70	58
Official creditors	125	16	25	13	4	181	70	58
Private creditors	15	8	14	0	0	5	0	0
of which: Bonds	0	0	0	0	0	0	0	0
Private nonguaranteed	46	0	66	66	843	1,398	1,363	1,652
of which: Bonds	..	..	..	..	..	..	..	..
Principal repayments	**211**	**45**	**54**	**66**	**337**	**1,096**	**440**	**2,494**
Public and publicly guaranteed	146	31	2	0	1	6	5	12
Official creditors	113	21	2	0	1	6	5	8
Private creditors	33	10	0	0	0	0	0	4
of which: Bonds	0	0	0	0	0	0	0	0
Private nonguaranteed	65	14	52	66	336	1,091	435	2,482
of which: Bonds	..	..	..	..	..	..	..	..
Interest payments	**81**	**7**	**10**	**30**	**31**	**43**	**273**	**133**
Public and publicly guaranteed	64	3	5	14	13	14	14	6
Official creditors	50	2	5	14	13	14	14	6
Private creditors	13	1	0	0	0	0	0	0
of which: Bonds	0	0	0	0	0	0	0	0
Private nonguaranteed	17	4	5	16	18	29	259	127
of which: Bonds	..	..	..	..	..	..	..	..
Net financial flows								
Net debt inflows	-329	-180	28	-299	666	616	1,254	-574
Official creditors (incl. IMF)	-58	-169	21	13	-1	175	57	48
Private creditors	-271	-11	7	-312	667	441	1,196	-622
Long-term	-37	-16	28	0	507	313	927	-834
Public and publicly guaranteed	-19	-2	14	..	0	5	..	-4
Private nonguaranteed	-19	-14	14	0	507	308	927	-830
Short-term	-233	5	-21	-312	160	128	269	212
Net equity inflows								
Foreign direct investment	23	103	52	105	166	387	400	400
Portfolio equity	..	..	..	..	..	..	..	..
Major economic aggregates								
Gross national income (GNI)	6,329	5,481	3,972	7,901	8,907	10,050	11,513	11,784
Exports of goods, services & prim. income	..	..	..	..	..	..	..	..
Imports of goods, services & prim. income	..	..	..	..	..	..	..	..
Primary income on FDI	..	..	..	..	..	..	..	..
Personal transfers & comp. of employees	..	..	..	..	..	..	..	..
International reserves	193	97	76	822	732	659	574	474
Ratios								
External debt stocks to exports (%)	..	..	..	..	..	..	..	..
External debt stocks to GNI (%)	60.7	81.1	143.8	75.9	74.2	72.7	75.2	69.5
Debt service to exports (%)	..	..	..	..	..	..	..	..
Reserves to external debt stocks (%)	5.0	2.2	1.3	13.7	11.1	9.0	6.6	5.8

Notes:

Data from 2001 include late interest fee owed to Paris Club and Commercial Creditors. Short-term debt is based on data from the BIS.

APPENDIX
About the Data

Data Sources and Methodology

Data Sources

The principal sources of information for the tables in *International Debt Statistics 2015* are reports to the World Bank through the World Bank's Debtor Reporting System (DRS) from member countries that have received either International Bank for Reconstruction and Development (IBRD) loans or International Development Association (IDA) credits. The DRS has its origin in the World Bank's need to monitor and assess the financial position of its borrowers. Since 1951, borrowers have been required to provide statistics on their public external debt and private sector debt that benefit from a public guarantee. In its design, consistency, and continuity of coverage, the DRS is a unique resource. Reporting countries submit detailed reports on the annual status, transactions, and terms of the long-term external debt of public agencies and that of private ones guaranteed by a public agency in the debtor country. The DRS maintains these records on a loan-by-loan basis. In 1973, coverage of the DRS was expanded to include private sector nonguaranteed borrowing, but for this category of debt, data are provided by borrowers in aggregate rather than loan by loan.

Data submitted to the DRS are processed in the World Bank External Debt (WBXD) system, along with additional information received from the files of the African Development Bank, the Asian Development Bank, the Inter-American Development Bank (IDB), the International Monetary Fund (IMF), institutions of the World Bank Group (IBRD and IDA), and the European Bank for Reconstruction and Development (EBRD). The WBXD is an internal system of the World Bank. Among its outputs is the International Debt Statistics (IDS) database, from which the tables in this publication and online database are produced.

Data on exports and imports (on a balance of payments basis), international reserves, current account balances, foreign direct investment (FDI) on equity, portfolio equity flows, and primary income of FDI are drawn mainly from the files of the IMF, supplemented by United Nations Conference on Trade and Development (UNCTAD) reports and country data. Balance of payments data are presented according to the sixth edition of the IMF's *Balance of Payments Manual* (BPM6). Official aid flows come from data collected and published by the Development Assistance Committee (DAC) of the Organisation for Economic Co-operation and Development (OECD). Short-term external debt data are as reported by debtor countries or are estimates based on the Bank for International Settlements (BIS) quarterly series of commercial banks' claims on developing countries. For some countries, estimates were prepared by pooling creditor and debtor information. Data on the gross national income of most developing countries are collected from national statistical organizations or central banks by visiting and resident World Bank missions.

Every effort has been made to ensure the accuracy and completeness of the external debt statistics. Coverage has been improved through the efforts of the reporting agencies and close collaboration between the Bank and our partners, Commonwealth Secretariat (COMSEC) and UNCTAD, which provide debt recording and reporting systems across the globe, as well as through the work of the World Bank missions, which visit member countries to gather data and to provide technical assistance on debt issues. Nevertheless, quality and coverage vary among debtors and may also vary for the same debtor from year to year. Data on long-term external debt reported by member countries are checked against, and supplemented by, data from several other sources. Among these sources are the statements and reports of several regional development banks, government lending agencies, and official government Web sites.

Methodology

Aggregations

Total debt stock and other aggregate measures are derived from the summation of loan-level data on stocks and flows after conversion to a common currency. Other tabulations are compiled using terms and conditions reported in the loan-level data, such as currency composition, cancellations, rescheduling of other liabilities into long-term public and publicly guaranteed external debt, and debt buybacks.

Aggregates for regional and income groups are based on the World Bank's operational classifications, which may differ from common geographic usage or income groups used by other organizations. Country classifications of DRS reporting countries in 2013 are shown in country groups in the back of the publication. The same classification is used for all historical data shown in *International Debt Statistics* and the online tables and online database.

Currency Conversion

Data on external obligations are normally reported to the World Bank in the currency of repayment and are converted into a common currency (U.S. dollars) using official exchange rates published by the IMF.

Commitments, disbursements, and debt service payments (flows) are converted to U.S. dollars at the annual average exchange rate for the year. Debt outstanding (disbursed and undisbursed) at the end of a given year (stock) is converted at the exchange rate in effect at the end of the relevant year. Consequently, year-to-year changes in debt outstanding and disbursed may not be equal to net flows (disbursements less principal repayments); similarly, changes in debt outstanding (including undisbursed debt) may not equal commitments less repayments. Discrepancies will be particularly significant when exchange rates have moved sharply during the year. Projected debt service is converted to U.S. dollars at rates in effect at the end of December 2012.

Beginning with 1991, all ruble debt owed to the former Soviet Union has been converted at a rate of US$1 = 0.6 ruble, except in cases where a bilateral agreement specifying a different conversion rate is in place. Adoption of this methodology does not constitute an endorsement by the World Bank staff of the appropriateness or validity of the exchange rate used. That matter must be resolved bilaterally between the Russian Federation and its debtor countries.

Starting with the 1988–89 edition of *World Debt Tables* (a predecessor of IDS), all data pertaining to IBRD loans from 1985 onward are recorded at their current market value. Starting with the 1991–92 edition, all data pertaining to Asian Development Bank loans from 1989 onward are recorded at their current market value. Starting with the 1998 edition, all data pertaining to African Development Bank and African Development Fund loans from 1997 onward are recorded at their current market value.

Debt Stock and Flow Reconciliation

Because of currency conversions and the timing of transactions, there may be differences between the change in aggregate stocks from one period to the next and flows during the relevant period; changes in debt outstanding, including undisbursed amounts, will therefore differ from commitments less repayments.

Changes in the stock of debt from one period to the next can be attributed to five factors: the net flow of debt, the net change in interest arrears, the capitalization of interest, a reduction in debt resulting from debt forgiveness or other debt reduction mechanisms, and cross-currency valuation effects. Any residual difference in the change in stock not explained by one of those five factors may indicate inconsistencies in the reported data or specific phenomena prevailing in an individual country (for example, an incomplete historical series for all categories of debt). Starting in 1989, the IDS includes the debt stock reconciliation, but not all components are shown in the IDS print edition and online tables.

External Debt Restructuring

Starting in 1985, the WBXD includes information on the restructuring of debt by official creditors in the context of the Paris Club, restructuring by commercial creditors, debt swap operations, buybacks, and bond exchanges. It attempts to capture accurately the effect of debt restructuring on both external debt stocks and external debt flows, consistent with the terms on which the restructuring takes place. In the compilation and presentation of external debt data, a distinction is made between cash flows and imputed flows. According to this criterion, restructured service payments and the shift in liabilities from one financial instrument to another as a result of debt restructuring are considered to be imputed flows. Both cash flows and imputed flows are recorded separately in WBXD.

The imputed flows and stock changes associated with debt restructuring are included in the IDS tables and online database to complement the cash-basis transactions recorded in the main body of the data. Such data encompass information on the debt stock and debt flows restructured each year, the amount of principal forgiven (interest forgiven is shown as a memorandum item), and the amount of external debt stock reduced either by forgiveness or by a debt buyback operation. Changes in creditors and debtors that result from debt restructuring are also reflected. For example, when insured commercial credits are rescheduled, the creditor classification shifts from private to official (bilateral), reflecting the assumption of the assets by the official credit insurance agencies in the creditor country. The IDS data will show a reduction in the external debt owed to the original private creditors equal or similar to the amount of debt restructured and a corresponding increase in the debt owed to the new official creditor. Similarly on the debtor side, when a government accepts responsibility for the payment of restructured debt previously owed by a private enterprise, the relevant change in the debtor category will be reflected. Likewise, if short-term external debt is restructured into a long-term obligation, the stock of short-term external debt will decline and the stock of long-term external debt will rise by the amount of short-term debt restructured. In the event of a debt swap of long-term external debt (external debt to equity, external debt for nature, or external debt for development), the face value of the external debt swapped will be recorded as a decline in long-term external debt stock, but no flow transaction (principal repayment) will be recorded.

Projections of Future Disbursements and Debt Service Payments

The WBXD system projects future disbursements and future debt service payments on the assumption that every existing loan commitment will be fully used and repaid in full.

Future Disbursements

Disbursement projections are made using one of the following methods:

- *Specific schedules.* Debtor countries are requested to submit a schedule of future disbursements, if available, at the time each new loan is first reported.
- *Standard schedules.* In the absence of specific schedules, the WBXD system projects the future disbursement schedule according to the undisbursed balance of each loan at the end of the most recent reporting period.

These projected schedules are based on profiles derived from the disbursement pattern of comparable loans that fully disbursed. Thirty different profiles have been compiled corresponding to each category of creditor and, in the case of official creditors, for concessional and nonconcessional loans. Each profile is derived by applying regression analysis techniques to a body of data on actual disbursements for each fully disbursed loan in the WBXD database. The profiles are periodically updated to take into account the evolving pattern of disbursements observed for fully disbursed loans.

Future principal payments are generated by the WBXD system according to the repayment terms of each loan. Principal repayments (amortization) are based on the amount of the loan commitment. If the amortization schedule follows a set pattern (for example, equal semiannual payments), the WBXD system calculates repayments automatically using the loan commitment amount, the first and final payment dates, and the frequency of the payments. If future payments are irregular, the WBXD system requires a schedule.

Future interest payments are generated by the WBXD system according to the disbursed and outstanding balance of the loan at the beginning of the period. Using the interest rate specified in the loan contract, the first and final interest payment dates, and the frequency of payments, the WBXD system calculates the stream of future interest payments due. If interest payments are irregular, the WBXD system requires a schedule.

Future debt service payments are the sum of future principal and interest payments due on existing commitments, including the undisbursed portion. They do not include debt service payments that may become due as a result of new loans contracted in subsequent years, nor do they take into account the effect of any change to future debt service obligations resulting from actions such as prepayment or rescheduling or from cancellations that occurred after the most recent year-end data reported to the DRS.

Both projected disbursements and future debt service payments are converted into U.S. dollars using end-December 2012 exchange rates. Likewise, future interest payments on loans with a variable interest rate (for example, loans from commercial banks tied to the London Interbank Offered Rate [LIBOR]) are based on the interest rate prevailing at end-December 2012.

Treatment of Arrears

The DRS collects information on arrears of both principal and interest. Principal in arrears is included in the amount of long-term external debt outstanding and is shown separately. Interest in arrears on long-term external debt and interest in arrears on the use of IMF credit are included as part of short-term external debt outstanding and are shown separately. Clearance of interest in arrears by repayment will be recorded as an interest payment in the relevant creditor category of the loan (or loans) on which the arrears were incurred, as a corresponding reduction in the level of short-term debt outstanding, and as a net reduction in interest arrears. Clearance of interest arrears through debt restructuring or forgiveness will be recorded as a reduction in the level of short-term debt outstanding and a net reduction in interest arrears. When interests are rescheduled, they will be capitalized: This change will be recorded as an increase in long-term debt outstanding equal to the amount of interest capitalized and the reduction in short-term debt outstanding noted previously.

External Debt and Its Components

This section describes the compilation of the major components of external debt included in the IDS tables and database and the relationship between them, as shown in figure A.1 on the next page. Information about general methods of compiling external debt data is discussed in the previous section titled "Methodology." For concise definitions, see the glossary.

Total External Debt

Total external debt shown in the IDS is the sum of long-term external debt, short-term debt, and IMF credit. It represents the total debt owed to nonresident creditors and is repayable in both foreign and domestic currency.

Short-Term Debt

Short-term debt is defined as external debt with an original maturity of one year or less. The DRS requires debtor countries to report only on their long-term external debt. However, to gain a comprehensive picture of total external obligations, the World Bank encourages debtor countries to voluntarily provide information on their short-term external obligations.

By its nature, short-term external debt is difficult to monitor: Loan-by-loan registration is normally impractical, and monitoring systems typically rely on information requested periodically by the central bank from the banking sector. The World Bank regards the debtor country as the authoritative source of information on its short-term debt. Unless otherwise specified in the country tables, the data for short-term debt are derived from the data provided by the quarterly external debt statistics (QEDS) database. QEDS was jointly developed by the World Bank and the IMF and provides detailed external debt data of countries that subscribe to the IMF's Special Data Dissemination Standard (SDDS) and a selected number of countries that participate in the IMF's General Data Dissemination System (GDDS). The data are compiled according to the External Debt Statistics, Guide for Compilers and Users. BIS data on international bank lending is the second source of the short-term debt. These data are reported on the basis of residual maturity, but an estimate of short-term external liabilities by original maturity can be derived by deducting from claims due in one year those that, 12 months earlier, had a

Figure A.1. **External Debt and Its Components**

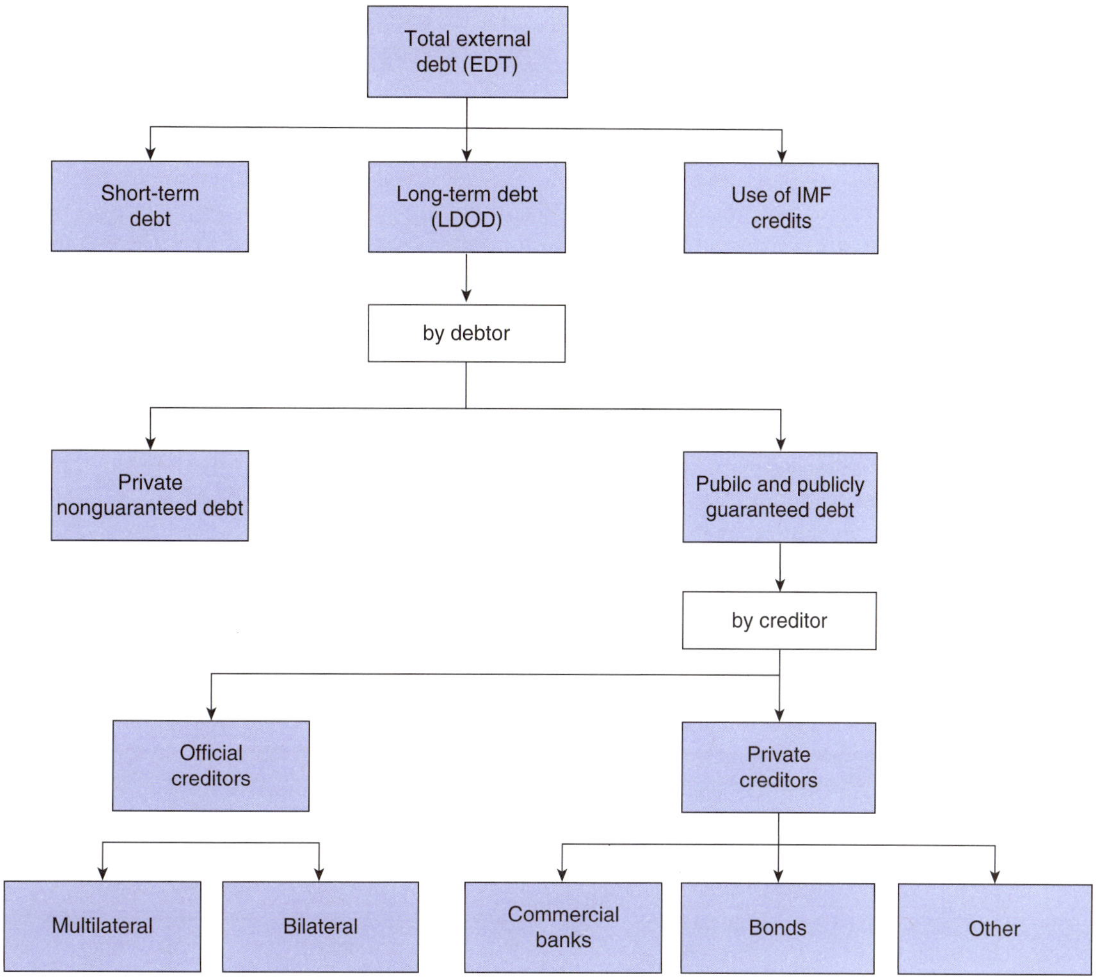

maturity of between one and two years. However, not all commercial banks report to the BIS in a way that allows the full maturity distribution to be determined, and the BIS data include liabilities only to banks within the BIS reporting area. Consequently, the results should be interpreted with caution.

The flow of short-term debt may be derived from the change in claims (stock) data in the BIS quarterly series over consecutive periods, but valuation adjustments resulting from exchange rate movements will affect the calculations, as will prepayment and refinancing of long-term maturities falling due. When short-term external debt has been rescheduled, lags in reporting and differences in the treatment of the rescheduled external debt by debtors and creditors may result in double counting.

Interest in arrears on long-term external debt and interest in arrears on the use of IMF credit are added to short-term debt and are separately identified.

Use of IMF Credit

Data related to the operations of the IMF are provided by the IMF Treasurer's Department. They are converted from special drawing rights (SDR) into dollars using end-of-period exchange rates for stocks and average-over-the-period exchange rates for flows. IMF trust fund operations under the Enhanced Structural Adjustment Facility, Extended Fund Facility, Poverty Reduction and Growth Facility, and Structural Adjustment Facility (Enhanced Structural Adjustment Facility in 1999) are presented together with all of the IMF's special facilities (buffer stock, supplemental reserve, compensatory and contingency facilities, oil facilities, and other facilities). SDR allocations are also included in this category. According to the BPM6, SDR allocations are recorded as the incurrence of a debt liability of the member receiving them (because of a requirement to repay the allocation in certain circumstances, and also because interest accrues). This debt item was introduced for the first time in IDS 2013 with historical data starting in 1999.

Long-Term Debt

Long-term debt has an original maturity of more than one year. It comprises the obligations of both public and private debtors. Private nonguaranteed debt comprises the external obligations of private debtors that are not guaranteed for repayment by a public entity in the debtor country.

Public and publicly guaranteed debt comprises the external obligations of public debtors and has two components: (a) public debt, which is borrowing by the national government or agency, by a political subdivision or agency, or by autonomous public bodies, and (b) publicly guaranteed debt, which is borrowing by a private agency that is guaranteed for repayment by a public entity.

Private Nonguaranteed Debt

The DRS reporting requirements were expanded in 1973 to include long-term private nonguaranteed debt. Data are reported annually on an aggregate basis and include, for the reporting year, the total amount of disbursed and outstanding debt; the amount of disbursements, principal repayments, and interest payments; the principal and interest rescheduled; and the projected principal and interest payments for future years. The aggregate data are usually reported in U.S. dollars, and no information on the underlying currency composition is given.

DRS reporting countries recognize the importance of monitoring borrowing by their private sector, particularly when it constitutes a significant portion of total external debt, but many countries acknowledge the difficulty of this process. Detailed data are available only when countries have registration requirements for private nonguaranteed debt in place, most commonly in connection with exchange controls. When formal registration of private nonguaranteed debt is not mandatory, compilers must rely on balance of payments data and financial surveys.

The data on private nonguaranteed debt in this publication is as reported or as estimated for countries where this type of external debt is known to be significant. The estimation of private nonguaranteed debt is based on the national data on quarterly external debt statistics (QEDS) or IMF data. Flows are derived from the change in stock over consecutive periods and are adjusted for the effects of exchange rate movements (assuming the currency composition mirrors that of public and publicly guaranteed debt) and for any known debt restructuring. Principal repayments are estimated on the basis of the average maturity observed for loans to private sector borrowers in countries reporting to the DRS and on the basis of the stock of debt outstanding. Interest payments are estimated on the basis of the stock of debt outstanding and interest rates prevailing in international capital markets.

Balance of payments data provide a useful guideline in the estimation process: private nonguaranteed external debt may be derived as a residual between net long-term external borrowing recorded in the balance of payments and net long-term public and publicly guaranteed external debt reported to the DRS.

Public and Publicly Guaranteed Debt

Data related to public and publicly guaranteed debt are reported to the DRS on a loan-by-loan basis. The data provide annual information on the disbursed and outstanding balance and the undisbursed balance of each loan, the cumulative disbursements, the principal and interest paid and principal and interest restructured in the reporting year, and the stock of any outstanding payment's arrears of principal and interest. Detailed information on the terms and conditions of each loan is also reported. Public debt and publicly guaranteed debt are shown as a single line in this publication and then further disaggregated by creditor type and, in the case of private creditors, by type of credit instrument.

Official Creditors

Official creditors include multilateral and bilateral lenders. In general, official creditors provide loans (and, in some cases, provide grants) to public bodies, although in some cases they may lend to other entities with a public guarantee.

Multilateral creditors are international financial institutions such as the World Bank, regional development banks, and other multilateral and intergovernmental agencies whose lending is administered on a multilateral basis. Funds administered by an international financial organization on behalf of a single donor government constitute bilateral loans (or grants). For lending by a number of multilateral creditors, the data presented in this publication are taken from the creditors' records. Such creditors include the African Development Bank, the Asian Development Bank, the IDB, IBRD, and IDA. (IBRD and IDA are institutions of the World Bank.)

Bilateral creditors are governments and their agencies, including central banks, aid agencies, official export credit agencies, and autonomous agencies such as the U.S. Department of Agriculture or the Federal Home Loan Bank. Member countries of the OECD Development Assistance Committee (DAC) and some other countries also report information on loans extended bilaterally or officially guaranteed to the Creditor Reporting System of the OECD.

Private Creditors

Private creditors include commercial banks, bondholders, and other private creditors. This line includes only publicly guaranteed creditors. Nonguaranteed private creditors are shown separately.

Bonds include publicly issued or privately placed bonds.

Commercial bank loans are loans from private banks and other private financial institutions.

Credits of other private creditors include credits from manufacturers, exporters, and other suppliers of goods, plus bank credits covered by a guarantee of an export credit agency. This line is included in the online database but is not shown in the published tables. It can be obtained as the difference between (a) credits of total private creditors and (b) bonds and commercial bank loans.

Sources of the Macroeconomic Indicators

The macroeconomic data are prepared by The World Bank from a variety of sources. Data on Personal Transfers and Compensation of Employees are prepared by World Bank staff based on IMF balance of payments statistics. Data on foreign direct investments are prepared by World Bank staff based on IMF balance of payments statistics and UNCTAD publication. Other macroeconomic data are from IMF balance of payments statistics.

Data on exports of goods, services, and primary income are gap-filled with countries' balance of payments statistics for the following countries:

Algeria (2013)
Burkina Faso (from 2011)
Comoros (from 2005)
Côte d'Ivoire (2011)
Fiji (2013)
Ghana (2013)
Guinea-Bissau (from 2011)
Indonesia (2013)
Kenya (2013)
Madagascar (from 2006)
Mali (2012)
Mauritania (from 2006)
Niger (2011)
Nigeria (2013)
Peru (2013)
São Tomé and Príncipe (2013)
Senegal (2012)
Serbia (2013)
Seychelles (2013)
Swaziland (2013)
Tanzania (2013)
Togo (2011)

Data on imports of goods, services, and primary income are gap-filled with countries' balance of payments statistics for the following countries:

Algeria (2013)
Burkina Faso (from 2011)
Comoros (from 2005)
Côte d'Ivoire (2011)
Fiji (2013)
Ghana (2013)
Guinea-Bissau (from 2011)
Indonesia (2013)
Kenya (2013)
Madagascar (from 2006)
Mali (2012)
Mauritania (from 2006)
Niger (2011)
Nigeria (2013)
Peru (2013)
São Tomé and Príncipe (2013)
Senegal (2012)
Serbia (2013)
Seychelles (2013)
Swaziland (2013)
Tanzania (2013)
Togo (2011)

Data on current account balance are based on countries' balance of payments statistics for the following countries:

Algeria (2013)
Benin (2012)
Bolivia (2013)
Burkina Faso (from 2011)
Central African Republic (from 2005)
Chad (from 2005)
Comoros (from 2005)
Côte d'Ivoire (2011)
Fiji (2013)
Gabon (from 2006)
Ghana (2013)
Guinea-Bissau (from 2011)
Indonesia (2013)
Kenya (2013)
Liberia (2012)
Madagascar (from 2006)
Mali (2011)
Mauritania (from 2007)
Niger (2011)
Nigeria (2013)
Peru (2013)
São Tomé and Príncipe (2013)
Senegal (2012)
Serbia (2013)
Seychelles (2013)
Swaziland (2013)
Tajikistan (2013)
Tanzania (2013)
Togo (2011)
Zimbabwe (from 2005)

Data on personal transfers and compensation of employees are based on countries' balance of payments statistics for the following countries:

Indonesia (2013)
Peru (2013)

Data on portfolio equity are based on countries' balance of payments statistics for the following countries:

Burkina Faso (from 2011)
Indonesia (2013)
Nigeria (2013)

Country Groups

Regional Groups

East Asia and Pacific

Cambodia (A)
China (P)
Fiji (A)
Indonesia (A)
Lao PDR (A)
Malaysia (E)
Mongolia (A)
Myanmar (E)
Papua New Guinea (A)
Philippines (A)
Samoa (A)
Solomon Islands (A)
Thailand (A)
Tonga (A)
Vanuatu (E)
Vietnam (A)

Europe and Central Asia

Albania (A)
Armenia (A)
Azerbaijan (A)
Belarus (A)
Bosnia and Herzegovina[a] (A)
Bulgaria (A)
Georgia (A)
Hungary (A)
Kazakhstan (A)
Kosovo (A)
Kyrgyz Republic (A)
Macedonia, FYR (A)
Moldova (A)
Montenegro (A)
Romania (A)
Serbia[a, b] (A)
Tajikistan (A)
Turkey (A)
Turkmenistan (E)
Ukraine (A)
Uzbekistan (A)

Latin America and the Caribbean

Argentina (A)
Belize (A)
Bolivia (A)
Brazil (A)
Colombia (A)
Costa Rica (A)
Dominica (A)
Dominican Republic (A)
Ecuador (A)
El Salvador (A)
Grenada (A)
Guatemala (A)
Guyana (A)
Haiti (A)
Honduras (A)
Jamaica (A)
Mexico (A)
Nicaragua (A)
Panama (A)
Paraguay (A)
Peru (A)
St. Lucia (A)
St. Vincent and the Grenadines (A)
Venezuela, RB (A)

Middle East and North Africa

Algeria (A)
Djibouti (A)
Egypt, Arab Rep. (A)
Iran, Islamic Rep. (A)
Jordan (A)
Lebanon (A)
Morocco (A)
Syrian Arab Republic (E)
Tunisia (A)
Yemen, Rep. (A)

South Asia

Afghanistan (A)
Bangladesh (E)
Bhutan (A)
India (A)
Maldives (A)
Nepal (A)
Pakistan (A)
Sri Lanka(A)

Sub-Saharan Africa

Angola (A)
Benin (A)
Botswana (A)
Burkina Faso (A)
Burundi (A)
Cabo Verde (A)
Cameroon (A)
Central African Republic (A)
Chad (P)
Comoros (A)
Congo, Dem. Rep. (P)
Congo, Rep. (A)
Côte d'Ivoire (A)
Eritrea (E)
Ethiopia (A)
Gabon (A)
Gambia, The (A)
Ghana (A)
Guinea (E)
Guinea-Bissau (E)
Kenya (A)
Lesotho (A)
Liberia (A)
Madagascar (A)
Malawi (A)
Mali (A)
Mauritania (A)
Mauritius (A)
Mozambique (A)
Niger (A)
Nigeria (A)
Rwanda (A)
São Tomé and Príncipe (A)
Senegal (A)
Seychelles (A)
Sierra Leone (A)
Somalia (E)
South Africa (P)
Sudan[c] (P)
Swaziland (A)
Tanzania (A)
Togo (A)
Uganda (A)
Zambia (A)
Zimbabwe (A)

Note: Letters in parenthesis indicate DRS reporters' status: (A) as reported, (P) preliminary, and (E) estimated. The status "as reported" indicates that the country was fully current in its reporting under the DRS and that World Bank staff are satisfied that the reported data give an adequate and fair representation of the country's total public debt. "Preliminary" data are based on reported or collected information, but because of incompleteness or other reasons, an element of staff estimation is included. "Estimated" data indicate that countries are not current in their reporting and that a significant element of staff estimation has been necessary in producing the data tables.
a. For Bosnia and Herzegovina, total debt before 1999, excluding IBRD and IMF obligations and short-term debt, is included under Serbia.
b. Data prior to 2006 include Montenegro.
c. Data include South Sudan.

Income Groups

Low-income economies

Afghanistan
Bangladesh
Benin
Burkina Faso
Burundi
Cambodia
Central African Republic
Chad
Comoros
Congo, Dem. Rep.
Eritrea
Ethiopia
Gambia, The
Guinea
Guinea-Bissau
Haiti
Kenya
Liberia
Madagascar
Malawi
Mali
Mozambique
Myanmar
Nepal
Niger
Rwanda
Sierra Leone
Somalia
Tajikistan
Tanzania
Togo
Uganda
Zimbabwe

Middle-income economies

Albania
Algeria
Angola
Argentina
Armenia
Azerbaijan
Belarus
Belize
Bhutan
Bolivia
Bosnia and Herzegovina
Botswana
Brazil
Bulgaria
Cabo Verde
Cameroon
China
Colombia
Congo, Rep.
Costa Rica
Côte d'Ivoire
Djibouti
Dominica
Dominican Republic
Ecuador
Egypt, Arab Rep.
El Salvador
Fiji
Gabon
Georgia
Ghana
Grenada
Guatemala
Guyana
Honduras
Hungary
India
Indonesia
Iran, Islamic Rep.
Jamaica
Jordan
Kazakhstan
Kosovo
Kyrgyz Republic
Lao PDR
Lebanon
Lesotho
Macedonia, FYR
Malaysia
Maldives
Mauritania
Mauritius
Mexico
Moldova
Mongolia
Montenegro
Morocco
Nicaragua
Nigeria
Pakistan
Panama
Papua New Guinea
Paraguay
Peru
Philippines
Romania
Samoa
São Tomé and Príncipe
Senegal
Serbia
Seychelles
Solomon Islands
South Africa
Sri Lanka
St. Lucia
St. Vincent and the Grenadines
Sudan
Swaziland
Syrian Arab Republic
Thailand
Tonga
Tunisia
Turkey
Turkmenistan
Ukraine
Uzbekistan
Vanuatu
Venezuela, RB
Vietnam
Yemen, Rep.
Zambia

Note: Low-income economies are those with a GNI per capita of $1,045 or less in 2013. Middle-income economies are those with a GNI per capita of more than $1,046 but less than $12,745. Italicized countries are IDA-only countries as of July 1, 2014; IDA-only excludes blend and IBRD countries.

Glossary

Debt Reporting System (DRS)

Average terms of new commitments provide information on the interest rate, maturity, and grace period of new commitments on public and publicly guaranteed external debt contracted with public and private creditors. Averages are weighted by the amounts of the loans.

Bilateral official creditors are official agencies that make loans on behalf of one government to another government or to public (and, in some cases, private) borrowers in another country.

Bonds are debt instruments issued by public and publicly guaranteed or private debtors with durations of one year or longer. Bonds usually give the holder the unconditional right to fixed money income or contractually determined, variable money income.

Commercial banks are private banks that provide loans and other financial services.

Commitments of public and publicly guaranteed debt constitute the total amount of new long-term loans to public sector borrowers or borrowers with a public sector guarantee extended by official and private lenders and for which contracts were signed in the year specified.

Concessional debt conveys information about the borrower's receipt of aid from official lenders at concessional terms as defined by the DAC, that is, loans with an original grant element of 25 percent or more. Loans from major regional development banks—African Development Bank, Asian Development Bank, and the Inter-American Development Bank—and from the World Bank are classified as concessional according to each institution's classification and not according to the DAC definition, as was the practice in earlier reports.

Contractual obligations on outstanding long-term external debt are the anticipated debt service payments on long-term external debt contracted up to December 31 of the reporting year.

Currency composition of public and publicly guaranteed debt provides information on the share of loans outstanding and disbursed by currency of repayment. For major multilateral creditors, the currency composition of the relevant unit of account is also taken into account. The principal currencies in which the external debt of low- and middle-income countries is contracted (the euro, Japanese yen, U.S. dollar, SDR, and all other currencies) are separately identified. Beginning in 2001, debt denominated in the currencies of the members in the Euro Area is included under the euro rather than the national currencies that previously prevailed.

Current account balance shows the difference between the sum of exports and income receivable and the sum of imports and income payable (exports and imports refer to both goods and services, while income refers to both primary and secondary income).

Debt buyback is the repurchase by a debtor of its own debt, either at a discount price or at par value. In the event of a buyback of long-term debt, the face value of the debt bought back will be recorded as a decline in stock outstanding of long-term debt, and the cash amount received by creditors will be recorded as a principal repayment. For example, if a country buys back long-term external debt of face value B at a price P, then long-term external debt will decline by B, and principal repayment will increase by P. The difference between the price at which the debt was bought back and the face value is recorded as a debt stock write-off (the related transactions are not separately identified in the International Debt Statistics [IDS] publication but are available in the online database).

Debt forgiveness grants include both debts canceled by agreement between debtor and creditor and reductions in the net present value of official nonconcessional loans resulting from concessional rescheduling or refinancing. Data are recorded on a disbursement basis and include debt forgiveness from bilateral and multilateral creditors.

Debt outstanding and disbursed is the value at year's end of long-term external debt owed by public and publicly guaranteed debtors and private nonguaranteed debtors.

Debt restructurings are revisions to debt service obligations agreed on by creditors and debtors. Such agreements change the amount and timing of future principal and interest payments.

Debt service to exports is the ratio of the sum of principal repayments and interest paid on total long-term debt (public and publicly guaranteed debt and private nonguaranteed debt) to the value of exports of goods and services and receipts of primary income from abroad.

Debt stock-flow reconciliation shows the indicators that affect the change in debt stocks from one period to the next.

Disbursements are drawings during the year specified on loan commitments contracted by the borrower.

Exports of goods, services, and primary income constitute the total value of exports of goods and services, receipts of compensation of nonresident workers, and investment income from abroad.

External debt flows are debt-related transactions during the year specified. They include disbursements, principal repayments, and interest payments.

External debt stocks comprise public and publicly guaranteed long-term external debt, private nonguaranteed long-term external debt, use of IMF credit, and short-term external debt, including interest arrears on long-term debt. The relation between external debt stock and its components is illustrated on page 159 (figure A.1).

External debt stocks to exports is the ratio of outstanding external debt to the value of exports of goods and services and receipts of primary income from abroad.

External debt stocks to GNI is the ratio of outstanding external debt to gross national income.

Foreign direct investment refers to direct investment equity flows in the reporting economy. It is the sum of equity capital, reinvestment earnings, and other capital. Direct investment is a category of cross-border investment associated with a resident in one economy having control or a significant degree of influence on the management of an enterprise that is resident in another economy. Ownership of 10 percent or more of the ordinary shares or voting stock is the criterion for determining the existence of a direct investment relationship.

Grace period is the time between the date on which a loan is committed and the date on which the first principal payment is due. The information presented in International Debt Statistics is the average grace period on all public and publicly guaranteed debt committed during the specified period.

Grants are legally binding commitments that obligate a specific value of funds available for disbursement for which there is no payment requirement. They include debt forgiveness grants and grants from bilateral and multilateral agencies (such as the International Development Association).

Gross national income (GNI) is the sum of value added by all resident producers, plus any product taxes (less subsidies) not included in the valuation of output, plus net receipts of primary income compensation of employees and property income from abroad. Yearly average exchange rates are used to convert GNI from local currency to U.S. dollars.

Heavily Indebted Poor Country (HIPC) Initiative is a program of the World Bank and the International Monetary Fund (IMF) to provide debt relief to qualifying countries with unsustainable debt burdens.

Imports of goods, services, and primary income constitute the total value of goods and services imported and income payable to nonresidents. Interest arrears on long-term debt are interest payments due but not paid, shown on a cumulative basis.

Interest arrears are due and payable immediately and are therefore regarded as short-term obligations. Thus, an increase in interest arrears on long-term debt will be recorded as an increase in short-term debt. Interest in arrears on the use of IMF credit is also considered to be part of short-term external debt.

Interest payments are the amounts of interest paid in foreign currency, goods, or services in the year specified.

Interest rate is the interest rate applicable to a loan commitment as specified in the loan contract. The information presented in International Debt Statistics is the average interest on all public and publicly guaranteed debt committed during the specified period.

International Bank for Reconstruction and Development (IBRD) is a multilateral official creditor. IBRD is the nonconcessional lending arm of the World Bank Group.

International Development Association (IDA) is a multilateral official creditor. It is the concessional financing arm of the World Bank Group. IDA also provides grant financing to qualified borrowers.

IMF charges are the amounts of interest paid in foreign currency in the year specified for transactions with the IMF.

IMF purchases are the total drawings on the general resources account of the IMF during the year specified, excluding drawings in the reserve tranche.

IMF repurchases are the amounts of principal (amortization) paid in foreign currency in the year specified for transactions with the IMF.

International reserves constitute the sum of a country's monetary authority's holdings of special drawing rights, its reserve position in the IMF, its holdings of foreign exchange, and its holdings of gold (valued at year-end London prices).

Long-term external debt is debt that has an original or extended maturity of more than one year and that is owed to nonresidents by residents of an economy and is repayable in foreign currency, goods, or services.

Long-term private sector debt is long-term debt owed by the private sector, whether publicly guaranteed or not.

Long-term public sector debt is long-term external debt owed by the public sector.

Maturity is the date on which the final principal repayment on a loan is due. It is the sum of the grace and repayment periods. The information presented in International Debt Statistics is the average maturity on all public and publicly guaranteed debt committed during the specified period.

Multilateral Debt Relief Initiative (MDRI) is a program of the World Bank, the IMF, the Inter-American Development Bank, and the African Development Bank that provides additional debt relief to countries that have completed the HIPC process.

Multilateral official creditors are official agencies owned or governed by more than one country that provide loan financing. They include international financial institutions such as the World Bank, regional development banks, and other intergovernmental agencies.

Multilateral to external debt stocks is the ratio of the stock of debt owed to multilateral creditors to total external debt.

Net flows on external debt are disbursements on long-term external debt and IMF purchases minus principal repayments on long-term external debt and IMF repurchases. Up to 1984, this calculation included only long-term external debt and IMF flows. Since 1985, the calculation includes the change in stock of short-term debt (excluding interest arrears on long-term external debt).

Official creditors are governments or other bilateral public entities, such as export-import agencies, development agencies, and multilateral financial institutions, such as the World Bank and regional development banks.

Personal transfers and compensation of employees is the sum of personal transfers and compensation of employees. Personal transfers consist of all current transfers in cash or in kind made or received by resident households to or from nonresident households. Personal transfers thus include all current transfers between resident and nonresident individuals. Compensation of employees refers to the income of border, seasonal, and other short-term workers who are employed in an economy where they are not resident and of residents employed by nonresident entities.

Portfolio equity is the category of international investment that covers investment in equity securities. Equity securities include shares, stocks, participation, or similar documents (such as American Depositary Receipts) that usually denote ownership of equity.

Present value of debt outstanding is the nominal value of all future debt service obligations on existing debt discounted at prevailing market rates of interest. The interest rates used in this calculation are the Commercial Interest Reference Rates (CIRR) for each relevant currency compiled and published by the Organisation for Economic Cooperation and Development.

Primary income on FDI are payments of direct investment income (debit side), which consist of income on equity (dividends, branch profits, and reinvested earnings) and income on the intercompany debt (interest).

Principal arrears on long-term debt are principal repayments due but not paid on long-term external debt, shown on a cumulative basis.

Principal repayments are the amounts of principal (amortization) paid in foreign currency, goods, or services in the year specified with respect to long-term external debt.

Private creditors are bondholders, commercial banks, and other trade-related lenders.

Private nonguaranteed debt is debt owed by private sector borrowers to external creditors on loans that do not benefit from a public sector guarantee by the debtor country.

Public and publicly guaranteed debt outstanding and disbursed is the value of debt at year's end of public sector borrowers, or borrowers with a public sector guarantee, owed to official and private lenders.

Public and publicly guaranteed external debt comprises public debt (an external obligation of a public debtor, such as the national government or agency, a political subdivision or agency, or an autonomous public body) and publicly guaranteed external debt (an external obligation of a private debtor that is guaranteed for repayment by a public entity).

Public debt is an external obligation of a public debtor, including the national government, a political subdivision (or an agency of either), and autonomous public bodies.

Publicly guaranteed debt is an external obligation of a private debtor that is guaranteed for repayment by a public entity.

Reserves to external debt stocks is the ratio of international reserves to outstanding external debt.

Reserves to imports (months) is the ratio of international reserves to the value of imports of goods, services, and primary income in the year shown and is expressed in months:

$$\frac{\text{Reserves}}{\text{Imports/12}}$$

Short-term external debt has an original maturity of one year or less. Available data permit no distinction among public, publicly guaranteed, and private nonguaranteed short-term external debt.

Short-term to external debt stock ratio is the ratio of short-term external debt to total outstanding external debt.

Special Drawing Rights (SDRs) refer to an international reserve asset that was created by the IMF in 1969 to supplement its member countries' official reserves. The value of SDRs is based on a basket of four key international currencies: the U.S. dollar, the pound sterling, the Japanese yen, and the euro. In addition to playing a role as a supplementary reserve asset, SDRs serve as the unit of account for the IMF and some other international organizations.

Technical cooperation grants include (a) free-standing technical cooperation grants, which are intended to finance the transfer of technical and managerial skills or of technology for the purpose of building up general national capacity without reference to any specific investment projects, and (b) investment-related technical cooperation grants, which are aimed at strengthening the capacity to execute specific investment projects.

Total amount forgiven is the total amount of principal and interest due, principal and interest in arrears, and debt stock forgiven in the year specified.

Total amount rescheduled is the total amount of external debt rescheduled, including principal and interest due, principal and interest in arrears, charges, penalties, and debt stock in the year specified.

Total change in external debt stocks is the difference in the external debt stock between two consecutive years.

Use of IMF credit denotes members' drawings on the IMF other than amounts drawn against the country's reserve tranche position. Use of IMF credit includes purchases and drawings under Stand-By, Extended, Structural Adjustment, Enhanced Structural Adjustment, and Systemic Transformation Facility Arrangements as well as trust fund loans. SDR allocations are also included in this category.

Quarterly Debt Statistics

Central bank sector is identical to the definition of that subsector in the 2008 System of National Accounts (SNA). The central bank is the financial institution (or institutions) that exercises control over key aspects of the financial system. It carries out such activities as issuing currency, managing international reserves, transacting with the IMF, and providing credit to deposit-taking corporations.

Central government subsector consists of the institutional unit(s) of the central government plus those nonmarket Non-profit institutions that are controlled by the central government. The political authority of the central government extends over the entire territory of the country.

Currency and deposits consist of notes and coins and deposits (both transferable and other). Notes and coins represent claims of a fixed nominal value usually on a central bank or government; commemorative coins are excluded. Deposits include all claims that are (a) on the central bank, deposit-taking corporations other than the central bank, and, in some cases, other institutional units; and (b) represented by evidence of deposit.

Debt liabilities owed by residents to residents of the same economy are classified as *domestic debt*, and debt liabilities owed by residents to nonresidents are classified as *external debt*. The definition of residence follows the current international standards (the System of National Accounts 2008 [2008 SNA] and the *Balance of Payments and International Investment Position Manual*, Sixth Edition [BPM6]).

Debt securities are negotiable financial instruments serving as evidence of a debt. The security normally specifies a schedule for interest payments and principal repayments. Examples of debt securities are bills, bonds, and debentures, including bonds that are convertible into shares, commercial paper, negotiable certificates of deposit, loans that have become negotiable from one holder to another, nonparticipating preferred stocks or shares, asset-backed securities and collateralized debt obligations, banker's acceptances, and similar instruments normally traded in the financial markets.

Deposit-taking corporations, except the central bank sector is identical with the corresponding subsector in the 2008 SNA. It includes commercial banks, institutions such as savings banks, savings and loan associations, credit unions or cooperatives, traveler's check companies, and specialized banks or other financial institutions if they take deposits or issue close substitutes for deposits Post office savings banks or other government-controlled savings banks are also included if they are institutional units separate from the government. Deposit-taking corporations that engage exclusively (or almost exclusively) with nonresidents, often called offshore banks or offshore banking units, are included in the deposit-taking corporations sector, but they may be excluded from the money-issuing sector because their liabilities are not included in broad money.

General government sector is identical with the definition of that sector in the 2008 SNA. The government units of a country consist of those authorities and their agencies that are units established by political processes and exercise legislative, judicial, and executive authority over other institutional units within a given territorial area. General government agencies that are residents of an economy include all departments, establishments, and bodies located in the economic territory of an economy's central, state, and local governments and all embassies, consulates, military establishments, and other entities, which are located elsewhere, of an economy's general government.

Insurance, pension, and standardized guarantee schemes comprise (a) nonlife insurance technical reserves, (b) life insurance and annuity entitlements, (c) pension entitlements, claims of pension funds on pension managers, and entitlements to nonpension funds, and (d) provisions for calls under standardized guarantees.

Loans include those financial assets created through the direct lending of funds by a creditor (lender) to a debtor (borrower) through an arrangement in which the lender either receives no security evidencing the transactions or receives a nonnegotiable document or instrument.

Other accounts receivable/payable covers items other than equity; currency and deposits; loans; insurance, pension, and standardized guarantee schemes; trade credit and advances; and SDRs.

Other sectors comprises other financial corporations (i.e., other than deposit-taking corporations), nonfinancial corporations, and households and nonprofit institutions serving households (NPISHs) subsectors.

SDR allocations are recorded as the incurrence of a debt liability of the member receiving them (because of a requirement to repay the allocation in certain circumstances, and also because of interest accrues).

Trade credit and advances consist of liabilities arising from the direct extension of credit by suppliers for transactions in goods and services, and advance payments by buyers for goods and services and for work in progress (or to be undertaken).

ECO-AUDIT

Environmental Benefits Statement

The World Bank is committed to preserving endangered forests and natural resources. The Office of the Publisher has chosen to print ***International Debt Statistics 2015*** on recycled paper with 50 percent post-consumer waste, in accordance with the recommended standards for paper usage set by the Green Press Initiative, a non-profit program supporting publishers in using fiber that is not sourced from endangered forests. For more information, visit www.greenpressinitiative.org.

Saved:

- 9 trees
- 4 million BTUs of total energy
- 724 lbs. of net greenhouse gases
- 3,926 gallons of water
- 263 lbs. of solid waste

green press INITIATIVE